T5-AGS-527

A HISTORY OF PENAL METHODS

PATTERSON SMITH REPRINT SERIES IN
CRIMINOLOGY, LAW ENFORCEMENT, AND SOCIAL PROBLEMS

A listing of publications in the SERIES *will be found at rear of volume*

PUBLICATION NO. 124: PATTERSON SMITH REPRINT SERIES IN CRIMINOLOGY, LAW ENFORCEMENT, AND SOCIAL PROBLEMS

A HISTORY OF PENAL METHODS

CRIMINALS, WITCHES, LUNATICS

BY

GEORGE IVES, M.A.

MONTCLAIR, N.J.
PATTERSON SMITH
1970

66110

Originally published 1914
Reprinted 1970 by special arrangement with
Hutchinson Publishing Group, Ltd., London
Patterson Smith Publishing Corporation
Montclair, New Jersey 07042

SBN 87585–124–X

Library of Congress Catalog Card Number: 70–108241

This book is printed on three-hundred-year acid-free paper.

PREFACE

CRIMINOLOGY is the study of the causes and treatment of crime. To track the offender is a problem for the police ; to determine his guilt or innocence is the work of the courts. Graphic accounts of his crime and capture, descriptions of his trial and conviction, or reports of the last scene when he stood upon the scaffold, are not criminology. The dreary records of convict mismanagement by the Governor of Gaolblank, and the ghastly-cheerful reminiscences of the Chaplain of Chokee—even the fascinating studies of, say, Edgar Poe, and Conan Doyle, in the art of Deduction—are not criminology. We know now, and are beginning to realize, that nothing ever happens without a *cause*. A man can no more exist underived from the Past or effectless upon the Future, than he can walk suspended in the air.

Therefore, when we look upon a person who is branded as a criminal, we have to *account* for him. He may be degraded enough as we find him, he may be a drunken, homeless wanderer or street-corner man, but what *made* him like this ?

He started some few years back as a helpless baby, with a little bright, wondering face looking out on life. What has been impressed into it since then ? It was a blank page, with only the water-mark of heredity, and a certain grade of quality and texture upon it. What have we written there ? what has the whole community been doing to make these lines, now so deeply graven, or whence came they ? How is this stain on him, and therefore on all of us, to be cleared away ? What must be done to help with a strong hand : that will be criminology.

I have sought to show how every act of aggression which might occur, was met by an instinctive counteract of retaliation, spontaneously undertaken by the injured party or group, unless appeased by adequate compensation. How later, revenge was left entirely to the State, the notion of restitution being lost sight of ; and how, ultimately, the original cause and mainspring of punishment—which was clearly, vengeance—became disguised in official forms ; its alleged purposes being then variously explained and justified by all sorts of theories, which were often conflicting and contradictory.

So that professional legislators and unthinking democracies altogether lost sight of penal law origins (if we go so far as to assume that they ever had realized them), and looked upon punishments as remedial measures, whereas they are really only survivals, concessions allowed to unreasoning cruelty.

So used are we to witnessing new laws made and fresh crimes created, as well as the constant punishing of all sorts of citizens—a punishment being always the cheapest and easiest substitute for a positive remedy—that it is scarcely remarkable that men generally acquiesce.

I have therefore tried to analyse the theories and assumptions on which the criminal laws are founded, and to exhibit their falsity ; and have collected a number of instances of archaic punishments which were manifestly instinctive ; the inference being that all others are similarly derived from evil (because pain-producing) desires.

While the question of the origin of punishment is a matter of profound historical and didactic interest, that of the causes which create criminals is of the utmost importance to the whole commonwealth. The very idea of the necessity for causation only arose with the spirit of scientific inquiry. In the olden days of theological Dualism all crimes were attributed to diabolical instigation ; a belief which was expressly stated on the legal indictments. But now we are beginning to seek out the actual sources of social troubles, and to discover them in circumstances rather than sins, and to find them to be by no means evils inevitable, due to human depravity, but much more to bad conditions which have been tolerated, if not maintained, through selfishness and neglect.

In the belief that such words as Chance and Accident are merely expressions which reveal our ignorance of catenary impulses ; and that the far-thrown pebble glancing over the swell, and skimming from wave to wave until it sinks into the ocean, must take a certain and undeviating course occasioned by the forces and resistances acting on it ; I have tried to examine and analyse the forces which play on people, the usual resistance to them, and the resultant conduct ; which may generally be predicted. I have attempted to show how offenders ought to be classified on rational principles in order that each may receive the treatment proper to his condition. It is, as most of the modern school are perceiving now (witness the works of Devon, Hopkins, de Quiros, Saleilles, etc.), the scientific sorting out of Society's Failures, and their individual treatment according to their various and widely differing needs, that will prove to be the greatest measure yet undertaken, to ensure the ultimate but certain elimination of crime.

The reader will perceive that many of the following chapters could have been lengthened enormously and there would still have remained much unused material. The literature on every subject is now so vast that one is conscious and fearful of having left out a number of works of reference which would have been valuable ; but the book has already taken so many years, that I have decided that it must stand as it is, and only be amplified at some future time, should this ever be feasible.

With a long experience of great catalogues, I have made it a rule to give each author's initials when quoting authorities, and, generally, the dates of their works. Also, I have usually indicated whence I have obtained historical facts, even in cases where they might have been assumed to be matters of common knowledge, in order that they may be easily verified or further explored ; for it has always been my hope and ambition to set other students at the task of investigating complex, neglected, or tabooed problems, so that light may be thrown on them.

CONTENTS

CHAPTER I

66110

CHAPTER XV

CHAPTER XVI

CHAPTER XVII

CHAPTER XVIII

CHAPTER XIX

CHAPTER XX

A HISTORY OF PENAL METHODS

CHAPTER 1

PENAL METHODS OF THE MIDDLE AGES

PRISONS as places of detention are very ancient institutions. As soon as men had learned the way to build, in stone, as in Egypt, or with bricks, as in Mesopotamia, when kings had many-towered fortresses, and the great barons castles on the crags, there would be cells and dungeons in the citadels.[1] But prisons as places for the reception of " ordinary " (as distinct from state or political) criminals for definite terms only evolved in England many centuries afterwards[2] ; whilst imprisonment as a punishment in itself,[3] to be endured under rules made expressly punitive and distressful, may be described as essentially modern, and reached its worst phase in the nineteenth century.[4]

[1] " In the early cuneiform writing . . . the symbol for a prison is a combination of the symbols for ' house ' and ' darkness ' "—Isaac Taylor, *History of the Alphabet*, p. 21. London, 1899.

[2] It has been said that imprisonment is not mentioned in Anglo-Saxon laws as a punishment ; it is, however, referred to in the laws of Æthelstan thus : " For murder let a man forfeit his life, if he will deny it and appear guilty at the threefold ordeal let him be 120 nights in prison ; afterwards let his relations take him out and pay the king 120 shillings and to his relatives the price of his blood. . . ." See J. Johnson, *Ecclesiastical Laws*. London, 1720. The same king ordained that " If a thief be brought into prison that he be 40 days in prison and then let him be released thereout with cxx. shillings and let his kindred enter into borh for him that he will ever more desist."—B. Thorpe, *Ancient Laws and Institutions of England*, fol. ed. p. 85. London, 1840.

[3] " In the reign of Henry III. imprisonment for a definite period was an unknown punishment."—G. J. Turner, *Select Pleas of the Forest*, p. lxv. London, 1901.

[4] " Imprisonment occurs in the Anglo-Saxon Laws only as a means of temporary security."—Pollock and Maitland, *Hist. Eng. Law*, vol. i. p. 26. Cambridge, 1895.

The Teutonic Tribes of the bays and forests were fierce and free. They exemplified, in fact, the theory of Nietzsche, that liberty cannot be granted but must be taken.[1] They had not cowered before Oriental superstitions,[2] and as they lived in widely scattered hordes a central government could not impose its yoke upon the savage warriors. With the wild clansmen of the fierce Norse nations, where every man was always ready armed [3] and boys received their weapons at fifteen,[4] the great desideratum was the maintenance of peace.

The instinct of retaliation throbs in all men, and vengeance swift and bloody would be sought for, which, where the kindred ties were close and strong, might spread a feud through villages and clans, such that the very children might be born devoted to the duty of a family revenge. The Teutonic nations, like the free peoples they were, always assumed that for a crime to have been committed, an individual must have suffered injury.[5] And they conceived the aggrieved plaintiff as no cowed weakling (or he would not have counted), but as a fighting freeman with spear and shield, who would repay a wrong with interest, and whom, if slain, his kinsmen would avenge.

Thus the placation [6] of the injured party was the objective of the oldest laws. Allowance was made for

---

[1] " In the nature of the Saxons in the most ancient times there existed neither a knowledge of the most high and heavenly King . . . nor any dignity of honour of any earthly king. . . ."—W. Stubbs, *Const. Hist.* p. 49. Oxford, 1880.

[2] *Ibid.* p. 75.

[3] " Nihil neque publicae neque privatae rei nisi armati agunt." —Tac. *Germ.* xiii.

[4] Among the Jutes, etc., see J. M. Lappenberg, *Hist. of Eng. under the Anglo-Saxon Kings*, i. p. 97. London, 1845   The Anglo-Saxon lad came of age at twelve ; see work just quoted, p 173, and J. Thrupp, *The Anglo-Saxon Home*, p. 108. London, 1862.

[5] The exceptions to this wise though primitive rule are to be found where occasionally " God " and even " Nature " would be cited as injured third parties, upon theological grounds. See, for instance, N. Marshall, *Penitential Discipline of the Primitive Church*, pp. 49, 190, Oxford, 1844 ; and the thirteenth-century *Mirror of Justice*, chap. xiv.

[6] " To keep the peace is the legislator's first object, and it is not easy. To force the injured man or the slain man's kinsfolk to accept a money compensation instead of resorting to reprisals is the main aim of the law-giver."—F. W. Maitland, *Constitutional History of England*, p. 4. Cambridge, 1908.

human feelings [1] and impulses. Some ancient codes [2] permitted him like for like : an eye for an eye, and a tooth for a tooth, in the sense of so much, and no more.[3] But the Teutonic laws offered him compensation,[4] and, when it is possible, compelled him to accept it.[5] Thus crimes were met by restitution, not by punishment.[6]

Every sort of injury which one freeman could do to another was first of all atonable by bōt (a money compensation paid to the injured man or his relations).[7] What this fine was depended firstly upon the nature and extent of the damage done, and secondly upon the rank and importance of the person injured.[8] For every man had his class and value ; and every form of aggression against a freeman, from a wound which killed him outright to a blow which deprived him of a single tooth,[9]

---

[1] Thus in the Laws of the XII. Tables the manifest thief would be killed if a slave, or if free become the bondman of the person robbed ; if, however, he were captured later, he had to refund double the value of what he had taken. By the Germanic codes a thief might be instantly chased and then hanged or decapitated, but fines for homicide would be imposed if he were slain after an interval. Henry Maine, *Ancient Law*, ed. of 1906, pp. 387, 388.

[2] For instance, Exodus xxi. 23, 24, 25.

[3] See E. Westermarck, *Moral Ideas*, vol. i. p. 178. London, 1906.

[4] At first it was not always necessary to accept the blood-fine. See E. W. Robertson, *Scotland under her Early Kings*, p. 287, Edinburgh, 1862, on this point ; and as to the treatment of female relatives, see J. Thrupp, *Anglo-Saxon Home*, p. 151.

[5] In the seventh century a law of Ine ordained that " If any one takes refuge before he demands justice, let him give up what he has taken to himself and pay the damage done and make bōt with xxx. shillings."—Thorpe, *Ancient Laws and Institutions*, fol. ed. p. 48.

[6] " The penal law of ancient communities is not a law of crimes ; it is a law of wrongs, or, to use the English technical word, of torts. The person injured proceeds against the wrongdoer by an ordinary civil action, and recovers compensation in the shape of money damages if he succeeds."—Maine, *Ancient Law*, p. 379.

[7] " It is curious to observe how little the men of primitive times were troubled with these scruples (as to the degree of moral guilt to be ascribed to the wrongdoer), how completely they were persuaded that the impulses of the wronged person were the proper measure of the vengeance he was entitled to exact, and how literally they imitated the rise and fall of his passions in fixing their scale of punishment."—Maine, *Ancient Law*, p. 389.

[8] " Every man's life had its value, and according to that valuation the value of his oath in a court of justice varied, and offences against his person and protection were atoned for."—Stubbs, *Const. Hist.* i. p. 188.

[9] A front tooth usually cost six shillings ; in Alfred's time, eight.

4 A HISTORY OF PENAL METHODS

as well as the theft of anything he possessed, had its appointed fine according to his wer.[1]

The tariffs varied with the different tribes,[2] but the main principle—of compensation—extends through all. In Mercia the wer-gild of a king was fixed at 7200 shillings or 120 Mercian pounds of silver,[3] to which great sum was added the cynebot of a similar amount which was payable to his people.[4] The wer-gild of a thane (i.e. county magnate) came to 1200 shillings, that of a ceorl (husbandman) was 200 shillings.[5]

These murder-fines, however, were much heavier than they look ;[6] those of the kings,[7] numerous as they were, would in most cases have been hopelessly unpayable by private people, and those of the thanes by humble families. Even the wer-gild of the ceorl, or labourer, which was 200 scillings, or about four pounds, was not inconsiderable when we remember that in Æthelstan's time one scilling would buy a sheep, and six scillings (or thirty pence)[8] an ox—the cost would be the price of a small herd.[9]

So that frequently the man-fines[10] were never paid, and then we perceive that the wise compensation system of the codes arose more out of the fear of the vendetta than from humane principles ;[11] if they were not paid, vengeance would be let loose.

[1] Laws of Æthelbert. If a freeman rob the king let him pay a forfeiture ninefold. If a freeman rob a freeman let him make threefold satisfaction.—J. Johnson, *Ecc. Laws*.

[2] For a collection of the various codes and for examples of their amazing minuteness as to all possible injuries, see F. Lindenbrog, *Codex legum antiquarum*, pp. 474, 498, etc. Frankfort, 1613.

[3] The Mercian pound was equal to 60 scillings, the Wessex to 48 ; see H. A. Grueber, *Handbook of the Coins*, p. ix. London, 1899.

[4] Stubbs, *Const. Hist.* i. p. 109.

[5] Thorpe, fol. ed. p. 80.

[6] W. S. Holdsworth, *History of English Law*, p. 13. London, 1903.

[7] J. M. Kemble, *The Saxons in England*, i. p. 149. London, 1876.

[8] R. Ruding, *Annals of the Coinage*, p. 110. London, 1840.

[9] F. W. Maitland, *Domesday Book*, p. 44. Cambridge, 1879.

[10] "It was at least theoretically possible down to the middle of the tenth century for a man-slayer to elect to bear the feud of the kindred. His own kindred, however, might avoid any share in the feud by disclaiming him ; any of them who maintained him after this, as well as any of the avenging kinsfolk who meddled with any but the actual wrongdoer, was deemed a foe to the king."—Pollock and Maitland, *Hist.* ed. of 1898, i. 48.

[11] When a ceorl had been frequently accused, if afterwards he were apprehended he might lose a hand or a foot.—Laws of Ine. R. Schmidt, *Gesetze*, p. 29. Leipzig, 1858.

If the offender were not slain or abused,[1] if he did not escape and live as an outlaw and a " wolf's head "[2] (which was frequently done,[3] for there were some ten men outlawed [4] to every one hanged [5]), he might be sold [6] as a wite theow [7] into penal slavery.[8] For there were slaves as a class in Christendom and in England up to the twelfth century,[9] and they being helpless, like our " submerged " masses, were of little account at all in the community.

Derived mainly from the conquered taken in wars and raids, [10] their ranks were recruited by men sold for their offences, and likewise, it is said, from those who sold themselves in times of starvation ; [11] many were sent as slaves beyond the seas,[12] and the fact that we find this custom repeatedly prohibited [13] testifies also to its prevalence.[14]

From the poor slaves there need be no fear of vengeance or retaliation ; they were a voteless minority amidst Saxon freemen. If a slave were slain only eight shillings were payable to his kinsfolk,[15] while a man-bot of thirty

---

[1] See Laws of Ine, sect. 12. Thorpe, fol. ed. p. 49.
[2] Pollock and Maitland, *Hist.* i. 476 and ii. 451, ed. of 1898.
[3] J. Thrupp, *Anglo-Saxon Home*, p. 145.
[4] G. G. Coulton, *Chaucer and his England*, p. 293. London, 1908.
[5] Pollock and Maitland, i. 478, ii. 450.
[6] And see *Early Assize Rolls for the County of Northumberland*, pp. xviii., xix., etc. Durham, Surtees Society, 1891.
[7] Stubbs, *Const. Hist.* p. 89.
[8] Dooms of Alfred, sect. 24. " If any one steal another's ox and slay or sell it, let him give two for it, and four sheep for one. If he have not what he may give be he himself sold for the cattle."—Thorpe, *Laws*, fol. ed. p. 23. Compare Exodus xxii. 3 ; Pollock and Maitland, *Hist.*, ed. 1895, vol. ii. 514.
[9] Pollock and Maitland, ii. p. 11.
[10] The intertribal wars at one time " filled the foreign markets with English slaves," says J. R. Green, relating the well-known story of Pope Gregory.—*Hist. Eng. People*, i. 37. London, 1881.
[11] Hovenden. H. T. Riley's ed. i. p. 143. London, 1853.
[12] A vigorous slave trade was carried on just prior to the Conquest. —Thrupp, *Anglo-Saxon Home*, p. 130.
[13] Pollock and Maitland, *Hist* i. p. 12. Cambridge, 1895.
[14] Law of Ine, seventh century. " If any one sell his countryman bound or free, though he be guilty, over sea, let him pay for him according to his wer."—Stubbs, *Charters*, p. 61. Oxford, 1884.
Law of Æthelred. " Christian men and condemned persons are not to be sold out of the country, at least not into heathen nations."— Thorpe, fol. ed. p. 135.
A law of William I. was to the same effect.—R. Schmidt, *Gesetze*, p. 347.
[15] F. W. Maitland, *Domesday Book*, p. 31.

shillings was claimed by his master.[1] And that, it would
seem, was all on the part of the State.[2] The Church,
however, to its credit, imposed a penance, a two years'
fast.[3] Other injuries to the theow (slave) were treated
with proportional mildness,[4] but of Church laws and
discipline I shall have to speak presently.[5]

For the damage done by his slave the master was liable,[6]
as for a trespass by his cattle.[7] For the more serious
offences the theow would be handed over to the kinsfolk
of the injured party, unless perchance his master should
redeem him by payment.[8] If upon accusation he failed
at the ordeal, he was to be forthwith branded the first
time ;[9] but the second conviction would be capital,
" seconda vice non compenset aliquid nisi caput." [10]

Apart from legal or revengeful penalties for wrongs
done to any freeman,[11] the theow was absolutely at the
mercy of his master.[12] If he were not allowed to " redeem
his hide " by such small compensation or atonement of
which he was capable, he might have one leg fastened by
a ring to a stake, round which he would be lashed with
a three-thonged whip.[13] It was composed of cords knotted
at the ends.[14] If a ceorl were goaded into homicide,

---

[1] Æthelbert. " If any one slay a ceorl's hlf-æta, let him make bōt
with vi. shillings."—Thorpe, fol. ed. p. 3.

[2] Thorpe, 8vo ed. i. p. 626.

[3] Thrupp, *Anglo-Saxon Home*, p. 127.

[4] See *Theodori liber poenitentialis*. Thorpe, fol. ed. p. 288. *Poeniten-
tiale Ecberti*, lib. ii. 3. Thorpe, p. 368.

[5] Compare Exodus xxi. 20, 21 : " And if a man smite his servant,
or his maid, with a rod, and he die under his hand ; he shall be
surely punished.

" Notwithstanding, if he continue a day or two, he shall not be
punished : for he is his money."

[6] Stubbs, *Const. Hist.* p. 89.

[7] " Omne damnum quod servus fecerit, dominus emendet."—Thorpe,
fol. ed. p. 11.

[8] Maitland, *Domesday Book*, p. 32.

[9] Or he might be scourged thrice, *temp.* Æthelstan. See Thorpe,
fol. ed. p. 88.

[10] Laws of Æthelred. D. Wilkins, *Leges Anglo-Saxonicae*, p. 103.
London, 1721.

[11] By Alfred's Dooms rape on a ceorl's female slave was punished
by a five-shilling bōt to the ceorl ; if a theow committed the offence,
he might be emasculated.—Thorpe, fol. ed. p. 35.

[12] Stubbs, *Const. Hist.* i. p. 25.

[13] Thrupp, *Anglo-Saxon Home*, p. 131.

[14] William Andrews, *Old-Time Punishments*, p. 146. Hull, 1890.

vengeance might then be taken upon six of his kinsfolk [1] (upon the principle that the thane had six times his value,[2] see wer-gilds, *ante*, and Maitland, *Domesday Book*, p. 53). If a theow killed his lord [3] he was to perish in torments; [4] for revenge was sweet,[5] and the strong took it without stint.[6]

Clearly, then, from the nature of early Saxon society, elaborate penal machinery had no place. The freemen atoned for their transgressions with fines when possible, and by slavery, mutilation, outlawry, or death when they could not pay. Cruelly as the slaves might be flogged or slaughtered, there were no prisons in the land even for them.[7] " The villages were mere groups of wooden homesteads with barns and cattle-sheds surrounded by rough stockades and destitute of roads or communications. Even the palace of the king was a long wooden hall with numerous outhouses, for the English built no stone houses and burnt down those of their Roman predecessors." [8]

The Teutons, according to Tacitus, abhorred walled towns as the defences of slavery and the graves of freedom. The Frisians forbade the construction of any walls more than twelve feet high.[9] In the course of time the crown, or central government, grew in power ; the king, and even the great lords, spiritual and temporal, were able to enforce obedience and order, at any rate upon those in their neighbourhood.[10] The royal authority could defy

---

[1] Thrupp, *Anglo-Saxon Home*, p. 144.

[2] E. W. Robertson, *Scotland*, ii. p. 450.

[3] Pollock and Maitland, *Hist*. ed. 1898, ii. p. 450.

[4] See Thorpe, 8vo ed. vol. i. p. 579 : " Si quis dominum suum occidet," etc.

[5] F. Lindenbrog, *Codex legum antiquarum*, p. 498.

[6] For similar laws in ancient Wales and eighteenth-century America, etc., see Westermarck, *Moral Ideas*, i. p. 518.

[7] " Imprisonment," say Pollock and Maitland, " would have been regarded in those old times as a useless punishment ; it does not " (as it was then employed and understood) " satisfy revenge, it keeps the criminal idle, and do what we may it is costly."—*Hist. Eng. Law*, ed. of 1895, vol. ii. p. 514.

[8] Grant Allen, *Anglo-Saxon Britain*, p. 47.

[9] E. W. Robertson, *Scotland*, p. 295.

[10] Laws of Ine. To fight in the king's house rendered the offender liable to be put to death.—J. Johnson.

Laws of Alfred. To fight in the presence of an archbishop meant a fine of 150 shillings.—Thorpe, p. 32.

To fight in the house of a common man meant a mulct of thirty shillings, and six shillings to the ceorl.—J. Johnson.

the vendetta, and from very early times had claimed a
share in the compensation,[1] so that, along with the wer-
gild, payable to the injured party, the wite, or additional
fine, had to be paid to the sovereign (or overlord) for the
disturbance of his peace.[2]

Sometimes he would take vengeance for the State or
for an aggrieved person.[3] Thus in the reign of Æthelstan
a man might forfeit his hand for coining, and have it
nailed over the door of the mint ;[4] and in the reign of
Cnut a woman might lose her nose and ears if she committed adultery. In the early period these mutilations
appear to have often been intended to be mortal, for in
the laws of Alfred and Guthrum we read that " If a male-
factor, having forfeited himself, has had a limb cut off,
and, being left to himself, survive the third night ; afterwards he that is willing to take care of his sore and soul
may help him with the Bishop's leave."[5]

But the maimed criminals were also allowed at large,
to be a living warning to others. That the Saxons could
be cruel enough when bōt was not made, and to habitual
criminals and slaves, we have seen already ; how barbarous the amputations were may be gleaned from the
words of our Danish monarch : " . . . At the second
time let there be no other bōt if he be foul " (at the ordeal)
" than that his hands be cut off or his feet, or both, according as the deed may be, and if then he have wrought
yet greater wrong, then let his eyes be put out, or his
nose and his ears and the upper lip be cut off ; or let
him be scalped . . . so that punishment be inflicted and
also the soul preserved."[6]

William the Norman enjoined that offenders should not
be slain outright, but hacked about.[7] " Interdicimus,"
he commands, " eciam ne quis occidatur vel suspenda-
tur pro aliqua culpa sed enerventur oculi, et abscin-
dantur pedes vel testiculi, vel manus ita quod truncus
remaneat vivus in signum prodicionis et nequicie sue."[8]

---

[1] Thrupp, *Anglo-Saxon Home*, p. 148.
[2] See example, *temp.* Cnut. Thorpe, fol. ed. p. 174.
[3] J. Johnson, *Ecc. Laws.*
[4] Thorpe, fol. ed. p. 174.
[5] J. Johnson, *Ecc. Laws.*
[6] Thorpe, Laws of Cnut, fol. ed. p. 169.
[7] *Ibid.* p. 213.
[8] See *Saxon Chronicle*, J. Ingram's ed. p. 295. London, 1823.

About the tenth century, after the ending of the Danish troubles, and in the eleventh under the Norman rule, the king was strong enough to extend his power and protection.[1] In the twelfth the old system of bōt and wer, designed to compensate the injured and keep the peace among the fierce and warlike race of freemen,[2] began to give place to one under which the king exacted punishment and tribute,[3] which he administered and collected through itinerant judges, sheriffs, and other officers.[4]

The heavy fines imposed on places and people[5] became an important source of revenue to the crown[6] and to the barons and the lords of manors[7] when they held rights of private jurisdiction[8] (Sake and Soke, Courts Leet,[9] etc.), which were frequently delegated.[10]

The State was growing strong enough to take vengeance; the common man was no longer feared as had been the well-armed Saxon citizen of old, and to the " common " criminal was extended the ruthless severity once reserved for the slaves.[11] Then likewise Glanville and the lawyers,[12] under the influence of Rome and Constantinople, drew a sharp and arbitrary distinction between the criminal

---

[1] Stubbs, *Const. Hist.* i. p. 204.

[2] Maitland, *Domesday Book*, p. 33.

[3] Often of death for serious offences, but the prisoner's goods were forfeited for felony ; hence it was to the profit of the government to have many felonies. See F. W. Maitland, *Const. Hist. Eng.* p. 111, and J. Britton, Nichols' ed. p. 35. Oxford, 1855.

[4] " To them " (the subject people) " a new tribunal seemed only a new torment."—L. O. Pike, *Hist. Crime*, i. 134. London, 1873.

[5] The hundreds were liable to be fined for undetected murders— as villages now are in India—and also officers for neglect of duty ; see T. Madox, *History and Antiquities of the Exchequer*, chap. xiv. p. 539, etc. London, 1769. J. Britton, F. M. Nichols' ed. p. 138. This liability was abolished in the reign of Edward III. ; see W. S. Holdsworth, *Hist.* p. 8.

[6] T. Madox, *Hist. Exch.* i. p. 425, etc.

[7] Maitland, *Domesday Book*, p. 52.

[8] *Infangthef*, the right to hang a thief, "hand having and back bearing." *Utfangthef*, the right to punish a thief beyond the particular boundary.

[9] Holdsworth, *Hist.* p. ii. ; and see Stubbs, *Const. Hist.* i. 452, 453, etc.

[10] " The lord exercised . . . jurisdiction in civil and criminal suits which, with all the profits—for in early times the pecuniary interests of justice formed no small part of the advantages of judicial power— was conferred on him by the original gift."—Stubbs, *Const. Hist.* i. p. 102, and Holdsworth, 13, 14.

[11] See Maitland, *Domesday Book*, p. 33.

[12] *Ibid.* p. 83.

and the civil pleas, and the idea of compensation began to wane before the revenge instinct now backed by power. If there was money obtainable, the king's judges would seize it ;[1] the idea of damage done to the individual was merged and lost in the greater trespass [2] alleged to have been committed by the offender against the peace, against the code and king.

Up to the middle of the twelfth century [3] some counties were without public gaols or prisoners' cages,[4] and Henry II. commanded their construction at the Assize of Clarendon, 1166. By the seventh article [5] gaols were to be made in the walled towns or erected within royal castles [6] with the king's timber or other wood that might be available.[7] They were evidently light improvised structures [8]—sheds knocked up beneath massive walls of city or castle. The king's strong places or the larger monasteries would be prisonous enough with little alteration. These early prisons of the Angevin kings were collecting depots or remand prisons for the safe custody of persons accused. Bracton, who died in 1268, expressly wrote that prison was to confine and not to punish.[9]

Bishop Britton [10] (thirteenth century) says that only those accused of felony were to be kept in irons, and none were to be ill-treated except according to sentence.

---

[1] " So intimate is the connection of judicature with finance under the Norman kings, that we scarcely need the comment of the historian to guide us to the conclusion that it was mainly for the sake of the profits that justice was administered at all."—Stubbs, Const. Hist. i. p. 438.

[2] After Henry II. " a crime is no longer regarded as a matter merely between the criminal and those who have directly suffered by his crime ; it is a wrong against the nation."—Maitland, Const. Hist. p. 109, ed. of 1898.

[3] L. O. Pike, History of Crime in England, i. p. 130.

[4] In the period of the Civil War, however, the barons had made their castles robbers' caves, from which they raided the unhappy English. Vide The Saxon Chronicle for the year 1137.

[5] See Stubbs, Charters, p. 143.

[6] The expenses for gaols at Canterbury, Rochester, Huntingdon, Cambridge, Salisbury, Malmesbury, Aylesbury, and Oxford are detailed in the Roll of 1166.

[7] See John Lingard, Hist. Eng. ii. p. 619. London, 1849.

[8] Pike, Hist. i. p. 130.

[9] " Carcer ad continendos et non ad puniendos habere debeat."
—De Legibus, lib. iii. cap. vi. f. 105

[10] F. M. Nichols' ed. p. 44.

In the *Mirror of Justice* we read that " every common prison [1] is a gaol and only the king has the keeping of it [2]; every other man's prison is private, etc. ; and because it is forbidden that any one be tormented before judgment, the law wills that no one be placed among vermin and putrefaction, or in any horrible or dangerous place, or in the water, or in the dark, or any other torment ; but it is lawful for gaolers to put fetters upon those whom they suspect of trying to escape, but the fetters must not weigh more than 12 oz.[?] . . ." [3]

The captives having been collected together within the gaols would have to wait till the next assize. It might be a long time—months (as even now) or years [4]— for the king's judges were dreaded—and of those who could not get mainpernors (bail),[5] many would die of want or disease before the justices were ready to try them.

Meanwhile the prisoners and their families were to be kept at their own expense ; according to Bishop Britton[6] the gaoler was required to take nothing from the poor— who would in general possess nothing to be taken—and not more than fourpence for the keep of any prisoner.[7] None were to be detained from inability to pay the fees. Such were the rules approved by Edward I. In practice, it appears probable that, for the next five hundred years

---

[1] And see 5 Hen. IV. c. 10.

[2] In 1295 a law was passed by which a man should no longer suffer death or mutilation for prison-breaking alone, unless his crime would have been so punished upon conviction. See statute, De Fragentibus Prisonam, 23 Edward I., Record Commission. *Statutes of the Realm*, vol. i. London, 1810.

[3] W. J. Whittaker's ed. p. 52.

[4] In the reign of Henry III. the judges set forth every seven years. —Pike, *Hist. Crime*, p. 135 ; and see G. J. Turner, *Pleas of the Forest*, p. xv. By 13 Ed. I. assizes were to be held three times a year at most. In the early part of the nineteenth century the gaols in the provinces were delivered only twice a year. See Blackstone, *Commentaries*, bk. iv. chap. xix. ; J. Stewart's ed. p. 352. London, 1854. W. Crawford's remarks in his *Penitentiaries of the United States*, p. 37. London, printed for the House of Commons, 1834.

[5] The gaol was his pledge or security that could find (or was allowed) none.—Glanville, J. Beames' ed. pp. 346, 348. London, 1812. For details as to who were or who were not replevisable in the thirteenth century, see 3 Ed. I. c. 15 and 27 Ed. I. c. 3.

[6] F. M. Nichols' ed. p. 46.

[7] Fourpence is mentioned as the gaoler's fee in the *Liber Albus* (early fifteenth century), H. T. Riley's ed. p. 448. London, 1861.

or so, the prisoners would be well fed if they had means, and might be starved to death if they had not.[1]

Those who survived until the opening of the court would be brought up, according to Bracton,[2] with their hands free, though sometimes in leg-irons. We find the description amplified by Britton ;[3] they were to be " barefooted, uncoifed and bare-headed, in their coat only, without irons of any kind,[4] so that they might not be deprived of reason by pain, nor be constrained to answer by force."[5] But thus far no punishments had been meted out ; these followed upon conviction, and were of a physical and sanguinary character.

According to Bracton, an offender might be broken on the wheel for treason, a crime so great that it was scarcely to be permitted that the relations should live.[6] For the " common " criminal there was hanging,[7] and the ghastly mutilations enjoined by the Norman kings were continued ; indeed they were made more savage for many offences after 1176.[8] Up to the reign of Henry III. the penalty for poaching in the king's forests was death or the loss of eyesight.[9] Rape up to the reign of Edward I. might also involve loss of eyes and emasculation.[10]

Stealing from a dwelling appears to have met with the same barbarous punishment. A glimpse of the gentle ways of twelfth-century " justice " is revealed in an

---

[1] On this point see F. A. Gasquet, *Henry VIII. and the English Monasteries*, p. 4. London, 1906.

[2] Lib. iii. f. 137.

[3] Nichols' ed. p. 35.

[4] See illustration given in Besant, *Mediæval London*, p. 349. 1906.

[5] " If, however, they refused to plead, they would be pinioned down on the bare ground and fed upon bread and dirty water ; but they were not to eat on the day they drank, or drink on the day they ate, etc."—Nichols' ed. p. 26.

[6] "Vix permittitur heredibus quod vivant."—*De Legibus*, lib. iii. f. 118.

[7] *Temp.* Henry I., see W. Dugdale, *Origines Juridiciales.* London, 1680.

Richard, see J. F. Stephen, *Hist. Crim. Law*, i. p. 458. London, 1883.

Henry III., see W. Page, *Early Assize Rolls*, p. xviii. etc.

[8] By the Assize of Northampton. See Stubbs, *Const. Hist.* i. p. 545.

[9] 2 Hen. III., Carta de Foresta ; and also 9 Hen. III. c. 10 : " No man henceforth shall lose either life or member for killing our deer."

[10] *Sax. Chron.*, Ingram's ed. p. 266.

Ibid. p. 295.

Mirror of Justice, Whittaker's ed. p. 141.

account of a supposed miracle. A certain Ailward being accused of housebreaking (committed apparently under considerable provocation to recover a debt), was lodged for some time in Bedford Prison.[1] After having failed in the water ordeal and being convicted, he was taken out to the usual place of punishment, where his eyes were blinded, he was mutilated, and the parts were buried in the ground. He is said to have been restored through St. Thomas of Canterbury.

By the time of Edward I. we begin to arrive at sentences of imprisonment, and read of such penalties as one year and then a fine, or two years in default of fine, in the first Statutes of Westminster. For such offences as carrying off a nun, allowing a prisoner to evade prison, or stealing tame beasts out of parks, a sentence of three years might be awarded besides the customary fine. As we have seen, the profits of " justice" were highly regarded ; the fines were perquisites of the Crown (and sometimes of subordinate administrators and officials as well). The prisons were used as " squeezers " to extort them. " Imprisonment," say Pollock and Maitland,[2] " was, as a general rule, but preparatory to a fine. After a year or two the wrongdoer might make fine ; if he had no money he was detained for a while longer. In the thirteenth century the king's justices wield a wide ' common law ' power of ordering that an offender be kept in custody. They have an equally wide power of discharging him upon his making a fine with the king."

In Henry III.'s reign " The wrongdoer but rarely goes to prison, even for a moment.[3] On the plea roll the *custodiatur* which sends him to gaol is followed at once by ' Finem fecit per unam markam ' (or whatever the sum might be), and then come the names of those who are pledges for the payment. The justices do not wish to keep him in prison ; they wish to make him pay money." The authors just quoted say that the fines were generally light, and give several instances [4]—it doubtless depended

---

[1] J. C. Robertson, *Materials for the History of Thomas Becket,* vol. i. p. 156. London, 1875. Referred to by Stephen, *Hist. Crim. Law,* i. p. 79.

[2] *Hist. Eng. Law,* ii. p. 515.

[3] *Ibid.* ii. p. 516.

[4] For example, a fine of one mark (13s. 4d.) for rape.

much upon the judges and the reign. But wherever there are enclosing walls, there are certain to be abuses behind them.[1] Judicial and administrative scandals kept on occurring.[2]

In the fourteenth century many persons are said to have perished of hunger and thirst,[3] and many died in prison about the time of the Black Death (1349).[4] Into the fifteenth century the complaints continue ; we read the following in the *Liber Albus* : [5] " Whereas great outcry has been made heretofore as to many wrongs and misprisons done by the gaolers of Newgate and Ludgate and their officers and servants, . . ." and new regulations were made (and no doubt broken, as the others had been) respecting fees the prisoners should pay.

The sixteenth century showed no advance in the matter of humanity.[6] Torture, which, legally or illegally, has always been a ready trick of statesmen, developed after 1468,[7] and under the Tudor sovereigns the rack was ever creaking to extort confessions. The " common " criminals were treated with the utmost severity ; in 1530 an Act was passed by which all poisoners were to be boiled alive.[8] Burning was the penalty appointed for heresy, high and petty treason [9] (*i.e.* murder of a husband by a wife, murder of a master or mistress by a servant,[10] and several offences against the coin), and, unlike the punishment of boiling, continued legal until 1790.[11] The right hand might

---

[1] See *Mirror of Justice*, Whittaker's ed., Introduction, pp. xxiv., xxxv., and 1st ed. iii. c. 7.
Holdsworth, *Hist. Eng. Law*, p. 39.
W. Page, *Early Assize Rolls*, p. xx.
[2] Of robbery by the judges, see Lingard, *Hist.* ii p. 217.
[3] For instance, at Northampton in 1323 ; see Coulton, *Chaucer and his England*, p. 284.
[4] Pike, *Hist. Crime*, i. p. 288.
[5] Riley's ed. p. 448.
[6] See Pike, *Hist. Crime*, i. p. 427.
[7] Maitland, *Const. Hist.* p. 221, ed. 1908.
[8] 22 Hen. VIII. c. 9.
On the Continent boiling alive was a very common punishment for coining ; the victim was generally strapped to a pole and so lay in the cauldron ; sometimes he was let down into it from above ; see Baring Gould, *Curiosities of Olden Times*, p. 95.
[9] W. Besant, *Tudors*, p. 380. London, 1904 ; and see 25 Hen. VIII. c. 14.
[10] Stephen, *Hist. Crim. Law*, p. 477.
[11] A man was boiled to death in 1531 ; a woman was burnt in 1571, and in 1575.—Holinshed, *Chron.* pp. 926, 1226, 1262.

be taken off before hanging for aggravated murder, or a man might be hung in chains and left to perish.[1] There was the drawing and quartering in some executions, and ordinary hangings were exceedingly numerous.[2] Men lost their hands for exporting sheep and for libel,[3] and there was branding, etc., for perjury, and sometimes for persistent vagrancy.[4]

A picture of the prisons has been left us in a work of 1545. "I see," observes the monk whose complaint[5] is given, "also a pytyful abuse for presoners. O Lord God, their lodging is to bad for hoggys, and as for their meat it is euil enough for doggys, and yet, the Lord knoweth, thei haue not enough thereof. Consyder, all ye that be kyngs and lordys of presons, that inasmoch as ye shut up any man from his meate, ye be bound to giue him sufficyant fode for a man and not for a dogge." He further declares that the charges were greater than any at the "dearest inn in Ingland," and says that men lay six and seven years in prison before the oncoming of their case.

About the year 1552 the City authorities selected what had been a palace at Bridewell[6] (given by Edward VI.) for (among other purposes) locking up, employing and (as heretofore, according to Holinshed) whipping beggars, prostitutes, and night-walkers of all sorts.[7] Later on similar detention places were also called Bridewells, after the first one at Blackfriars just alluded to. In 1597 they planned Houses of Correction,[8] and in 1609 it was ordered that they should be builded in every county.[9] Though they became, in practice, one with the common gaols, they lasted, at least in name, till 1865.[10]

[1] Besant, *Tudors*, p. 379.
[2] Stephen, *Hist. Crim. Law*, p. 468.
[3] Besant, *Tudors*, p. 380.
[4] W. Andrews, *Old-Time Punishments*, p. 92.
[5] Henry Brinklow's *Complaynt of Boderwyck Mors*, J. M. Cowper's ed. London, E.E.T. Society, 1874.
[6] See Holinshed, *Chronicles*, pp. 1081, 1082.
J. Wilkes, *Enc. Londinensis*, iii. p. 891. London, 1810.
E. C. S. Gibson, *Life of John Howard*, p. 47. Lond, 1901.
[7] See Besant, *Tudors*, p. 387.
[8] 39 Eliz. 4 and 5.
[9] 7 Jac. I. c. 4.
[10] Departmental Committee on Prisons. *Minutes of Evidence,* Appendix ii. p. 457. London, 1895.

But to resume our survey of ordinary prisons. The seventeenth century affords the usual evidence of what walls can hide. The gaolers, as of old, appear to have been all-powerful ; [1] sometimes friendly, often the reverse, always extortionate. John Bunyan, during his twelve years' incarceration, was allowed to work for his family —for a large part of the time in tolerable surroundings ; but while in the Gate House prison he was charged huge fees.[2] The prisoners hung collecting bags out of their windows on Sunday mornings.

George Fox,[3] the Quaker, agreed with the keeper and his wife for meat and drink, chamber, and other accommodation at a certain rate. But he refers to one of their party being put " down in the Doomesdale [4] amongst the felons, and this, it appears, was a " noysome, filthy, stinking hole, where was a puddle of . . . and filth over their shoes and the . . . of the felons, the straw almost broken to chaffe with their long lying thereon and full of vermin, wherein is neither chimney nor easing house." Confirmatory evidence as to how felons fared in 1667 may be deduced out of a Statute of Charles II.[5] "Whereas," it says, " there is not yet any sufficient provision made for the relief and setting to work of poor and needy persons committed to the common gaol for felony and other misdemeanours, who many times perish before their trial, and the poor there living idly and unemployed become debauched and come forth instructed in the practice of thievery and lewdness," etc.

The excellent plan was proposed that the profits of the prisoners' labour should be placed to their relief. But we find useful labour within prison walls has always been a most difficult problem, and the world outside was always far too busy to see to it. The prisons of the eighteenth century were very much like those that had been before, but perhaps we know more about them

[1] As very early in the sixteenth century ; see 19 Hen. VII. c. 10.

[2] See John Brown, *John Bunyan, His Life and Times*, pp. 169, 182, etc.

[3] *The West answering the North : Relation of the Sufferings of George Fox, Edw. Pyot, and William Salt*, p. 34. Printed 1657.

[4] As to the pits and dungeons of an old English prison, see Charles Creighton, *History of the Epidemics in Britain*, p. 386. Cambridge, 1891.

[5] 19 Car. II. c. 4.

through the great work of John Howard, *The State of the Prisons*. It is a matter of history how that grim, conscientious Puritan went where the ruling classes neither cared nor dared to venture.[1] For, besides the dreadful stench which stuck to his notes and garments, deep in the windowless (window tax), airless rooms and dungeons through which he went, down in the stale, cramped yards [2]—when there were any—without space or sun, and in which even the supply of water was mostly beyond the bounds, and so inaccessible,[3] rising amidst the putrefaction of those places, there lurked the dreaded typhus or gaol fever, which was spread mainly by the vermin.

It had always been about since prisons were used, and sometimes proved the Nemesis of neglect.[4] In 1522, at the assize in the castle at Cambridge,[5] many of the knights and gentlemen attending caught the infection from the " sauor of the prisoners or the filthe of the house." Writing of the year 1577, we read in *Baker's Chronicle*: [6] "About this time, when the judges sate at the Assize in Oxford, and one Rowland Jenks, a book-seller, was questioned for speaking opprobrious words against the queen, suddenly they were surprised with a pestilent savour, whether rising from the noisome smell of the prisoners or from the damp of the ground is un-certain ; but all that were present, almost every one, within forty hours died." Much the same happened at Exeter in 1586 [7] and at Taunton in 1730, and some hundreds perished at both these places.

Thomas Allen, in his *History of London*,[8] relates that in 1750 " The Lord Mayor, some of the aldermen, two of the judges, the under sheriff, many lawyers, and a number of lookers-on, died of the gaol distemper." The prison

---

[1] *The State of the Prisons*, pp. 8 and 9. Warrington, 1780.
[2] Many prisons had no yards or courts of any kind. See J. B. Bailey, *The Condition of the Gaols as described by John Howard*, chap. ii. London, 1884.
[3] *Ibid.* p. 16.
[4] See E. F. Du Cane, *Punishment and Prevention of Crime*, chap. iii. p. 43. etc. London, 1885.
[5] *Hall's Chronicle*, p. 632, ed. of 1809.
[6] P. 353. London, 1730.
[7] Creighton, *Epidemics*, chap. vii. p. 383.
[8] Vol. ii. p. 48. London, 1827.

was afterwards cleansed ! Howard asserts that in 1773–4 more people died from the gaol fever than were executed in the kingdom ; [1] we lost 2,000 sailors (criminals were often given the choice between punishment and the services) with the fleet in the war with America.[2] He quotes Lord Bacon as saying that the most pernicious infection next to the plague is the smell of the jail.[3] Such were the mephitic dens into which were cast men, women, and children of all sorts ; and there they would rot away or survive, as the case might be, until the expiration of their (generally short) sentences of imprisonment, if they could pay the fees charged on their coming out ; or until they ultimately came up for trial, after which they would either be acquitted and discharged (again when they paid the fees), or they would be convicted and transported or executed.[4]

The number of capital offences was truly enormous. Onward from 1688 they steadily increased,[5] owing, as has been well remarked, to the "unhappy facility afforded to legislation by Parliamentary government."[6] Members who could not become ministers, and who yet wanted to do something, often had interest enough to hang somebody, or at least to get a law passed creating a new capital felony.[7]

Thus, through the ambitions of private members and

---

[1] *State of the Prisons*, p. 10, ed. of 1780.
[2] *Ibid.* p. 13.
[3] *Ibid.* p. 12.   See also Jacob Ilive, *House of Correction*.   London, 1757.
[4] There were always a few poor creatures who, although sentenced to transportation, were left behind to remain in prison, a fate worse than exile, and perhaps worse than death.   See Dept. Com., 1895, Appendix, p. 459, and E. F. Du Cane, *Crime*, p. 115.
[5] ". . . Of the 160 offences referred to by Blackstone as punishable by death, four-fifths had been made so during the reigns of the first three Georges."—J. A. M. Irvine, *Chambers's Encyclopædia*, ii. p. 743, art. "Capital Punishment." London, 1888.
[6] James Mackintosh, *Miscellaneous Works*, p. 718.   Speech on the state of the Criminal Law, House of Commons, 2nd March, 1819. London, 1851.
[7] "The anecdotes which I have heard of this shameful and injurious facility I am almost ashamed to repeat.   Mr. Burke once told me that on a certain occasion when he was leaving the House one of the messengers called him back, and, on his saying that he was going on urgent business, replied : 'Oh, it will not keep you a single moment ; it is only a capital felony without benefit of clergy.' "—Mackintosh, *Miscellaneous Works*, p. 718.

the general callousness of the ruling class, the number
of capital offences kept ever growing, until, in theory,
there were more than two hundred of them.[1] The law,
however, had overreached ; rough and often most brutal
as the people of that day were, they would not enforce
the penalties provided,[2] so that the hangman's ministrations were invoked for only twenty-five classes of offences
in London,[3] and for not more than thirty throughout
England.[4] In fact, it was found that conscientious people
refused to prosecute for the lesser crimes, dreading to
have a share in taking life. But actually the gallows load
was heavy ; an instance appeared in a *Times* [5] paragraph—18th January, 1801—which tells how a certain
Andrew Branning, a luckless urchin aged only thirteen,
had broken into a house and carried off a spoon. Others
were with him, but they ran away, and only he was
captured and brought to trial. His story ended in two
words, which were short and customary : Guilty—
Death. Thus transportation and the extreme penalty
kept clearing the prisons, but those within them were
the while exploited, being entirely the prey and property
of warders, keepers, and assistant gaolers, all of whom
made the most of their positions—which might be given
out like pensions or be purchased [6]—to wring out fees [7]
and make their places pay ;[8] and having what amounted
to unlimited power, and being, by the nature of their
office, used and inured to witnessing suffering, the gaolers,[9]
from the beginning and right into the eighteenth century,
shrank from no means, however mediæval, by which

---

[1] Mackintosh, *Miscellaneous Works*, p. 718.
[2] There grew up, as an eminent judge of those days has declared,
" a general confederacy of prosecutors, witnesses, counsel, juries,
judges, and the advisers of the Crown, to prevent the execution of the
criminal law."—Sir William Grant, quoted by Mackintosh, p. 719.
[3] Irvine in *Chambers's Encyclopædia*, ii. p. 743.
[4] Mackintosh, p. 718.
[5] Reprinted in the *Times*, 18th January, 1901.
[6] Du Cane, *Crime*, pp. 35, 36.
[7] Howard, *State of the Prisons*, p. 22.
[8] See 8 & 9 Will. III. c. 27, A.D. 1697.
[9] See, for instance, the removal of Governor Bambridge by 2 Geo. II.
c. 32.
　　T. Bird, *Letters from the Shades*. London, 1729.
　　Re Governor Huggins, etc., see *Report of a Committee of the House
of Commons*, pp. 25, 26, 27. London, 1729.

they could extract their fees and charges.[1] Thumb-screws and iron skull-caps were sometimes used,[2] and were produced in court as evidence.[3]

Prisoners might be loaded with heavy irons unless they would pay to be allowed lighter ones.[4] They were liable to be flogged with ropes or whips or anything that came handy,[5] the common instrument of flagellation, however, being the formidable *membrum tauri*.[6] They might be kept in damp dungeons and darkness; the living were sometimes locked up with the dead. They could be set apart and purposely exposed to utter starvation,[7] gaol fever, and small-pox, or actually done to death by their keeper's violence.[8]

The prisoners were robbed for room, squeezed for food,[9] and dealt with for drink of all kinds, spirits, and tobacco, in which the officials did a roaring trade.[10] Lastly, the new arrivals at a prison were fleeced and pillaged by their fellow gaol-birds for " chummage " or " garnish " money,[11] and failing this, they were frequently stripped of their very clothing, a process termed " letting the black dog walk." [12]

And in all these vile places there was generally no

[1] Gaol fees were abolished in 1774 by 14 Geo. III. c. 20.
[2] J. M. D. Meiklejohn, *Hist. Eng.* ii. p. 276. London, 1890.
[3] See *The Tryal of William Acton, Deputy-Keeper of the Marshalsea Prison*, p. 4, etc. London, 1729.
And also *Cases in Parliament*, 1684–1737. *British Museum*, 515, l. 5 (39), *re* Bambridge, etc.
[4] Howard, p. 17.
[5] *Tryal of Acton*, p. 5.
[6] See Murray, *English Dictionary*, under " Bull," iv. B.
[7] See *Report of the Committee of* 1729, p. 9. *Brit. Mus. Cat.* 522, m. 9 (28).
[8] There were seven trials for murder in 1730.—Du Cane, p. 36.
[9] The old-time prisoners depended mainly upon their friends and upon outside charity for their sustenance (*vide* Britton ; Bracton, lib. iii., etc.). After the reign of Elizabeth they were supposed to receive 1d. or 2d. a day, or seven to eight ounces of bread. (Du Cane, p. 40.)
From 1759, by 32 Geo. II. c. 28, each debtor was ordered to receive 2s. 4d. a week from his detaining creditor, but Howard found (p. 6) that, in practice, they could not get it, and numbers actually starved.
[10] By an Act passed in 1784 (24 Geo. III. c. 54) the gaolers were to receive payment as compensation for the loss of their former profits made out of alcohol, which they were thereby forbidden to sell to prisoners from the year 1785.
[11] Howard, p. 16.
[12] *Report of the Committee of* 1729, **p.** 2.

66110

production of anything. The prisons and Bridewells were supposed originally to set rogues to work,[1] but the authorities took no trouble to organise it, and throughout the detention-places useful employment (if we except occasional work done for the gaoler, or permitted in particular instances) was impossible. It was found in 1818,[2] that out of the 518 prisons in the United Kingdom, in 445 there was no employment, and that in the remaining 73 it was of the slightest possible description.

Such were the bad old prisons of the past. Their faults were many, glaring, and obvious, but they had yet a human side, too, and a better one. Though the idiot might be laughed at and the new-comer despoiled, though the keepers might be brutal and the atmosphere poisonous, still in the midst of evil there would be individual acts of kindness and self-sacrifice. If the captives were in chains and rags,[3] they were not cut off from the outside world or striped and spotted in a livery of shame.[4] If gaols were hotbeds of infection and cesspools of corruption,[5] at least they were not the ghastly whited sepulchres which were built in the nineteenth century.

MITIGATIONS AND PECULIARITIES

So far we have endeavoured to trace the course of the usual punishments inflicted in various ages on the " common" criminals when they were brought up charged with the graver crimes. There were, however, ways of escape open, which are sufficiently general and important to be dealt with separately.

The Ordeals.—The invocation of miraculous guidance, to determine the guilt or innocence of a person accused, has been resorted to from time immemorial by all manner of methods throughout the four continents.

There were many ordeals in mediæval England. There

---

[1] Howard, p. 5.
[2] Mayhew and Binny, "Criminal Prisons of London" (quoting from the *Fifth Annual Report of the Prison Discipline Society*), p. 97. London, 1862.
[3] Du Cane, p. 43.
[4] London Prisons (*British Museum Catalogue*, 6056, b. 74), bound pamphlets, p. x. London, 1789.
[5] Du Cane, p. 41, etc.

was the corsned, or consecrated barley-cake, which was supposed to choke a perjurer if he tried to swallow it ; when mouth and throat were dry from fear or excitement this was quite possible. There was a test by immersion, in which the accused had to sink two ells deep—over seven feet. A rope was attached round the body, and it is interesting to notice that Archbishop Hincmar (ninth century) gave express directions for the rescuing of those who, by thus sinking, were declared to be innocent.[1] There was a test tried with hot water, in which a stone had to be picked up out of boiling liquid without the arm being scalded. There was a test, to pass which the hand had to be inserted into a glove of hot iron without being burned by it. There was a test in which the suspected person must walk through flames without being scorched. There was a test which consisted in having to walk over nine red-hot ploughshares, blindfolded and unseared.[2]

Perhaps, however, the best-known ordeal was that which was worked out with a heated iron bar or ring.[3] This generally weighed three pounds, and had to be carried—they were always personal and picturesque in the middle ages—for a distance of nine times the length of the bearer's foot.[4] His hand was then bound up and left alone for three days.[5] At the end of these it was examined, and if found clean and free from suppuration[6] the accused was acquitted.

Doubtless, in deeply superstitious times the ordeals, with their solemn prayers and incantations, were fairly effective. But yet they do not seem to have been altogether trusted, at any rate in the later period,[7] since even those who passed successfully through them were obliged to quit the country within forty days.[8] Most people, however, who underwent ordeals had been

---

[1] E. B. Tylor in *Ency. Brit.* ninth ed. art. " Ordeal."
[2] For account of the elaborate ritual, see W. Besant, *Mediæval London*, vol. ii. chap. vi.
W. Dugdale, *Origines Juridiciales*, chap. xxix.
[3] Stubbs, *Charters*, p. 71.
[4] Besant, *Mediæval London*, ii. p. 193.
[5] Thorpe, fol. ed. p. 517.
[6] Glanville, J. Beames' ed. p. 350, note.
[7] Maitland, *Const. Hist.* p. 128.
[8] Reeves, *Hist. Eng. Law*, i. p. 234. London, 1860.

arraigned by twelve knights of the county (who thus resembled a Grand Jury) and were already under grave suspicion ; [1] the ordeal, then, could only say not proven. Moreover, it would appear from various sources that the tests and trials were frequently tampered with,[2] the elaborate ritual giving plenty of opportunity ; [3] at least one king scoffed at priestly acquittals.[4]

After incurring the disapproval of many Popes, the ordeals were condemned at the fourth Council of Lateran in 1215, and by the eighteenth canon priests were forbidden to pronounce their blessing upon them.[5] The ordeals were abolished in England in the reign of Henry III. and the juries took their place.[6]

Another species of ordeal, and certainly another means of escape from the criminal law, was the wager of battle. This very ancient mode of trial [7] was introduced into England by the Normans under William I. If a man made a charge against another, and proofs of guilt were not obvious and overwhelming, the latter could demand trial by battle,[8] unless the complainant were over sixty years old or were sick and infirm,[9] or laboured under some physical disability,[10] in which case he might choose the ordeal.[11] Priests, infirm persons, and women might have champions to represent them.[12] The knights fought with their usual weapons,[13] the plebeians with staves

---

[1] Pike, *Hist. Crime*, p. 131.
[2] Madox, *Hist. Exchequer*, i. p. 546.
[3] *Ency. Brit.*, art. " Ordeal," p. 820, ninth ed.
[4] E. A. Freeman, *History of the Reign of William Rufus*, i. pp. 156, 157. London, 1882.
[5] P. Labbé, *Sacrorum Conciliorum*, tom. xxii. p. 1007. Venice, 1778.
[6] Stubbs, *Charters*, p. 25.
[7] Id., *Const. Hist.* i. 314.
[8] Unless he went to the ordeal, or, in the later period, to a jury. See W. Forsyth, *History of Trial by Jury*, p. 202. London, 1852. Twiss's Bracton, ii. 403.
[9] Peers, on account of their position, and citizens of London, on account of their supposably peaceful avocations and by charter, were exempt from having to accept a challenge.—Blackstone, *Commentaries*, lib. iv.
[10] The loss of certain teeth was looked upon as a handicap—the peasant fighters made a horrible use of them. *Vide* H. C. Lea, *Superstition and Force*, p. 131. Philadelphia, 1878.
[11] Lingard, *Hist. Eng.* ii. p. 224.
[12] Reeves, *Hist.* i. p. 61.
[13] Lingard, ii. p. 222.

forty-five inches long, which were tipped with iron heads shaped like rams' horns.[1] They were to be bareheaded, barefooted, and close-shaven ; and so they fought till death or surrender,[2] at first with the clubs, and afterwards, failing them, in hideous grapple, killing as best they could. If the accuser were defeated he could be committed to gaol as a calumniator,[3] but was not to lose life or limb ; he was, however, fined sixty shillings and lost civil rights.[4]

If the person who was accused—were he knight or peasant—yielded, he was then forthwith hanged or beheaded as being guilty.[5] If, however, he prevailed in the combat or defended himself till the stars came out,[6] he might leave the field as being acquitted,[7] unless, perchance, the justices desired to put him on trial for something else, which they occasionally did.

The custom of trial by battle, along with all other kinds of ordeals,[8] dropped out of practical usage during the thirteenth century,[9] but continued the law for five hundred years afterwards. In 1818 it was recalled into action.[10] One Abraham Thornton was strongly suspected of having outraged and murdered a girl, Mary Ashford. Although he was acquitted when tried by a jury, he was immediately accused by her brother and heir-at-law, and claimed to defend by the wager of battle. The fight was refused by the plaintiff, and shortly afterwards

[1] Besant, *Mediæval London*, ii. p. 198.
[2] *Ibid.* p. 196.
[3] Twiss's Bracton, ii. p. 405. London, 1879.
[4] Lingard, ii. p. 223.
[5] Id., *Hist.* p. 224.
[6] Blackstone, bk. iv., Sharswood's ed. ii. p. 348. Philadelphia, 1878.
[7] Bracton, Twiss's ed. p. 405.
[8] It grew to be condemned by the Church. See, for instance, *C. Valentinum*, iii. c. 12, held A.D. 855.
[9] Unhappily to be succeeded by a dreadful revival of torture all over Europe, where it was in full blast in the fourteenth century, and in England from 1468. Having abandoned supernatural means of extracting men's secrets, Church and State made ruthless and pitiless use of more material methods. The Inquisition took up torture, and the custom spread to the lay courts towards the end of the thirteenth century. Consult, for instances, Lea, *Superstition and Force*, pp. 421, 458 ; Maitland, *Const. Hist.* p. 221 ; Lea, *History of the Inquisition in the Middle Ages*, i. p. 423, etc. New York, 1906.
[10] Barnwall and Alderson, *Report of Cases*, i. pp. 405, 426, etc. London, 1818.

there was passed " An Act to abolish Appeals of Murder, Treason, Felony, or other Offences . . . and Wager of Battel," [1] so it could not be claimed again.

Another haven of refuge from the clutches of the State was found within the pale of SANCTUARY. Although, like prayer or sacrifice,[2] existing round the globe from the beginning,we may confine ourselves to Christian shelters, as they alone affected our laws.

The early Church doubtless afforded refuge as soon as it possessed the power to do so, and gave asylum from the reign of Constantine.[3] Laws were made on the right of refuge by Theodosius in 392,[4] and the boundaries of sanctuary were extended by Theodosius junior in the fifth century,[5] while many kinds of offenders were debarred from it under Justinian (483-565).[6]

The saving power of sanctuary [7] would seem to have been but feeble and tentative in the earlier period, since debtors to the State, Jewish converts who were debtors, heretics and apostates, the slaves of orthodox masters (the slaves of heretics and heathens obtained their freedom [8]), and persons guilty of the more serious offences, were refused privilege.[9]

But the protection of the mighty Roman Church was to be something more than a mere respite for the lesser grades of offenders.   In the year 511 a Council of Orleans [10] ordered that criminals who sought refuge in a church or house of a bishop should not be dragged forth from it.

[1] 59 Geo. III. c. 46.
[2] See, for instance, Westermarck, *Moral Ideas*, ii. 628 seq.
[3] J. Bingham, *Antiquities of the Christian Church*, iii. p. 203.   Oxford, 1855.
[4] *Ibid.* p. 204.
[5] *Ibid.* pp. 205, 217.
[6] *Ibid.* p. 213.
[7] H. H. Milman, *History of Latin Christianity*, ii. p. 59. London, 1864.
[8] Bingham, iii. pp. 209, 211.
[9] By the Dooms of Alfred there was but a three days' sanctuary in a mynster-ham.   A fugitive was not to be dragged from a church for seven days, though none were to bring him any food the while.— Thorpe, fol. ed. pp. 27, 28, 29. If he delivered up his weapons, however, it appears he might dwell in safety for thirty days, while his relations were got together to ransom him.—Thorpe, p. 29 ; Reeves, i. p. 32. On this thirty days' refuge allowed in the early Church, see Bingham, iii. p. 207.   A deliberate murderer might be plucked from the altar, just as by Hebrew law.—Thorpe, p. 27.
[10] *Concilium Aurelianse*, Labbé, tom. viii. p. 350.

Even the slave given up to his master was not to be hurt by him. About a century later Pope Boniface V. (619–625) [1] commanded that none who had taken refuge should be abandoned. The same spirit is found in the *Decretum Gratiani* compiled in 1151. Pope Innocent III., in a letter written in 1200,[2] ordered that only night robbers, bandits, and persons doing violence within the church should be given up.[3] And this we find reaffirmed by Gregory IX. in the year 1234.[4] In 1261 Boniface, Archbishop of Canterbury, in his Constitutions,[5] expressly forbade that any obstacle should be placed in the way of food being brought to such as were in a sanctuary— so much had the Church increased in power since Alfred's time—and that any should be molested, who, having taken it, had forsworn the country.[6]

The exiles to whom this thirteenth-century archbishop alludes were persons who had fled into churches, where they could then claim refuge for forty days.[7] The buildings were watched that no one should escape, and if a man got away the parish was fined. At the end of this period the refugees must surrender,[8] but they might make an oath before the coroner admitting their guilt, and also promising to quit the realm. A road and port of destination were then assigned them,[9] and they might travel thither " with a wooden cross in their hands, barefooted, ungirded, and bareheaded, in their coats only.[10] And," said the king, " we forbid any one under peril of life and limb to kill them so long as they are on their road pursuing their journey." [11] But they would forfeit goods and chattels if they had any.[12]

---

[1] J. L. Mosheim, *Ecc. Hist.* i. p. 461. London, 1863.

[2] Migne, *Patrologiae*, tom. 216 ; " Regni Carraclae," p. 1255.

[3] Bingham, iii. p. 214.

[4] A. Friedberg (*Decretal Gregor. IX.* lib. iii. tit. xlix. cap. vi.), *Decretalium Collectiones*, ii. pp. 655, 656. Leipzig, 1881.

[5] John Johnson, *Ecc. Laws*, quoting Spelman, ii. p. 305.

[6] The Statute 9 Ed. II. c. 10 (1315) is also to this effect.

[7] Besant, *Mediæval London*, p. 201.

[8] *Ibid.*, p. 212.

[9] Frequently Dover, where numbers congregated awaiting shipment. See Pike, *Hist. Crime*, i. p. 232. Clerks were not forced to go.

[10] Britton, lib. i. ch. xvii.

[11] And see 9 Ed. II. c. 10: "They that abjure the realm shall be in Peace so long as they be in Church or Highway."

[12] Blackstone, *Commentaries*, bk. iv., Sharswood's ed. ii. p. 332. Philadelphia, 1878.

Under the masterful tyranny of Henry VIII. it was held that too many British subjects escaped this wise, and it was enacted in 1530 [1] that those who had taken sanctuary should not leave the realm, but should be sent to one of the privileged places (if it were not full, which at that time meant if it contained not more than twenty people), there to remain as sanctuary persons for the rest of their lives; and they were also to be branded on the thumb. [2]

The great sanctuaries comprised Westminster Abbey, and at least thirty other celebrated monasteries, [3] amongst which were St. Martin-le-Grand, Beverley, Hexham, Durham, and Beaulieu, which possessed special charters and immunities. [4] Though traitors, Jews, infidels, and those guilty of sacrilege were not to be received, and though even the peace of a minster might, in the strifes of State, be broken through as in 1398, or evaded as in 1483, yet those within were generally safe from all men. A follower of Jack Cade [5] was protected against the king, and even one of the murderers [6] of the little princes in the Tower found refuge in St. Martin's Sanctuary. [7]

There were whole colonies of these fugitives round the great abbeys already mentioned, "The right of asylum," says Dean Stanley, [8] "rendered the whole precinct a vast Cave of Adullam for all the distressed and discontented in the metropolis who desired, according to the phrase of the time, to take Westminster." But the power of the State increased more and more, and the dominion of the Church was sapped away. In 1487 [9] King Henry VII. obtained a Bull from Innocent VIII. which allowed malefactors to be taken from the sanctuaries if it were proved that they had sallied out from them to commit crimes. In 1504 he procured a Bull allowing him to take out persons suspected of treason. In 1534 King Henry VIII. said that lese-majesty was

[1] 22 Hen. VIII. c. 14.
[2] As to branding, *vide* 21 Hen. VIII. c. 2.
[3] A. P. Stanley, *Westminster Abbey*, p. 346. London, 1882.
[4] Besant, *Mediæval London*, p. 202.
[5] *Ibid.* p. 206.
[6] Bingham, iii. 215.
[7] Besant, p. 208.
[8] Stanley, p. 346.
[9] H. A. L. Fisher, *Pol. Hist. Eng.*, p. 21. London, 1906.

treason, and deprived those guilty of privilege.[1] In
1535 sanctuary persons were forbidden to carry weapons
or to go out between sunset and sunrise.[2] In 1540 many
sanctuaries were extinguished, and several offences, such
as wilful murder, rape, burglary, and arson, were excluded from privilege.[3]

The sanctuary at the Abbey was broken up in 1566,[4]
and doubtless all the others came to a sudden end upon
the dissolution of the monasteries. In 1604 the old
rules and laws about sanctuaries were repealed.[5] In the
year 1623 all rights of refuge were taken away.[6] The
idea lingered in the popular imagination, however, and
in 1697 it had to be pointed out by statute that arrests
for debt could be made in " pretended privileged places."[7]
These districts (such as the Mint, Suffolk Place, etc.) were
alluded to again in 1722,[8] and likewise in 1724[9] as regards
Wapping, Stepney, in Middlesex—more than a century
after legal abolition.

Yet another way was open to people of good position
or repute by which they could extricate themselves from
the ordinary course of law[10] (but not against the suit
of the king, and there were also other limitations), and
that was by means of formal COMPURGATION. We have
seen that in Teutonic communities the oath of a slave had
no legal value, while the oath of a thane was worth those
of six labourers. Thus kings and bishops might sometimes rebut accusations by means of their word alone.[11]
The Visigoths allowed an accused person (of credit) to
reply in this manner,[12] but the practice was condemned
by the Church as inciting to perjury.[13]

The usual course[14] was for the accused to obtain eleven

---

[1] 26 Hen. VIII. c. 13.
[2] 27 Hen. VIII. c. 19.
[3] 32 Hen. VIII. c. 12.
[4] Stanley, p. 352.
[5] 1 Jac. I. c. 25, s. 34.
[6] 21 Jac. I. c. 28, s. 7.
[7] 8 & 9 Will. III. c. 27, s. 15.
[8] 9 Geo. I. c. 28.
[9] 11 Geo. I. c. 22.
[10] *Ency. Brit.* art. " Wager of Law."
[11] Lea, *Superstition and Force*, p. 23.
[12] *Ibid.* p. 21.
[13] C. *Valentinum*, iii. c. xi., A.D. 855.
[14] Forsyth, p. 76.

or twelve compurgators [1]—relations, neighbours, or
fellow-craftsmen who would swear with him to the
justice of his cause.[2] Perjury was indeed often suspected
in these compurgations, and if a man of bad character
got his co-witnesses [3] (and if he could not he was generally sent to the ordeal) he was frequently banished in
spite of their testimony.[4]
In the beginning of the thirteenth century Pope
Innocent III. modified the oath,[5] and afterwards witnesses swore only to character, to their belief in the
accused's credibility. Compurgation appealed especially
to the clergy,[6] and was even called the *Purgatio Canonica*.[7]
Cut off by their calling from all lay connections, they
could rely more upon their own brethren. It was by
solemnly swearing with twelve priests as compurgators
that Pope Leo III. elected to clear himself from certain
accusations, in the presence of Charlemagne (in A.D. 800) ; [8]
and in 803 that emperor ordered priests to defend themselves by taking an oath with three, five, or seven compurgators. The practice began to decline towards the
close of the twelfth century,[9] but still lingered on into
the sixteenth century in England, and in isolated cases
to later times. The Wager of Law was not formally
repealed till 1833.[10]

The Rule of the Church

The Christians had always been an exclusive body of
people, at first from fear, and afterwards from fanaticism.
They excommunicated all offending members, thus not
only cutting them off from fellowship, but also depriving
them of those rites which in their creed were necessary
for salvation. This custom of excluding from communion
was from the first a formidable spiritual weapon among
believers ; what it became when the Christians could

[1] Reeves, *Hist.* i. p. 33.
[2] Holdsworth, *Hist.* i. p. 138.
[3] Reeves, p. 33.
[4] Holdsworth, p. 139.
[5] Lea, *Superstition*, pp. 66, 81.
[6] Holdsworth, *Hist.* i. p. 138.
[7] Lea, p. 35.
[8] *Ibid.* p. 33.
[9] *Ibid.* p. 64.
[10] 3 & 4 Will. IV. c. 42, s. 13.

also wield the sword of temporal power we shall see in the course of time. In the early days they were a world within the world—vehement in convictions, stimulated by persecutions, and extremely well organised.

Their bishops arbitrated and ruled in ecclesiastical matters,[1] and also in civil suits between individuals who were unwilling to go to law before unbelievers; and doubtless they sat in judgment on their own followers before the advent of the regular Ecclesiastical Courts of subsequent ages.[2] From the Apostolic times they had resented resort to external tribunals,[3] and, in a series of Councils,[4] the Church had forbidden appeal to the civil powers against the decisions of Christian Courts; by the eighty-seventh Canon of the Fourth Council of Carthage (A.D. 398) no Catholic was to bring any cause, whether just or unjust, before an heretical judge.

The time came when the State accepted Christianity, and when that religion influenced the laws.[5] Under Constantine the civil officers were obliged to carry out the decrees of the Christian bishops, who exercised a wide jurisdiction. In 376 their Courts were given the same status as belonged to those of the imperial magistrates.[6] From the beginning, and under the Theodosian and Justinian Codes the bishops possessed great disciplinary powers; and after the death of Charlemagne, in the midst of a period of violence and disruption, the Ecclesiastical Courts were firmly established and gained in power as the centuries went by.[7] They had their own rules and codes to determine cases,[8] and came to adjudicate upon many things which do not concern us, such as tithes, breaches of covenant, births, marriages, and wills.[9]

[1] S. Cheetham, *History of the Christian Church during the First Six Centuries*, p. 171. London, 1894.
[2] Stubbs, *Const. Hist.* i. p. 267.
[3] 1 Corinthians vi.
[4] In A.D. 341 by the eleventh and twelfth Canons of the Council of Antioch; in 397 by the ninth Canon of the Third Council of Carthage; and in 451 by the ninth Canon of the Council of Chalcedon.
[5] Lingard, *Hist.* ii. p. 120.
[6] Cheetham, p. 171.
[7] H. C. Lea, *History of the Inquisition in the Middle Ages*, i. p. 309. New York, 1906.
[8] Canons of Council, Papal Decrees, and the many Collections.
[9] See Lingard, ii. 126.
J. Johnson, *Laws and Canons*, ii. p. 189, note F, ed. 1851.
N. Marshall, *Penitential Discipline*, p. 136.

After the appearance of the Collection of Ivo of Chartres (*b.* 1035, *d.* 1115),[1] and still more upon the compilation of Gratian's Decretals (A.D. 1151), they began to rival, if not surpass, the Secular Courts in reputation and influence.[2] The Courts Christian were the defenders of dogma ; in those times, without right believing nothing else profited. The Church Courts also enforced Christian morality. " The bishops," says Archdeacon Cheetham,[3] " took cognizance, as was natural, of matters which were rather offences against the moral law than against the State, and sometimes succeeded in overawing even high-placed offenders." ·" The doctrine of penance," says Mr. Thrupp, " dealt with a series of immoralities which the laws disregarded." [4]

It used to be a custom in ancient times for the bishop to go journeying through his diocese. As he entered each parish he would be met by the inhabitants, from amongst whom he would select seven men of mature age and strait character,[5] who were then sworn on holy relics to relate all they knew, or possibly imagined, about their neighbours and their shortcomings. The bishop or his archdeacon [6] would then investigate and summon suspected persons before them for examination and sentence.[7]

It would appear that these inquisitions with the *Testes Synodales* could be extremely punitive when undertaken by a vigilant and censorious Christian moralist. We find that an energetic Bishop of Lincoln so harried his diocese,[8] and with amazing and minutely personal examinations unearthed so many scandals among all

---

[1] Stubbs, *Charters*, p. 136.
[2] Lingard, *Hist.* ii. p. 126.
[3] *History of the Christian Church*, p. 171.
[4] *Anglo-Saxon Home*, p. 254.
[5] Lea, *Inquisition in the Middle Ages*, i. p. 312.
[6] They would be brought before the Court by its apparitors, of whom there were many ; citations were not to be made through the vicars, rectors, or parish priests, lest the secrecy of the confessional should become mistrusted and the people cease to confess their sins.— *Vide* Archbishop Stratford, A.D. 1342, *C. Lond. Can.* 8. J. Johnson, *Laws and Canons*, ii. p. 371. Chaucer has given us a specimen of one of those " moral " agents in his accounts of the *sumptnour* or *summoner*.
[7] As usual, blackmailing was not infrequently resorted to. *Vide* H. W. C. Davis, *England under Normans and Angevins*, p. 209. London, 1909.
[8] See S. Pegge, *Life of Bishop Grosseteste*, p. 183.

ranks of the people,[1] that he was checked by Henry III.[2] Although the nations and the laws of Europe ceased to be pagan, and became Christianised, the Church, with its haughty claims and well-learned rulers, sought for autonomy. Had not the Apostle Paul said that they should judge angels,[3] and that the saints some day should judge the world ?[4] After such a text it was easy to claim that the Emperor Constantine had declared at the great Council of Nicaea[5] (in A.D. 325) that priests could be judged by God, but not by men. The clergy wanted to be tried by their peers, and looked askance at the other Courts ; the times were given over to violence, the punishments were always sanguinary, and the lay lords and judges were exceedingly rapacious.[6] If there were no more open pagans in high places, there came along various heretics certain to be abhorred at least equally.

So the Church started on a long contention, in which there were many struggles, with local victories and defeats in different countries. In the earlier period the State was the stronger ; a law of Gratian[7] (fourth century) reserved to the Secular Court all but the slight offences of the clergy. It was laid down at the Council of Agde in 506,[8] and again at the Council of Epaone in 517,[9] that while the clergy should not appeal to the civil power as plaintiffs,[10] they were to attend if summoned to the Secular Courts. At a Council of Macon in 581[11] it is implied that criminal cases were to be conceded to them. At the same

[1] Some years later Archbishop Boniface, in his Constitutions, declared (17) that the State must not interfere with moral inquisitions. *Vide* J. Johnson, *Laws and Canons*, ii. p. 205, ed. 1851 ; and observe " Note on Anselm's Canons," p. 28 of the same volume.

[2] The visitations of the archdeacons were highly unpopular, creating any number of spies and informers ; see *Ecclesiastical Courts Commission*, p. xxiv. London, 1883.

[3] 1 Cor. vi. 3.

[4] *Ibid.* 2.

[5] Rufinus, *Hist. Ecc.* lib. i. cap. ii. p. 184, ed. of Basel. 1611.

[6] On the packing and intimidating of juries until, as Wolsey observed, " they would find Abel guilty for the murder of Cain," see W. Eden (Lord Auckland), *Principles of Penal Law*, p. 176. London, 1771.

[7] H. C. Lea, *Studies in Church History*, p. 171. Philadelphia, 1869.

[8] *C. Agathense*, c. 32.

[9] *C. Epaonense*, c. 11.

[10] The same was also referred to by the eighteenth Canon of the Council of Verneuil about 755.

[11] *C. Matisconense*, i. c. 7.

time the clergy were forbidden to accuse one another
before civil magistrates.[1]
The fear and jealousy of the Secular Courts persisted ;
by a Canon of the Third Council of Orleans (A.D. 538),[2]
the bishop's permission was to be given before a cleric
could attend as plaintiff or defendant. By the fourth
Canon of the Fifth Council of Paris (A.D. 615),[3] no judge
was to try any ecclesiastic without first giving notice
to his ordinary ; this order is repeated in a Capitulary
of Charlemagne of A.D. 769. Pope Gregory the Great
(540–604)[4] had contended for the principle that a clerical
defendant was entitled to be tried by his own Court,
and this was established by Welsh Canons of the seventh
century.[5]

A Capitulary of Charlemagne gave the bishops criminal
jurisdiction over the clergy,[6] though the emperor reserved
to himself the right of final decision in all cases.[7] By
the year 853 his grandson, the superstitious Charles the
Bald, was appealing to the bishops at Soissons against
the person of a humble clerk who was accused of forging
the royal signature.[8] In A.D. 866[9] Pope Nicholas I., in
his advice to the Bulgarians, declared that laymen had
no right to scrutinize or condemn any priests, who were
to be left to the control of their prelates. The Council
of Ravenna in 877[10] ordered that none who were under
the bishops' guardianship should be seized by the seculars.
The two systems drifted farther and farther apart ;[11]
clerks were forbidden under pains and penalties to attend
secular summonses. The Emperor Frederic II.[12] decreed
in 1220 that no one might drag a clerk before a secular

[1] C. Matisconense, i. c. 8.
[2] C. Aurelian, iii. c. 32.
[3] C. Parisiense, v. c. 4.
[4] Gregor. I. lib. vi. Epis. xi.
[5] Haddan and Stubbs, Councils and Ecclesiastical Documents, i.
p. 133. Canones Wallici, c. 40 (37). Oxford, 1869.
[6] Lea, Studies p. 178.
[7] Ibid. p. 179.
[8] Ibid. p. 182.
[9] Epis. xcvii. 70. Migne, Patrologiae, tom. 119, p. 1006.
[10] C. Ravennense, c. 4.
[11] For instance, by Charlemagne in 789 and at the Synod of Bamberg A.D. 1491 ; vide Lea, Studies, pp. 178, 192, 196.
[12] Privilegia Clericorum Constitutio Frederici Imperatoris, p. iii.
B. M. Cat. i. a. 6515, Constitutio Caroli, 1498.

tribunal ; any lay judge who convicted one was to forfeit his place, besides incurring spiritual penalties.[1] The Emperor Charles IV. made similar laws in 1359 (*Constit. Caroli IV.* 5), and punished the imprisonment of a clerk with outlawry and loss of possessions.[2] This was confirmed by Pope Martin V. in 1418. The right to clerical immunity[3] was reasserted at the twenty-fifth session (20) of the General Council of Trent in 1563.[4]

The Church, as we have already seen, had been allowed and appointed to regulate the faith and morals of all men. It also claimed, and, in the long-run, secured, the right to demand all clerics accused of crimes,[5] except in cases of high treason, highway marauding,[6] and deliberate house burning,[7] offences against the laws of the forest (that is hunting the king's deer, etc.),[8] and misdemeanours. (*i.e.* slight offences).[9] In time all clerks claimed privilege of clergy, and these consisted not only of those in priests' orders[10] (of minor orders there were four degrees below subdeacons[11]), but of all those who were tonsured and had their hair cut in the clerical fashion.[12]

All anywise connected with Church work, such as the readers, acolytes, and door-keepers, could claim clergy.[13] So that the state of clerkship was frequently claimed,[14] both justly and fraudulently, by extremely humble people, and the existence of the tonsure, and also its genuineness, were very important in criminal cases, for it was sometimes assumed as a claim to immunity,[15] and occasionally

[1] G. H. Pertz, *Monumenta Germaniae Legum*, tom. ii. p. 244. Hanover, 1837.
Lea, *Studies*, pp. 191, 196.
[2] *Ibid.* pp. 191, 192.
[3] P. F. Lecourayer, *Histoire du Concile de Trente*, tom. ii. p. 658 ; and see p. 585, etc. 1736.
[4] For post-Tridentine claims, *vide* Lea, *Studies*, p. 216, etc.
[5] Holdsworth, *Hist. Eng. Law*, iii. p. 253.
[6] Even *insidiatores viarum et depopulatores agrorum* were ultimately allowed clergy by 4 Hen. IV. c. 2, A.D. 1402.
[7] Matthew Hale, *Pleas of the Crown*, ii. p. 333. London, 1800.
[8] Lingard, *Hist.* ii. p. 192, etc.
[9] Holdsworth, i. p. 382.
[10] Lea, *Studies*, pp. 213, 218.
[11] Lingard, ii. p. 127.
[12] D. Rock, *The Church of our Fathers*, i. p. 144. London, 1903.
[13] J. F. Stephen, *Hist. Crim. Law*, i. p. 461.
[14] A. S. Green, *Henry II.*, p. 85. London, 1903.
[15] Lea, *Studies*, pp. 178, 203.

the accused would have their heads shaved by the prosecutors in order to obliterate it.[1]

By the statute *Pro Clero* of 1350,[2] " all manner of clerks, as well secular as religious, which shall be from henceforth convicted before the secular justices aforesaid for any treasons or felonies touching other persons than the King himself or his royal majesty, shall from henceforth freely have and enjoy the privilege of Holy Church, and shall be, without any impeachment or delay, delivered to the ordinaries demanding them." This came to mean immunity for all who could read.[3]

A man who claimed clergy was examined as to his scholarship, being required to read a passage,[4] usually from the 51st Psalm, which was called his " neck verse."[5] Then said the lay Court to the bishop's representative, " Legit ut clericus ? "; and the examiner replied, " Legit,"[6] or " Non legit " ; [6] and the person would either be remitted to the ordinary or sentenced by the judge, although it was forbidden to teach an accused person his letters [7] while he awaited trial (and he might have to lie five or six years in the bishop's prison until he could be presented at the assizes—Pollock and Maitland, *Hist. Eng. Law*, p. 442); yet foreigners might read from books in their own language,[8] and the blind could claim clerkship if they could speak in the Latin tongue.

Clearly, to be tried by the Ecclesiastical Courts was looked upon as being a privilege and an advantage by the person accused.[9] He had every chance of acquitting himself [10] by means of the Canonical Purgation (see Compurgation, *ante*) ; [11] and even if he happened to be condemned by bishop[12] or abbot, in case he failed to obtain

---

[1] Johnson, *Laws and Canons*, ii. p. 194.
[2] 25 Ed. III. c. 4.
[3] Stephen, *Hist. Crim. Law*, i. p. 461.
[4] Meiklejohn, *Hist. Eng.* vol. i. p. 165. London, 1895.
[5] Lord Auckland, *Principles*, p. 173.
[6] Thomas Smith, *De Republica Anglorum*, Alston's ed. p. 103. Cambridge, 1906.
[7] D. Barrington, *Observations on the More Ancient Statutes*, p. 443.
[8] Hale, *Pleas of the Crown*, ii. p. 372.
[9] Stephen, *Hist. Crim. Law*, i. p. 460.
[10] Pollock and Maitland, *Hist. Eng. Law*, i. p. 426.
[11] W. Stanford, *Plees de Coron.*, lib. ii. cap. 48. London, 1560.
[12] Holdsworth, *Hist. Eng. Law*, i. p. 382.

the necessary compurgators, or were delivered over *absque purgatione* (*i.e.* not allowed to make his purgation),[1] or even if, from religious fears, he refused to swear innocence,[2] the ecclesiastical punishments were generally merciful, except for such deadly sins as heresy or witchcraft.

The clergy were forbidden by the Canons to impose sentences of death or mutilation ; [3] the injunction was repeated by Archbishop Ecgberht.[4] " We threaten anathema," wrote Archbishop Richard in the year 1175,[5] " to that priest who takes the office of sheriff or reeve." Again in 1215 were the clergy forbidden the judgment of blood.[6] They were not, said a Council of Toledo,[7] to sit as judges, even at the command of a ruler, in cases of treason, unless he first promised to remit the red penalties. At the Council of Auxerre [8] the clergy were prohibited from witnessing the usual torturing of the prisoners, or from lingering round the trepalium when it was in progress. In fact, except for acts or thoughts which it considered to be high crimes against the soul, the Church was milder than the mediæval State.

The Church, being debarred from the employment of the swift and sanguinary penalties of those times, had to resort to other methods of disapproval, and it evolved the penitential discipline. At first it wielded only spiritual weapons—none the less terrible in those days because they were ghostly—and by refusing access to Church or Communion, and thereby (as all concerned fully believed) closing on kings the everlasting doors, it sometimes brought the mightiest to their knees to implore pardon from the priests of God.[9] On confessing a crime, or upon being condemned, all manner of tasks and toils

---

[1] Stephen, *Hist. Crim. Law*, i. p. 461.
[2] See Bingham, *Antiquities of the Christian Church*, v. p. 459.
[3] *Concilium Tarragonense*, c. 4, A.D. 516.
   C. Autissiodorense, c. 34, A.D. 578.
   C. Toletanum, xi. c. 6, A.D. 675.
[4] *Excerptiones Ecgberti*, *Arch. Ebor.* 156.
[5] Johnson, *Laws and Canons*, ii. p. 60.
[6] *C. Lat.* iv. c. 18.
[7] *C. Toletanum*, iv. c. 31, A.D. 633.
[8] *C. Autissiodorense*, c. 33, A.D. 578.
[9] As, for instance, Theodosius, fourth century ; Emperor Henry IV., eleventh century ; King Henry II., twelfth century.

were laid upon the penitent. Sometimes they were capricious and poetic ; thus if a man had slain his near kindred,[1] the weapon with which the deed was committed could then be forged into a penal chain, and, bound therewith, arrayed in the sclavinia,[2] or, it might be, naked, he would have to trudge away, staff in hand, to his destination, which might be some local shrine, or that of St. Thomas of Canterbury ; but which might be far off, across and beyond the seas, to Compostella, Rome, or Palestine.[3] The ordinary penitent wore no chains, but he was usually required to go unarmed, to eat no flesh, to take no strong drink, and to abstain from warm baths, and sometimes he had to fulfil weird and painful conditions particularly imposed by his penitentiary ;[4] as, for instance, when Robert, called the Devil, was ordered by a certain hermit[5] to eat only bones and scraps which had been thrown to dogs, and to be dumb and act like one insane. Our own King Edgar[6] was condemned not to wear his crown for seven years. Examples could be multiplied indefinitely. A much-employed form of correction consisted in imposing penitential fasts,[7] during which the offender was to subsist upon bread and water,[8] and was subject to many disabilities and restrictions.[9] These sentences might be for any period ranging from a single day to twenty years, and even longer, and all the while the penitent was supposed to drag out his existence in shame and disgrace, making prayers for deliverance.[10]

[1] Thrupp, *Anglo-Saxon Home*, p. 238.
[2] *Ibid.* p. 243.
[3] King Æthelwulf, in the ninth century, obtained an ordinance from the Pope that no Englishman was to be condemned to make a pilgrimage in irons outside his own country.—Lappenburg, *Saxon Kings*, ii. 26. A pilgrim from Canterbury would be recognized by his carrying back a bottle or a bell ; a shell if he had arrived from Santiago de Compostella (Spain), and a palm from the Eastern Land. —R. F. Littledale, *Ency. Brit.*
[4] Thrupp, *Anglo-Saxon Home*, p. 256.
[5] See W. J. Thoms, *Early English Prose Romances*, i. p. 31, etc. London, 1858.
[6] Johnson, *Laws and Canons*, ii. p. 449.
[7] So much would depend upon the view taken by the penitentiary. See, for instance, Charles Reade's historical story, *The Cloister and the Hearth.*
[8] Usually for half the time, and often for three days in a week for the second half. Vide *Pen. Ecgberti, Arch. Ebor.* etc.
[9] Lea, *Studies in Church History*, p. 245.
[10] Thorpe, fol. ed. pp 280, 315.

The Church allowed class distinctions in several ways ; [1] offences might be punished according to the rank of the aggrieved party, so that the penance for the murder of a bishop was for twelve or fourteen years, or longer, upon bread and water, while the slaying of a deacon could be atoned for by seven or ten years', and of a layman by four, five, or seven years' discipline. On the other hand, people, and especially the clergy, were liable to be sentenced more severely in proportion to their rank.[2] Thus, for homicide, where a layman would get four or five years' penance from the ordinary,[3] a clerk would receive six years, a priest ten, and a bishop as much as twelve years (seven on bread and water).[4] These long-enduring penances sound severe, and doubtless were for devout believers. But the Roman Church, always a marvel of organization, allowed its bishops very great latitude, both in imposing and removing penances. " I require not the continuance of time," said Chrysostom, " but the correction of the soul ; demonstrate your contrition, demonstrate your reformation, and all is done." By the authority of the Councils [5] they could increase or mitigate sentences,[6] so that the infirm and the over-sensitive might have their tasks modified.[7]

[1] See the Penitential of Archbishop Theodore of Canterbury (A.D. 673), Thorpe, p. 278.
In the year 1139 a Council of Lateran condemned murderers of the clergy of excommunication, removable by the Pope alone (Labbé, tom. xxi. p. 530). Nevertheless we find Archbishop Richard complaining of want of protection (Petrus Blesensis, *Opera*, Epistola 73, Giles's ed. i. p. 217, Oxford, 1847 ; also Hook, *Lives of the Archbishops of Canterbury*, ii. p. 577, London, 1862) ; and Henry II. provided lay penalties (Reeves, *Hist. Eng. Law*, i. p. 133 ; Lingard, *Hist.* ii. p. 193 ; Carte, *Hist.* i. p. 689 ; C. H. Pearson, *History of England during the Early and Middle Ages*, p. 511. London, 1867).
[2] *Vide Penitential* of Theodore, *De Temperantia Poenitentium*, etc.
[3] Penitential of Ecgberht, Archbishop of York (eighth century), Thorpe, p. 377.
" The common penance for murder " (ninth century) was seven to ten years.
[4] J. Johnson, *Laws and Canons*, note E, ii. p. 11.
[5] *C. Ancyranum*, c. 5, A.D. 314.
  C. Nicaeni, c. 12, A.D. 325.
  C. Chalcedonense, c. 16, A.D. 451.
  C. Ilerdense, c. 5, A.D. 524.
[6] For England, see Thorpe, i. p. 278 ; Johnson, *Laws and Canons*, ii. pp. 10, 11, note D.
[7] Johnson, p. 446.

But they dealt gently with the men of might ; [1] the wind was tempered to the woolly lamb. [2] In spite of Cuthbert's Canons at Cloves-Hoo in the eighth century, [3] the rich were generally enabled to perform their pilgrimages vicariously (whereby there had arisen a class of professional pilgrims ; Thrupp, p. 239, etc.), and to atone for sins by almsgiving and payment. [4] "Thou hast money, buy off thy sin," Ambrose had written in the fourth century. [5] "The Lord is not for sale, but thou thyself art for sale. Restore thee by thy works. Buy thyself back by thy money."

This exhortation was followed and given the lowest possible interpretation in the Canons made (by Dunstan, probably) in the reign of King Edgar in the year 963. [6] When a great man had been condemned to fast, say seven years, he was to lay aside his weapons, and take his staff in his hand and walk barefoot, clad in wool or haircloth, and he was not to go to bed or banquet for three days.

He was to take to his assistance twelve men, and they were to fast three days on bread, raw herbs, and water : thus thirty-six fasts were kept. He was to get together seven times 120 men and set them to fast three days ; thus he secured $7 \times 120 \times 3 + 36$ fasts, or 2,556 which meant as many fasts as there were days in seven years, counting a leap year ! And thus his penance was done, or rather evaded. [7]

But the Church did not usually allow its penalties to be disregarded ; against heretics there were, even in England, severe statutes, [8] and they would be seized by

---

[1] Marshall, *Penitential Discipline*, pp. 109, 110.

[2] The king's familiar friends and associates were to be received into the communion of the Church and were not to be cast out, decreed a Council of Toledo.—*C. Toletanum*, xii. c. 3, A.D. 681 ; Labbé, tom. xi. p. 1030 ; Marshall, *Penitential Discipline*, p. 126.

[3] *C. Clovenhonense*, cc. 26, 27, A.D. 747.

[4] Maitland, *Domesday Book*. p. 281.

[5] St. Ambrose, *De Elia et Jejunio*, c. xx. ; Migne, *Patrologiae*, tom. xiv. p. 724.

[6] See J. Johnson and B. Thorpe ; also Lea, *Middle Ages*, i. pp. 464, 473.

[7] Carte, *Hist.* i. p. 581. I think it was Herbert Spencer who remarked how completely mere outward material performance or conformity could generally satisfy the mediaeval claims.

[8] 5 Rich. II. c. 5, A.D. 1382.
2 Hen. IV. c. 15, A.D. 1400.
2 Hen. V. c. 7, A.D. 1414.

the civil forces and burned alive. Any one who had offended against the Canons, and who refused to do penance, could be excommunicated, and then he became liable to arrest.[1] In this country if the offender ignored it for forty days,[2] the King's Court, on the request of the bishop,[3] issued a Writ of Significavit,[4] or some similar injunction, ordering the sheriff to imprison him until he had satisfied the claims of the Church.[5]

The hierarchy, although, as we have seen, debarred from directly inflicting such penalties as death or amputation of members, resorted to many forms of corporal punishment. Floggings for penance or discipline were administered frequently; [6] the younger monks in the monasteries commonly received thirty-nine stripes.[7]

But the bishops had other and worse penalties in reserve, and, unlike the secular rulers, they employed imprisonment as a means of punishment in itself. The Catholic Church, with its ideals of cloistral life and ascetic seclusion, sought to produce remorse through mental affliction, and in its high-walled abbeys and gloomy courts had buildings ready to immure any one. The first cells were among the *exedrae* round churches and bishops' houses and were called the *decanica*,[8] while refractory

[1] *C. Triburiense*, c. 3, A.D. 895.
Lea, *Studies*, p. 384.
Stubbs, in Appendix II. *Ecc. Courts Comm.*, 1883, pp. 55, 56.
[2] He might even be proceeded against on suspicion of heresy if he continued contumelious. See twenty-fifth session of the Council of Trent, Lecourayer, tom. ii. pp. 648, 653.
[3] Stubbs, *Const. Hist.* iii. p. 374.
[4] Chaucer, John Saunders's ed. p. 83. London, 1889.
" Significavit is a Writ which issues out of the Chancery upon a Certificate given by the Ordinary of a man that stands obstinately excommunicate by the space of forty days, for the laying him up in prison without Bail or Mainprice, until he submit himself to the Authority of the Church." " And it is so called because Significavit is an emphatical word in the Writ."—T. Blount, *Law Dictionary*. London, 1717.
[5] See A. Abram, *Social England in the Fifteenth Century*, p. 111 (London, 1909); also *Chancery Warrants for Issue, The Patent Rolls*, etc.; J. Johnson, *Laws and Canons*, ii. p. 192, *De Excommunicato Capiendo*, and p. 399; Holdsworth, *Hist.* i. pp. 358, 433.
[6] Henry II. of England was severely scourged by eighty ecclesiastics ; the bishops present gave each five strokes, and every monk gave three. The king's penance brought on illness.—Lea, *Middle Ages*, p. 464; Meiklejohn, *Hist.* i. p. 102.
[7] Bingham, *Antiquities of the Christian Church*, vi. p. 172.
[8] *Ibid.* ii. p. 128. I once saw a cell belonging to a Spanish prelate at Majorca ; it was a little dark lock-up and was untenanted.

monks were freely imprisoned in the great monasteries.[1] Though the ecclesiastical punishments [2] were accounted generally merciful—as we shall see presently from English comments on them—they could be pitiless enough on occasions, especially against heretics. The secret and dreadful Inquisition had its own prisons,[3] in which it tortured its victims by every means that subtlety could suggest, and in which the mind-wrecking results of solitary confinement were probably first discovered, and at any rate utilized.

Already back in the thirteenth century the authorities had frowned on prison association.[4] In 1229 a Council of Toulouse ordered that the " converted " heretics (*i.e.* those who had recanted from the fear of execution, and who were even then sentenced to imprisonment for life ; *vide* Lea, on Laws of Frederic II., Bull of Gregory IX., etc., in his *Middle Ages*, i. pp. 321, 484) should be kept from corrupting others. The new prisons built for the Church and the Inquisition [5] were ordered to have small dark dungeons for solitary confinement. In 1246 a Council of Beziers [6] ordered that the captives should be kept separate in secret cells, so that no one might corrupt another. It speaks of the " enormis rigor carceris."

The prisoners of the Church [7] were subjected to various kinds of incarceration. There was the *Murus Largus*, under which they were allowed about the place ; [8] the *Murus Strictus*, *Durus*, or *Arctus*, by which they were

---

[1] For instance, Tinmouth Priory was employed as a prison by the abbots of St. Albans. See W. Dugdale, *Monasticum Anglicanum*, iii. p. 309. London, 1846.
Bingham, vii. p. 43.
Ingulph's *Chronicle of the Abbey of Croyland.* Riley's ed. p. 98.
[2] Lea, *Middle Ages*, i. p. 488.
[3] *Ibid.* p. 290.
Charles Molinier, *L'Inquisition au XIIIe et au XIVe siècle*, pp. 435, 440, etc. Paris, 1880.
Concilium Albiense, c. 24, A.D. 1254.
Lea, *Superstition and Force*, p. 426.
Findings of the Commission of Cardinals sent by Pope Clement V. in 1306 ; see Molinier, p. 450, and B. Hauréau, Bernard Delicieux, p. 134, etc. Paris, 1877.
[4] *C. Tolosani*, c. 11.
[5] Lea, *Middle Ages*, i. p. 491.
[6] *C. Biterrense*, c. 23, et *C. Biterrense*, A.D. 1233; *De Custodia Claustria*, Labbé, tom. xxiii. p. 275.
[7] Lea, *Middle Ages*, i. p. 487.
[8] *Ibid.* p. 486.

supposed to be confined in separate cells upon bread and water ;[1] and the *Murus Strictissimus*, where they were kept in dungeons and in heavy irons.[2] The Inquisition employed, besides, innumerable torments, and could learn little from the imaginings of Dante ; but that dread organisation has a history of its own.

Apart from it, the bishops[3] possessed their prisons, and the great convents had penal cells,[4] and these they would use to inflict penance or punishment.[5] Thus at Canossa, in 1077, Pope Gregory VII.[6] consigned the rebellious German prelates to solitary cells with bread-and-water dietary.

Again we may read of another example occurring in the year 1283. A certain Brother John had, it appears, bitten his prior's finger " like a dog," it was said ; and for this we find the bishop ordering the outraged prior[7] " to keep the said Brother John in prison under iron chains, in which he shall be content with bread, indifferent ale, pottage, and a pittance of meat or fish (which on the sixth day he shall do without) until he is penitent." A worse fate befell Alexander de Langley in the same century.[8] This unfortunate creature was a man of great culture and was the keeper of the abbot's seal. Either from approaching general paralysis, or from some other form of insanity, he passed into a state of extreme exaltation, perhaps to the extent of being, as they would take

---

[1] In 1234 a Council of Albi decreed that the holders of confiscated property of heretics should make provision for the imprisonment and maintenance of its former owners.

[2] For instance, in A.D. 1300 we find certain prisoners at Albi condemned " Ad perpetuum carcerem stricti muri ubi panis doloris in cibum et aqua tribulationis in potum, in vinculis et cathenis ferreis solummodo ministrentur."—Molinier, p. 94, quoting Doat, tom. xxxv.

[3] " We do with special injunction ordain that every bishop have one or two prisons in his bishopric ; he is to take care of the sufficient largeness and security thereof for the safe keeping of clerks according to canonical customs that are flagitious, that is, caught in a crime or convicted thereof. And if any clerk be so incorrigibly wicked that he must have suffered capital punishment if he had been a layman, we adjure such an one to perpetual imprisonment. . . ."—J. Johnson, ii. pp. 207, 208 ; *Constitutions of Archbishop Boniface*, A.D. 1261.

[4] Dugdale, *Monasticum Anglicanum*, vi. p. 238.

[5] Lea, *Middle Ages*, p. 487.

[6] James Stephen, *Studies in Ecclesiastical Biography*, p. 38. London, 1907.

[7] J. W. Willis Bund, *Episcopal Registers*, ii. p. 182. Oxford, 1902.

[8] H. T. Riley, *Gesta Abbatum Monasterii Sancti Albani*, i. p. 266. London, 1867.

it, mutinous or blasphemous. A severe flogging having failed to restore his sense of proportion, he was consigned in fetters to a cell in which he ultimately died, and was buried, the corpse still chained.

There had also existed within the monasteries the dreadful punishment of solitary confinement known as *In Pace.* " Those subjected to it," says Dr. Lea,[1] " died in all the agonies of despair. In 1350 the Archbishop of Toulouse appealed to King John to interfere for its mitigation, and he issued an ordinance that the superior of the convent should, twice a month, visit and console the prisoners, who, moreover, should have the right, twice a month, to ask for the company of one of the monks. Even this slender innovation incurred the bitterest resistance of the Dominicans and Franciscans, who appealed to Pope Clement VI., but in vain."

There could indeed be abuses and cruelties in ecclesiastical prisons, as there always are where high walls conceal. For instance, we may read [2] that in A.D. 1283 certain monks were seized by the Abbot of Westminster, " and so greatly beaten that one of them has miserably expired." There were cases where the Church took the extreme step of degrading from orders. In the very early period this often meant that degraded clerics would be immediately claimed by the secular authorities and set servile tasks [3]—after which they could not be reinstated. Very often they were shut up in the monasteries,[4] a course which the bishops preferred to remitting them to lay punishment.[5] Innocent III. (1198–1216), however, directed that clergy who had been degraded should then be handed over to the secular powers.[6]

But in actual practice clerks were not often totally degraded.[7] To be deprived of orders was looked upon as

---

[1] *History of the Inquisition in the Middle Ages,* i. 487 and note ; and see H. R. Luard, *Annales Monastici,* t. ii. p. 296, t. iii. p. 76 ; F. W. Maitland, *Law Quarterly Review,* ii. p. 159.
[2] Bund, *Epis. Registers of the Diocese of Worcester,* ii. p. 189.
[3] Bingham, *Antiquities of the Christian Church,* vii. p. 18.
[4] *Ibid.* p. 12.
[5] Addis and Arnold, *Cath. Dict.* p. 276.
[6] S. Luzio, *Cath. Ency.* iv. p. 678. New York, 1908.
[7] Coulton, *Chaucer and his England,* p. 288.
Lea, *Studies in Church History,* p. 189.
" Degradation was a penalty rarely inflicted, since the Church

a terrible punishment ; [1] it was the final casting from the fold and was inflicted with great difficulty.[2] Three bishops were required to degrade even a deacon ; six were necessary to unfrock a priest ; and it took twelve prelates to adjudicate upon a bishop.[3] When any were degraded, excommunicated, and sent to the seculars, the sanguinary lay penalties took their course.[4] The chief offence for which the Church withdrew all protection was obstinate or repeated heresy. In the earlier period those found guilty were branded on the forehead [5] and cast out [6] (as once from Oxford, to die of cold and starvation) excommunicate, or they might be imprisoned and have their property confiscated.[7] But with the rise and multiplication of militant sectaries, the Church urged the State to proceed to extremities.

Heretics were ruthlessly burned alive by popular custom [8] (and were sometimes " lynched " like negro

was reluctant to admit that the sacred office once conferred could be taken away for any offence short of heresy."—Davis, *Normans and Angevins*, p. 207. See also W. Fanning in *Catholic Ency.*, art. " Prisons," vol. xii.

[1] Degraded clerks were forbidden to live in the world as laymen by a Council of Rouen.—*C. Rothomagense*, c. 12, A.D. 1074.
Those who threw off their habit were not to be admitted into the army or into any convent of clerks, but were to be esteemed excommunicate.—Lanfranc's *Canons*, c. 12, A.D. 1071 ; J. J. ii. 9.

[2] Lecourayer, *Concile du Trente*, tom. i. p. 543.

[3] Stubbs, *Ecc. Courts Comm.*, 1883, Appendix ii. p. 57.

[4] A lay officer was supposed to be present to take over the fallen cleric into his custody.—*Cath. Ency.* iv. p. 678.

[5] *C. Remense*, A.D. 1157.

[6] *C. Oxoniense*, A.D. 1166.

[7] *C. Turonense*, A.D. 1163.

[8] Lea, *Hist. Inq. Middle Ages*, i. p. 222.
A deacon was burned at Oxford in 1222, having been tried before Archbishop Langton for embracing Judaism in order to marry a Jewess.[*] From that time until 1400 no one is said to have been burned to death for heresy in England.—Maitland, *Law Quarterly Review*, ii. p. 153. London, 1886.

[*] Professor E. P. Evans throws an interesting sidelight on this offence. " It seems rather odd," he observes, " that the Christian lawgivers should have adopted the Jewish code against sexual intercourse with beasts, and then enlarged it so as to include the Jews themselves. The question was gravely discussed by jurists whether cohabitation of a Christian with a Jewess, or *vice versa*, constitutes sodomy. Damhouder (*Prax. rev. crim.* c. 96, n. 48) is of the opinion that it does, and Nicolaus Boer (*Decis*, 136, n. 5) cites the case of a certain Johannes Alardus or Jean Alard who kept a Jewess in his house in Paris and had several children by her ; he was convicted of sodomy on account of this relation and burned, together with his paramour, ' since coition with a Jewess is precisely the same as if a man should copulate with a dog ' (*Dopl. Theat.* ii. p. 157). Damhouder includes Turks and Saracens in the same category."—*The Criminal Prosecution and Capital Punishment of Animals*, p. 152. London, 1906. Cf. William Eden, Lord Auckland : *Principles of Penal Law*, p. 95.

criminals in the United States [*vide* Lea, *Middle Ages*, i. pp. 219, 222, 308,]) and in time this became formally recognized.[1] Pedro of Aragon in 1197, the Emperor Frederick II. by the *Edict of Cremona* in 1238, Louis IX. of France by his *Établissements* in 1270, and Henry IV.[2] of England in 1400, made burning at the stake the legitimate punishment of persistent or relapsed heretics.[3]

But it was not the severities of the Church that kept arousing the jealousy and opposition of the secular power. It was the immunity it afforded to those under its protection [4] which moved the State to attack clerical privileges, and, in the course of ages, to remove them entirely. In Saxon times lay and episcopal authorities acted closely together, but William of Normandy, doubtless continuing the Continental movement already alluded to, separated the ecclesiastical from the secular courts.

King Henry II. had succeeded to the throne after a period of civil war and devastating brigandage, in which the Church had fortified its position and extended its jurisdiction,[5] and was bent upon reasserting the power of the central government. He found that the clergy and the clerks [6] were outside his control, and in the middle ages they were a numerous body,[7] as many people were received into orders who had little or nothing to do in their own profession, and who were debarred by rule from obtaining a livelihood otherwise.[8] So the king employed all his efforts to place the clerks under his justices.

A crucial case arose in 1163. A certain Philip de

---

[1] Lea, *Middle Ages*, i. pp. 220, 221, etc.

[2] 2 Hen. IV. c. 15.

[3] A pious old lady left a bequest to the city of London to defray the expenses of incinerating misbelievers.—Meiklejohn, *Hist.* i. 223.

[4] W. Stubbs, *Charters*, p. 136.

[5] G. B. Adams, *Political History*, p. 279. London, 1905.

[6] It was represented to him that in the nine years through which he had reigned innumerable offences and one hundred murders had been committed by clerks, who had escaped all punishments save the light sentences of fine and imprisonment inflicted by their own courts.—W. R. W. Stephens, *The English Church*, p. 165. London, 1901. *William of Newburgh*, lib. ii. p. 130, H. C. Hamilton's ed. London, 1856.

[7] In the thirteenth century there were, for instance, twelve clerks in the village of Rougham.—Augustus Jessopp, *Coming of the Friars*, p. 84. London, 1889. See also J. E. Thorold Rogers, *Six Centuries of Work and Wages*, i. pp. 24, 160, 161.

[8] Carte, *Hist.* i. p. 381.

Broi or de Brois,[1] who was probably an Archdeacon of Bedford and a Canon of Lincoln, had previously escaped personal punishment on a charge of manslaughter, but was afterwards denounced as a murderer by Simon FitzPeter, who was one of the king's justices. On this he protested vehemently and abused the judge. There had been several other cases about that time, including a bad one of murder and rape by a cleric from Worcester,[2] and another of homicide out of Salisbury,[3] in which the offender escaped with imprisonment, and King Henry took action with great fury.[4] He claimed to have been insulted in the person of his delegate, and ordered that de Broi should be brought to trial, not only for this, but for the original manslaughter ; he wished, in fact, to send him to the gallows. The archbishop refused to reopen the matter already tried and decided ; but for having insulted the king's officer the rebellious priest was severely dealt with,[5] as he was stripped and flogged before the angry judge, and lost his office and stipend on being banished for two years.[6] The king was dissatisfied, desiring nothing less than the death of the canon, and vigorously proceeded towards the subjugation of the clergy.

In 1164 he promulgated the *Constitutions of Clarendon,* by which he desired that criminous clerks should incur the lay penalties. The offender was first to be accused in the temporal court ; [7] then tried, convicted, and degraded by the ecclesiastical tribunal ; thence sent back for sentence to the secular court, to receive the customary draconic punishments. But Archbishop Becket and the English hierarchy declared that to degrade a clerk and then remit him to the secular judges was to punish him

[1] Eirikr Magnusson, *Thomas' Saga Erkibyskup,* i. p. 144, note.
[2] William FitzStephen ; J. C. Robertson's *Materials for the History of Thomas Becket,* iii. p. 45.　London, 1881.
David Hume, *Hist. Eng.* i. p. 391.　London, 1818,
[3] See Herbertus de Boseham ; Robertson, *Materials,* iii. pp. 264, 265.
[4] Magnusson, *Thomas' Saga Erkibyskup,* i. p. 145.
[5] William of Canterbury ; Robertson's *Materials,* i. pp. 12, 13.
Edward Grim ; Robertson, ii. p. 375.
Anonymous ; Robertson, iv. p. 24.
K. Norgate, *England under the Angevin Kings,* ii. p. 21.　London, 1887.
[6] R. de Diceto, *Works,* Stubbs's ed. i. p. 313.　London, 1876.
[7] F. W. Maitland, *Eng. Hist. Rev.* vii. p. 226.　London, 1892.

twice for the same offence.[1] "Affliction," they said, quoting a Hebrew prophet,[2] "shall not rise up a second time." All they would concede was that if a clerk after being degraded [3] committed the offence again he might be handed over as an ordinary layman.[4]

The death of Archbishop Thomas stayed all Henry's plans as regards the Church. "The temporal courts maintained their claim to bring the criminous clerk before them ; they abandoned their claim to punish the degraded clerk."[5] In the thirteenth century it had become the custom that the clerk [6] should first be indicted and inquired upon before he could claim his clergy ;[7] by the reign of Henry VI.—1422–1461—he must first be convicted [8] before being passed into the hands of his bishop.[9]

In 1261 Archbishop Boniface [10] ordered that the clerks in their bishops' custody for capital crimes should suffer perpetual imprisonment. In 1275 Edward I. expressly ordered that the bishops were to allow no clerks to depart without purgation.[11] In 1276 [12] the *Bigami, i.e.* the persons who had been twice married or those who had married widows [13] (highly respectable acts at the present time), were excluded from claiming clergy.[14] In 1279 Archbishop Peckham decreed in his *Constitutions* :[15] "Let not clerks that are in prison for their crimes, and afterwards de-

---

[1] Stephens, *Hist. Eng. Church*, p. 166.
[2] Nahum, i. 9.
[3] Norgate, *Angevin Kings*, ii. p. 23.
[4] Stephens, *Hist. Eng. Church*, p. 166.
[5] Holdsworth, *Hist.* i. p. 382.
[6] Pollock and Maitland, *Hist.* i. p. 442, and note 2, ed. of 1898.
[7] James Gairdner, *The English Church*, p. 42. London, 1902.
[8] Reeves, *Hist Eng. Law*, iii. p. 41.
[9] If a clerk were accused, the Crown got his goods till he had completed purgation, after which they were usually returned (Hale, *Pleas of the Crown*, ii. p. 384). If, however, he was delivered over *absque purgatione*, or if he had first pleaded guilty, the king retained them, and had the produce of his lands for the prisoner's life.—A. T. Carter, *History of English Legal Institutions*, p. 255. London, 1906.
[10] Johnson, *Laws and Canons*, ii. p. 208.
[11] 2 Ed. I. c. 2.
[12] 4 Ed. I. c. 5.
[13] Following a Canon of the Council of Lyons, A.D. 1274. *C. Lugd.* c. 6.
[14] For other instances of the dislike to remarriage, see Westermarck, *Moral Ideas*, ii. pp. 450, 451 ; and E. S. Hartland, *Primitive Paternity*, i. p. 134.
[15] Johnson, *Laws and Canons*, ii. p. 267.

livered to the Church as convicts, be easily enlarged,
or admitted to purgation upon too slight pretence, but
with all solemnity of law and with such provident deliberation that it may not offend against the king's majesty
or any that have a regard to equity."

In 1350 there came the statute *Pro Clero*.[1] Many
persons had, it appears, been seized by the seculars.
By this Act the Church's privileges were reaffirmed[2] and
the offending clerks were ordered to be handed over to
the spiritual court. But for this grant the King demanded that the clerical convicts should thenceforth be
safely kept and duly punished, " so that no clerk shall
take courage to offend for default of correction." Thus
urged by the Crown, and perhaps fearful of other enact-
ments, Simon Islip, Archbishop of Canterbury, endeavoured
to make things harder for the Church's prisoners. " They
are," he complains, " with so much backwardness and
favour committed to gaol, and are so deliciously fed
there, that the prison intended for a punishment for their
crimes is turned into a refreshment and delicious solace,
and they are pampered in their vices by ease and such
inducements and yet make their escape out of custody as
injurious to them. . . . And some notoriously infamous
criminals, that are in truth wholly without excuse, are
yet so easily admitted to their purgations, that every
clerk thus delivered (by the secular judge) hath sure
hopes of returning to his former evil life by one means
or other. . . . Therefore we have thought fit thus to
ordain concerning the imprisoned clerks[3] . . . (they are)
to be closely imprisoned with all proper care and expedition according to the quality of their persons and the
heinousness of their crimes, that they may not to the
scandal of the Church return to their former way of life
from an imprisonment intended for a punishment."
Clerks guilty of bad offences are, on Wednesday, Friday,
and Sabbath day, to have bread and water ; on the other
days, bread and small beer ; " but on the Lord's day,
bread, beer, and pulse, for the honour and eminence of

[1] 25 Ed. III. c. 4.
[2] See, for instance, a law passed in 1378 (1 Ric. II. c. 15) against
arresting priests during divine service.
[3] Archbishop Islip's *Constitutions*, A.D. 1351. Johnson, *Laws and
Canons*, ii. p. 414, etc.

that day. And let nothing else be given them by way of alms or gratuity from their acquaintance and friends, or for any pretence or reason whatsoever ; nor let any purgation be granted them." These severe rules, which, coming from the archbishop,[1] were, of course, repeated by all the prelates, resembled the penal systems of discipline which reached their maximum of cruelty in the nineteenth century.

But there seems good reason to believe that the Church's treatment of its prisoners remained, on the whole, mild and humane. The clergy were not hardened prison officials ; their calling was spiritual rather than military. They were dealing with men belonging more or less to their own order, and were prone to class loyalty.[2]

In the light of subsequent criticism and legislation,[3] it seems that even after Islip's ordinance the Church's convicts were much better treated than were the laymen in the common gaols. Moreover, either (or both) from a sense of humanity,[4] or because the bishops disliked having to pay for the keep of their prisoners,[5] long sentences were avoided and life sentences were inflicted as rarely as possible ; the prisoners would be pardoned [6] on jubilees and special occasions, and sometimes released on their friends paying ransom (apparently of such sums as £20 or £40 ; vide Lea, Studies in Church History, p. 202, and the statute 23 Hen. VIII. c. 1). The State all along appeared on the side of severity, and, from the thirteenth

[1] See, for instance, F. C. Hingeston-Randolph, Register of John de Grandisson, Bishop of Exeter, Part ii. p. 1118. London, 1897.
[2] For instance, they could not be accused by disreputable persons ; vide C. Carthag. A.D. 390 ; Labbé, tom. iii. pp. 694, 870 ; C. Chalced. c. 21, A.D. 451 ; Labbé, tom. vi. p. 1229 ; C. Trident. Ses. 13, c. 7, A.D. 1551. It was complained that the clergy could not be accused by the laity and would not accuse each other.—Lea, Studies in Church History, pp. 208, 211.
[3] For instance, Simon Fish in his Supplicacyon of Beggars, written about 1529, J. M. Couper's ed. p. 12. London, 1871.
Shakespeare, writing of the fifteenth century, refers to the matter :
. . . You know our king
Is prisoner to the bishop here, at whose hands
He hath good usage and great liberty.
Third Part of King Henry VI. iv. 5.
See also Hook, Archbishops of Canterbury, ii. p. 398.
[4] J. C. Robertson, Materials, iv. p. 49 ; Epist. Nicolaus de Monte.
[5] Coulton, Chaucer, p. 288.
[6] Lea, Studies in Church History, p. 196.

century, was in the habit of sending clerks to their bishop *absque purgatione*, who, in theory at least, were to be life prisoners. Indeed, if the ordinary should attempt to release such persons, he could be restrained from doing so by a writ out of the Chancery.[1]

So early as 1238 a Bishop of Exeter [2] was in trouble for having sent a certain clerk to purgation. Later on an Abbot of St. Albans [3] was accused of allowing some prisoners to escape ; and there are doubtless other instances. But evidently the prisoners of the bishops were continually being released, for we find a special statute [4] passed in the year 1402 forbidding that clerks found guilty of treason (of less degree than plotting against the king himself), or who were known to be common thieves, should be allowed any sort of purgation. In 1485 an Act [5] was passed by which the bishops might commit priests, clerks, and religious men to ward and prison for advowtry (*i.e.* adultery), fornication, incest, or any other fleshly incontinence, and they were not to be liable for actions for wrongful imprisonment.

In 1487 a severe blow was aimed at immunity. By this Act,[6] clerks (*i.e.* such as could read, but who were not actually within orders) were to enjoy their privilege only once ; and to ensure that they should no longer be " continually admitted as oft as they did offend," it was ordained that clerks not within orders, who should hereafter be convicted of murder, should be forthwith branded [7] by the gaoler in open court with the letter M upon the brawn of the left thumb, and, if found guilty of theft,[8] with the letter T, before being handed over to the ordinary officer.

An ordained priest could appeal to his Church again, but if he should claim his clergy a second (or other) time he was to have his letters of ordination ready at hand, though he might be allowed one day's grace in which

---

[1] Hale, *Pleas of the Crown*, ii. p. 384.
[2] Pollock and Maitland, p. 444, ed. 1898 ; p. 427, ed. 1895.
[3] Riley, *Chronica Monasterii S. Albani*, iii. p. 48. See also Britton, Nicols' ed. p. 27.
[4] 4 Hen. IV. c. 3.
[5] 1 Hen. VII. c. 4.
[6] 4 Hen. VII. c. 13.
[7] Stephen, *Hist. Crim. Law*, i. p. 463.
[8] Holdsworth, *Hist.* i. p. 382.

to obtain them—or equivalent evidence from the nearest bishop—and if they were not forthcoming he forfeited all clerical privileges.[1] In 1496 lay persons who should murder their lord, master, or sovereign immediate were deprived of their clergy ; and in the fourth year of the following reign more exceptions were made, and clergy was taken from all, not actually within orders, who committed a felony in a church, or upon the king's highway, or who slew anybody in his own house.[2]

We have already seen with what exceeding difficulty a clerk, and more especially a priest, could be degraded and cast out of orders. To remedy this, Cardinal Wolsey, Archbishop of York, obtained a Bull[3] (as regarded England) from Pope Clement VII. in 1528, by which a single bishop, assisted by two abbots or other high dignitaries, could perform the ceremony.[4]

The statute 23 Hen. VIII. c. 1 (1531) alludes to the monition of Edward I. (1275), to the effect that no Church prisoners should depart without strict purgation, on which Henry VIII. observes that, nevertheless, they were released very easily. It cites the statute of Henry IV. (1402), which ordered that notorious criminals should make no purgation, and goes on to say that the ordinaries kept releasing offenders speedily and hastily " for corruption and lucre," or because the clergy will in no wise consent to take charge of prisoners. The law then proceeds to take away the benefit of clergy from the various petit treasons previously referred to, and also for arson, from all clerks—subdeacons and the grades above them still excepted. The clergy within orders were to have lifelong imprisonment for these crimes, unless they could find guarantees for good conduct—the accused to the extent of £40, with two substantial sureties in £20 apiece. By this statute it was also intended to relieve the bishops of

[1] 12 Hen. VII. c. 7.
[2] 4 Hen. VIII. c. 2, A.D. 1512.
[3] T. Rymer, *Foedera*, tom. xiv. p. 239. London, 1712.
[4] Lea, *Studies in Church History*, p. 189.
By the fourth Canon at the thirteenth session of the Council of Trent in 1551, it was decreed that a bishop or his vicar-general could condemn, and even degrade criminous clergy, with the assistance of as many mitred abbots, or. in default of them, as many high ecclesiastics as there would have been bishops under the old system.—Lecourayer, i. p. 550 ; Luzio, *Cath. Ency.* iv. p. 678.

the burden of maintaining their prisoners, and they were empowered to degrade such offending clerks, and to hand them over " in sure and safe keeping into the King's Bench," with a certificate certifying their degradation —now so much easier—upon which the king's judges were to pass such sentences (usually of death) as would have been passed upon the convicted if, at the time of their accusation, they had been laymen and not clerks of any kind.

Nor was this all, for in the same year (1531) an Act [1] was passed by which escapes from the bishop's prison were made felony for the clerks ; those within orders were to be sent back to their prison, to abide there without release. In 1533 [2] clergy was taken away from all who refused to plead, or who challenged above twenty jurymen peremptorily. In 1536 [3] clergymen within orders were to be placed on the same footing with other clerks, but this law only lasted about a decade. But now the immunity of the clergy began to be taken away by a long series of statutes exempting particular crimes from any indulgence.[4]

In 1576 convicted clerks ceased to be handed over to the bishops to make purgation.[5] For all " clergy-able " felonies, Lords of Parliament [6] (even when they could not read) and the clergy in orders were immediately released. The rest who could read were discharged for a first offence upon being branded, but the Court might also order their detention in prison for not more than a year ; the captives who could not read were speedily hanged.[7]

[1] 23 Hen. VIII. c. 11.
[2] 25 Hen. VIII. c. 3.
[3] 28 Hen. VIII. c. 1, s. 7.
[4] " In 1533 unnatural offences, in 1541 witchcraft, were made felonies. In 1603 bigamy was made a felony."—Holdsworth, *Hist.* i. p. 388.
[5] 18 Eliz. c. 7.
[6] Special, and moral prosecutions were carried out through the Court of Star Chamber (3 Hen. VII. c. 1) (*vide* Lingard, *Hist.* vii. p. 377 ; Carter, *Outlines of English Legal History*, p. 101 ; Hudson, *Treatise on the Star Chamber*), and by the hated Court of High Commission (1 Eliz. c. 1) (see Hale, *Precedents and Proceedings in Criminal Cases*, p. l., and *Ecc. Courts Comm.*, 1883, p. xxxviii.), which imposed some enormous fines and inflicted various painful penalties, till they, with the ecclesiastical courts, were overthrown in the year 1640 (16 Car. I. cc. 10 and 11).
[7] Blackstone, iv. p. 28.

As the privilege of clergy became less worth having it was extended: to the *bigami*, or twice married, in 1547, and to women [1] (professed nuns had always lived under the Church's rule) in 1692. Upon conviction they were to be treated in the same way as the men in similar cases, that is, branded upon the hand, and then discharged, either at once or after imprisonment not exceeding one year.

In 1699 [2] it was ordered that the branding should be done upon the face, but this cruel marking was found to prevent the victims from obtaining employment and to render them desperate, and the law was repealed six years afterwards in the reign of Anne.[3] In 1705 the reading test was abandoned. The distinction had come to lie between offences, not offenders,[4] and all were admitted to " clergy " who had been convicted of any of these minor felonies which still remained clergyable.[5] The Act of 1705 also provided that such convicts should be liable to be sent to houses of correction or to public workhouses, for periods of not less than six months or exceeding two years, at the discretion of the magistrates.

In 1717 [6] it was enacted that persons (other than peers or clerks in orders) guilty of clergyable offences might be transported for seven years [7] (the usual sentence was for fourteen), instead of being branded or whipped.[8] In 1779 [9] persons liable to be burned in the hand might escape with a fine, or they might be whipped in public or private, not more than three times ; women were to be flogged in the presence of females. By this Act the branding was abolished in practice ; [10] and about half a century later all that remained of the old privilege was done away with in the reign of George IV.[11]

[1] Women received certain allowances by 21 Jac. I. c. 6 in 1623.
[2] 10 & 11 Will. III. c. 23.
[3] 5 Anne c. 6.
[4] Carter, *Hist Eng. Legal Inst.* p. 247, ed, 1902.
[5] Stephen, *Hist. Crim. Law*, i. 463.
[6] 4 Geo. I. c. 11.
[7] Holdsworth, *Hist.* p. 383.
[8] Stephen, *Hist. Crim. Law*, p. 463.
[9] 19 Geo. III. c. 74, s. 3.
[10] But was continued in New South Wales up to the year 1797, *vide* D. Collins's *Account*, vol. ii. p. 54.
[11] 7 & 8 Geo. IV. c. 28, s. 6, A.D. 1827.

It has been customary to condemn all these old rights for so many years accorded to clerkship, because they are supposed to have constituted infringements of the principle that all men should be equal before the law.[1] But when we consider the barbarities they prevented, and after we have examined and ascertained the aimlessness and inutility of mere punishments, we may be forced to think that they were not an unmixed evil, and that, perhaps, they rather made for good.

SUMMARY AND " POETIC " PUNISHMENTS

Since the poor human body has always been sensitive, so at the promptings of the revenge instinct it has always been assailable and most readily beaten. Naturally enough, the Duke of Gloster exclaims—in that most subtle second act of *Henry VI.*—" Have you not beadles in your town and things called whips?" Of course they had. The serf, the varlet, the vagabond, the lunatic, and the petty offender were all whipped with uncertain severity;[2] most likely until the victim was bloody and until the operator was tired and felt he had earned his fee. Doubtless the whips were of all sorts and sizes. They are frequently represented as having three thongs;[3] Titus Oates was flogged with a whip of six.[4] I have seen and handled a lash of transportation times, which had a thick leather thong bound with wire.[5] The cat-o'-nine-tails is alluded to in the eighteenth century.[6]

Both men and women (the latter up to 1817) were flagellated in public,[7] being either tied up to a post, or fastened behind a cart and so thrashed along the road. Perhaps the most obvious thing to do, next to flogging

[1] Yet, as Professor Menger expressed it, " Nothing can be so unequal as the equal treatment of unequals."
[2] Stephen, *Hist. Crim. Law*, iii. p. 27.
[3] William Andrews, *Old-Time Punishments*, p. 153.
[4] *Dictionary of National Biography.* There was an Act of Henry VIII, which has been called the whip with six strings, which may have some reference to the hangman's usual weapon.
[5] On the old convict ship *Success.*
[6] See Murray, *Dictionary*, vol. iv.
[7] *Vide* H. B. Irving, *Life of Judge Jeffreys*, p. 42.
57 Geo. III. c. 75.

an offender, was to exhibit him to the populace. The country was immeasurably more parochial than it is now in these times of travel, and to be rendered infamous in one's village or neighbourhood was no trifling penalty ; and so we find the stocks set up in the towns and hamlets,[1] and, for more serious misdemeanours, there was the lofty pillory or neck-catcher (the *heals-fang*).

This well-known instrument [2] was made of all shapes and sizes, and varied from a forked post or a slit pillar [3] to what must have looked like a penal dovecote made to hold several prisoners.[4] The convicted were sometimes drawn thither on hurdles, and might be accompanied by minstrels on the way.[5] The hair of the head and beard was shaved off, and sometimes the victims were secured by being nailed through the ears to the framework, and might also be branded.[6] With faces protruding through the strong beams, and with hands through two holes, secured and helpless, they were made to stand defenceless before the crowd as targets for any missiles that might be thrown. To those who were hated this was a serious ordeal, for they would be so pelted and knocked about by the mob as to be badly wounded, if not actually done to death.[7] At length those who had stood their time were released, and those who had had their ears nailed would be cut free, and then they might slink away from the scene of shame, or be carried back to prison to endure additional punishment. The pillory was abolished for all offences except perjury and subornation in 1816,[8] and altogether in the year 1837.[9]

Before leaving the middle ages we must examine what I have classed as the poetic punishments. These were the spontaneous reprisals with which the community strove to repay the criminals in kind, and by

[1] See Statute of Labourers, 25 Ed. III. c. 2.
[2] L. Jewitt, "The Pillory and who they put in it," *The Reliquary*, i. p. 210, April 1861.
[3] Besant, *Tudors*, p. 381.
[4] Andrews, *Old-Time Punishments*, p. 68.
[5] Jewitt, p. 213.
[6] *Ibid.* p. 221.
[7] On one occasion two informers were killed in the pillory for getting certain lads hanged for the sake of reward. See J. Villette, *Annals of Newgate*, vol. iv. p. 116. London, 1776.
[8] 56 Geo. III. c. 138.
[9] 7 Will. IV. and 1 Vict. c. 23.

which, if strict taliation were seldom attainable, our ancestors succeeded in contriving many chastisements that were, at any rate, associable equivalents. Of these a few examples may be given. For instance, a baker who sold loaves which were short of weight was shown with the bread tied round his neck.[1] A fishmonger who had been selling bad fish was paraded with a collar of stinking smelts slung over his shoulders.[2] A grocer who had been selling much-adulterated spices was placed in the pillory and had the powders burned beneath his nose (A.D. 1395).[3] A heretic who had advocated strict Judaism was sentenced to prison and to be fed entirely upon pork.[4] The Inquisition attached two pieces of red cloth in the shape of tongues to the breast, and two more upon the shoulders of a false witness, which were to be worn for life.[5] Indeed, badges and crosses were often imposed, and were in these times a dreadful mark of Cain.[6] In 1505 two men were sentenced by the archbishop to wear a faggot (or a badge representing one) upon the left shoulder, to show that they stood in danger of the flames.[7] It would seem they did, for they were burned alive in 1511.

Louis IX. ordered that those who had spoken indecently should have their tongues pierced and their upper lips cut away.[8] Pope Innocent IV. remonstrated with the king against this barbarity. The mutilation of the tongue was a punishment known and inflicted in England for blasphemy. In 1656 one James Nayler, "the mad Quaker," had his tongue pierced with a hot iron for claiming to be the Messiah.[9] He was also whipped at the cart's tail, and kept in prison for two years. A drunkard was sometimes walked about in a barrel, his head protruding from the top and his hands from two holes made in its sides.[10]

---

[1] Pike, *Hist.* i. p. 237.
[2] Besant, *Mediæval London*, p. 354.
[3] J. A. Rees, *The Grocery Trade*, p. 57. London, 1910.
[4] W. Hudson, *Treatise on the Court of Star Chamber*, ii. p. 225.
[5] Lea, *Hist. Inq. Middle Ages*, i. p. 441.
[6] Hudson, *Treatise on the Court of Star Chamber*, p. 225.
[7] James Gairdner, *English Church*, p. 53.
[8] Barrington, *Ancient Statutes*, p. 422.
[9] C. H. Firth, *Last Years of the Protectorate*, p. 101. London, 1909.
[10] Andrews, *Old-Time Punishments*, p. 140.

For the village scold [1] they kept the brank or bridle of iron, which contained a flat (and for the unfortunate witches [2] occasionally a spiked and painful) gag that went into the mouth and pressed down the tongue. They might also be placed in the local ducking chair [3] and immersed in water. A remarkable illustration [4] of the intensely individual and personal aspect of primitive penalties [5] is furnished where—as it sometimes happened—the prosecutor had himself to execute his convict assailant, " or dwelle in prison with the felon unto the time that he wyll do that office or else find a hangman."[6]

---

[1] Jewitt, "Scolds and how they cured them," *Reliquary*, October 1860.

[2] Andrews, *Old-Time Punishments*, p. 45.

[3] See Jewitt, "A few Notes on Ducking Stools," *Reliquary*, January 1861.

[4] Andrews, *Old-Time Punishments*, etc., etc.

[5] Holdsworth, *Hist.* ii. p. 327.

[6] At some of the American lynchings the injured woman applies a match to the wood upon which the offending negro is to be burned to death.

CHAPTER II

THE WITCH TRIALS

TOWARDS the middle of the seventeenth century there lived at Manningtree a certain Matthew Hopkins, whose name deserves perhaps to be recorded. Not that he stands by any means apart, a veritable Lucifer among the devils. Sprenger in Germany, Torquemada in Spain, Grillandus in Italy, de l'Ancre in France, and other persecutors over Christendom, were better known and had killed more people. But Hopkins went to work on English ground. The people were then professing the same creed that the majority do now. Shakespeare had been in his grave more than a generation, and trees may have been standing as bushes in the fields and lanes of Essex which will yet renew leaves and branches at the kiss of coming spring. Hopkins reveals the spirit of his time, for it has been wisely observed that every society has the criminals it deserves. His kind remain with us still as spies and blackmailers, traitors and " friendly natives " of the tribe of Judas generally. But they derive their power to harm from the community in which they live. Parasites need a proper " host " to flourish in. A dark and superstitious age it must have been to countenance this man ; for he was a professional " discoverer," or, as he was sometimes called and styled, Witch-Finder General. He began with the destruction of some half-dozen persons in his native hamlet. We cannot determine what had marked them down—perhaps they were his private enemies—moral reform has always been a ready pretext to work vengeance with, and has been much employed in these latter days. They may have been old, eccentric, isolated, or insane ; in any case, once seized they had to die, and in their torments implicated others, most likely any names conveniently suggested to them. The fame of the new discoverer spread far and wide. Towns and hundreds in the eastern county, and even places far outside its boundaries, sent to this fell apostle, saying " Come over and help us," and on the track of blood the monster went. It was his wont to ride upon these expeditions accompanied by another man, and by a female searcher, whose services would be required in the minute personal examinations which were carried out, especially on women. He made an open charge of twenty shillings for each village visited, but no doubt in this nefarious calling there were other and more profitable ways of extorting money. Can we not well imagine what sums may have been paid to him (as they are to the "sex" blackmailers of to-day) to avoid accusation? How many may have yielded their little all to save some one who was dear to them from common ill-usage, probable death, and certain disgrace, which such a charge involved? Who knows how extorted gold might influence the ordeals enforced? Who shall say what may have come by stealth to the witch-finders to bring ruin upon some enemy, perhaps upon some rival? Who, indeed? From place to place swooped this bird of prey, descending on peaceful homesteads and capturing whom he chose. Woe to the man, and still more to the woman, who lived alone, who kept a black cat, or who was found to carry birthmarks on her body, or to be the least out of the normal in physical structure! Woe to the person who was eccentric, subject to fits or trances, or who might be in any way deranged or of weak intellect! Woe, in fact, to the unhappy creature who by any means came in for accusation! The Pishogue mark would thenceforth be upon them ; relations would drop away as from contamination with the plague [1] ; and the most brutal rabble of that time would jostle round, intent upon the chase, with their fierce lust for blood not the less keen from the idea that there was something Christian in their cruelty. The victim would then be seized and carried off to further interrogation, ill-treatment,

---

[1] " They died alone and unpitied," says Lecky ; " . . . their very kinsmen shrank from them as tainted and accursed."—*History of Rationalism*, p. 149. London, 1865.

and torture.   Parents and children, comrades and lovers,
might weep in secret, and the boldest might even venture
to denounce the senseless iniquity of the proceedings—
at which they would incur no little danger.   But they
would speak unheeded, and have to linger around the
gallows till the final act, when something swayed and
dangled from a cord.

But somehow good Master Matthew began to be
unpopular, and many reasons might account for it.
Perhaps he had been unwise in the selection of his "subjects"—it looks like it, for one was an old clergyman—
and lived to find out that some of them had not been quite
so friendless as he may have counted on.   Perhaps the
supply of lonely or defenceless folk had given out,
or that in pushing his profession so far afield he
could not estimate the new material.   " Discoveries," of
course, had to be made to keep up his reputation and
his income, and as he pursued his way through a wide
area it may be that quite a large number of people began
to feel themselves open to accusation, and so were ready
to consider it suspicious that he alone had such an eye
for witches.   And then a whispering rose amongst them,
until it reached the persecutor's ears :   For sure this
man is aided by the Devil, or else he would not ferret out
so many.   And he may well have started when he saw
the anger-light in the fierce eyes around him, and when
he felt at last the frightful superstitions, which he had
kindled and well thriven on, were out of hand, turned
hard against himself.   So he produced a little book which
bears the date of 1647, printed, he tells us, " For the
benefit of the whole Kingdome."   It has upon the title-
page the somewhat troublesome quotation, " Thou
shalt not suffer a witch to live" (Exodus xxii. 18).   We
cannot do better than glance through its pages and at
the " Certain queries answered which have been and
which are likely to be objected against Matthew Hopkins,
in his way of finding out witches."

" *Querie I.*—That he must needs be the greatest witch,
sorcerer, and wizzard himself, else hee could not doe
it.

" *Answer.*—If Satan's Kingdome be divided against
itself how shall it stand ? "

The next paragraph is interesting as once more emphasizing the crude and absolutely material notions conceived of the spiritual world.

" *Querie II.*—If he never went so farre as is before stated, yet for certaine he met with the devill and cheated him of his booke, wherein were written all the witches' names in England, and if he looks at any witch he can tell by her countenance what she is ; so by this his helpe is from the devill.

" *Answer.*—If he had been too hard for the devill and got his booke it had been to his great commendation and no disgrace at all."

It will be noticed that he does not exactly deny even this report, or appear to consider it at all unusual to meet the devil walking about casually. " We must needs argue," he continues later, " he is of long standing, above 6,000 years, then he must needs be the best scholar in all knowledge of Arts and tongues, and so have the best skill in Physicke, etc." Mr. Hopkins's own skill, he pleads, was really forced on him. " This discoverer never travelled for it," he writes in reply to Querie V., " but in March 1644 he had some seven or eight of that horrible sect of witches living in the towne where he lived . . . who every six weeks, in the night (being always on a Friday night), had their meetings [1] close by his house, and had their severall solemne sacrifices there offered to the devill, one of which this discoverer heard speaking to her imps one night and bid them go to another witch, who was thereupon apprehended and searched by women who had for many years known the devill's marks, and found to have three teats about her, which honest women have not. So upon command from the Justice they were to keep her from sleep two or three nights, expecting in that time to see her familiars, which the fourth night she called by their severall names [2] and

---

[1] Meetings of a more or less bacchanalian character really took place in Europe through the middle ages, survivals of old rites and nature-worship. See Professor Karl Pearson's long and learned account of these in *The Chances of Death*. London, 1897.

[2] These were often domestic pets or animals about the yard. Even feeding the sparrows on the winter snow would have been dangerous for a suspected person. See kind of evidence sought for by R. Bernard in his *Guide to Grand Jurymen*, p. 235. London, 1627, etc. The miserable witches, in the agony of sleeplessness and torment, ultimately

told them in what shape a quarter of an hour before they came in, there being ten of us in the roome.[1] " The first she called was (1) Holt, who came in like a white Kitling. (2) Jamara, who came in like a fat Spaniel without any legs at all. . . . (3) Vinegar Tom, who was like a long-legged greyhound with a head like an Oxe with a long taile and broad eyes, who, when this discoverer spoke to and bade him go to the place provided for him and his angels, immediately transformed himself into the shape of a child foure years old without a head and gave half a dozen turns about the house and vanished at the dore. (4) Sacke and Sugar, like a black rabbet. (5) Newes, like a Polcat. All these vanished away in a little while. Immediately after this witch confessed several other witches from whom she had her imps, and named to diverse women where their marks were . . . and imps' names such as Elimanzer Pyewacket, Peck-in-the-crown, Grizzell Greedigut, etc. ; which no mortall could invent. Twenty-nine were condemend at once, four brought twenty-five miles to be hanged where their discoverer lives, for sending the devill like a beare to kill him in his garden ; so by seeing diverse of the men's papps and trying various wayes with hunderds of them, he gained the experience."

Although his dealings must be described as mild compared with the ghastly, inconceivable tortures in vogue with the inquisitors upon the Continent,[2] his victims were yet baited and handled with the grossest cruelty. They were supposed not to weep,[3] being witches,

doing or saying anything that was already expected of them. See, for instance, F. Hutchinson, *An Historical Essay concerning Witchcraft*, pp. 37, 57. London, 1718.

[1] On the power of suggestion and imagination, see, for instance, G. le Bon, *Revue scientifique*, March 26 and April 2, 1910.

[2] The whole hideous and devilish procedure is given by J. Sprenger and H. Institor in their *Malleus Maleficarum*, about 1485–89. Frankfort ed., 1580.
Paulus Grillandus, *De sortilegiis*, lib. 4, *De questionibus et tortura*. Lyons, 1533.
J. Bodin, *De la démonomanie des sorciers*. Paris, 1580.
R. Scot, *The Discoverie of Witch-craft*. London, 1584. B. Nicholson's edition. London, 1886.
H. Boguet, *Discours des sorciers*. Lyons, 1608.

[3] Esquirol gives this as a symptom in some forms of insanity. See

though indeed cause enough was given them. It is remarkable in this connection that Shelley,[1] with how much accuracy I am not aware, alludes to " the dry, fixed eyeball " of the tortured. Hutchinson [2] held this phenomenon to have been due to prolonged deprivation of sleep and exhaustion. Doubtless the weary length of the investigations, and often the age and senile desiccation of the victims, might easily explain a state of tearlessness whenever it was really prevalent.

They were supposed to possess an insensible part in their bodies,[3] and the examiners would prick over them to try to find it out. Especially, a witch was affirmed to have somewhere upon her person the " Devil's mark." " Some bigg or place upon their body where he " (the familiar, imp, or spirit) " sucketh them." [4] This alleged " mark " might be almost anything or nothing ; from an abnormal, and perhaps atavic, teat, down to a birthmark, mole, old scar, or even a tiny vein under an eyelid. They were supposed also to float upon being " swum."

They were, for the most part, wizen, old creatures, clad in old long-used, greasy garments.[5] Such skirts would retain much air ; they might be bound so as to favour this, or spread, as with Ophelia, widely inflated. It was quite likely they should thus be upborne (and also, for they were mostly poor and thin, that the heavy, sometimes chained, Bible should outweigh them in the

E. K. Hunt's translation of *Mental Maladies*, p. 245. Philadelphia, 1845.
R. Scot, *Descoverie Booke*, ii. chaps. v.-viii.
Bodin, *Démonomanie*, p. 170.
James I., *Daemonologie*, p. 81.
H. Boguet, chap. xlvi.
[1] *The Cenci.*
[2] *Historical Essay*, p. 139.
[3] See J. P. Migne, *Encyclopédie théologique*, vol. xlix. tome seconde, p. 72. Paris, 1848.
Charles Mackay has observed : " It was no unusual thing then, nor is it now, that in aged persons there should be some spot on the body totally devoid of feeling " (p. 137). In Scotland there were a number of witch-finders who were known as " common prickers " (p. 146).—*Popular Delusions*, London, 1869.
[4] Michael Dalton, *The Countrey Justice*, p. 242. London, 1618.
James I., *Daemonologie*, p. 80.
Matthew Hopkins quoted, p. 33, *ante*.
Sinistrari of Ameno Demoniality, p. 27. J. Liseux, trans. Paris, 1879.
D. Neal, *History of New England*, p. 137. London, 1747.
[5] Hutchinson, *Essay*, p. 138.

ordeal with scales). But ordeals are uncertain and dangerous unless they can be carefully manipulated. Mr. Hopkins had been keen on the water test ; it was the finishing touch and proof at the end of a long series of torments and examinations. But a day came, it is said, on which a few brave Englishmen, who had perhaps lost some one near and dear to them at his hands, laid hold upon the witchfinder himself, and binding him in a sack, cast him into a pool. It was a bold act, in those savage days, to interfere with any kind of inquisition, Catholic or Puritan, and was no doubt attended with great risk. But only for a moment in this case, for there before them bobbed the dread discoverer of witches, floating upon the surface of the water ; and all declared the devil got his own. But such an end was altogether unexpected and unusual ; it was downright bad luck and misfortune, from Mr. Hopkins' point of view. His position appeared unassailable, and indeed probably would have been, if he had kept to the right sort of people, and practised on the isolated or unpopular, who could have been legitimately sacrificed. All he had done was quite lawful and regular.

Witchcraft, like many acts against religion and morality, had always been an ecclesiastical offence, and had been punished in the secular courts as leading to murder and personal injury,[1] and it was made a felony in 1541.[2] But it was the (then) recent law of 1603 that was much in force,[3] by which, in the quaint language of the statute, it was forbidden, upon pain of death, to " employ, feed, or reward any evil and wicked spirit." [4] And since the High Court of Parliament had recognized witches,[5] it became necessary to investigate accusations and probe for " spirits " through the forms of law. Thus Hopkins could claim to be a moral reformer, putting in force the statute of the realm ; he could quote Scripture

[1] T. Wright, *Dame Alice Kyteler*, London, Camden Society, vol. xxiv., 1843.
[2] H. L. Stephen, *State Trials*, vol. i. p. 211. London, 1899.
[3] Hutchinson, p. 34.
[4] See long and interesting essay on witchcraft in the *Ency. Brit.* ninth ed.
[5] The Act is quoted at length in R. Royston's *Advertisement to Jurymen of England*, in which he criticizes del Rio's and Perkins' "·proofs."

clearly to his purpose, the justices and gaolers obeyed his call, assizes waited to condemn his prisoners. And if his method seemed superstitious or barbarous, he could perhaps cite Mr. Perkins' way,[1] or could refer to Mr. Kincaid's custom in these matters,[2] and could quote standard works with precedent on his side.[3] So he seemed truly to have a safe task and a paying one, built up upon the prejudices of the people. But as by their superstitions he rose, so also by them he fell— utterly, and unpitied.[4] It was not his monstrous cruelties, but "God's ordeal," which showed him up, delivered to the devil ; and, in the caustic words of Samuel Butler, as one "who after proved himself a witch, and made a rod for his own breech."[5]

But now, dismissing this particular parasite, we may review the course of thought upon the question. Belief in witchcraft is so ancient and so universal,[6] that the existing religions, and perhaps all religions whatsoever, must have arisen in its atmosphere.

From time to time the Christian Church dealt with the question,[7] and had elaborated quite a ritual of tests and remedies. And it was after nearly fifteen hundred years of Christianity that Pope Innocent VIII.[8] issued a special Bull against all supposed witches (December 5, 1484), naming one Sprenger, a Dominican, and Kramar—

[1] Alluded to by Cotton Mather, *The Wonders of the Invisible World.* Boston, 1693.

[2] James Williams, *Ency. Brit.* ninth ed. vol. xxiv. p. 622. Kincaid was one of the "common prickers" or professional finders, who in those superstitious times were numerous.

[3] For instance, Michael Dalton, *The Countrey Justice,* p. 242 ; Richard Bernard, *A Guide to Grand Jurymen,* p. 240.

[4] Whether the story of his immersion is true or not, he undoubtedly died despised and discredited.

[5] *Hudibras,* Part III. chap. iii.

[6] Coming down, maybe, from the prehistoric mother cult. See Karl Pearson, "Woman as Witch" in his *Chances of Death,* and O. M. Hueffer, *Book of Witches.*

[7] Exorcism, etc. Paul Regnard, *Les Maladies épidémiques de l'esprit,* is full of engravings of old pictures illustrating the point. Paris, 1887.

[8] Although the Popes, such as John XXII., Innocent VIII., Julius II., and Adrian VI., legislated on witches, the Protestants were quite as vindictive. See, for instance, J. Michelet, *Life of Luther,* bk. v. chap. vi. : "The crazed, the halt, the blind, and the dumb are all possessed with demons. Physicians who treat these infirmities as arising from natural causes are fools who know not the power of the devil." We shall deal later with the works of Puritan divines in England and America.

whose name latinised to Institor—inquisitors to seek and punish them ; and this they did with frightful cruelty. They wrote a text-book on their methods and discoveries about 1489, and kept the torture chambers busy and the faggots fiercely burning.

Their book was answered by John Wier, physician to the Duke of Cleves, in 1563.[1] He refuted many of the grosser superstitions prevailing, and also suggested that the devil deceived people and made many confess to impossible practices ;[2] likewise, that the witches did not really occasion the illnesses and calamities which they were accused of causing and even admitted having brought about.

At first the work awakened only controversy and condemnation—a stage in advance, however, since the most wronged are generally undefended, and pass to their doom in silence and with no one to speak for them.

In 1580 Bodin, a French writer, published a most furious attack on Dr. Wier, declaring him to have been the pupil of the sorcerer and that he wrote inspired by the devil. He reiterated all the old fantastic stories as being true, and in the hideous procedure of investigation which he set forth, applied such diverse and such agonising torments as could not have been surpassed by any of the earlier inquisitors.

Bodin in turn was answered, from England, by Reginald Scot, in 1584, who wrote a long and powerful review of the witch persecutions, in which he quotes extensively from Sprenger, Bodin, and the Continental tormentors. Full of wise saws and modern instances, he cast doubts on the rationale of the witchcraft tests and trials.

But although just a century had gone by since Innocent launched his Bull from the Papal throne, many poor people, some at that time unborn, were destined still to suffer trial and torture. And more than another century had to pass before the law would leave " witches " alone ; before afflicted, half-mad, or unpopular old

---

[1] Chapters xi., xiv., etc. ; French edition of 1579.
[2] This theory was advanced by George Gifford in *A dialogue concerning witches and witchcraft. In which is laid open how craftily the Devill deceiveth not only the witches but many others.* London, 1603. And by John Webster, who was sceptical of the miraculous in his *Displaying of supposed Witchcraft*, 1677.

women could throw crumbs to the sparrows upon the snow, or keep a cat, without danger of death. King James, as a young man, fell foul of both Scot and Wier in 1597. Speaking of them he said : " One called Scot, an Englishman, is not ashamed in publicke print to deny that there can be such a thing as witchcraft, and so he maintains the old error of the Sadducees in denying spirits. The other called Wierus, a German phisition, sets out a publick apologie for al these crafts-folkes—whereby procuring for their impunitie he plainly betrayes himselfe to have been one of their profession " ; and six years later came his grotesque law already alluded to, sanctioned with all the weight of Parliament.[1] The trials in Germany were severely criticised in 1631 by Father Spee, who published his book at first anonymously,[2] and checked the ardour and the cruelty of the courts.

But they were defended again by Joseph Glanvill,[3] chaplain to the King, in 1681. About this time Dr. Bekker, a clergyman, living in Holland, compiled four lengthy volumes about witchcraft,[4] in which he contended that neither devils nor spirits could act on mankind. In England, ten years later, wrote Richard Baxter,[5] author of *The Saint's Rest* and other evangelical works which were widely read, supporting the weird beliefs of the witchcraft schoolmen.

By this time the persecutions, which were waning in England, had broken out at Salem in America ; and we find Cotton Mather (like Glanvill, a divine, and F.R.S.) writing a little book [6] to justify their existence (and [7]

---

[1] In 1609, a terrible commission scourged the regions round Bordeaux and Labourt in Western France. See P. de l'Ancre, *Tableau de l'inconstance des Mauvais Anges*, 1612. Under Louis XIV. the lurid *Chambre Ardente* was set up in 1679, and lasted till 1682. La Reynie. the Lieutenant-General of Police, was an active inquisitor. See F Funck-Brentano, *Princes and Poisoners* ; G. Maidment, trans. London, 1901.

[2] *Cautio Criminalis*, 1631.

[3] *Saducismus Triumphatus*, 1681.

[4] In Dutch, 1681 ; French translation, *Le Monde enchanté*. Amsterdam, 1684.

[5] *The Certainty of the World of Spirits*. London, 1691.

[6] *The Wonders of the Invisible World : Observations upon the Nature, the Number, and the Operations of the Devils.*

[7] R. Calef, *More Wonders of the Invisible World*. London, 1700.

his own conduct, for many were sceptical), upon that
continent where, as he quaintly says, the Pilgrim Fathers
" imagined that they should leave their posterity
in a place where they should never see the inroads of
Profanity or Superstition." The records of the nineteen
executions in this neighbourhood, of one poor creature
who was pressed to death, and of the crowd of unhappy
suspects who were cast into the prison,[1] show how the
frenzy of this murderous " revival " swept like an epidemic down upon the settlement,[2] so that for fifteen
months the air seemed charged and laden with hysteria
and are a grim commentary. But evolution operates
even on taboos and superstitions, and this was probably
the last general persecution, and Bishop Hutchinson
called his learned work *An Historical Essay*,[3] for it was
dealing mainly with the past. The law lagged behind,
however, as it generally does, the statute of James I.
(1603) being, when Hutchinson wrote, " now in force "
in 1718. And so it continued for eighteen years longer,
until repealed in 1736.[4] In Ireland the law lasted until
1821.

Witchcraft was clearly kept alive by theology. People
who really believed in a personal devil (and even
those who questioned the witch-convictions assumed
the devil to be very much alive, designing mischief
and disguised everywhere), could easily accept tales of
familiar spirits.[5]

Those who received the Hebrew and Christian records

---

[1] D. Neal, *History of New England.*—" The prisons were hardly able
to hold the number of the accused."

[2] As it did as late as 1861, round the little village of Morzines in
Savoy ; see A. Constans, *Une Relation sur une épidémie d'hystério-
démonopathie.* Paris, 1863.

Dr. R. Madden gives a long account of various historical outbreaks in
his *Phantasmata*, chap. x. " Maniacal Epidemics, etc." London, 1857.

E. Pronier, *Etude sur la contagion de la Folie.* Lausanne, 1892.

L. F. Calmeil, *De la Folie.* Paris, 1845.

[3] *An Historical Essay concerning Witchcraft.*

[4] Lecky, *History of Rationalism.*

[5] One mediæval writer was said to have estimated the exact number
of the various devils, which he stated as 7,405,926 ; see Jules Garinet,
Histoire de la Magie, p. xxviii. Paris, 1818. Another declared that
there were six principal genera of demons ; R. Madden, *Phantasmata*,
p. 293. Another author puts the devils at 2,665,866,746,664 ; see
P. Carus, *History of the Devil*, p. 346. London, 1900.

as altogether inspired, could not ignore possession and sorcery.[1] "Après que Dieu a parlé," says de l'Ancre, "de sa propre bouche des magiciens et sorciers, qui est l'incrédule qui en peut justement douter?"[2] And Sir Matthew Hale said in his summing up: "That there were such creatures as witches, he made no doubt at all. For, first, the Scriptures had affirmed so much; secondly, the wisdom of all nations had provided laws against such persons, which is an argument of their confidence of such a crime."[3] Speaking of a particular case, Mr. H. L. Stephen[4] quotes Campbell as follows: ". . . During the trial the imposture practised by the prosecutors was detected and exposed. Hale's motives were most laudable; but he furnished a memorable instance of the mischief originating from superstition. He was afraid of an acquittal or a pardon, lest countenance should be given to a disbelief in witchcraft, which he considered tantamount to disbelief in Christianity." Glanvill[5] follows on the same side, arguing with great ingenuity from the scriptural point of view (for instance, in dealing with certain doctrines as to the fate of unbaptized children, p. 22). "The question whether there are witches or not," he begins in Part ii., "is not a matter of vain speculation or of indifferent moment, but an inquiry of very great and weighty importance. For on the resolution of it depends the authority of our laws, and, which is more, our religion, in its main doctrines, is nearly concerned." And what may be called the religious belief in witches[6] —a very different thing from the torturing of them—outlived the penal laws concerning them.[7] The Rev. John Brown of Haddington (1703–1791) complained of the

---

[1] "Quae quidam nefandissima opera si non vere fierent, sed delusoria, vane contra ea fuissent promulgatae leges et in legum ipsarum auctores, etiã in ipsum Deum, ista retorqueretur vanitas: quod extrema blasphemia est."—B. de Spina, *Quaestio de strigibus*, p. 8. Rome, 1576.

[2] *Sortilège*, p. 599. Paris, 1622.

[3] *A Tryall of Witches*, 10th March 1664, Sir Matthew Hale, Kt. Appendix by C. Clark, p. 20. London, 1838.

[4] *State Trials*, i.

[5] *Saducismus Triumphatus*.

[6] The Roman Catholic view of sorcery and evil spirits is treated at length by R. R. Madden, *Phantasmata*, chap. ix.

[7] A. Chalmers, *Biographical Dict.*, art. "Cotton Mather." London, 1815.

repeal of King James's Act,[1] and even John Wesley (1722–1787) declared that giving up witchcraft is, in effect, giving up the Bible.[2] On page 366 of the journal,[3] which he edited we read : " With my latest breath will I bear testimony against giving up to infidels one great proof of the invisible world : I mean that of witchcraft and apparitions, confirmed by the testimony of all ages " ;[4] and Huxley[5] alluded to a contemporary clergyman who had been preaching diabolical agency. Nor did the actual persecutions cease altogether, and though the last legal trial in England took place in 1712[6] (the last execution in Europe is given by Lecky[7] as occurring in Switzerland in 1782 ; another authority mentions Posen,[8] with date 1793), sporadic outrages continued in the country, and persist in a modified form to the present day.[9] At Clonmel, Ireland, in 1895,[10] a poor old woman was placed upon the kitchen fire by her own family and burned, so that she died from the effects.[11] But what were once pious customs and duties had at length become crimes, and the chief mover in this latest witch trial got (to the best of my recollection) twenty years' penal servitude.

A belief so universal as that in witchcraft must clearly be founded upon positive phenomena. It will not serve our purpose to discuss what yet unknown supernormal powers might be attained under special

[1] " We cannot help lamenting that a sect among us looks upon the abolition of the penal statute against witchcraft not only as an evil but as a sin. . . . The Seceders published an Act. . . in 1743 (reprinted at Glasgow, 1766). In this Act is contained the annual confession of sins. . . . Among the sins national and personal there confessed are . . . (that) the penal statutes against witchcraft have been repealed by Parliament, contrary to the express law of God."—H. Arnot, *Criminal Trials in Scotland*, p. 370. Edinburgh, 1785.

[2] Lecky, *History of Rationalism*, p. 134.

[3] *Arminian Magazine*, v. p. 366. London, 1782.

[4] Dr. H. More, employed the same argument in his *Antidote against Atheism*, lib. iii. chap. ii. London, 1653.

[5] *Lay Sermons*. London, 1870.

[6] H. L. Stephen, *State Trials*.

[7] *History of Rationalism*, chap. i.

[8] J. Williams, *Ency. Brit.*, ninth ed., art. " Witchcraft."

[9] Mackay, *Delusions*, pp. 184, 187, etc.

[10] *History of Rationalism*, p. 4, etc.

[11] See article on the case by E. F. Benson, *Nineteenth Century*, vol. xxxvii. June 1895. A somewhat similar case occurred at Tarbes in 1850.—*History of Rationalism*, p. 4.

conditions, or how much more there may be to discover beyond X-rays and wireless telegraphy. For while old ideas as to imps and devils, brooms and black cats, were manifestly ridiculous, and although the abnormal powers, whatever they may have been, could work no rescue in the hour of need, there may be many things in heaven and earth undreamed of in our present state of knowledge. But ordinary witch cases appear to have been resolvable into the examination of—

(a) Hysterical subjects—sometimes crowds of them—who might imagine anything and accuse anybody, including themselves. Such people were (and are) often given to swallowing needles and other things, some of which found their way through the body and emerged from all parts of it.[1] This would have been considered strong evidence of diabolical agency. Many of these would be subject to epilepsy, catalepsy—accompanied sometimes by that strange insensibility to pain [2] which was remarked on by the torturers—and to obscure nerve diseases generally.

(b) "Wise women," [3] midwives, doctors good and bad, who may, according to the custom of the times in which, as among savages, magic [4] and medicine were inextricably mingled, have resorted to charms [5] (as are still employed by old women to cure warts), and sometimes, doubtless, to preparing and administering actual poisons; [6] and who, whenever anything remarkable

[1] "What sort of distemper 'tis shall stick the body full of pins ? " —Quoted by Calef, More Wonders, p. 5.
[2] Scot quotes a ghastly passage from Grillandus, who writeth " that when witches sleepe and feel no paine upon the torture, Domine labia mea aperies should be said, and so, saith he, both the torment will be felt and the truth will be uttered."—Discoverie of Witchcraft, p. 17. And we find in del Rio : " Narravit mihi . . . anno 1599 captam puellulam strigatricem, quae nec pedum ustulationem saevissimam, nec flagra validissima sentiebat ; donec Sacerdos cujusdam monitu illi Agni benedicti ceream imaginem in collum injecere, tum enim vi sacra amuleti daemonis praestigiosa ludibria depulsa et illa vim doloris coepit persentiscere."—Disquisitionum magicarum, p. 184. Venice, 1616. See also E. Gurney, Phantasms of the Living, p. 181, who considers the insensibility to pain may have been due sometimes to autohypnotism.
[3] Mentioned, for instance, in Twelfth Night.
[4] " Les sorcières furent les sages-femmes et les sorciers les médecins du moyen âge."—P. Christian, Histoire de la magie, p. 400. Paris, ? 1871.
[5] E. Gurney, Phantasms of the Living, p. 183.
[6] Lecky, History of Rationalism, p. 77.

occurred, were always liable to be accused of having in some way trafficked with the all-explaining devil.[1] They sometimes claimed to possess the powers of witches, and tried to gain support or protection from being feared, deceiving others and often themselves as well.[2]

(c) Private enemies,[3] whom an accusation of witchcraft,[4] or of any of the little group of offences [5] which were always supposed to be closely allied with it,[6] was the readiest way to ruin.[7]

(d) People accused for the sake of gain by means of deliberate plots and conspiracies. Feigning to be bewitched, and naming some (known to be) innocent person as the cause of the mischief, was a mean crime that was by no means uncommon, and many flagrant instances are given of it by early criticisers.[8]

(e) The main body of the victims.[9] Old women who had outlived family and friends, who were helpless and solitary,[10] ugly from age, unclean from infirmities,

---

[1] R. Calef, the opponent of Cotton Mather, quotes an instance of this kind. One Margaret Rule, having been seized with fits, " . . . some of the neighbours were forward enough to suspect the rise of the mischief in a house hard by, where lived a Miserable Woman who had been formerly imprisoned on the suspicion of witchcraft, who had frequently cured very painful hurts by muttering over them certain charms which I [? C. M.] shall not endanger the Poysoning of my Reader by repeating."—*More Wonders of the Invisible World*, p. 3. Boston, 1700.

[2] See O. M. Hueffer, *The Book of Witches*. London, 1908.

[3] See action of Richard III.

[4] The full indictment against Lord Hungerford, who was beheaded on Tower Hill along with Thomas Cromwell, by Henry VIII.

[5] P. de l'Ancre, *Seconde Considération*. As to the kind of offences " qui se trouvent enveloppés dans le sortilège," *Tableau de l'inconstance des Mauvais Anges*. Paris, 1612.

[6] J. Bodin, *Démonologie*, p. 60. Paris, 1580.

[7] Shamanism, etc. See, for instance, Elie Reclus, *Primitive Folk*, pp. 68, 70. London, 1889.

It was a crime imputed with so much ease and repelled with so much difficulty, that the powerful, whenever they wanted to ruin the weak . . . . had only to accuse them of witchcraft to secure their destruction.—C. Mackay, *Popular Delusions*, p. 109. A certain G. Naudé, " late Library Keeper to Cardinal Mazarin," wrote a book, entitled *The History of Magic*, " By way of apology for all the wise men who have unjustly been reputed magicians from the creation to the present age." Englished by J. Davies. London, 1657.

[8] The most tainted or prejudiced evidence was received in these kinds of cases. See *Concilium Biterrense* of A.D. 1246, c. 12. Labbé, tom. xxiii. p. 718.

[9] Scot, *Discoverie*, bk. i. chap. iii.

[10] Mostly poor, miserable old women, Glanvill admits.—*Saducismus*, p. 29.

eccentric in wisdom, crazy with delusions, palsied in limbs, or wandering in mind.[1] All these, or nearly half the old folks in the land, were always liable to accusation on account of their misfortunes.[2] They were the wretched scapegoats of those times, on whom was laid whatever might befall, from epileptic fits to summer hail.[3]

(*f*) The people denounced by prisoners under torture. As we have seen, accusation meant examination, and this had two objects : to extort a " confession " from the suspected witch, and to compel her to reveal accomplices. Some might confess at once, and did so in the hope of execution (the *kind* of confession required was already well known), and the more monstrous and elaborate it might be, the better would be the chance of escaping torture. Others would naturally deny taking part in abominations in which they had not engaged, and most of which were beyond possibility. And no doubt nearly all would make a long and desperate struggle against incriminating their unfortunate friends, who might, however innocent of crime, be also other people's enemies. And so the accursed ingenuity of man was practised on these miserable victims of his ignorance and superstition. One hideous device [4] tried by a Frankish king was to drive sharp spikes underneath the nails ; [5] this, he contended, always induced confession from the intense anguish. Very likely it did.

Other inquisitors went their own sweet way, and used all possible varieties of the question, that they might

---

[1] " None ever talked to themselves who were not witches," asserted one of the common prickers.—Mackay, *Delusions*, p. 147.

[2] Especially as they often pretended, or really believed in, powers and curses, and, being quite helpless on the material side, invoked the aid of supernatural terrors to get assistance and be looked upon with fear.

[3] Various persons accused of witchcraft, says Boguet, " ont confessé qu'ils faisoient la gresle en Sabbat afin de gaster les fruicts de la terre."—*Discours des sorciers*, p. 144. Storms were supposed to be occasioned by the devils. " Telle est l'origine de l'habitude de sonner les cloches pendant les orages."—L. F. A. Maury, *La Magie*, p. 102. Paris, 1860.

[4] Bodin, *Démonologie*, p. 171.

[5] Scot, *Discoverie*, p. 17. And this was also practised on a prisoner accused of sorcery before James I.—Lecky, *History of Rationalism*, p. 114.

make out of the shrieks and ravings the sort of story
they expected and prompted,[1] and lash more suspects
down upon the rack.   No wonder, then, that persecution
spread;[2] the aged and the disordered were always
there, and any one of these might be thought a witch,[3]
or find herself denounced from the torture-room—perhaps by a lifelong friend.

The readiness with which all "evidence" was ac-
claimed and the appalling means by which it was got
together placed any abnormal person in constant peril,
and will account for the enormous numbers of the implicated.   Tens of thousands of victims, says Lecky,[4]
perished by the most agonising and protracted torments
without exciting the faintest compassion.   In a single
German city they used to burn 300 witches annually.[5]
In Nancy, 800 were put to death by a judge in the course
of sixteen years.[6]   Zachary Gray,[7] who edited an edition
of *Hudibras*, claims that during the Long Parliament
500 witches were executed each year, and that he read
through a list of no less than 3,000 of them.[8]   The total
of Great Britain has been estimated at 30,000,[9] and it
has been estimated that during the sixteenth and seventeenth centuries the witch death-roll for Europe[10] reached
200,000 people.[11]

Perhaps the sidelights give a more graphic conception
of what went on in those dark days of error.   Listen to

[1] One of the early inquirers as to the witch trials took a friend in
with him to witness a torturing.   As an experiment, he asked the
prisoner if his companion, an entire stranger, had not been one of her
accomplices, and the poor creature moaned out that he had.

[2] "Le diable est si bon maistre que nous n'en pouvons envoyer
si grand nombre au feu, que de leurs cendres il n'en renaisse de nouveau
d'autres."—Florimonde de Raemond, *Antichrist*, p. 103.   Lyons, 1597.

[3] It became a common prayer, with women of the humbler class,
that they might not live to be old.   It was sufficient to be aged, poor,
or half-crazed to ensure death at the stake or on the scaffold.—Mackay,
Delusions, p. 116.

[4] *History of Rationalism*, p. 3.

[5] Mackay, *Delusions*, p. 159.

[6] Lecky, *History of Rationalism*, p. 4.

[7] Quoted by W. B. Gerish, *A Hertfordshire Witch*.   London, 1906.

[8] Mackay, *Delusions*, p. 139.

[9] H. C. Lea, *History of the Inquisition in Spain*.   New York, 1907.

[10] W. F. Poole, *Salem Witchcraft*.   Boston, 1869.

[11] 300,000 women are said to have been slaughtered since Innocent's
Bull of 1484.   See an important article in *Chambers's Encyclopædia*,
x. p. 698, ed. of 1901.

this complaint of a French writer [1] who evidently thought
he was approaching the "last days." "Was it [sorcery]
ever so much in vogue as here in this unhappy [six-
teenth] century? The benches of our courts are all
blackened by them ; there are not sufficient magistrates
to hear the cases. Our prisons are gorged with witches,
and not a day passes but our warrants are ensanguined
with them, and we return saddened to our homes,
shocked at the ghastly and appalling things that they
confess." And in our own land, about fifty years later,
we come upon a letter written to Sir Edmund Spencer
in 1647 : "Within the compass of two years near upon
300 witches were arraigned, and the greater part executed, in Essex and Suffolk only. Scotland swarms
with them now more than ever, and persons of good
quality executed daily." [2]

It was in Scotland, likewise, that there used to be
kept a chest "locked with three severall locks and
opened every fifteenth daie," [3] which might receive, as
did the Lion's Mouth at Venice, denunciations slipped
in secretly ; and that in 1661 the justices were ordered
to attend certain towns to hear cases of witchcraft at
least once a week. [4]

The witch trials are ended. So far as *they* are concerned, we can look back from the heights of history
over this vast red sea of superstition which has swallowed
up such multitudes. And to think it was all so useless,
so unnecessary ! [5] but yet by no means hard to be explained. The underlying and provocative phenomena
had really been present in a huge number of cases (and
when they were not, were fervently conceived, and so
suggested, looked for, and enforced as to set up all kinds
of hallucinations in the accusers and sometimes in the
accused), and in default of tracing out their causes, [6]

---

[1] F. de Raemond, *L'Antichrist*, p. 102.
One writer estimated the number of sorcerers living in Europe at
1,800,000. See Calmeil, tom. i. p. 217.
[2] James Howell, *Familiar Letters*, 1688.
[3] Scot, *Discoverie*, p. 16.
[4] *Ency. Brit.* ninth ed. vol. xxiv. p. 622.
[5] "On the enactment of the statute to repeal the law, vanished all
those imaginary powers so absurdly attributed to old women oppressed
with age and poverty."—H. Arnot, *Criminal Trials*, p. 369.
[6] The late Mr. Gurney, of the Psychical Research Society, found,

evident or recondite, clergy and jurists, and of course the populace, gave out a false and thaumaturgical account of them. They were correct in affirming many amazing facts and phenomena (and all these persist, for nature has not changed.[1] There are at least as many abnormal and half-mad people amongst us now as there ever were, only we treat the clearer cases kindly, and are no longer afraid of mythical influences), although these were magnified and multiplied million-fold, for Superstition is a monster that grows by feeding. They were fantastic in their fabulous explanations of them. The rest—in those cruel times when torture was as common as is cross-examination—followed quite naturally. The doctors, theological and legal, erred in their diagnosis, mistaking diseases for devils and abnormality for magic. We shall come upon this again, crass and close at hand. May the future condemn the Present, as we now deplore the Past.

after a most extensive investigation, " a total absence of respectable evidence, and an almost total absence of any first-hand evidence at all, for those phenomena of magic and witchcraft which cannot be accounted for as the results of diseased imagination, hysteria, hypnotism, and occasionally, perhaps, telepathy."—*Phantasms of the Living*, i. p. 172.

[1] See E. B. Tylor, *Primitive Culture*, ii. p. 130.

CHAPTER III

TREATMENT OF THE INSANE

As the abnormal and the rationally eccentric were considered witches, and held to have been disciples of the devil, so the more obviously sense-bereft were thought to be controlled by the fiends within them. Both witches and lunatics were held to be beneath the sway of infernal powers, but the former as willing agents of the devil, and the latter as involuntary victims, who were deemed to be possessed. In ancient Egypt, by the Temple of Saturn,[1] in classic Greece with the Asclepieia, and by the laws of Pagan Rome,[2] the mentally afflicted were treated with humanity, and, if without the aid of our present science, at least upon the same broad principles which we adopt to-day.

In the warm sunlight of the Eastern lands the life of the population was spent in the open air. As we read in the Scriptures and in books of travel, the lunatic might dwell amidst the tombs. He could wander through the soothing cypress groves in the moonlight or lie under shading palm in the noontide heat. He dwelt apart, like the leper, cut off by his terrible infirmity from the kinship of reason, but free at least in the air and sunlight, and often allowed a quite especial licence [3] as being in the guardianship of God.[4] But the troublesome conduct into which lunatics were ever liable to be led [5] would

---

[1] J. B. Tuke in the *Ency. Brit.*
[2] E. Westermarck, *The Origin and Development of the Moral Ideas*, i. p. 269.
[3] Westermarck, *Moral Ideas*, i. p. 270.
[4] E. B. Tylor, *Primitive Culture*, ii. p. 117.
[5] See, for instance, the story called "The Sleeper Awakened" in the *Arabian Nights*.

frequently rouse the instinct of retaliation, and bring down swift and heavy punishment upon them.[1]

In Europe also and in England the less-dangerous lunatics " were allowed to wander about the country,[2] beggars and vagabonds, affording sport,[3] and mockery. We get a vivid glimpse from Shakespeare of that " poor Tom [4] that eats the swimming frog, the toad, the tadpole, the wall newt and the water newt, that in the fury of his heart, when the foul fiend rages, eats cow-dung for sallets, swallows the old rat and the ditch dog, drinks the green mantle of the slimy pool ; [5] who is whipt from ty thing to tything, and stocked, punished, and imprisoned."[6]

This was the lot of sufferers in those times, and beyond doubt a certain number of them, unmindful or unheedful of savage laws, obeyed the obsessing suicidal impulse which is so common among mad people ; and through this many of the most afflicted must have been taken, in the mercy of nature, out of the world of men in which they had no part. But if the half-witted poor were allowed to wander,[7] those of the richer class were less fortunate. Their families were shy and ashamed of them ; they were concealed and locked in garrets and cellars, or penned apart, secured in sheds and outhouses—fastened up anywhere about the premises,[8]

Medicines there were indeed for the insane patients, and some of them might have added to the witches' cauldron.[9] Among the less nauseous of these came

[1] The severities to which the insane were subjected by various tribes are mentioned by Westermarck in *Moral Ideas*, i. p. 271.

[2] John Conolly, *Treatment of the Insane*, p. 4.   London, 1856.

[3] F. Beach, *Psychology in John Hunter's Time* : " they served as a sport to visitors at assizes, fairs, and other times " (p. 4). Hunterian Oration.   London, 1891.

[4] For an account of these wandering Tom o' Bedlams, see Isaac D'Israeli, *Curiosities of Literature*, ii. p. 343.   London, 1849.

[5] " Come, march to wakes and fairs and market-towns. Poor Tom, thy horn is dry."—*Lear*, iii. 6.

[6] *Lear*, iii. 4.

[7] Walter Besant, *London in the Eighteenth Century*, p. 378.   London, 1902.

[8] This lasted right into the nineteenth century : see D. H. Tuke, *Chapters in the History of the Insane*, p. 128.   London, 1882.

[9] See, for instance, W. Besant, *London in the Time of the Stuarts*, p. 236.   London, 1903.   And for a particularly filthy mixture advised " For a man haunted by apparitions," Cockayne, i. p. 365.

wolf's and lion's flesh,[1] and as our Saxon forefathers were
skilled herbalists, we find the clovewort, polion, and
peony recommended,[2] also the mandrake, round which
many stories were woven from its resemblance to the
human form. They said : " For witlessness, that is,
for devil sickness or demoniacal possession, take from
the body of the same wort mandrake by weight of three
pennies, administer to drink in warm water as he may
find convenient ; soon he will be healed." [3]
Doubtless in all civilisations the more acutely insane
would have to be a care for the community.[4] The early
Christians tended them in their churches, in which they
stood in a special part,[5] and where they were provided
with food " while they abode in the church, which, it
seems, was the chief place of their residence and habitation." [6]
The monks to some extent looked after them in their
monasteries.[7] But whatever medicines or other remedies
they may have employed, the main idea of those days
about lunacy was that it came through demoniacal
possession. The object was to drive the devils out.
To accomplish this they seem to have resorted to all
sorts of incongruous " cures," both ghostly and physical.[8]
The great spiritual weapon has always been exorcism.
This was the primal art of all religions, and it was practised
also by the early Christians.
In the third century the exorcists were formed into
a special order.[9] " When an exorcist is ordained," we
read, " he shall receive at the hands of the bishop a book
wherein the forms of exorcism are written. These forms
were certain passages together with adjurations in the
name of Christ commanding the unclean spirit to depart

[1] Oswald Cockayne, *Leechdoms, Wort Cunning, and Starcraft*, pp. 361,
365. London, 1864.
[2] Cockayne, pp. 101, 161, 169.
[3] Cockayne, i. p. 249.
[4] Tylor, *Primitive Culture*, ii. p. 127.
[5] Joseph Bingham, *Antiquities of the Christian Church*, i. p. 322.
[6] Bingham, p. 323.
[7] F. A. Gasquet, *Henry VIII. and the English Monasteries*, p. 463.
[8] There were, says Maury, " de véritables litanies d'anthèmes contre
Satan."—*La Magie*, p. 319.
[9] J. Bingham, *Antiquities of the Christian Church*, i. p. 321. See also
Paul Verdun, *Le Diable dans la vie des saints*, p. 2 ; *Ency. Brit.* ninth
ed. vol. viii. p. 806.

out of the possessed person." This custom has continued through the centuries,[1] forming the subject of innumerable legends and pictures relating to saints and teachers in the Middle Ages ; and though the practice seems to be in abeyance,[2] the old idea of exorcism is not dead. We must perceive this when we read,[3] for instance, " Water and salt are exorcised by the priest, and so withdrawn from the power of Satan, who, since the Fall, has corrupted and abused even inanimate things.[4] But besides the weapons, mystic and spiritual, employed by the Church, were others of a more corporeal character.

The patients were bound to venerated crosses at evening, to be released as cured in the morning.[5] They were chained fast to stones in various churches ; they were dipped into holy wells—this custom lasted in Cornwall to modern times ; and they were sent as pilgrims to shrines,[6] at some of which they underwent a regular course of treatment ; music was often an important element.[7] And remedies far more drastic might be provided, which relied not so much upon the power of the saints as on the human weakness of the devils.

Thus, scattered among the recipes for herbs and all the indescribable filthy mixtures which were advocated for insanity,[8] we come across the following prescription, the effects of which would prove anything but imaginary :—" In case a man be a lunatic, take skin

---

[1] " The so-called Fourth Council of Carthage (anno 396) prescribes a form for the ordination of exorcists the same in substance as that given in the Roman Pontifical, and used at this day."—Addis and Arnold, *Catholic Dictionary*, art. " Exorcism." London, 1903.
A man who was said to have been possessed by seven devils was exorcised by seven clergymen at the Temple Church, Bristol, in 1788. —Tylor, *Primitive Culture*, ii. p. 128. See also L. A. Maury, *La Magie*, p. 331.

[2] Already in the fifth century Pope Innocent I. forbade the exorcists from exercising their ministry without the express permission of the bishop, and that order is in force. See also Louis Duchesne, *Christian Worship*, M. L. Maclure's trans. p. 349. London, 1904.

[3] Addis and Arnold, *Cath. Dict.* p. 444.

[4] Or this prayer of Pope Leo XIII. : " S. Michael Archange . . . repoussez en enfer par la vertu divine Satan, et les autres esprits mauvais, qui errent dans le monde cherchant des âmes à perdre." Quoted by P. Verdun, ii. p. 314.

[5] D. H. Tuke, *Hist. Insane*, p. 14.

[6] F. Beach, *Psychology in John Hunter's Time*, p. 2.

[7] L. A. Maury, *La Magie*. p. 329.

[8] Cockayne, *Leechdoms*, ii. bk. iii. p. 335.

of a mereswine or porpoise, work it into a whip, swinge the man well therewith, soon he will be well. Amen." At one monastery the lunatics in the charge of the monks are said to have received ten lashes every day.[1] The insane have been flogged for various reasons :— (1) Superstitiously, to drive out the devil, and even to scare away a disease ; (2) therapeutically, because pain and shock would often subdue the ravings of the patients, although only temporarily ; (3) instinctively, as a relief to their keepers' feelings. The medical and the brutal whippings we shall meet again later on, long after devil-driving had been abandoned, though it prevailed through Christendom for probably over sixteen hundred years. To understand it we must turn aside to savages.

Primitive peoples,[2] like children, *personified* everything. Disease appeared to be a sort of personal entity— like that deceitful dream [3] Zeus sent to Agamemnon— " thing " " to be drawn out in an invisible form, and burnt in the fire or thrown into the water." A foe invisible, but yet so human in its limitations as to be stopped by thorns placed in its path.[4] And if all manner of physical ailments were looked upon as being, or, at any rate, as emanating from personal demons, much more would such a fearful and mysterious affliction as insanity be held to indicate a devil's presence and immediate handiwork.[5] Moreover, to the primitive mind the demons of all sorts were much too near, too vividly conceived, too real, too commonplace, to be regarded as spiritual beings within the modern meaning of the word. They were conceived as obviously living and moving about,[6] and therefore as being human in their

---

[1] W. A. F. Browne, *What Asylums were, are, and ought to be*, p. 101. Edinburgh, 1837.

[2] See Tylor, *Primitive Culture*, i. p. 258.
R. Routledge, *Hist. Science*, p. 5. London, 1881
Edward Carpenter, *The Art of Creation*, p. 36. London, 1904.

[3] It may be interesting to compare 1 Kings xxii. 20. John Lubbock (Lord Avebury), *Origin of Civilization*, p. 32. London, 1889.

[4] Certain savages mentioned by Tylor endeavoured to stay the progress of small-pox germs after this fashion.—*Primitive Culture*, ii. p. 115.

[5] See, for instance, Abbot Richalmus, *Liber revelationum de insidiis et versutiis daemonum inversus homines.*

[6] " . . . but as I knew it was the Devil," wrote Luther, " I paid no attention to him and went to sleep."

character. Thus among savages " the souls of the dead
are thought susceptible of being beaten, hurt, and driven
like any other living creatures,"[1] and demons could be
hunted out of the houses and scared away to woods and
outer darkness.[2]

The ideas of the profoundly superstitious Middle
Ages resembled these. Even the great opponent or
accuser, Satan, who was restored by Milton to the rôle
of Ahriman,[3] was but a wretched creature, a poor devil,[4]
in the popular imagination. " He " is continually out-
witted like the pantomime policeman,[5] and nonplussed
by the shallowest equivocations.[6] He beats a man,[7]
and is beaten and vanquished.[8] He aims a stone at
Dunstan and misses,[9] and when seized by the nose with
pincers, his bellowings are heard for three miles round.[10]
He howls when sprinkled with holy water,[11] and Luther
hurls an inkstand at his head.[12] This man-like and
material monster of course felt pain, and when he took
up his abode in a human body he was supposed to feel
the blows inflicted on the sufferer.[13] It was the devil
(or his representative) who might be driven out of man
or woman ; the demons could be commanded to quit
each portion of the invaded body, member by member.[14]
The fiends were supposed to writhe in anguish [15] when

[1] *Primitive Culture*, i. p. 409.
[2] E. B. Tylor, *Ency. Brit.* ninth ed vol. vii. p. 63, etc.
[3] Cheyne and Black, *Ency. Bib.* art. " Satan," by Gray and Massie.
F. T. Hall, *The Pedigree of the Devil.* London, 1883.
J. Tulloch in *Ency. Brit.* ninth ed. art. " Devil."
[4] Satan, said Tertullian, is God's ape. He was indeed supposed
to possess a tail ; this might be severed, but it would grow again.
[5] A. Reville, *The Devil*, pp. 40, 42. London, 1871.
[6] L. W. Cushman, *The Devil and the Vice.* London, 1897.
[7] Tylor, *Primitive Culture*, p. 77.
[8] P. Verdun, *Le Diable dans la vie des saints*, p. 97.
[9] S. Baring Gould, *Lives of the Saints*, v. p. 278. London, 1897.
[10] P. Carus, *The History of the Devil*, pp. 255, 256. London, 1900.
[11] John Ashton, *The Devil in Britain and America*, p. 87. London,
1896.
[12] Carus, *The History of the Devil*, p. 343.
[13] R. Burton, *Anatomy of Melancholy*, Pt. i. sec. ii. p. 57, ed. 1806.
[14] Maury, *La Magie*, p. 310.
[15] The same idea is found among many savages. In a certain
tribe referred to by Dr. Tylor, " The dancing of women by demoniacal
possession is treated . . . by the doctor thrashing them soundly with
a stick—the demon, and not the patient, being considered to feel the
blows."—*Primitive Culture*, ii. p. 124.

the possessed cowered beneath salt water or the whip.[1] On *them* the curses and the stripes were meant to descend,[2] until at last, through unendurable torments, they fled the body by the nearest orifice.[3] This crude and savage way of expelling " devils " was long continued ; belief in it is probably by no means dead in the minds of some country-folk. Hawthorne, writing of the seventeenth-century Puritans,[4] makes the gaoler say of his prisoner, " Verily she hath been like a possessed one, and there lacks but little that I should take in hand to drive Satan out of her with stripes." But there were times enough when exorcism failed and flogging proved unavailing. Then the insane would have to be restrained and subjected to some sort of treatment [5] —to say some sort of *ill-treatment* were nearer the truth. Doubtless they always aimed at quieting the more troublesome patients, and bringing them into order, if not back to reason.

Says Andrew Boorde in his strange *Regyment of Health* : [6] " I do advertyse every mā the which is mad or lunaticke or frenticke or demoniacke, to be kept in save garde in some close house or chambre where there is lytell lyght. And that he have a keper the which the mad man do feare." The same idea we see expressed by Shakespeare : [7] " We'll have him in a dark room and bound," is the immediate cry towards the mad. Shut up and bound they were, in all manner of ways and places, by relatives, monks, and keepers. As we have seen, many were executed as witches or malefactors, and would be thrown into gatehouses and prisons,[8] where they might furnish horrible diversion for the other

---

[1] See, for instance, Abbot Richalmus, caput **xxvi.**, *De efficacia salis et aquae.*

[2] D. H. Tuke, *History of the Insane,* p. 21.

[3] In many ancient drawings they are depicted blown from the mouth, little black monsters mingled in a cloud ; there were other manners of egress.

[4] *The Scarlet Letter,* chap. iv.

[5] The people of those early days, says Maury, " bien qu'attribuant la folie à une cause imaginaire n'en avaient pas moins connu que c'était une véritable maladie."—*La Magie,* p. 309.

[6] Chap. **xxxvii.** London, 1542.

[7] *Twelfth Night,* Act iii. Sc. 4.

[8] W. Besant, *London in the Eighteenth Century,* p. 536.

prisoners,[1] and where they were sometimes drugged to make them silent and to cease from raving.[2] Sometimes they were placed in such hospitals as there were,[3] along with fever and accident cases.[4] In the course of time, as population spread and townships grew, the old resorts were found to be inadequate. The number of the lunatics was increasing, and the whole country was filling up and enclosing. Whipping from place to place became ineffective, and there had been no public institutions available but monasteries, gaols, and hospitals.[5] In the year 1247 was founded by Bishopsgate the Priory of St. Mary of Bethlem,[6] and here insane people were kept and tended, at any rate from 1403. Doubtless there came to be other places thus put to use, such as, for instance, one St. Katherine's by the Tower,[7] where, we are told, " they used to keep the better sort of mad folks." But it was not until about the middle of the eighteenth century [8] that grim and sombre circumvallate buildings began to be erected to intern the troublesome.[9] " They were," says Dr. Conolly,[10] " but prisons of the worst description. Small openings in the walls, unglazed, or whether glazed or not, guarded with strong iron bars, narrow corridors, dark cells, desolate courts, where no tree nor shrub nor flower nor blade of grass grew.[11] Solitariness, or companionship so indiscriminate as to be worse than solitude ; terrible attendants armed with whips . . . and free to impose manacles and chains and stripes at their own brutal will ; uncleanness, semi-starvation, the garrotte, and unpunished murders—these were the characteristics

---

[1] W. E. H. Lecky, *History of England in the Eighteenth Century*, vi. p. 257. London, 1887.
[2] Andrew Halliday, *Lunatic Asylums*, p. 10. London, 1828.
[3] W. A. F. Browne, *What Asylums were*, p. 105.
[4] J. Conolly, *Treatment of the Insane*, p. 7.
[5] See J. E. D. Esquirol, *Mémoire sur la Maison Royale de Charenton*, p. 10.
[6] D. H. Tuke, *Hist.* p. 52.
[7] W. Besant, *London in the Time of the Stuarts*, p. 237.
[8] J. B. Tuke, art. " Insanity," *Ency. Brit.* ninth ed.
[9] Many asylums were built under the Act of 1808, but before that the pauper patients had been "crowded into the damp dungeons of our public workhouses, or shut up in houses of detention and ill-regulated prisons."—A. Halliday, *Lunatic Asylums*, p. 10.
[10] *Treatment of the Insane.*
[11] Oscar Wilde, *Ballad of Reading Gaol*, p. 24.

of such buildings throughout Europe." What may be called the theoretical treatment was bad enough. Those who could not be cured must be subdued ;[1] the teaching of Boerhaave and Cullen admitted this, and the latter wrote : " Fear being the passion that diminishes excitement, may therefore be opposed to the excess of it, and particularly to the angry and irascible excitement of maniacs ; these being more susceptible of fear than might be expected, it appears to me to have been commonly useful."[2]

It was desired " to acquire some awe over them,"[3] and he declares that " sometimes it may be necessary to acquire it even by stripes and blows."[4] This was the therapeutic flogging already alluded to.[5] Shock, terror, blistering, bleeding, purging, the use of chains and all manner of manacles[6]–these were the means employed and set down in the textbooks to heal the disordered mechanism of the brain.[7]

In the *Gentleman's Magazine* of 1765[8] we read of the private asylums that " persons were taken forcibly to these houses without any authority, instantly seized by a set of inhuman ruffians trained up to this barbarous profession, stripped naked, and conveyed to a dark room." So ignorant were the doctors of those days as to the nature of insanity that the harsh cruelties practised on private patients were carried out even upon the king. Of the eighteenth-century practice Mr. Massie has written :[9]

[1] Robert Jones, *An Inquiry into the Nature of Nervous Fevers.* London, 1785.
[2] W. Cullen, *First Lines of the Practice of Physic*, iv. p. 153. Edinburgh, 1789.
[3] Cullen, p. 171.
[4] *Ibid.* p. 154
See also R. Mead, *Monita et praecepta medica*, p. 67 ; he says, however, that fast binding is sufficient. London, 1751.
[5] Page 81, *ante.* Dr. Haslam flogged lunatics at stated periods to avert outbreaks.—Conolly, p. 12.
[6] D. H. Tuke, *Hist.* p. 107. F. Beach, *Psychological Medicine.* He also alludes to John Wesley's *Prescriptions*, p. 6, etc. Andrew Wynter, *The Borderland of Insanity*, J. M. Granville's ed. p. 70. London, 1877.
[7] " The vagrant action of the limbs was suppressed, but the source of irritation in the brain was left out of consideration."—Conolly.
[8] Quoted by Beach, Hunterian Oration, 1891.
[9] W. Massie, *A History of England during the Reign of George III.*, iii. p. 207. London, 1865.
See also J. M. D. Meiklejohn, *Hist. Eng.* Pt. ii. p. 330.

" Mental disease was at that time a branch of art little understood, and the specific treatment of lunatics was worthy of the barbarous age of medicine. The unhappy patient " (King George III.) " upon whom this most terrible visitation of Heaven had fallen, was no longer dealt with as a human being. His body was immediately enclosed in a machine, which left it no liberty of motion. He was sometimes chained to a staple. He was frequently beaten and starved, and at least he was kept in subjection by menacing and violent language." That, like most lunatics, he was very annoying is certain ; he once talked for nineteen hours unceasing. But all his troubles were intensified by ill-treatment ; [1] they left him to be knocked about by a German servant,[2] and the first doctors kept him even from his own children, at which the poor old man complained " very heavily." [3] Such, then, was the orthodox treatment applied against the highest in the land. But the worst deeds were done behind thick walls. " Sane people," says Beach,[4] writing of private establishments, " were frequently confined in these asylums, for persons frequently availed themselves of the facilities [5] then in use in order to get rid of a troublesome relative or to obtain some selfish object."

And what of the really mad ? [6]—irritable, violent, irrational, helpless, often with as little control over the functions of the body as on the workings of the mind. We can imagine what their state became when left in the hands of ignorant practitioners and brutal attendants, with chains and instruments of restraint convenient and ready. Screened off from all kith and kin, they writhed with sores and rotted in ordure.[7] Sometimes—mostly on Monday mornings after the Sabbath rest and accumu-

---

[1] Massie, *Hist.* p. 208.
[2] Wynter, *Insanity*, p. 80.
[3] J. H. Jesse, *Memoirs of the Life of George III.*, iii. pp. 95 and 274. Later on he was placed in the better care of Dr. Willis, a clergyman who was much celebrated for his management of mad people ; see Jesse, iii. p. 90, etc.
[4] Hunterian Oration, p. 5.
[5] Besant, *London in the Eighteenth Century*, p. 377. See also Charles Reade's book, *Hard Cash*.
[6] See Conolly's description of the old-time reception of a private patient.—*Treatment of the Insane*, p. 138.
[7] D. H Tuke, *Hist.* p. 171.

lations—they might be carried out into a yard[1] to be mopped and soused from pails in the coldest weather.[2] The condition of the living-rooms and wards[3] was often such that visitors grew physically sick from going into them;[4] but they were rare within those private prisons,[5] strangers are never welcome behind the walls. At York Asylum,[6]—an especial plague spot opened in 1777, and burnt,[7] it is said, to avoid disclosures that might hang its keepers,[8] in 1814—a rule was adopted in 1813 " that no person[9] shall be allowed to visit any of the patients without a special written order signed by the physitian." Official visitors were generally harmless.[10] At York the worst rooms were not shown them.[11] For most of the small asylums there were none at all.[12]

Even the larger public asylums during the eighteenth, and also far into the nineteenth century, were horrible monuments of cruelty and neglect. The miserable patients lay upon straw in cells,[13] or upon wooden shelves to which they were fastened. Many were naked or decked over with one blanket.[14] In the wards they were frequently chained to the wall by wrist or ankle,[15] and occasionally by both. One patient at Bethlem,[16] a fierce, powerful man whose name was Norris, after a fracas with a drunken keeper, had his arms and shoulders encased in a frame

---

[1] D. H. Tuke, *Hist.* p. 171.
[2] R. Gardner Hill, *Lunacy* ; *its Past and its Present*, p. 7. London, 1870.
[3] *Ibid.* p. 6.
[4] J. B. Sharpe, *Report and Minutes of Evidence on the Madhouses of England* ; evidence of G. Higgins, pp. 12 and 13 ; of R. Fowler, p. 308 ; and of H. Alabaster, p. 326. London, 1815.
[5] *Edinburgh Review*, xxviii. p. 445. Edinburgh, 1817.
[6] Jonathan Gray, *History of York Asylum*, p. 12. York, 1815.
[7] See Conolly's amazing denunciation in his *Treatment of the Insane*.
[8] A female patient was got with child by the head keeper ; he was subsequently given a piece of plate, and kept a private madhouse of his own ; see Sharpe, *Report and Min. of Ev.* p. 14.
[9] Gray, chap. iv. ; *ibid.* p. 26 ; Beach, p. 4.
[10] S. W. Nicoll, *An Enquiry into the Present State and Visitation of Asylums*, p. 10, etc. London, 1828.
[11] Sharpe, p. 12 ; Gray, p. 23.
[12] Sharpe, *Report and Min. of Ev.* pp. 277, 290, 297.
[13] *Ibid.* p. 46
[14] For instance, at Bethnal Green Asylum.—Beach, p. 12.
[15] As late as 1837.—Tuke, *Hist.* p. 81.
[16] Sharpe, p. 46.

of iron obtained from Newgate.[1] This instrument [2] was attached by a twelve-inch chain to a collar round his neck, from a ring round a vertical iron bar which had been built into the wall by the head of his bed.[3] His right leg was secured to the frame upon which he lay. The effect was that the patient could move up and down as far as the ring and short chain round the upright bar permitted, but he could not stir one foot from the wall, and could only rest lying upon his back. " In this thraldom," says Dr. Conolly,[4] " he had lived for twelve years. During much of this time he is reported to have been rational in his conversation. At length relief came, which he only lived about a year to enjoy. It is painful to add that this long-continued punishment had the recorded approbation of all the authorities of the hospital. Nothing can more forcibly illustrate the hardening effect of being habitual witnesses of cruelty, and the process which the heart of man undergoes when allowed to exercise irresponsible power."

The medical men were poorly paid and proportionately neglectful. At the time of which we are speaking—the end of the eighteenth and the beginning of the nineteenth century—the physician at Bedlam got only £100 a year.[5] However, he kept a private asylum, and sometimes left the public institution for months together.[6] One of the surgeons is described as having been " generally insane and mostly drunk," in spite of which he was retained there for ten years.[7]

With such shameful neglect and callousness on the part of the doctors—there appear to have been no chaplains in those days [8]—it is not to be wondered that the unhappy patients fell entirely into the hands of the keepers and immediate attendants, and most of these were quite ignorant people, rendered impatient and brutal by the exasperating ways of the demented inmates, and by

[1] Sharpe, p. 85.
[2] *Ibid.* p. 48.
[3] See Besant, *London in the Eighteenth Century*, where a print is given of this prisoner in his cell at p. 375.
[4] *Treatment of the Insane*, p. 28.
[5] Sharpe, *Report and Min. of Ev.* p. 120.
[6] *Ibid.* p. 59.
[7] Tuke, *Hist.* p. 153.
[8] Sharpe, *Report and Min. of Ev.* p 68.

their boundless power over them. Instinctive and retaliative floggings (the third kind, alluded to on p. 81), assaults, and possibly even murders, were not uncommon, as well as the distressing and unlimited restraints already referred to.[1] One doctor invented and introduced a special instrument to prise open the patients' mouths at compulsory feeding. He mentions that, by the usual process, teeth were apt to be broken, and some were left " without a front tooth in either jaw."[2]

In the eighteenth century [3]—up to 1770—and in some places, doubtless, even to later times, the mad people were reckoned among the " sights."[4] The public paid [5] to go round the asylums, as they do now to gaze upon wild beasts.[6] The baser and more mischievous among them would irritate and purposely enrage the secured patients, as their descendants tease caged animals to this day ; [7] and thus reproduced for their ghastly diversion " exhibitions of madness which are no longer to be found, because they were not the simple product of malady, but of malady aggravated by mismanagement."

Such conduct appears to have been general in those times.[8] At Geneva [9] some lunatics would be given grass and horrible things to eat to amuse visitors. This also happened at the Bicêtre,[10] in certain parts of Germany, etc.[11] " Les Fous de Charenton " became, for a time, notorious for their plays,[12] which were presented with

---

[1] For an account of some of these, especially as used in Portugal into later times, see G. A. Tucker, *Lunacy in Many Lands*, pp. 16, 1346, etc. Sydney, 1887.

[2] John Haslam, *Observations on Madness*, p. 317. London, 1809.

[3] Besant, *London in the Eighteenth Century*, p. 377. There is also a reproduction of Hogarth's " Scene in Bedlam " from " The Rake's Progress."

[4] R Gardner Hill, *A Concise History of the Non-Restraint System*, p. 139. London, 1857.

[5] W. A. F. Browne, p. 119.

[6] One large asylum is said to have made £400 a year from exhibiting lunatics, but this would probably not include the keepers' tips ; see Tuke, *Hist*. p. 73.

[7] Conolly, p. 33. See also P. Pinel, *Traité Médico-philosophique sur l'Aliénation Mentale*, p. 65. Paris, An. IX.
J. B. Tuke, *Ency. Brit*. ninth ed. vol. xiii. p. 111.

[8] See E. Westermarck, *Moral Ideas*, i. p. 274.

[9] H. W. Carter, *Principal Hospitals*, p. 42. London, 1819.

[10] P. Pinel, *Traité*, p. 64.

[11] A. Halliday, *Lunatic Asylums*, p. 76.

[12] J. E. D. Esquirol, *Mémoire de Charenton*, pp. 46, 48.

much sound and fury, attracting spectators from very grotesqueness. They were forbidden in 1811.

High walls kept things dark for years, but the light stole through in the end, as it always will.[1] In 1793 Pinel removed the chains from patients in the Bicêtre. At home, the York Asylum, already alluded to, began to bear an evil reputation. In 1788 it incurred the *Animadversions*[2] of the Rev. William Mason.[3] In the year 1791 some friends of a female patient desired to visit her, but were not allowed, upon the plea that she was not in a suitable condition to be seen by strangers (she probably was not !). A few weeks after this she was reported dead.[4] The woman belonged to the Society of Friends, and the suspicious circumstances of her incarceration caused much resentment among the Quakers. Soon after, William Tuke resolved that they should have a hospital of their own. The Retreat was started in the year 1792, and its humane and enlightened methods were soon contrasted with the barbarous and secret administration prevailing at the older institution. But the years rolled by while patients languished and died. It was in 1813 that Samuel Tuke—a grandson of the founder of the Retreat—brought out a little work [5] describing the system there. It " excited universal interest, and, in fact, achieved what all the talents and public spirit of Mason and his friends had failed to accomplish. It had still better effects. A very inoffensive passage in this book roused, it seems, the animosity of the physician to York Lunatic Asylum, and a letter which this gentleman published in one of the York newspapers [6] became the origin

[1] F. Beach, p. 11. J. Conolly, p. 10. R. Gardner Hill, *Concise Hist.* p. 141.
[2] *Animadversions on the Present Government of York Asylum.* York, 1788. It deals mainly with the question of finance.
Edinburgh Review, vol. xxviii. p. 433.
These produced *A Letter from a Subscriber to the York Lunatic Asylum.* York, 1788, etc.
[3] He died in 1797, and an inscription was erected to him in Westminster Abbey. See *Dict. Nat. Biog.*, and Jonathan Gray, *History of York Asylum*, p. 18.
[4] Samuel Tuke, *Description of the Retreat*, p. 22. York, 1813.
[5] The *Description of the Retreat* near York, already alluded to.
[6] To the *York Herald*, dated September 23, 1813. It was signed merely " Evigilator," but had been written by Dr. Best, the head of the York Asylum.
See J. Gray, *Hist.* p. 28 ; also D. H. Tuke, *Hist.* pp. 129, 148.

of a controversy among the governors of that establishment, "which terminated in August 1814, after a struggle of nearly two years, in the complete overthrow of the old system, and the dismission of every officer of the asylum, except the physician himself." [1] The conflict was taken up by others and carried on. Towards the close of that same year (1813), a case of alleged misconduct was brought forward by Mr. Godfrey Higgins, a magistrate for the West Riding. "Mr. Higgins' statement was read" (before twenty-seven governors), "after which the accused servants of the house were called in and sworn. They denied upon oath the truth of the charges. No other evidence was called for ; nor was any minute committed to writing of what had been sworn by the servants. The following resolution was passed :—The governors having taken into consideration the statements published in the York and other newspapers respecting the treatment of William Vicars, lately a patient in this asylum, . . . are unanimously of opinion that . . . he was treated with all possible care, attention, and humanity." [2]   It was of no avail ; thirteen gentlemen of the county came forward with donations, in virtue of which they qualified as governors. These new men brought their votes to bear to force on an inquiry, and though the old gang of scoundrels never got their deserts, and, to conceal their guilt, are said to have set the premises on fire, yet they were driven out of their situations, and soon investigation became national.

In 1814 Mr. George Rose brought in a Bill to regulate asylums, which passed the House of Commons. But the authorities at Bedlam opposed the measure,[3] spending over £600 in so doing. They had good cause, as we shall see presently. The York Asylum governors—nineteen of them, including the archbishop—sent in a petition against it ; and the intrepid Mr. Higgins sent one in its favour, signed by himself.[4] The Bill was thrown out by the House of Lords,[5] but a committee

[1] *Edinburgh Review*, vol. xxviii. p. 433. Edinburgh, 1817.
[2] S. W. Nicoll, *An Enquiry*, p. 11 ; and see Jonathan Gray, *Hist.* p. 31.
[3] D. H. Tuke, *Hist.* p. 79.
[4] J. Gray, *Hist.* chap. vi.
[5] D. H. Tuke, p. 161.

of the House of Commons was then appointed, and collected the inconceivable and horrible evidence from which we have quoted. Its report was presented by Mr. Rose in 1815,[1] and though the committee at Bedlam formally exonerated its officials for all things they had done and neglected to do, including even the dreadful instrument placed round Norris,[2] the unofficial mind of the public had been roused to indignation, and many of the worst abuses were presently remedied.

Mr. Rose died in 1818, but in the following year Mr. Wynn brought forward another Bill, which was, however, opposed by Lord Eldon, who observed[3] that " there could not be a more false humanity than over-humanity with regard to persons afflicted with insanity," a line of argument which we shall come on again. That Bill shared the fate of its predecessor. It was not until nine years afterwards that Mr. Gordon secured the passing of an Act[4] to improve the asylums, in the year 1828. Though abuses continued into the middle of the nineteenth century,[5] and many Acts of Parliament were subsequently brought in,[6] the monstrous evils of which we have spoken continued as crimes where previously they had been customs, and took place on a much diminished scale.

At Lincoln Asylum,[7] about 1838, Dr. Gardner Hill removed mechanical restraints, and Dr. Conolly[8] followed at Hanwell in the succeeding year. In this they were, of course, opposed in the Profession,[9] but new ideas and new conceptions were coming, which are still working in the treatment of insanity. All along, heretofore, the Mind and the Body had been conceived as two separate things. People had ceased to believe in the interference of devils, but they spoke vaguely of " a mind diseased." There often being no physical injury that could be

---

[1] D. H. Tuke, p. 157.
[2] Nicoll, p. 21.
[3] D. H. Tuke, *Hist.* p. 162.
[4] *Ibid.* p. 173.
[5] J. B. Tuke, *Ency. Brit.* ninth ed. ; D. H. Tuke, *Hist.* p. 85 ; R. Gardner Hill, *Lunacy*, p. 5.
[6] See, for instance, Hunterian Oration, 1891, etc.
[7] R. Gardner Hill, *Lunacy*, p. 42.
[8] Andrew Wynter, p. 100.
[9] Hill, pp. 87, 88.

detected, " the common opinion seemed to be confirmed that it " (mental disorder) " was an incomprehensible, and consequently an incurable, malady of the mind." [1] A medical writer [2] of the early nineteenth century could allude to lectures he had attended, at which the doctor had declared that treatment and physic were useless in a case of *furor uterinus*, because it was a disease of the mind, not of the body. No doubt there loomed the fear of Free Will and Theology. " . . . Many very able men," says Dr. Halliday,[3] " led away by what appeared to be the general opinion of mankind, shrank from a strict investigation of a subject that seemed to lead to a doubt of the immateriality of mind, a truth so evident to their own feelings and so expressly established by divine revelation." It is not for us to turn aside into labyrinths, or to attempt to settle what " mind " may mean. But we know that, to our present power of comprehension, the mind can only function through the body. How it first formed, and if it can yet rekindle, are vital questions which may never be answered ; at any rate they lie beyond our range.

Gradually metaphysics and moral concepts were left behind as experts examined facts. " . . . Derangement," says a nineteenth-century writer,[4] " is no longer considered a disease of the understanding, but of the centre of the nervous system, upon the unimpaired condition of which the exercise of the understanding depends. The brain is at fault and not the mind."

" The old notion," says Dr. Wynter,[5] " that derangement of mind may happen without any lesion of the instrument of thought being the cause or consequence, has long been exploded."

The physical origin of insanity " became gradually accepted. Its mental phenomena were more carefully observed, and its relation was established to other mental conditions which had not hitherto been regarded as insane in the proper sense of the word. . . . Hitherto the criteria of insanity had been very rude, and the evidence

[1] Halliday, *Lunatic Asylums*, p. 2.
[2] F. Willis, *A Treatise on Mental Derangement*, p. 6.   London, 1823.
[3] *Lunatic Asylums*, p. 2.
[4] W. A. F. Browne, p. 4.
[5] *Borderland of Insanity*, p. 11.

was generally of a loose and popular character ; but whenever it was fully recognized that insanity was a disease with which physicians who had studied the subject were peculiarly conversant, expert evidence obtained increased importance, and from that time became prominent in every case. The new medical views of insanity were thus brought into contact with the old narrow conceptions of the law courts, and a controversy arose in the field of criminal law, which, in England at least, is not yet settled."[1]

The instinct of retaliation was not readily restrained by reasoning or proofs of irresponsibility. In postulating freedom of choice under all physical conditions ; in assuming plenary responsibility in men and women under all circumstances ; in refusing to recognize any abnormal state unless it were so extreme and obvious as to render the person before the court unconscious of his actions and surroundings, the judges were defending their own position. Thus the new theories [2] were disputed and sneered at, and arbitrary standards as to sanity were set up at variance with all facts and expert evidence.[3]

Some contended that the more subtle and amazing forms of madness or abnormality perceived by the specialists were but new names for old perversities.[4] Others averred that nothing physical ought to exculpate. Smollett wished that all lunatics guilty of grave offences might be subjected " to the common penalties of the law." Upon this Mr. Tuke observes in comment that " The entire inability to distinguish between voluntary and involuntary acts, . . . between motives and consequences, is singularly well shown. Unfortunately it was not peculiar to Smollett." [5]

[1] Alexander Gibson, in *Ency. Brit.* ninth ed. art. " Insanity (Law)."
[2] " That " [kleptomania] " is one of the diseases I was sent here to cure," a certain judge is said to have observed ; but he did not cure it.
[3] One of these legal tests had been a knowledge of the multiplication table.—W. A. F. Browne, p. 3.
[4] The " robust " attitude has been shown by Dickens. " That young Pitcher's had a fever." " No ! " exclaimed Mr. Squeers. " Damn that boy, he's always at something of that sort." " Never was such a boy, I do believe," said Mrs. Squeers ; " whatever he has is always catching too. I say it's obstinacy, and nothing shall ever convince me that it isn't. I'd beat it out of him."—*Nicholas Nickleby,* chap. vii.
[5] D. H. Tuke, *Hist.* p. 96.

And I might add that this instinctive feeling continued—as everything instinctive generally does. Turning to the work of a writer still living (in 1908), we come upon the following : "Of late years a certain school of thinkers [1] . . . have started some theories respecting the responsibility of many dangerous criminals and murderers, which have very properly been objected to by more practical observers." And the writer continues with all the sweet simplicity of ignorance : "Even the inmates of lunatic asylums know well the distinction between right and wrong. And it is precisely upon this knowledge that the government and discipline of such establishments are based. Hence no theories of criminal irresponsibility should be permitted to relax the security and strictness of the detention of dangerous offenders, whether sane, or partially insane, or wholly mad. And it is important to observe that the treatment and condition even of mad murderers should not be made attractive to others outside." But the hard scientific facts persisted. Injustice and cruelty, practised upon the weak and helpless, do not, alas ! and *pace* good Mrs. Stowe, bring down upon nations the visible wrath of God ; but the manifest falseness of the old assumptions, and the continued failure of the mediæval methods, could not be hidden through unending years. Slowly the light of science began to penetrate into the dark places of punishment. The entirely mad were first rescued and treated as patients, and these now, happily, no longer concern us ; their case belongs to Medicine, not to Criminology. With regard to the half-mad we are in a state of slow change and transition. Their wrongs, long known to the alienists, are being brought before the law-makers. "Crime," says the Report of Mr. Secretary Gladstone's Committee,[2] "its causes and treatment, has been the subject of much profound and scientific inquiry. Many of the problems it presents are practically at the present time insoluble. It may be true that some criminals are irreclaimable, just as some diseases are incurable, and in such cases it is not unreasonable to acquiesce in the

---

[1] W. Tallack, *Penological and Preventive Principles*, pp. 249, 250. London, 1896.

[2] *Departmental Committee on Prisons Report*, p. 8. London, 1895.

theory that criminality is a disease and the result of physical imperfection. But criminal anthropology as a science is in an embryo stage. . . ." With regard to the abnormal we are only on the threshold of justice ; a multitude of causes, theological and instinctive, prevent the facts from being faced and known.

We may take comfort in the course of evolution ; in that the violently mad (employing the word in a wide and general sense) are no longer exorcised and tormented ; in that the eccentrically mad are no longer burned and tortured for what was imagined against them ; in that the weak-minded and the partially deranged are being considered, with a view to their segregation in special places apart from healthy offenders ; in that innate and absolute abnormality of emotions has been established by the specialists upon overwhelming evidence ; and that the knowledge of this is quietly spreading, and being recognised and admitted among educated people throughout the civilized world.

CHAPTER IV

BANISHMENT

THERE was a time when the whole expanse of this great island upon which we live stood out unspoiled and beautiful, much as Nature made it. The tides swept up their channels as they do now, and the waves tumbled and hissed along sand and shingle, as they lap round the shore to-day. The estuaries were not then contaminated with sewage, the great rivers had not become opalescent with oil, and the rapid streams were not coloured with chemicals. The roads were not disfigured by telegraph poles and the commons were not vulgarised with the garish gas lamps. The moon and the stars gave light, and the hours of darkness peace over the world. Encircling all the towns and villages, as the great sea encompasses its atolls, the forest stretched unbroken, far and wide. The brown bear shambled through the fastnesses of the hills, the shy wolf was abroad at night, alert for his prey, and the wild boar, afraid of nothing, rooted about under oaks and beeches. Huge herds of wandering deer grazed over the pastures, and innumerable rabbits scampered among the dells. But the forest concealed men, too-wild youths who ill bore elders' discipline; brigands descended from the savage invaders; homicides escaping from blood-revenge, thieves and affrighted theows who could not pay fines, and men of all sorts whom the tribe had banished. For the outlaws were the ancestors of the convicts, and the wilderness was the first penal colony. But it was banishment to nature, not to degradation; once outside organized communities " the world was all before them where to choose," and there was room enough in those distant days, for up to the fourth century the population of

Britain was under a million,[1] and for another thousand years, and longer, it totalled less than half the multitude of people who live within our present capital.[2] There must have been real joyousness in the outlaw's life, beneath the green wood in the summer time; there were so many bands of them,[3] and the forest folk would tend to fraternise with each other, being made sympathetic from common fear, as our outcasts are in the slums of cities to-day. The chase was real hunting then, not a walk among poultry, and the poachers could sport like kings.

Withal, they had to pay heavily for their freedom; their chattels, as those of felons, had been forfeited to the king; [4] their land was his for a year and a day, and then went to the over-lords of whom they were tenants, and they were houseless and homeless through all the bitter months of the northern winter. Well might the outlawed lover say to his would-be waive: [5]

> " Yet take good hede for euer I drede
> That ye coude not sustein
> The thorney wayes the depe valeis,
> The snowe, the frost, the reyn,
> The cold, the hete, for drye or wete
> We must lodge on the playn
> And us aboue noon other roue
> But a brake bussh, or twayne.
> Which sone shulde greue you I beleve,
> And ye wolde gladly than,
> That I had too the grene wode goo,
> Alone a banyshyd man."

And again :

> " I councel yow remembre hou
> It is noo maydens lawe
> Nothing to dowte but to renne out
> To wod with an outlawe :
> For ye must there in your hende bere
> A bowe redy to drawe
> And as a theef thus must ye lyue
> Euer in drede and awe."

[1] Meiklejohn, *Hist.* i 14.

[2] The population in the reign of Henry VII. was about 3,000,000. " The two cities of London and Westminster had about 60,000 inhabitants between them, and they were joined by a country road lined with trees."—*Ibid.* ii. 288.

[3] See, for instance, the tales about Robin Hood and his men and the adventures of Queen Margaret.

[4] See Stephen, *H. C. L.* i. p. 472.
Holdsworth, *Hist. E. L.* iii. p. 62.

[5] The " Nut Brown Maid" (circa A.D. 1500) in W. W. Skeat's *Specimens of English Literature*, 4th ed. Oxford, 1887.

It was indeed a life of danger and romance for the strongest man, and a hard, rough place for any woman, even though she "cut her hair up by her ear and her kirtle at the knee," as the poem says.[1] For all those who had been outlawed thenceforth would [2] hold their lives like the animals, and all men might kill them, at any rate if they showed fight or resisted capture,[3] and their children were outlaws too.[4]

Strictly speaking, an outlaw could only be reinstated through the king's pardon,[5] and even that did not give back the forfeitures. Sometimes the sovereign tried to make soldiers of them, as for instance when, in 1324, Edward II. issued a proclamation at Nottingham offering to receive and pardon outlaws and felons [6] who would fight for him in Gascony. Doubtless there were multitudinous ways by which the banished people betook themselves, for though the agricultural life of the hamlets was more or less stagnant and intensely parochial, yet it was probably more easy to disappear then than now. The wandering population was very large—indeed one eminent authority has remarked, "There was much less journeying for mere pleasure's sake, but very much more, comparatively, out of necessity."[7]

Along the roads went traders with pack-horses, journeying with their merchandise ; pedlars carrying their small

[1] At first the bare fact of flight appears to have constituted the evader an outlaw; later on, however, he was proclaimed and summoned in the neighbouring counties and was allowed five months in which to appear.—Stephen, *Hist. C. L.* i. pp. 468, 469.

[2] ". . Utlagatus et weyviata capita gerunt lupina, quae ab omnibus impune poterunt amputari ; merito enim sine lege perire debent, qui secundum legem vivere recusant."—*Fleta.* J. Selden's ed. lib. i. p. 41. London, 1647.

[3] Stephen, *H. C. L.* i. 472.

[4] At first all the offspring were dragged down into outlawry, but in later times only those born after their parents' banishment were held to become involved. See Westermarck, *Moral Ideas,* i. 46; *Leges Edwardi Confessoris,* 19, in Thorpe, fol. ed. p. 194 ; Thrupp, *Anglo-Sax. Home,* pp. 116, 145.

[5] Stephen, *Hist. C. L.* i. p. 472.

[6] F. Palgrave, *Parliamentary Writs,* vol. ii. p. 690. London, 1830. All through the centuries criminals have been pardoned upon condition that they should become soldiers, see Act of 1779. F. Grose, *Military Antiquities,* vol. i. pp. 74, 100. London, 1786. J. D. Lang, *Transportation and Colonisation,* pp. 9, 14. London, 1837.

[7] J. J. Jusserand, *English Wayfaring Life in the Middle Ages,* p. 244. London, 1892.

wares; poor students with letters testimonial from their universities;[1] pilgrims real and false who were seeking shrines;[2] labourers who were looking for better work,[3] and also the usual tramps and loafers[4] who would be trying to avoid any, runaways, and prospective mercenary soldiers[5] who wished to ply "the hired assassins' trade" either on land or sea.[6] In fact an unending line of people of all qualities and callings.[7]

Into the stream of this moving multitude the various kinds of outlaws might be absorbed. Many offenders were allowed to abjure the realm,[8] including those who had passed through the ordeals,[9] and, prior to the year 1530, lay criminals who had quitted the Sanctuaries under the Church's protection.[10] Most of them would be making for the narrow crossing from Dover, that port and Plymouth being specially designated for them by the Statute passed in 1389.[11]

From thence they generally got across, and doubtless, from being a common custom, such migrations were to some extent prepared for and organized.[12] For instance, at Dover "The Maison Dieu was a hospital for the reception of poor priests, pilgrims, and strangers,[13] both

[1] See 12 Ric. II. c. 7 A.D. 1388.
14 Eliz. c. 5; *Statutes of the Realm*, vol. iv. pt. i. p. 592 : "And all Scollers of the Universityes of Oxford & Cambridge yt goe about begginge not being aucthorysed under the seal of the said Univ'sities by the Commyssarye Chauncelour or Vicechauncelour of the same."
[2] Jusserand, pp. 361, 395.
[3] *Ibid.* 259. For the strict laws against wandering by the working classes, see 12. Ric. ii. c. 3 A.D. 1388.
[4] Peter Force, *Collection of Historical Tracts*, vol. i. p. 22. Washington, 1836.
[5] J. W. Fortescue, *Hist. of the British Army*, pp. 78, 42, 44. Lond., 1889.
Enc. Brit. art. "Army," ix. ed. p. 569
[6] "These professional warriors of no country and no principles served only for pay, and could always be bought by a higher bidder." Oscar Browning, *The Age of the Condottieri*, p. 31.
[7] As to the numbers and audacity of the pirates, *vide* W. Laird Clowes, *Royal Navy*, vol. i. p. 371, ii. p. 49, etc. London, 1898.
[8] Auckland, *History of New Holland*, p. vi. London, 1787.
[9] *Ante*, pp. 21, 23.
[10] Clerks who had taken Sanctuary need not quit the realm. See Statute 9 Ed. II. c. 15, A.D. 1315.
[11] 13 Ric. II. c. 20.
[12] Hostlers at the ports were sworn to search their guests for bad money, etc.—Ruding, *Coinage*, i. p. 211.
[13] M. E. C. Walcott, *Inventories of St. Mary's Hospital, Dover*, p. 2.

men and women, and there were similar establishments, the Holy Trinity at Arundell (now in ruins), at Portsmouth, where the hall and chapel remain ; and at Southampton, where St. Julian's Norman Chapel has been lately restored and the Early English Gallery remains.'' At one time the fare for a passage over the Channel was determined by statute,[1] and was to be 2s. for a man and horse, and 6d. for a person alone. This would amount to about (or rather less than) 30s. and 7s. 6d. respectively, according to present values.

Even these small charges would have proved insurmountable obstacles to penniless fugitives, and it has been said [2] that the poorer passengers were often neglected and allowed to accumulate,[3] but pilgrims and travellers were assisted by pious persons upon their road,[4] and the Church would look after refugees from its sanctuaries.[5] At Calais there was a Maison Dieu, or receiving-house like the one at Dover, and the monasteries were ready havens of refuge everywhere. The shrine-seekers might be passed on from one to another ; poor travellers could perhaps join on to other parties and work their way. The dishonest and criminal would pose as pilgrims or rob people when they dared. So in various ways the adventurers would spread forth : [6] to Amiens, Cologne, Paris ; [7] to Italy, Spain, North Africa, Palestine ; and some took service under Byzantine emperors.[8]

After 1530, the sanctuary refugees were retained at home, and upon the spread of Protestantism pilgrimages went very much out of vogue.

There was, however, another way of dealing with those who had not been slain on the battlefield or executed in the ordinary course. The captives might be made

[1] 4 Ed. III. c. 8.
See Meiklejohn, *Hist.* i. p. 212 ; J. H. Ramsay, *Dawn of the Constitution*, p. 539. London, 1908.
[2] S. P. H. Statham, *History of Dover*, p. 66. London, 1899.
[3] They used to tarry but one ebb and flood if they could get passage, and were to walk every day into the sea up to their knees and above, crying "Passage for the love of God and king."—Besant, *Med. Lond.* p. 212.
[4] Jusserand, p. 379.
[5] *Ibid.* p. 363.
[6] *Ibid.* 395.
[7] P. Force, i. 22.
[8] Fortescue, *Hist. Army.* i. p. 7.

into galley slaves. The original habitat of the galley was the Mediterranean, existing under a variety of names and also in many different shapes and sizes.[1] It was a heavy ship, carrying masts and (usually lateen) sails, but it was mainly propelled by oars ; great sweeps that were pulled by slaves.[2]

Sometimes there were two or three banks of them.[3] The true galley was essentially a long and narrow ship ; [4] the large ones might be about 150 feet, or about the length of a frigate, but yet with hardly a fifth of its cubic capacity.[5] It would be raised somewhat at the stern [6] in order to make a platform or quarter-deck for the principal officers. In front was another but lower platform or bridge, whereon the soldiers, and in time of peace musicians, could stand, this deck forming a low roof over the galley's artillery, which was pointed forward. Beyond the cannon came a short turtle-deck, the stem of the ship finally jutting out as a spur or ram, which extended above the water and also served as a sort of bowsprit.[7]

The rowers were seated in the waist of the boat, either in the open air, or, in the larger ships, between decks.[8] There were often twenty-seven great oars a side, each twelve meters in length ; [9] fifty-four in all ; and every oar was pulled at by four men, or more,[10] who were chained and fastened one to another,[11] and generally to the bench as

[1] The Viking pirate boats were small and narrow, the typical specimen discovered at Gokstad and supposed to have belonged to the ninth century, A.D., was 78 feet long, 16½ broad and but 4 feet deep ; its rowers would be picked warriors. See Clowes, i. 20.

[2] At an earlier period, when the ships were lighter, with but a single man on each oar, they were generally rowed by freemen. The Moors manned their own ships up to A.D. 1500. Stanley Lane-Poole, *Barbary Corsairs*, pp. 205, 214. London, 1890.

[3] Clowes, *Navy*, i. p. 102.

[4] Jurien de la Gravière, *Les Derniers Jours de la Marine à Rames*, p. 5. Paris, 1885.

[5] Lane-Poole, *Barbary Corsairs*, p. 213.

[6] The large and round-built sailing ships of the North were very high at the poop and sometimes had castellated structures upon the bows as well ; we still speak of a vessel's " forecastle."

[7] See J. Furtenbach, *Architectura Navalis*, from whose illustrations of a galley the above description is mainly derived. Ulm, 1629.

[8] In ancient drawings of the Spanish Armada the oars may be seen protruding out of the port-holes in the middle of the ships' sides. Clowes, *Royal Navy*, 560, 572, etc. And, *de la Gravière*, p. 65.

[9] *Chambers's Enc.* art. " Galley," ed. 1901.

[10] De la Gravière, *Marine à Rames*, p. 4.

[11] Lane-Poole, *Corsairs*, p. 214.

well.[1] Above and between the groups of oarsmen were raised plank-paths,[2] along which walked boatswains or warders with heavy whips, with which they could reach the bare backs of the rowers.[3] Each of these stood, when pulling his hardest, upon one foot, the other foot being planted on the next bench in front. The huge sweeps were shoved forward in perfect time, then, as the blades touched water, the slaves struck back, throwing their weight as well as their pulling-power into the tug they gave on the creaking oars.[4]

The victims were frequently maritime prisoners who had been taken at sea and who were then consigned to the oars for years or even for life, the Eastern nations devoting their Christian slaves or captured prisoners to this use, and the Northern Powers returning the injury ; so that the miserable benchmen [5] on either side must have frequently found themselves obliged to fight their own countrymen, and sometimes they even contrived to turn against their oppressors, particularly at the battle of Lepanto (1571).[6] But while among the crews of the Orientals and even of the Western Powers as well, there were purchased slaves,[7] the Europeans put their convict fellow-citizens on the chain. In France during the seventeenth century the law courts were enjoined to refrain as much as possible from killing, torturing, mutilating, or even fining, their prisoners, in order to provide the galleys with crews. All who might anywise be compelled to row were to be forthwith swept up and secured, including loafers, the " possessed," and mad people.[8]

Queen Elizabeth appointed a commission in 1602 to arrange that prisoners, " except when convicted of wilful

---

[1] De la Gravière, p. 47.
In 1513 after the action at Le Conquest between English and French ships, in which the former were repulsed, we find it suggested that the rowers, who had become demoralised, should in future be secured to their benches, implying that they were not always so fastened previously.—Clowes, *Royal Navy*, i. p. 457.
[2] Lane-Poole, *Corsairs*, p. 216.
[3] There would be 10 warders to some 270 galley slaves in a ship of the larger sort. *Chambers's Ency.* v. 63.
[4] De la Gravière, p. 13.
[5] Lane-Poole, *Corsairs*, p. 39.
[6] De la Gravière, p. 54.
[7] *Ibid.* pp. 21, 26.
[8] *Ibid.* p. 20, etc.

Murther, Rape, & Burglarye," might be reprieved from execution and sent to the galleys " wherein, as in all things, our desire is that justice may be tempered with clemency & mercy . . . our good and quiet subjects protected and preserved, the wicked & evill disposed restrayned & terrefyed, and the offenders to be in such sort corrected & punished that even in their punishments they may yeld some proffitable service to the Comon welth." [1]

According to this English proclamation, the galleys were considered more merciful than ordinary civil punishments—though, if Queen Elizabeth needed rowers, that recked but little, one way or the other—and they gave rise, especially in the Mediterranean usage, to a most frightful form of slavery. The condemned might be sentenced to serve for years, and, if they had been thereby reprieved from hanging,[2] to bondage in chains for life ; [3] in those inhuman times such sentences were quite customary,[4] and a contemporary writer has told us that those who were serving [5] life-sentences on the ships were always considered the best-behaved oarsmen. Slaves of an alien race purchased or carried off would have but a slender chance of regaining their liberty, and when they were not thrown brutally overboard, would be worked on shore and elsewhere disposed of as, with increasing years and infirmities, they were rendered too weak to row.

What sort of life did they actually undergo ? Doubtless it varied much under different overseers. We must imagine them chained to their crowded benches, often for six months at a time and perhaps for longer, or penned in prison-like barracks at the seaports.[6] Their heads and their beards were shaved every month,[7] and their garments ranged from non-existence in the African waters,[8] to red caps, coats, shirts, and rough

[1] Rymer, *De Commissione Speciali pro Condempnatis ad Galleas transferendis*, tom. xvi. p. 446.
[2] *Chambers's Encyclopædia.*
[3] J. de la Gravière, p. 22.
[4] M. Collet, *Vie complète de S. Vincent de Paul*, tom. iv. p. 57. Paris, 1818.
[5] De la Gravière, quoting Captain Pantera, p. 34.
[6] Joseph Morgan, *Hist. of Algiers*, p. 517. London, 1729.
[7] De la Gravière, pp. 29, 60.
[8] R. Hakluyt, *Navigations*, vol. ix. p. 464. Glasgow, 1904.

canvas breeches[1] for those enslaved in colder, more decorous latitudes.[2] The rowers were exposed to all weathers, and were fed on hard fare, and frequently much stinted in water-supply. Captives of all ranks were herded [3] and chained together promiscuously, and doubtless grew to be as filthy and verminous as their shaven heads and paucity of clothing permitted them to become. But the worst horrors of their position appeared in action, whenever their boat was either pursuing or being chased. We know how men will strain themselves in a contest, we know how a race-horse may be punished with whip and spurs. We can only imagine, and happily have not seen, how slaves could be urged by their overseers when they rowed for their rulers' lives. In the battle-race they were lashed by the overseers with whips,[4] and indeed, by the fighting men generally, with rope-ends or anything that came handy. They were stimulated by sops of bread soaked in wine [5] ; in the frenzy of flight they were sometimes implored and entreated by those who might share their doom if the ship were taken ; [6] they were knocked about till covered with blood and wounds, and if, from any possible cause, one could work no further, all that was left of him would be thrown overboard. The galley in war-time was indeed a dreadful picture of pain and struggle ; to be fastened there was a fate far worse than that endured in all the grime and dust of a steamship's stokehole. It was a phase of pitiable human agony which has gone to return no more.

In time of peace, and under humane commanders, there were conceivably many mitigating conditions, so that the lot of the galley slaves [7] may have been really and ultimately less miserable than that of those condemned to prolonged imprisonment. Although it was

---

[1] De la Gravière, pp. 13, 47.
[2] Hakluyt, ix. 464.
[3] The Turkish Captain and Governor Draguet (Torghut) ; John Knox, the Protestant preacher, and St. Vincent de Paul, the Catholic missionary, all served for a time as galley slaves at the oars.
[4] J. Morgan, *Algiers*, p. 517.
[5] De la Gravière, p. 14.
[6] Morgan, p. 517.
[7] The slaves at Algiers are described as having been fairly contented ; see De la Motte and Bernard, J. Morgan's translation, *Voyage to Algiers and Tunis for the Redemption of Captives*, p. 42. London, 1731.

found, as we should have expected, that men became hardened and embittered in the course of their servitude,[1] yet, as Admiral Jurien de la Gravière has pointed out,[2] the teams (*chiourmes*) would be tended to some extent, as poor horses are, in their masters' own interest. Men weakened beyond a point could not pull, so they must needs have been kept in a state of efficiency, and [3] we find recorded many cases of individuals who served long terms, yet ultimately emerging, lived to extreme old age in spite of all hardships.[4]

Francis Bacon remarked [5] that " Galley Slaves, notwithstanding their misery, are generally Fat and Fleshy," at least they worked in the open air, and saw the sun fill heaven by day and the cold silver sickle journey through night. They had the common fellowship of distress, and felt the free wind blowing upon their faces, and when they lay down together, fixed to a narrow, over-crowded trough of deck they would be rocked by the endless waves which rolled in from the limitless horizon, defying the chains of men.

After the battle of Lepanto in 1571 and an English naval victory in 1590,[6] the round or sailing-ships with their heavier batteries gradually supplanted boats moved with oars, though these latter endured some time as auxiliaries. Towards the end of the sixteenth century the Galley merged into the Galleas ("un bâtiment mixte")[7] and finally into the Galleon or true sailing-ship, and the convicts were kept in the bagnes (in France from 1748 [8]), prisons, barracks or hulks round about the great harbours, and were set to work in chained gangs as Government prisoners.

But even when not employed as living machinery, convicts were frequently taken away to sea, and the great explorers and adventurers carried them in their vessels.[9]

[1] Collet, *St. Vincent de Paul*, iv. p. 56..
[2] *Marine à Rames*, p. 15.
[3] Hakluyt, *Navigations*, ix. pp. 464, 465.
[4] De la Gravière, p. 12.
[5] *Sylva Sylvarum*, 733.
[6] De la Gravière, pp. 55, 56.
[7] *Ibid.* p. 65.
[8] P. Zaccone, *Histoire des Bagnes*.   Paris, 1857.
[9] Barrington, *Statutes*, p. 446.

Columbus, Vasco de Gama, and our own Frobisher possessed them on board.[1]
The time arrived when the other half of the globe was
found beyond the trackless waste of the Atlantic Ocean,
and into it poured adventurers seeking gold and eager
for riches. At first they made slaves of the simple
savages whom they captured,[2] but as these were rapidly
decimated and withered away, or, in other parts, were
found to be aloof or intractable, they came to rely on
labourers sent from home; and of these some were
prisoners. In 1597 was passed a measure sanctioning
transportation.[3] It was called An Acte for Punyshment
of Rogues, Vagabonds and Sturdy Beggars.[4] Idlers were
to be taken and flogged, receiving a "testymonyall" to
that effect as a sort of passport, and were then to be
handed on to their place of birth or last residence, or they
might be put into the common gaol or house of correction
for a year or till placed, and those who were really too de-
crepit to be employed were to be relegated to almshouses.
"Provided always, & be it enacted," the Bill continues, "that Yf any of the said Rogues shall appear to
be dangerous . . . or otherwyse be such as will not be
reformed, That in every such case it shall & may be
Lawfull to commit that rogue to the Howse of Correccion
or otherwyse to the Gaole . . . there to remain untill
the next Quarter Sessions . . . & then such of the Rogues
so committed as . . . shalbe thought fitt not to be delivered, shall . . . be banyshed out of this Realme and
all the domynions thereof . . . and shall be conveied
unto such partes beyond the seas as shalbe at any tyme
hereafter for that purpose assigned by the Privie Counsell.
. . . And if any such Rogue so banyshed as aforesaid
shall returne agayne into any part of this Realme . . .
without lawfull Lycence or Warrant so to do, that in
every such case the offence shalbe Fellony and the Party
offending therein Suffer Death as in case of Felony."
Quite early in the seventeenth century, the new lands
of the West began to be exploited energetically. In

---

[1] Hakluyt, vii. p. 286.
[2] E. A. Ober, *Life of Columbus*, p. 244, etc. New York, 1906.
[3] 39 Eliz. c. 4.
[4] *Statutes of the Realm*, vol. iv. pt. 2, p. 899. London, 1819.

1606 the Virginia Company was created by James I. and by it a number of servants were emigrated, who bound themselves to serve the Company for five years (apparently for seven[1] after 1609), in return for their passage, maintenance, and the alluring prospect of becoming free landowners. The Company kept a tight hold over them until 1617, and over many until two years after that, when most of the original planters obtained their freedom, having actually served the Colony under conditions which were described as being " in noe way better than slavery " for nine or ten years.[2] Meanwhile others appear to have been conveyed over compulsorily. Sir Thomas Dale, writing to Lord Salisbury in August 1611, alludes to " the 300 disorderly persons he took with him," saying, " They are profane and mutinous," and that " their bodies are so diseased and crazed that not sixty of them may be employed upon labour." [3]

In spite of this, he asks for more labourers,[4] and " on account of the difficulty of procuring (2,000) men in so short a time, all offenders out of the common gaols condemned to die should be sent for three years to the Colony (Virginia) ; so do the Spaniards people the Indies." It would appear that the first batch of 300 whom Governor Dale condemned so unsparingly were loafers, tramps, and hopeless degenerates ; for, speaking about other prisoners Mr. Ballagh quotes him as saying that they " are not always the worst kind of men either for birth, spirit, or body, and would be glad to escape a just sentence and make this their new country, and plant therein with all diligence and comfort." [5]

From about 1618[6] the regular shipping of convicts became a customary expedient.[7] In 1619 James I.

[1] J. C. Ballagh, *White Servitude in the Colony of Virginia*, p. 12. Baltimore, 1895.
[2] *Ibid.* p. 24.
[3] W. N. Sainsbury, *Calendar of State Papers, Colonial Series*, 1574–1660. p. 11. London, 1860.
[4] Sainsbury, p. 11.
[5] Ballagh, p. 35.
[6] *Ibid.* p. 36.
[7] W. Stith, *Hist. of Virginia*, p. 167. Williamsberg, 1747.
E. D. Neill, *Hist. of the Virginia Company*, p. 154. Albany, 1869.
A number of waifs and strays were also sent out as apprentices. Ballagh, p. 28 ; Neill, p. 163.

ordered 100 dissolute persons to be conveyed out by the Company, and from 1618 to 1622 a number arrived,[1] and these continued to be dispatched for some fifty years longer.[2] But in the year 1663 there had been a mutiny, and this influenced local feeling against the convicts.[3] In 1671 [4] it was ordered that no more Newgateers were to be admitted into Virginia,[5] though they continued to be dispatched to the West Indian Islands.[6] Some convicts were sent to Minorca after the peace of Utrecht in 1713, but in 1717 appeared a new Act of Parliament [7] re-establishing transportation to America, and that on a much-extended scale.

Whereas, says this Act (which is sometimes referred to as of 1718), "many offenders to whom the royal mercy hath been extended,[8] upon condition of transporting themselves to the West Indies, have often neglected to perform the said condition, but returned to their former wickedness and have at last, for new crimes, [been] brought to a shameful, ignominious death ; and whereas in many of His Majesty's Colonies and Plantations in America there is great want of servants," etc., persons henceforth convicted of offences within Clergy were to be liable to seven years' transportation, and those reprieved from execution for graver crimes were to serve fourteen years,[9] or it might be longer, and the contractors for their transportation [10] were to possess a property in their services, and this was considered to be sufficient reward, though at one time the Government had paid £5 a head [11]

---

1 Ballagh, p. 36.
2 *Ibid.*
3 James Grahame, *Hist. United States*, p. 421.   Philadelphia, 1845.
4 Sainsbury, *State Papers*, 1669–1674, p. 242.   London, 1889.
Ballagh, p. 37.
Sainsbury, *State Papers*, 1675–1676, p. 346.   London, 1893.
5 Maryland followed suit in 1676.
6 Barrington, p. 446.
7 4 Geo. I. c. 11.
8 Prisoners often gave securities to transport themselves ; see Sainsbury, *State Papers*, 1669–1674, p. 6.
9 W. Hawkins, *Pleas of the Crown*, vol. iv. p. 304.   London, 1795.
10 P. Colquhoun, *Police of the Metropolis*, pp. 454, 455.   London, 1800.
11 Those who undertook the transportation of the convicted were generally bound in sums of money to carry out their undertaking effectively.   Thus, in the reign of Charles I. we find two persons giving pledges of £40 apiece to convey a certain convict then in the House of Correction safely to Barbadoes.   *Vide* J. C. Jeaffreson, *Middlesex*

passage-money. (See *Journal of the House of Commons,* vol. xl. p. 1161.)

In 1767 an Act [1] was passed for the more speedy and effectual transportation of offenders. In later times the ranks of the transported were greatly swelled by prisoners of war. After the battle of Dunbar (1650) a number of the routed Scottish army [2] were sent to New England for periods of six, seven, or eight years, and after the battle of Worcester (1651), Cromwell found a fresh batch of prisoners on his hands. For these all sorts of measures had been proposed : [3] they were to be sold as soldiers to foreign Powers ; [4] they were to be sent to work in the gold mines of Guinea; but actually they were more fortunately disposed of. Some appear to have been received in Virginia.[5] Others were selected by, and distributed among, members of Parliament and well trusted persons [6] who gave security for their safe custody, and doubtless employed the prisoners for their profit. At first 1,000 [7] and afterwards other parties were given over to assist some adventurers who were draining fen lands, and most of those still left over were dispatched to Bermuda.[7] In 1655 the Penruddock rebels were sent to Barbadoes,[8] and in 1653–1656 a great number of Irish bandits,[9] including young people, were carried away to Jamaica and other Plantations.[10]

In the year 1685 the fall of the Duke of Monmouth at Sedgemoor placed all his unhappy followers from the

County Records, vol. iii. p. 184. London, 1886. Occasionally the contractors failed to perform their part of the business and dropped their prisoners nearer home. See Sainsbury, *State Papers,* 1661–1668, p. 259. The contractors might secure their prisoners as they chose, and it would be felony to try to rescue them. See Statute 6 Geo. I. c. 23, s. 5.

[1] 8 Geo. III. c. 15.

[2] S. R. Gardiner, *Hist. of Commonwealth,* vol. i. p. 328. London, 1894.

[3] *Ibid.* pp. 464, 465.

[4] " Troops were bought and sold like cattle by their sovereign masters and dukes."—Meiklejohn, *Hist.* ii. p. 236, ed. 1890.

[5] Ballagh, p. 35.

[6] Gardiner, *Commonwealth,* i. p. 465.

[7] *Ibid.* p. 466.

[8] Gardiner, vol. iii. p. 194.

[9] Thomas Burton's *Diary,* 1656–1659. Rutt's ed., vol. i. p. iv London, 1828.

[10] Sainsbury, *State Papers,* 1574–1660, pp. 401, 409, 441.
Ibid. p. 407.

West within the grip of Jeffreys and his master.[1]
Hundreds were sold and sent away into bondage. " The
courtiers round James II. exulted in the rich harvest
which the rebellion promised, and begged of the monarch
frequent gifts of their condemned countrymen." Jeffreys
heard of the scramble, and indignantly addressed the
king : " I beseech your Majesty that I may inform you
that each prisoner will be worth ten pounds if not fifteen
pounds apiece, and Sir, if your Majesty orders these as
you have already designed, persons that have not suffered
in the service will run away with the booty."[2] They were
handed over as slaves, like the Commonwealth prisoners ;
and fearing that they might be treated too leniently—
for there were people of all grades among them—
the bigoted king wrote to the Plantation authorities,
"Having shown mercy to some of the late rebels by
ordering them to be transported to the Plantations,
we hereby instruct you that those sent to Jamaica shall
be kept there, and shall serve their masters for ten years
without permission to redeem themselves by money or
otherwise, till that term be expired."[3]

The attempted invasion of 1745[4] occasioned more
banishing,[5] and in 1747 an Act[6] was passed forbidding
deported rebels from coming home without special licence,
and threatening to hang them like other escaping
convicts if they dared do so.[6] The Act also forbade their
sojourning in any of the Dominions of France or Spain ;
all those who had fled thither were to be held proscribed,
and none were to correspond or communicate with them
on pain of the gallows tree.

[1] Meiklejohn, *Hist.* ii. p. 158, ed. 1890.
[2] G. Bancroft, *Hist. U. S.*, vol. ii. p. 250, ed. of 1834.
[3] Sainsbury, *State Papers*, 1685–1688, p. 105, sec. 404. London,
1899.
[4] " A great number of prisoners who were not executed were shipped
off as slaves to the Plantations, a fate scarcely less terrible than death ;
some were pardoned on consideration of their entering the service of
the king as sailors, some were pardoned later on, a few, it is said,
escaped."—Justin McCarthy, *Hist. Four Georges*, vol. ii. p. 309. London,
1890.
[5] 20 Geo. II. c. 46.
[6] Prisoners returning before their time were all along liable to be
executed.—See the *Statutes* 39 Eliz. c. 4 ; 4 Geo. I. c. 11 ; 6 Geo. I. c. 23,
and 16 Geo. II. c. 15, by which a reward of £20 was offered for securing
a conviction in the year 1743. See also *Journal of the House of Commons*
of 1752, p. 345.

The young and growing colonies hungered for labourers, and did their best to stimulate importation. In the early days, whosoever conveyed a servant at his own expense to Virginia [1] might receive a grant of 100 acres of land for each servant imported,[2] and this appears to have been the custom in other colonies.[3] Fifty acres was the more usual grant, and in the seventeenth century we find a certain Captain Cornwallis [4] claiming land for having imported seventy-one servants, and one Councillor Talbot receiving 32,000 acres for having brought over 640 persons in a period of twelve years ; [5] which works out at fifty acres for each person carried over.

The existence of such allurements and the satisfying of such claims reveal how strong was the call for labour, and led to an extensive export trade in white servants, which came to be undertaken by sea-captains and speculators. The law of 1717, already alluded to,[6] permitted merchants and others to contract with young persons between the ages of fifteen and twenty-one to convey them over and keep them out in the colonies in consideration of having the right to their services for any period not exceeding eight years. An extensive trade was also carried on with people who desired to be transported across the Atlantic, but who had not the means to pay for a passage. They were known as Redemptioners or Freewillers, it being a common custom to allow them on landing to sell their services to the best master they could procure, for three, four, or five years.[7] Their new owner would then redeem them by paying their passage-dues.

Many made themselves altogether over to their transporters, and were then bound to work for them (or for their assigns) for the length of time stipulated. The

[1] R. Hildreth, *Hist. of the United States*, vol. i. p. 99. New York, 1849.
[2] E. I. McCormack, *White Servitude in Maryland*, 1634–1820. Baltimore, 1904.
[3] E. D. Neill, *Virginia Carolorum*, p. 56. Albany, 1856.
[4] McCormack, p. 13.
[5] *Ibid.* p. 21.
[6] 4 Geo. I. c. 11.
[7] J. Boucher, *Causes and Consequences of the American Revolution*, p. 184. London, 1797.

terms set down in the indentures [1] ranged from one to five years, and four or five were usual periods of servitude. When persons were brought into a colony with no definite contract beyond having to work for the payment of their passage, [2] the terms of bondage were fixed by the legislature of the colony, and were generally for five years; or if the imported person were under nineteen, [3] until he or she attained the age of twenty-four. The contractor who had carried the serf across the ocean had absolute right to dispose of his passenger for the number of years that were fixed by indenture or local law, [4] and to invoke the civil power to hold his slave. Even if a convict were pardoned the Crown compensated the owner for the loss of his bondman's services. [5] The servants were frequently sold on a ship's arrival, like other slaves, and commanded a price of £10 apiece for a five-years contract. [6] The prisoners of war, with their longer sentences, appear to have been valued at from £10 to £15 ; [7] the negro slaves, who were held for life, fetched £25 [8] and sometimes £30. [9] With servants or serfs fetching a ready price, [10] it became a regular and profitable business to supply them, and they were often obtained by piratical kidnapping.

By the middle of the seventeenth century [11] we find these illegal press-gangs widespread and organized, their victims, [12] as usual, being seized from the proletariat ; children and young persons of both sexes, with men and women of the casual classes, [13] and sometimes people

[1] McCormack, pp. 38, 39.
John Hammond, *Leah and Rachel*, p. 8. London, 1655.
John Fiske, *Old Virginia*, vol. ii. p. 177. London, 1897.
[2] J. C. Hurd, *Law of Freedom and Bondage*, p. 220. Boston, 1857.
[3] W. W. Hening, *Laws of Virginia*, vol. iii. p. 447. New York, 1823.
[4] Ballagh, p. 34.
[5] 4 Geo. I. c. 11.
[6] Bancroft, *Hist.*, vol. i. p. 125, ed. 1885.
[7] *Ibid.* ii. p. 251, ed. 1834.
[8] *Ibid.* i. p. 125, ed. 1885.
[9] R. Ligon, *History of Barbadoes*, p. 46. London, 1657.
[10] Another estimate, of A.D. 1664, puts the price at £20 for negroes and £6 for whites. See Sainsbury, *State Papers*, Col. series, p. 229.
[11] Ballagh, p. 38.
[12] But in the time of revolts and rebellions, even people of " quality " might be carried off and lost sight of, which caused complaint ; see Sainsbury, *State Papers, Colonial Series*, 1661–1668, p. 221.
Journal of the House of Commons, vol. viii. p. 403.
[13] W. Bullock, *Virginia*, p. 14. London, 1649.

of superior positions [1] whom their relations desired to put away and get rid of, were pounced upon and carried on board vessels, and if not promptly rescued or ransomed, [2] conveyed as slaves to distant colonies.

In 1645 we read of an Ordinance from the House of Lords. " Whereas," it says, " the Houses of Parliament are informed that diverse lewd persons do go up and down the city of London and elsewhere and in a most barbarous and wicked manner steal away many little children : It is ordered by the Lords and Commons in Parliament assembled, that all Officers and Ministers of Justice be hereby streightly charged and required to be very deligent in apprehending all such persons as are faulty in this kind. . . . It is further ordered that the marshals of the Admiralty and the Cinque Ports do immediately make strict and deligent search in all ships and vessels upon the river and at the Downes for all such children. It is further ordered that this Ordinance be forthwith published in print." [3] But many who dealt with kidnappers were well placed [4] and amongst them were yeomen, tradesmen, doctors, courtiers and fine ladies. [5] Even mayors and justices would sometimes " intimidate small rogues and pilferers who, under terror of being hanged, prayed for transportation as the only avenue to safety, and were then divided among the members of the court." [6] In later times this was once exposed at the Bristol assizes held by the dreaded Lord Chief Justice Jeffreys, [7] who placed the offending mayor and aldermen, [8] robes and all, in the dock, [9] and, with that eruptive vehemence for which he was notorious, he told them in mordant words just what he thought

---

[1] J. Grahame, *Hist. U.S.*, p. 421.

[2] For instance, we find a private citizen writing to Sir A. Ashley Cooper that there are three ships in the Thames doing kidnapping work " and though the parents can see their children in the ships, yet without money they will not let them have them."—Sainsbury, *State Papers*, 1661–1668, p. 555.

[3] *Journal of the House of Lords*, vol. vii. p. 361.

[4] Ballagh, p. 38.

[5] Meiklejohn, *Hist.* ii. 158.

[6] Bancroft, *Hist. U.S.*, vol. ii. p. 251, ed. 1834.

[7] September 21, 1685.

[8] Bancroft, p. 251.

[9] Roger North, *Life of Lord Keeper Guilford*, vol. ii. p. iii. Lond., 1808.

of them." . . . I find they can agree for their interests . . . if it were but a kid (for I hear the trade of kidnapping is in much request in this city); they can discharge a felon or a traitor (this is the part that appears to have shocked him most!) " provided they will go to Mr. Alderman's plantation in the West Indies."

Then turning upon the mayor he roared, " Kidnapper, you I mean, Sir, do you see the keeper of Newgate ? If it were not in respect for the sword which is over your head I would send you to Newgate." And speaking of another hoary sinner who had sat upon the bench, the fiery judge declared he would have his ears off before he went out of the town.[1]

But this was altogether tardy and exceptional, and beyond doubt great numbers had been stolen. One large exporter is said to have spirited away 500 persons annually to Barbadoes, for a period of twelve years,[2] and another man is mentioned as having taken over 840 kidnapped people in the course of a single year. Although the persons thus illegally captured were mainly taken from the unimportant populace, yet these outrages became extensive enough to attract attention and to rouse fierce resentment in the people's minds. A Bill was introduced in the House of Commons on July 30, 1661, and was discussed in 1662 but never got home.[3] In 1664, says Ballagh, the abuse had grown so bad that tumults were frequently raised in the streets of London.[4] It was only necessary to point the finger at a woman and call her a common Spirit to raise a " ryot " against her.[5]

In 1662 the Mayor of Bristol—presumably not the magistrate who was to stand before Jeffreys more than

[1] H. B. Irving, *Life of Judge Jeffreys*, p. 300. London, 1898.
[2] Sainsbury, *State Papers, Colonial Series*, 1574–1674, p. 521, sec. 1214.
[3] See *Journal of the House of Commons*, vol. viii. pp. 316, 401, 403, 412.
[4] *White Servitude*, p. 39.
[5] An illustration of this appeared in 1649, when we find a person bound over " to answer for assaulting and pumping of one Margaret Emmerson upon the false report of (being) a Spiritt or an inticer or inveagler of children from their parents, there being noe such charge or accusation against her."—Jeaffreson, *Middlesex County Records*, vol. iii. p. 181.

twenty years afterwards—petitioned the King. " Among those, he said, " who repair to Bristol from all parts to be transported beyond the seas, some are husbands that have forsaken their wives, others wives who have abandoned their husbands ; some are children and apprentices run away from their parents and masters ; oftentimes unwary and credulous persons have been tempted on board by man-stealers, and many that have been pursued by hue and cry for robberies, burglaries, or breaking prison, do thereby escape the prosecution of law and justice." [1] He prayed for power to examine all masters of ships . . . and also all servants and passengers whether they go by their own free will and to keep a register of them. In 1664 there was another petition,[2] this time from merchants, planters, and masters of ships, trading to the Plantations. " There is a wicked custom," they said, " to seduce and spirit away young people to go as servants to the Plantations which petitioners abominate the very thought of. This gives the opportunity to many evil-minded persons to enlist themselves voluntarily to go the voyage, and having received money, clothes, diet, etc., to pretend they were betrayed or carried away without their consent. They pray that persons may be appointed under the great seal who may enter the name, age, quality, place of birth, and last residence, of those desiring to go to the said Plantations, which will be the means to prevent the betraying and spiriting away of people."

Sir Heneage Finch reported upon this matter, and found that the mischiefs complained of were very frequent,[3] there being scarce any voyage to the Plantations but some were carried away against their wills, or pretend to be so, after they have contracted with the merchants, and so run away. A little later in the same year (1664) [4] the Lord Mayor and the Court of Aldermen sent a memorial to the Sovereign, saying " That usually for the supply of soldiers to diverse parts and sending of men to the several Plantations beyond the seas without lawful

---

[1] Sainsbury, *State Papers*, 1661–1668, p. 98.
[2] *Ibid.* p. 220.
[3] *Ibid.* p. 220, sec. 769.
[4] *Ibid.* sec. 770.

press, certain persons called Spirritts do inveagle and by lewd subtilties entice away youth." At length the Registry Office, which had been talked about since the year 1661, took practical shape,[1] as in the year 1664 there were Proposals to the King in Council " to constitute an office for transporting to the Plantations all vagrants and idle persons that can give no account of themselves . . . such persons to be transported from the nearest seaport and to serve four years according to the laws and customs of those islands." (Virginia was sometimes spoken of as an island and is evidently included.) " For want of such an office no account can be given of many persons of quality transported in the late times of rebellion, wherefore in future all such persons to be registered under penalty of £20, no person under twelve years of age to be transported unless their friends and relations shall first personally appear at the office and give good reasons. . . ."[2]

On September 7 of the same year (1664)[3] there came an Order in Council and a commission to the Duke of York, who was Lord High Admiral, to see that those proposals were put in force ; but kidnapping appears to have gone on merrily all the same.[4] In 1668 Ashley was implored to make kidnapping a capital offence, as it had already been in the border counties, i.e. Northumberland, Cumberland, and Durham, by 43 Eliz. c. 13 ; and on March 11, 1669,[5] a Bill having this end in view was read a first time in the House of Commons. It was passed by the House on March 18, 1669,[6] on which day it went up to the Lords,[7] but would seem afterwards to have got lost in the lobbies of the Circumlocution Office.

On April 9, 1670, the Lords[8] were to be " put in mind of the Bill against spiriting away the Children," and again on November 17 or 18 the Peers are reminded[9]

[1] Sainsbury, *State Papers, Colonial Series*, Preface, p. xxvii. and p 11. sec. 32, 35 ; sec. 101.
[2] Sainsbury, p. 221, sec. 772.
[3] *Ibid.* p. 232, sec. 798.
[4] Sainsbury, *State Papers, Colonial Series*, p. 555, sec. 1720.
[5] *Commons Journal*, p. 137.
[6] *Ibid.* p. 142.
[7] *Lords Journal*, vol. xii. p. 313.
[8] *Commons Journal*, p. 156. *Lords Journal*, vol. xii. p. 346.
[9] M. A. E. Green, *Domestic State Papers*, p. 541. London, 1895.

of the " Bill against stealing and transporting children."[1]

The Bill passed the House of Lords on March 18, 1670,[2] and twenty-three days later (for up to 1751 the legal new year began on March 25) on April 10, 1671, it was returned from the Lords.[3]

It was read a second time on February 13, 1672 ;[4] continued on March 5,[5] and withdrawn on November 3, 1673.[6] So that although a " law " of March 18, 1670, is sometimes alluded to,[7] the various Bills appear to have been abortive and the punishments were generally light.[8]

Blackstone remarks that kidnapping was punished by fine, imprisonment, and the pillory. The *Middlesex Records* furnish numerous examples of sentences that were actually given, and we may therefore select a few specimens.[9] " 24 Feb., 1672, Mary Newport for kidnapping Mary Holmer and putting her on board a ship for Jamaica ; fined twenty marks." " October, 1680 ; John Morris for kidnapping Thomas Russells [10] and by force conveying him on board the ship *Cambridge*, bound for Virginia, to sell him. Found guilty and fined 40 marks ; committed to the new prison, there to remain till he should have paid the fine." The sting of that sentence may have been in its tail, for we do not know how long a term of imprisonment it might mean. On another occasion two persons were convicted of having

---

[1] *Commons Journal*, p. 166.

[2] *Lords Journal*, vol. xii. p. 462.

[3] " Mr. Speaker, the Lords have returned you down a Bill intituled An Act to prevent stealing and transporting children and other persons, with some alterations and amendments."—*Commons Journal*, p. 233.

[4] " A Bill to prevent the stealing away and selling of children beyond the seas was read a second time, etc." *Commons Journal*, p. 251.

[5] *Commons Journal*, p. 262.

[6] " A Bill being tendered and read to prevent stealing and transporting children and other Persons ; but the Manner of it being disliked, the Bill was withdrawn upon the Question."—*Commons Journal*, p. 286.

[7] For instance by Sainsbury, *State Papers*, 1661–1668, Preface, p. xxix. Ballagh, p. 39, *Dict. Nat. Biography*, Art. " Ashley Cooper," p. 1043.

[8] In the Colonies the penalties appear to have varied considerably. Sometimes a fine was inflicted of twice the value received for the person sold (*vide* Hening, *Laws*, iii. p. 448), but elsewhere death was, at least nominally, appointed for the offence of man-stealing. Hutchinson, *Papers*, p. 174.

[9] Jeaffreson, vol. iv. p. 38.

[10] *Ibid.* p. 94.

pounced upon a girl of sixteen and carried her upon ship-board ; they were to be in prison till their fines should be paid ; [1] the fine each had to pay was but twelve pence. When a certain William Haverland was convicted of kidnapping and sentenced to pay 40 marks and to be kept in gaol until they were paid [2] (besides to stand three times in the pillory) he appears to have been locked up for nearly six months, at the end of which period he received a pardon.

So that we are entitled to say that for those times, when the criminal law recked little of human life, the penalties for kidnapping were of a very lenient character. But economic forces, ever more powerful in the long run than penal laws, began to operate against kidnapping, and even against white servitude generally. The social evil of coloured slavery—the long-accumulated account for which has yet to be paid—was implanted, and gradually spread over the colonies. This plague was developed late, and from small beginnings, by slow degrees. The Spaniards had imported negroes to their own colonies from 1701 ; [3] in the year 1619 twenty negroes were sold from a ship to Virginia.[4] In 1625,[5] more than five years after the introduction, and when the white population numbered 25,000, there were but twenty-three black slaves in the colony ; [6] even in 1640 there were but 300 negroes to be found in Virginia.

From the year 1635 land grants were apportioned to importers of negroes as well as of white people, and the large estates thus accumulated increased the demand for slave labour of all sorts. In 1662 a new company was founded to undertake slave trading. In 1671 there were 2,000 slaves in Virginia,[7] but, so far, the white servants outnumbered them, as they totalled 6,000. The importation of negroes increased with time ; in 1708 there were 12,000 slaves ; [8] about fifty years later there

[1] Jeaffreson, p. 245.
[2] *Ibid.* Preface to vol. iv. p. xliii.
[3] Hurd, *Freedom and Bondage*, p. 205.
[4] J. C. Ballagh, *History of Slavery*, p. 7. Baltimore, 1902.
[5] Fiske, *Old Virginia*, p. 188.
[6] Ballagh, *Slavery*, p. 9.
[7] Neill, p. 330.
[8] Ballagh, *Slavery*, p. 11.

were 120,156, the white population numbering 173,316,[1] and just before the war of the American revolution Great Britain had 192 ships engaged in the trade and they were transporting 47,000 annually.[2]

The advent of such enormous numbers of lifelong slave-workers gradually took off the edge of colonial hunger for labourers,[3] although indentured servitude endured into the first quarter of the nineteenth century.[4] The war between the colonies and the mother-country [5] closed the door upon transportation to America about the year 1779.[6] Virginia forbade the importation of convicts who were wont to be brought in and then sold,[7] in 1788.[8]

What then had been the actual condition of those transported to the American and island plantations ? The colonial evidence is extremely various : many, if not most, convicts desired and urgently petitioned to be sent out ; [9] yet others dreaded it more than death.[10] Although the pioneers underwent very great hardships,[11] yet the conditions of those who came afterwards were largely determined by their personal qualities and equally by those of the masters they served under.[12]

Often the food was meagre and the life rough and hard,[13] and these conditions pressed with fatal severity upon those who were in any way degenerate and sickly, and numbers were.[14] We can still read the piteous lamenta-

[1] Ballagh, *Slavery*, p. 12.
[2] *Ibid.* p. 5.
[3] McCormack, pp. 77, 107, 111.
[4] W. E. H. Lecky, *Hist. Eighteenth Century*, vol. vi. p. 253.   Lond., 1887.
[5] McCormack, p. 105.
[6] See also the Statute 19 Geo. III. c. 74.
[7] Ballagh, *White Servitude*, p. 38.
[8] Hening, *Laws of Virginia*, vol. xii. p. 668.
[9] For example, Sir John Towers, " having long lain in a loathsome prison," prays for speedy transportation (*State Papers, Colonial Series* A.D. 1666, p. 409), and there are many such cases.
[10] See Captain John Smith, *New England's Trials* (1622) in Peter Force's *Collection of Historical Tracts*, vol. ii. p. 16.   Washington, 1838.
T. C. Gambrall, *History of Early Maryland*, p. 84.   New York, 1883.
[11] Hammond, *Leah and Rachel*, p. 3.
Fiske, *Old Virginia*, 153, 154.
[12] R. Ligon, *Hist. of Barbadoes*, p. 44.
[13] In the early days of Barbadoes the servants are said to have had no meat " unless an oxe died." Ligon, *Hist.*, p. 43.
[14] See J. H. Lefroy, *History of the Bermudas*, p. 204.   London, 1882.

tions of one Richard Frethome. He wrote that since he landed he had eaten nothing but pease and cobboly, "and had to work both early and late for a mess of water gruel and a mouthful of bread and beef; a mouthful of bread for a penny loaf cannot serve four men." He had nothing at all, not a shirt to his back but two rags, nor no clothes but one poor suit, nor but one pair of shoes, but one pair of stockings, but one cap, but two bands. "Oh that you did but see my daily and hourly sighs and groans, tears and thumps that I afford mine own breast, and rue and curse the hour of my birth with holy Job. I had thought no head had been able to hold so much water as hath and doth daly flow from my eyes." [1] The poor creature died but a few months afterwards.

Besides the inevitable hardships of their situation, the indentured servants had frequently to endure their masters' violence. In Virginia [2] their lives are said to have been protected only in theory, and of Barbadoes in the early period a witness exclaims, "Truly I have seen such cruelty there done to servants as I did not think one Christian could have done to another." [3] The most common punishment was, of course, flogging; [4] servants were generally flogged where freemen were fined; and in Virginia, ten to thirty lashes were the usual number inflicted, [5] but the actual severity would depend on the overseers and the instruments they employed. [6]

In 1705 [7] a law made it necessary to get a Justice-of-the-Peace order to be allowed to flog a Christian white servant naked; under a penalty of 40s. The servants would frequently run away from [8] bad masters, and be-

[1] Neill, *Virginia Carolorum*, p. 58.
[2] Fiske, *O. V.*, p. 178.
[3] Ligon, *Hist.*, p. 44.
[4] Ballagh, *White Servitude*, p. 45.
[5] McCormack, p. 66.
[6] There were gallows and chained gangs, too, for those who committed crimes in the colony. *Vide* H. C. Lodge, *Hist. of the English Colonies in America*, p. 125. New York, 1881.
    Ballagh, p. 35.
[7] Ballagh, *W. S.*, p. 59.
    Hening, iii. p. 448.
[8] *Ibid.* ii. p. 35.

came liable to severe penalties if recaptured: [1] to whipping, branding, and to having their serving time extended by from one to seven years ; [2] and they might have to labour in chains. Yet from the natural facilities of the country they escaped in great numbers, and some of them fled to the woods and mountains and stayed there, [3] and so went out of civilisation for good and all.

But were they not better off than those in prison or penal servitude ? As a class, they were beyond measure happier than the inmates of any walled-in penal institutions. In the early days the struggle was mainly with nature, for food and shelter, when master and slaves contended together in common cause. In later times the serfs' position grew worse in some ways from their association with the down-trodden negro slaves ; on the other hand, they gained advantages from some later laws. Except in those cases where they served under the worst masters, their position had many aspects that were human and even hopeful for their future in the colonies. An old writer on the state of Virginia has remarked about the convicts that " Their being sent thither to work as Slaves for Punishment is but a mere notion, for few of them ever lived so well and so easily before, especially if they were good for anything." " These are to serve seven and sometimes fourteen years and they, and servants by indenture, have an allowance of corn and cloathes when they are out of their time." [4]

As soon as they (the convicts) were landed in America, says another author, [5] they were no longer convicts but servants by indenture or custom of the country, and at the end of their term of bondage it was the custom to give them the plant to start with, [6] including raiment, tools, and implements, and also three barrels of corn. [7]

---

[1] By an Act passed in Virginia in 1670 servants when captured were to be severely flogged by every constable through whose district they were conveyed on the way back to their masters.
  Hening, ii. p. 278.
[2] Ballagh, *White Servitude*, p. 52.
[3] Fiske, p. 189.
  McCormack, p. 106.
[4] Hugh Jones, *The Present State of Virginia*, p. 53.   London, 1724.
[5] McCormack, p. 104.
[6] *Ibid.* p. 24.
[7] Hammond, *L. and R.*, p. 8.

Sometimes a grant of fifty acres was added ; and in any case land was obtainable easily.[1] In the year 1690 Governor Howard directed that every servant should receive a patent of fifty acres in fee on attaining his freedom. So that a man or woman had a real chance to retrieve past faults or misfortunes and was not merely cast forth to attempt the (almost) impossible. And in consequence many did well, and out of the fifty thousand or more who had been sentenced to transportation [2] some rose to attain high honour and position.[3]

AUSTRALIAN PERIOD.—The outbreak of war with our American Colonies in the year 1775 and their Declaration of Independence in 1776, was to have far-reaching consequences for all English prisoners. The broad Way of the West, the only outlet for the stream of convicted exiles, was to be closed by impassable barriers, and soon it began to silt up at home in ever-increasing volume, and no one knew how to deal with it. Some very wild proposals, indeed, were made : the convicts were to be exchanged for Christian slaves of near Eastern nations.[4] It was proposed to have them delivered over—as soldiers and food for powder—to Foreign Powers ; and though this plan was not approved of by a House of Commons Committee, it duly reported that such a course would not be unprecedented.[5] West Africa was looked upon as a likely spot, whence but few returned.

In the year 1782 [6] three men-of-war escorted a transport containing 300 convicts to Cape Coast Castle, West Africa, where they were enlisted as soldiers. Twenty or thirty died on the voyage, many deserted over to the Dutch, and a score seized a Portuguese ship and sailed in her away out to sea to be heard of no more. Nearly all the others died or escaped, so that but three were found where they had been landed, in the year 1785.

[1] Ballagh, *Servitude*, pp. 78, 84, 85.
[2] Lang, *Transportation*, p. 39.
[3] Fiske, p. 186.
    McCormack, p. 79.
[4] Marion Phillips, *A Colonial Autocracy*, p. 2. London, 1909.
[5] *Commons Journal*, vol. xl. p. 1162, A.D. 1785.
[6] *Ibid.* p. 959.

There appear to have been several outposts and garrisons [1] made up of such convict soldiers round Goree, Sierra Leone, and regions adjacent. Thither were sent many pro-British negroes from Northern America and returned slaves from various places, including 400 masterless blacks deported from England; [2] also strangely enough, sixty prostitutes out of London, who were to be made " honest women " through marriage with some of them [3]; however, the African fever destroyed these unfortunates.

The island of Lemane, [4] 400 miles up the Gambia river, was spoken of as a Settlement, [5] and H.M.S. *Nautilus* was sent to explore the south-west coasts [6] of the continent, but found nothing promising. Meanwhile the prisons at home were packed with prisoners, [7] many of whom, though sentenced to transportation, were kept in the gaols for two or even three years longer, [8] and " being closely ironed, they could not walk," explained My Lord, the Minister in the House of Commons. [9]

In 1776 the county authorities were told to prepare and enlarge the gaols to meet new conditions, [10] an order to which they do not appear to have paid much attention. And as there was still not room enough within walls, new Acts were passed from the year 1776, [11] authorising that prisoners, failing the possibility of their being transported, should be kept upon hulks. These, as their name implies, were old sailing-vessels, generally men-of-war, permanently made fast in rivers or harbours; within,

---

[1] See *Dict. Nat. Biography*, article "Charles O'Hara."
Horace Bleackley, *Distinguished Victims of the Scaffold*, pp. 115, 122. London, 1905.
J. D. Lang, *Transportation*, p. 14.
Historical Records of New South Wales, vol. i. pp. 6, 7. Sydney, 1892.
[2] H. H. Johnston, *History of the Colonization of Africa*, p. 107. Cambridge, 1899.
[3] *Ibid.* p. 108.
[4] *Commons Journal*, vol. xl. p. 955.
[5] G. B. Barton, *History of New South Wales*, p. 22. London, 1899.
[6] *Historical Records N. S. W.*, p. 14.
[7] *Vide* Lord Sydney, letter to the Lords Commissioners of the Treasury, August, 18 1786, *Historical Records*, pp. 14, 281.
[8] Commission of 1837.
[9] *Commons Journal*, vol. xl. p. 954, A.D. 1785.
[10] 16 Geo. III. c. 43, sec. xiii.
[11] 16 Geo. III. 1776.
19 Geo. III. c. 74, 1779.
24 Geo. III. c. 12, 1783.

they were as like the old-fashioned prisons as possible, being crowded, dirty and verminous, with the men and boys all in irons, often in double irons, for greater security.[1] Those who were able to do rough work were employed on shore on various dockyard tasks, such as digging and dredging, and worked the same number of hours as the free labourers.[2] They were allowed some beer ;[3] (without which nobody in those days was considered able to live !), generally small beer, a weaked variety, when they were set to do anything specially arduous, and when they got back to the ship at evening they appear to have had a good deal of freedom in spite of fetters[4] and to have been allowed a little tobacco with which to console themselves.[5] There prevailed, indeed, the usual stagnation of prison life, particularly for those who were unable to go outside with the land parties ; bad language, some pilfering, and occasional violence, both by convicts and overseers.

The former[6] were all liable to be flogged with a severe sort of cat, to the extent of two dozen lashes,[7] but applications of the birch[8] were common enough and were not considered worth noticing or recording. There were a great number of feeble degenerates placed on board,[9] including some dazed and deadened by solitary confinement sent out from Millbank and other prisons ; and there were a good many palpable lunatics on the ships as well, who were often troublesome[10] and who were soundly flogged just like other captives ; the authorities evinced neither surprise nor objection to the presence of mad people,[11] only the very violent ones being sent to asylums, and the condition of these has been already described.[12]

[1] J. H. Vaux, *Memoirs*, p. 261. London, 1827.
[2] *Reports and Minutes of Evidence on the Hulks at Woolwich*, p. xix. London, 1847.
[3] *Report of the Select Committee on Secondary Punishments*, p. 47. London, 1831.
[4] DuCane, *Punishment*, pp. 120, 121,
[5] Report of 1831, p. 48.
[6] *Report on the Hulks*, 1847, p. xix.
[7] *Ibid.* evidence, p. 323.
[8] *Ibid.* p. xviii.
[9] *Report of 1847*, pp. xxvi, 254.
[10] *Ibid.* p. xiii.
[11] *Ibid.* p. xv.
[12] In Chapter III. *ante*.

The prisoners of the hulks were, as usual, sadly neglected. Upon the hospital ship at Woolwich,[1] for instance, neither towels nor even combs were provided, and most of the patients were infested with vermin. Whenever new cases had to be taken in, the previous occupants of the beds were turned into hammocks, and then the recent arrivals used the old sheets, which had not been changed,[2] and some of the sick, especially if insane, lay in a horrible condition of filth and wretchedness. The senior medical officer of the hulks on the Thames had a private practice to distract his attention, and the assistant surgeon was not a qualified man at all, but a medical student who was working for his degree.[3] Among the criminals, lunatics, feeble-minded, and outcasts of all kinds who were cooped up for periods generally varying between one and seven years [4] (the latter sentence was to be equivalent to fourteen years' transportation ; all persons respited after sentence of death were to be specially dealt with by the Home Secretary) were young boys. An old table gives the number upon the hulks at that time, and we find the record of : one child of 2, two of 12, four boys of 14, four of 15, and altogether twenty persons less than 16 years old.[5] About 1824 they appear to have placed the boys on a special ship, the hulk *Euryalus*, and there the youngest " villain " was nine years old ; [6] some of the boys, the inspector reported, " are so young that they can hardly put on their clothes." [7] Two-thirds of them are described as having been natural or neglected children. The Government had a place for at least a few of the Nation's babies, in convict prisons. For some thirty years after their [8] inception the hulks received a large proportion of the condemned,[9] and were used until 1858, or between eighty and ninety years.[10]

[1] *Report* 1847, p. 15.
[2] *Ibid.* p. xv.   [3] *Ibid.* p. xxx.
[4] See 19 Geo. III. c. 74.
[5] A. Graham, *Report on Hulks to the House of Commons*, 1814.
[6] *Report Select Committee on Secondary Punishment*, p. 51.
[7] *Report of* 1831, p. 52.
[8] DuCane, *Punishment*, p. 118.
[9] Royal Commission of 1863, *Report*, p. 13.
[10] DuCane, p. 123.   There was a hulk employed at Gibraltar until the year 1875.   DuCane, p. 118.

For some ten years the prisons and hulks [1] had been filled up and overcrowded with prisoners. Lord Sydney, writing on August 18, 1786,[2] complained that the gaols were overflowing with captives who had accumulated since our loss of America. The oligarchical Government would most willingly have consigned the convicts to the devil or the dust destructor, had such methods been feasible ; in actual fact, it was intended to shut them up, and huge cell-prisons were being planned in which to immure them.

In the year 1770 Captain Cook had seen and examined the fringe of the eastern coast of Australia, and presently people thought of that great lone land,[3] away upon the farthest rim of the globe, and prepared to send convicts there. In the year 1786 the Government selected Naval Captain Arthur Phillip to take command of an expedition.[4] He appears to have been a man of high character, and, for those times, not devoid of humanity. " I doubt," he wrote, " if the fear of death ever prevented a man of no principle [5] from committing a bad action," Yet though he had found that men were never deterred from desperate deeds by fear of being executed for them, he seems to have fancied that they might be appalled at the threat of being sent away to be eaten ! At any rate, he made the extraordinary proposal—which, as far as I know, was never once acted upon—that if any of the people under his charge should be convicted of murder or another offence, they should be kept in bonds until they could be handed over to the New Zealand savages to be killed for meat.[6]

But, as is usually the case with every form of primitive vengeance, something very similar had been tried before. In his regulations for the crusading navy, made out in the year 1190, King Richard [7] ordered that if any man

[1] *Commons Journal*, vol. xl. p. 964 A.D. 1785.
[2] *Historical Records N. S. W.*, vol. i. pt. 2 p. 14.
[3] This course was especially urged by Mr. J. M. Matra, for whose proposals see *Historical Records*, i. 2, p. 7.
[4] *Dict. Nat. Biography*.
[5] *Historical Records*, i. 2, p. 52.
[6] *Ibid.*
[7] " Qui hominem interfecerit, cum mortuo legatus projiciatur in mari, si autem in terra interfecerit, cum mortuo legatus in terra infodiatur."—Benedict of Peterborough, *Gesta Regis Ricardi*.

on the ships committed a murder, he should be bound to the victim's body and thrown overboard, while if the deed had been done on shore, the aggressor was to be buried alive with the corpse, and this was a fate which seems even more horrible than being served up to make a canniballic holiday.

Captain Phillip when he was in command employed no strange or specially monstrous punishments, and made only moderate use of those of the period, which were, however, severe and sanguinary. Upon his appointment he proceeded, like the good sailor he was, to organize the equipment of the ships that were to set sail ; meanwhile the convicts were gradually collected in the Thames and at Plymouth and Portsmouth and placed on board, all the men in irons.[1] Some of them, we are told, were confined to bed on account of the cold [2]—it was early in the year 1787—against which their " wretched clothing " gave no protection ; [3] others through enfeeblement and depression occasioned by long periods of imprisonment in the gaols, but many of them looked forward to their long journey hopefully.[4]

The various prison authorities of those days moved in a very leisurely manner, as is their habit, and some of the convicts were kept on board ship for nearly four months upon salt provisions.[5] At length they got together 564 male and 192 female prisoners,[6] or in all 756,[7] and placed them on board six transports escorted by two vessels of war and accompanied by three store-ships.[8] Along with the human freight were sent a large number of farmyard animals, including horses and cattle,[9] besides seeds, implements and tools ; and the expedition, which was to go down in Australian history as the First Fleet, set forth in the month of May in the year 1787.

[1] Watkin Tench, *Narrative of the Expedition to Botany Bay*, p. 1. London, 1789.
[2] John White, *Journal of the Voyage to New South Wales*, pp. 2, 4. London, 1790.
[3] Some of the convicts were very nearly naked : see Phillip to Nepean, *Records*, 1, 2, 112.
[4] Tench, p. 2.   [5] John White, *Journal*, p. 5.
[6] David Collins, *An Account of the English Colony in New South Wales*. London, 1798.
[7] Collins, p. 111.
[8] Griffiths, *Millbank*, p. 243.
[9] Charles White, *Convict Life*, p. 10. Bathurst, 1889.

After a voyage lasting eight months,[1] 1030 persons arrived at what is now the great city of Sydney in the year 1788.[2] At first there was the hard, but healthy, struggle with nature in which all laboured ; there stretched before them a continent to be conquered, and honest Governor Phillip possessed but a tatterdemalion army under his orders. Rough soldiers ; [3] rapacious and unscrupulous officers, who, in later times, as trading monopolists, exploited the colony ; [4] and the untrained and largely defective crowd of the convict outcasts.[5] But he was a British sailor and got to work.[6]

Composed of such elements, it is not surprising that the little community was sometimes inclined to become criminous and disorderly, and offenders were flogged with unsparing severity.[7] A condemned man with the hanging-rope actually round his neck [8] was offered his life to be made executioner, and after some hesitation he accepted the post. A primitive prison was put together with logs ; [9] a patrol made up of convicts was organized as a watch,[10] and six marines were captured and sternly hanged for robbing the public store ; [11] some convicts were afterwards hanged for the same offence.[12]

Famine at one time threatened the settlement ; [13] in February 1790 there were not four months' provisions left even upon half-rations, and all the men,[14] including the Governor, shared the same allowances quite impartially.[15]

[1] Griffiths, *Millbank*, p. 243.
[2] Collins, p. 6.
[3] Charles White, *Convict Life*, p. 78.
[4] Report of the Select Committee of 1812, p. 4.
[5] The greater part of the 102nd Regiment, or New South Wales Corps, disembarked in June, 1790. Vide *Official History of New South Wales*, p. 22. Sydney, 1883.
Historical Records, vol. i. pt. 2, p. 353.
Lang, *Hist. Acct. of N.S.W.*, p. 47, etc. London, 1852.
[6] *Historical Records*, vol. i. pt. 2, p. 359.
[7] John White, *Journal*, pp. 55, 76, 129, 159, 216.
[8] *Ibid.* p. 129.
[9] Charles White, *Convict Life*, p. 234.
[10] *Historical Records*, vol, i. pt. 2. p. 288.
[11] John Hunter, *Historical Journal*, p. 135. London, 1793.
[12] *Records*, vol. i. pt. 2. p. 297.
[13] Lang, *Hist.* p. 34.
[14] *Historical Records*, vol. i. pt. 2, p. 327.
[15] A wealthy merchant declared that for three years under Phillip he all along expected to die of starvation.—Lang, p. 38.

So feeble had the little garrison grown from want of food,[1] that Government work was temporarily suspended or allowed to slack down, and each man was told to do as much as he could, while all hunted and fished for their very dinners. Relief at length came in June 1790.[2] Meanwhile, just about this period (1789) on the hulks at home, the convicts continued to accumulate more and more,[3] and might be kept two, three, four, or even five years upon them[4] (or in the prisons), although they had been sentenced to transportation,[5] and the authorities hastened about dispatching the second fleet. Where the hulks were full, they used to select, in the first place, people supposed to be under fifty years of age,[6] and out of these, those with the longest sentences, or who were the most troublesome. The required numbers were made up with seven-years men, and occasionally, although not frequently,[7] with young boys of fifteen and under.[8]

The women convicts were taken without any special selection, provided they appeared to be below the age of forty-five.[9] Convicts above fifty were not supposed to be sent out to the colony,[10] but I fancy that most of those in good condition managed to go, since we read that the aged and infirm were greatly tried by the hardships

[1] Watkin Tench, *A Complete Account of the Settlement at Port Jackson*, p. 42. London, 1793.
[2] Lang, pp. 39, 40.
Barton, *Hist.* i. p. 250 (ed. 1889).
Tench, p. 49.
[3] *Historical Records*, vol. i. pt. 2. p. 281.
[4] *Report Select Committee on Transportation of* 1837, p. 294.
[5] Tench, *Complete Account of the Settlement*, p. 80.
[6] Committee of 1812, p. 9.
[7] A Graham, *Report on Hulks to the House of Commons* 1814, p. 215.
[8] A convict of fifteen on Norfolk Island was given 100 lashes for stealing rum. *Vide* J. Hunter, *Historical Journal*, p. 311.
See also L. Macquarie, *Letters to Viscount Sidmouth*, pp. 35, 44. London, 1821.
In later times the boys were sent out in ships apart from adults, and a special prison was founded for them at Point Puer, Van Diemen's Land, in 1834. *Vide Select Committee of* 1838, pp. 216, 218, etc.
James Backhouse, *Visit to the Australian Colonies*, p. 57. London, 1843.
On one occasion a child of seven was transported for life, another of ten arrived in Van Diemen's Land in 1829 after three years' imprisonment. See John West, *History of Tasmania*, vol. ii. pp. 246, 247, etc. Launceston, 1852.
[9] *Report of* 1812, p. 10.
[10] *Report of* 1812, p. 77.

of the long journey.[1] Those who were really considered
too old or too ill would be left to linger in hulks and
prisons until they had served their terms,[2] or were pardoned, or till they died ; for nobody cared about them.
The voyage out was looked upon by the exiles with
varied feelings.[3] The sturdy and adventurous longed
for it, both as a relief from the stagnation of prison,[4] and
as a real opportunity for another start ; but to the timid
and the sensitive, especially women,[5] or those who had
marriage ties or children at home, the distance that lay
between them and their unexplored destination, which
thenceforth would sever every human bond of love and
memory, must have appeared almost as far and final as
that unknown gulf of space and darkness which yawns
beyond the limits of the grave.

The Second Fleet then was got together, and the ships
straggled into Port Jackson in June 1790.[6] The convicts had this time undergone horrible sufferings, having
fallen into the hands of rascally contractors who were
paid an allowance for each man embarked,[7] and when
people perished there were less mouths to feed and more
would remain over to be disposed of.[8] It is said, too, that
deaths were sometimes concealed by the other convicts,
so that they might obtain the rations of the deceased ;
as it was, many of them were starved to death.[9]

The usual weight [10] of the irons employed on ship-
board was $3\frac{1}{2}$ to 4 lb.[11] and consisted of a chain of moderate length ending in a ring fitting round the ankles,
which was mostly hitched up to the waist-belt.[12] But
the present contractors had previously been employed
in the Guinea slave trade—then quite a respectable
occupation—and had retained the use of the old slave

[1] J. T. Bigge's Report, 1822, p. 9.
[2] DuCane, *Punishment*, p. 125.
[3] C. A. Browning, *The Convict Ship*, p. 250. London, 1847.
[4] Tench, *Narrative of the Expedition*, p. 2.
[5] Lang, *Transportation*, p. 22.
[6] *Historical Records*, vol. i. pt. 2, pp. 355, 367.
[7] C. White, p. 106.
[8] *Hist. Records*, vol. i. pt. 2. p. 367.
[9] Lang, *Hist.* p. 41.
[10] Griffiths, *Millbank*, p. 270.
[11] C. White, p. 83.
[12] *Hist. Records*, vol. i. pt. 2, p. 367.

irons, which consisted of ankle rings joined by a solid
bolt some nine inches long,[1] which permitted merely a
cramped shuffle.[2]

In the well-managed ships both before and afterwards,[3]
the chains were removed after the first week or fortnight [4]
of the voyage from England,[5] but on the Second Fleet
the shackles were not removed until it was within a
few days of the journey's end,[6] and the unfortunate
prisoners were penned down below.

Often they were drenched to the waist by the breaking
seas.[7] When the *Neptune, Scarborough,* and *Surprise*
entered Sydney Harbour, the Chaplain, Mr. Johnson,
climbed on board the last-named. "Went down amongst
the convicts," he writes, " where I beheld a sight truly
shocking to the feelings of humanity—a great number of
them lying, some half, and others entirely naked, without
either bed or bedding, unable to turn or help themselves.
Spoke to them as I passed along, but the smell was so
offensive that I could scarcely bear it.[8] I then went on
board the *Scarborough,* and proposed to go down amongst
them, but was dissuaded from it by the Captain. The
Neptune was still more wretched and intolerable, and
therefore I never attempted it." The convicts sometimes concealed the fact of a death amongst them, in order
to devour the dead man's rations, and then each hidden
carcass added its quota to the pestilential atmosphere.[9]

---

[1] *Hist. Records,* vol. i. pt. 2, p. 367.

[2] I have seen very similar fetters at a prison in Morocco, the inmates
of which, however, were probably less miserable than the convicts in
" model " European establishments.

[3] Tench, *Narrative of the Expedition,* p. 7.

[4] Griffiths, *Millbank,* p. 400.

[5] J. T. Bigge's *Report,* 1822, p. 3.

[6] The practice, however, varied enormously : some masters retained
the irons for the greater part of the voyage and never allowed more
than half the convicts to be on deck at a time for fear of what they
might do. Others, like Dr. Browning, employed neither irons nor
whips ; when he was sick he had his bed placed down in the convict
hospital, where they nursed him devotedly. *Vide* Bigge, p. 3. For
death-rate on the *Hillsborough,* see Report of 1812, p. 18 ; Appendix.
For allusion to the *General Hewit, Surrey and Three Bees,* in 1814, see
Bigge, *Report,* p. 1. With reference to the *Friendship* and *Chapman,*
see Phillips, pp. 175, 177. For reference to *Hercules* and *Atlas* in 1802,
see G. W. Rusden, *History of Australia,* pp. 392, 393. London, 1883,
etc. For Dr. Browning, see *Convict Ship,* p. 8, etc.

[7] Johnson to Thornton, *Hist. Records.*

[8] *Ibid.*   [9] *Ibid.*

" Some of these unhappy people died after the ships came into the harbour before they could be taken on shore. . . . The landing . . . was truly affecting and shocking ; great numbers were not able to walk, nor move hand or foot ; such were slung over the ship's side in the same manner as they would sling a cask, a box, or anything of that nature. Before their being brought up to the open air some fainted, some died upon deck, and others in the boat before they could reach the shore. When they came on shore many were not able to walk, to stand, or to stir themselves in the least, hence, some were led by others. Some creeped upon their hands and knees. . . ." [1] The existing sick at Port Jackson had been under fifty ; the new comers swelled the list up to close on five hundred.[2]

In March 1791 Governor Phillip [3] commenced to make grants of land to certain prisoners who had served their time, the usual amounts being thirty acres [4] for a single man and fifty acres for such as were married,[5] with ten acres more for each of their children. They were also to receive tools, seeds,[6] and Government rations for the first eighteen months.[7]

In March 1791 [8] a Mr. Scheffer, who had come out as a superintendent of convicts, received 140 acres of land and had also four convicts assigned to him. Convicts were also bestowed on the settlers [9] who arrived on January 16, 1793.[10] In the course of a year the demand for convict labour both on the part of the Settlers—some of whom received a number of convicts proportionate to the amount of land which they held [11]—and of the

---

[1] *Hist. Records*, p. 387.
[2] Phillip to Grenville, July 13, 1790.
[3] M. Phillips, *Colonial Autocracy*, p. 62.
[4] Some of the convicts received only twenty acres.
[5] Instructions from the Crown to Governor Phillip, April 25, 1787.
Hunter, *Journal*, p. 537.
[6] C. White, p. 11.
Tench, *Complete Account*, p. 149.
[7] Hunter, *Journal*, p. 537.
Hist. Records, i. 2, p. 540.
[8] Tench, *Complete Account*, p. 152.
[9] *Official History*, p. 23.
[10] More immigrants came in 1796, and a free settlement was begun at Portland Head in the year 1802.—Lang, *Hist.* p. 40.
[11] C. White, p. 11.

Emancipists (*i.e.* prisoners who had earned their freedom and land-grants) developed enormously, and ultimately exceeded the available supply.[1]

We appear now to have arrived at a period in which the circumstances of those transported to Australia strongly resembled those on the American Plantations as they existed in the previous century. Yet they differed widely : in Virginia the convicts ceased to be convicts and were turned into indentured labourers or leased slaves. They were poured, as it were, into the solid matrix of a settled society. In Australia, for a long period, the prisoners themselves were the population ; the only others present being their natural enemies, the British officials sent out to govern them. In Virginia the practical standard of values and currency medium was tobacco : men were paid in tobacco units and also were fined in them.[2] Now, in New South Wales[3] at first it was alcohol, much as gin still is, in some parts of West Africa.[4]

The spirit generally sold was either Bengal or Jamaica rum ;[5] wages were paid in this ;[6] lands were purchased therewith.[7] Rich pastures, or ground on which streets were afterwards builded, were sold in drink and bought for so many gallons by crimps and speculators.[8] A wife upon one occasion went for four gallons, but the value of wives is an uncertain criterion ; they have been sold or exchanged in the midland towns for half-crowns. We get a clearer idea of this fluid currency from the following, which appeared in the *Sydney Gazette* January 19, 1811 : " Notice of a reward for each whole skin of a native dog [a Dingo, no doubt]: one gallon of spirits or one pound sterling. Half a gallon of spirits or ten shillings sterling for every skin of a native pup."[9]

[1] Griffiths, *Millbank*, p. 269.
[2] Lang, *Hist.* p. 92.
[3] The Bank of New South Wales was opened for business, and issued notes ranging in value from 2s. 6d. to £5 in 1817. Phillips, p. 162.
[4] Phillips, p. 19.
[5] M. Phillips, p. 96.
[6] *Report of the Committee on Transportation of 1812*, p. 5.
[7] R. Therry, *Thirty Years' Residence in New South Wales*, p. 71. London, 1863.
    Phillips, p. 19.
[8] Therry, p. 72.
[9] J. O'Hara, *History of New South Wales*, p. 373. London, 1817.

Though the main reason for the prevalence of this objectionable medium of exchange is to be found in the utter absence of money,[1] so that transactions had to be carried on by means of barter of some kind or other ;[2] yet this ready acceptance of spirits as a standard of value shows the demand for them. Indeed the whole colony—composed as it was at first of just the two classes most given to drinking,[3] the military and the prisoners in their charge—gave itself over to orgies of drunkenness ; and consequently crimes of violence, squalor and the deepest degradation were thoroughly rampant throughout the community.

These conditions were destined to endure for many years, being, of course, at their worst in the city and townships, and least destructive in the " back blocks " up country, where both the masters and the convicts assigned to them led more primitive lives. As succeeding shiploads of convicts came, and fresh batches of exiles were landed at Sydney's quays, a certain number were always claimed by the Government for the public works. This branch was not at all popular with the convicts, and was avoided whenever possible,[4] especially by the mechanics and skilful workmen.[5]

The hours of labour were light in the early days,[6] being from six to three—we shall have to speak of the penal gangs later on. The men were generally clad in grey,[7] and were supposed to be housed and locked in barracks at night,[8] unless they got special leave to sleep in the town, which a great number often managed to do.[9]

The rest were assigned as servants to such as applied for them.[10] They wore no distinctive dress when in private hands, but where they went was as uncertain as

1 " In the early days there had been no metal coinage at all." Phillips, p. 160.
2 *Report of the Committee of* 1812, p. 4.
3 Phillips, p. 17.
4 *Report of* 1837, p. 300.
5 Bigge, *Report*, p. 13.
6 *Report of* 1812, p. 11.
7 Griffiths, *Millbank*, p. 289.
8 *Report of the Committee of* 1837, p. 29.
9 Griffiths, *Millbank*, p. 280.
10 Phillips, p. 73.
Griffiths, *Millbank*, p. 289.

what they were.[1] Some got to friends and associates in the city.[2] Some even contrived to be assigned to their wives,[3] when the latter had followed them and possessed the means. Others might be sent to the distant stations up country to be shepherds and labourers ; and whenever they were delivered over to brutal masters, they served as black slaves or dumb beasts of burden, having as little hope of redress or rescue as ill-used dogs.[4]

The masters were, in practice, all-powerful: many of the employers in the country districts were magistrates, and though they might not flog their own convict servants,[5] they were always able and willing to oblige one another and order the lash for their neighbours' culprits or victims, when they were brought before them.[6] In fact it has been officially admitted[7] that the assigned convicts were completely at the mercy of the master and the household, and indeed of anybody set over them ;[8] a man once received fifty lashes for failing to take off his hat to a magistrate on the road,[9] and another was sentenced to do ten days' treadmill for insulting demeanour towards Mr. Mudie,[10] an employer who had shortly before been rebuked by the Government for his harshness, and who, with a number of others, was removed from the magistracy.

They could complain, of course—a mouse may run to the cat next door if it likes ; but officials generally and country magistrates—neighbours—particularly, stand by their order, and they would only have received harder treatment for doing so.[11] Beyond doubt there existed

---

[1] *Report Select Committee of* 1837, p. 5.
[2] T. H. Braim, *Hist. of New South Wales*, i. p. 242. Lond., 1846.
[3] Griffiths, *Millbank*, p. 291.
Therry, pp. 46, 47.
[4] Occasionally, however, some local Thwackums were removed from the Bench. *Vide* Therry, p. 177.
Charles White, p. 215.
Brain, vol. i. p. 254.
[5] *Vide* 3 Will. IV. No. 3, sec. xxix.
[6] Eric Gibb, *Convict System in Australia*, p. 19. London, 1885.
Therry, p. 48.
[7] James Mudie, *Vindication*.
Report of 1837, p. 286.
[8] Griffiths, *Millbank*, p. 286.
[9] Therry, p. 43.
[10] Mudie, *Vindication*, p. 81.
[11] Therry, 46, 47.

grave abuses and evils in the colonial life that might have been so open and healthy ; and the worst social weeds had their roots in alcohol. But all the cruelty and viciousness we have heard of could not altogether outweigh the natural advantages of the situation. Compared with the prisoners confined in the gaols and hulks,[1] and with those turned adrift [2] with the broad-arrow brand of criminality upon them [3]—for people in those dark days knew less, cared less, and, perhaps consequently, dogmatised more harshly about "felons" than we do now—compared even with the machine-driven factory-slaves, and with some of the small house-drudges in the England of those times, the chances of the transported convicts were distinctly more hopeful.

We can see in our minds the clustering convict crowd, composed of nearly all sorts and conditions, upon the ships. Many would certainly be broken down and defective creatures (sub-normal).[4] Of the whole, the vast majority would of course be thieves—using that word in its widest sense : smooth pickpockets, rough burglars, and the still more dangerous parasites, forgers, coiners, sharpers and exploiters, who robbed by brains. Some men of blood and violence we should have seen— ruffians whom bad surroundings, and especially alcohol, had made worse than beasts—and there might have been a weird little collection composed of those whom we could roughly call Passionates ; some of these had done dreadful deeds, but they would not usually be brutal or villainous in themselves ; in this small group, so different from the rest, we might have met madmen or even a superman![5]

---

[1] *Report of the Select Committee on Transportation of* 1861, p. 5.

[2] "When they [prisoners] gain their liberty no Parish will receive them and no Person set them to work . . . being shunned by their former acquaintants and baffled in every Attempt to gain their Bread, the danger of starving almost irresistibly leads them to a Renewal of their former Crime."—Report from a Committee, *Commons Journal*, vol. xl. p. 1161, July 28, 1785.

[3] "What should a man without a character do at home when thousands, nay millions of our poor fellow countrymen . . . find it so difficult to provide the means of subsistence throughout the year for their little ones ? "—*The Times*, April 17, 1850.

[4] See Governor Phillip in *Hist. Records*, i. 2, p. 355.

[5] The Rev. Dr. Lang refers to a certain convict who was working in double irons, who could quote aptly from Lucretius ; his offence is not stated.—*Transportation and Colonisation*, p. 122.

There would have been a great number of first offenders; lads who in these days would never be sent into penal servitude,[1] and if to prison, only for very short terms, or to Borstal for the new course of treatment. Such cases are very frequently released on probation, or bound over to come up for judgment if called upon, which means, Don't do it again! From time to time we should also have found a sprinkling of Politicals, Irish revolutionaries [2] of 1798, who were reprieved from hanging and sent out on life sentences. A few Cato Street conspirators of 1820—one of whom became a chief constable![3] and in the course of years—for example 1811–1812, 1816–17, 1833, etc.—a number of Luddites, and other machine breakers were added to the long lists of the transported ones.

All these different kinds of people really had a new start—at any rate in the earlier period.[4] Up to the year 1812 no particulars of their crimes were sent out to the colony. It was wiser to have no list, Macquarie considered,[5] lest dislikes and prejudices should be occasioned in particular instances; it was better to start afresh. As we have stated, the convicts were assigned either to the Government or to private people, and they generally had to serve a proportion of the period for which they had received sentence. Thus a lifer became eligible to receive a ticket of leave after the lapse of eight years ; [6] a fourteen-years man after six, and a seven-years man after four years' good conduct.

The state of the agenerate or subnormal was of course always precarious ; there were a certain number of the convicts who came from the " unemployable " class at home and who were continually falling back into crime from their own physical and mental infirmities. But a large proportion of even the unskilled elements had good

---

[1] In 1830 there were, in round numbers, 50,000 convicts ; in 1912 there are about 3,000. See R. F. Quinton, *Modern Prison Curriculum*, p. 52, London, 1912 ; and his *Crime and Criminals*, p. 35. London, 1910.

[2] Robert Peel to J. Beckett, Dublin Castle, Sept. 5, 1812 (Record Office) ; see also Therry, p. 93.

[3] Therry, pp. 96, 97.

[4] *Report of* 1812, p. 11.

[5] Macquarie, *Letter to Sidmouth*, p. 57.

[6] *Report of* 1837, p. 280, and Appendix, p. 264.

hopes before them, unless they had the misfortune to fall
into the hands of a master whose persistent ill-usage
shortened their lives or drove them into the Chained
Gangs or the Penal Settlements—of which details later—
and they might reasonably aspire to settle down on the
land and to become respected if always humble squatters
and citizens. Moreover the personal and emotional
side of life was not always altogether neglected. Convicts were sometimes allowed to select their own messmates,[1] and the authorities rather encouraged the practice
of wives [2] and families being sent to rejoin husbands and
fathers out in Australia [3] when the latter were declared
by the Governor to be in a condition to keep and look
after them,[4] a favour which we find continually being
petitioned for in the convicts' letters [5] and frequently
granted by the governing powers.[6] It is said that sons
and brothers occasionally contrived to get transported
on purpose,[7] in order to join their people in the new
world. But if the unskilled workers had certain prospects,
those of the trained and educated were very much better.
Able men were well paid ; they were valuable to their
masters and frequently worked their way into partner-
ship. They also filled places in the learned professions : [8]
some became doctors,[9] many acted as schoolmasters ; [10]
whilst in the field of journalism, the Emancipists, led by
such men as O'Shaughnessy and Watt, became easily
paramount.[11]

In business too some large fortunes were got together,
no doubt frequently by sharp practices. But it is more

---

[1] Charles White, p. 111.
[2] Griffiths, *Millbank*, p. 291.
[3] C. White, p. 129.
[4] Macquarie to Sidmouth, pp. 25, 73, and Appendix ii. p. 89.
[5] *Vide Colonial Office Papers*, 201, 67, 70, etc., Record Office.
[6] Letter from Lord Sidmouth to Henry Goulburn, Nov. 20, 1812.
Macquarie to Goulburn, Aug. 20, 1813.
[7] C. White, p. 123.
[8] The first convict emancipated became an assistant surgeon.—*Hist.
Records*, i. 2, p. 555.
[9] Tench, *Complete Account*, p. 44.
[10] *Commission of* 1837, p. 255.
Ibid. Appendix, p. 260.
[11] *Ibid*, Report, pp. 235, 241
Griffiths, *Millbank*, p. 292.
R. Flanagan, *Hist. N. S. Wales*, p. 485. London, 1862.

satisfactory to remember that those who were on the spot and able to judge considered [1] that many convicts were really reclaimed through the new life transportation afforded them, and that occasionally they earned such good reputations as to be placed on the magisterial Bench. [2]

But as the Colony, founded and made, as it had been, by convict labour, [3] increased in wealth and prosperity, it began to attract a stream of free settlers; and though the American Colonists had been content to make use of and tolerate the gradual absorption into the Plebeiance of the convict servants gradually drafted over, the free immigrants refused to fraternize with a class tabooed, and declined, as far as circumstances permitted, to be in any way impatriated with them. At first the convicts, though in a far better situation than circumvallated prisoners, [4] had no rights or liberties, but as years went by, and their sentences terminated, the best of them sought to attain the status of Colonists. Through the earlier period the freed convicts had the place pretty much to themselves, the officials doubtless holding aloof, and there being very few other settlers.

Thus the social friction which appeared afterwards must have been to a great degree non-existent, since the peccant Pot could scarcely complain of the nigritude of the criminal Kettle. But as the free immigrants began to arrive in augmenting numbers, things became different. The wise and far-seeing Governor, Lachlan Macquarie, appears to have known what would occur, and used all his influence to commend and receive well-conducted Emancipists and even to discourage the flow of free passengers. But the cleavage grew wider and deeper as years went by, and probably, in those times and circumstances, there could have been no way of closing it. The Emancipist party is said to have arisen in 1809; [5] it was not without wealth and great influence in the colony; [6] its press, complained the Rev. Dr. Lang, was

---

[1] Macquarie to Sidmouth, p. 16.
[2] *Ibid.* pp. 36, 38, 47.
[3] Macquarie to Sidmouth, p. 69.
[4] J. Finney, *History Australian Colonies*, ch. 2, v. Sydney, 1901.
[5] *Report Select Committee on Transportation of* 1838, p. xxviii.
[6] *Report Committee* 1837, p. 101.

" perpetually endeavouring [1] to impress on the community that the mere fulfilment of a man's term of transportation restored him . . . to the same condition in society as the man who never had been a convict."
On the other hand the Committee asserted [2] that " under a good system of punishment an offender should, at the expiration of his sentence, be considered to have atoned for his crimes, and should be permitted to commence a new career without any reference to his past one." This was the view upheld by Macquarie, but on the whole the authorities sided against the Emancipists. The contending parties fought fiercely for many years ; the Immigrants accusing the Emancipists of sharp practices and demoralisation, and the latter charging the former with injustice and pharisaism. Each side said probably much that was true and cruel about the other, as enemies have a habit of doing both in Australia and in all parts of the globe.[3] Gradually, in the course of years, the numbers of the free immigrants crept up to,[4] and ultimately surpassed, those of the convicts emancipated.[5]

The freemen were, on the whole, made up of sounder and better-balanced material ; they included in their ranks the official, wealthier, and governing elements, and were continually being recruited from the people at home. With this great increase in the population and wealth, there came, as a natural consequence, the ambition of Statehood. The Colony was now the country of its people, and they began to resent the idea of being known and spoken of as a mere convict settlement. A league was formed against it in 1830,[6] and by 1835 the colonial fight against the Institution which had laid its foundations was in full blast.[7] But there was another danger always threatening the practice of transportation, and that was the watchful eye of the English Government, which was always afraid that it would not be penal

[1] *Committee of* 1837, p. 241.   [2] *Report* 1838, p. 29.
[3] The unseemly wrangle is held to have persisted until the gold rush of 1851. Finney, p. 75.
[4] *Report Committee of* 1838, p. 28.
[5] In 1834 there are said to have been some twenty-one thousand free immigrants, against fifteen or sixteen thousand Emancipists.
[6] T. A. Coghlan and T. T. Ewing, *Progress of Australasia*, p. 31. Lond., 1903.
[7] Flanagan, *Hist. New South Wales*, i. p. 474.

enough.[1] During the first phase, the journey out, with
its enormous mileage, its indefinite destination, and the
utter and lifelong banishment which it appeared to
involve, was looked upon as being in itself a great punishment.[2] But as the passage out grew more familiar, and as
the poor, or " criminal," class got friends and relatives on
the other side, no doubt the terrors of the actual journey
abated, and Downing Street, though relieved to be
enabled to get rid of the prisoners, was always timorous
lest at any time, transportation should become less
dreaded than the grim hardships of home. For there
were lean years gone through in the land ; a great war
had been brought to a close (1816), entailing disbanded
armies, bread riots and misery.[3] Machinery had come
in, displacing the cottage workers and filling its factories
with white slaves ; [4] so that (in the absence of prisons
which are always so much worse than anything else)
the Government required something very infernal to be
contrasted against such conditions of poverty. This we
find clearly set forth by Sir George Arthur, Governor
of Van Diemen's Land. " In England, while employment
is so scarce that the operative must starve though the
convict is well fed and taken care of, it cannot be but
that under every restriction, every severity of discipline
that ingenuity can contrive or vigilance execute, the
condition of the convict must present to the lower class
that which they will be too apt to consider complete
evidence of the inutility of virtue and the paramount
advantage of vice." [5]

Richard Whately, Archbishop of Dublin, argued on
the same side.[6] Stimulated by such opinions, and likewise
alarmed at the restiveness of the immigrants, the Government proceeded, about 1837, to stop the assignment of
convicts to private persons,[7] alleging, amongst other

[1] See Griffiths, *Millbank*, p. 209.
[2] *Report of* 1812, p. 10.
[3] Meiklejohn, *Hist.* ii. p. 261.
[4] Therry, p. 24.
[5] *Report of Committee*, 1837, p. 289.
[6] *Thoughts on Secondary Punishment*, p. 3, etc. London, 1832.
[7] John Russell to Glenelg, April 15, 1837 ; Glenelg to R. Bourke,
May 26, 1837.
　　Coghlan and Ewing, p. 31.　　　　　　Finney, *Hist.* p. 75.
　　It appears to have lingered up to 1841.—Braim, i. 257, Grey, p. 6.

reasons, its inequality of effect. But very soon the Home authorities went further than this,[1] and there appeared in 1840 [2] an Order in Council prohibiting the sending of convicts to New South Wales. The new destination for the convict population was to be Van Diemen's Land. The discipline on that island had been severe all along,[3] indeed it had proved far more arduous than the transported exiles expected.[4] But the Lieutenant-Governor, Sir George Arthur, "had been long, assiduously, and successfully, endeavouring to render transportation a painful punishment, and to make the convict feel his position to be a disagreeable and degraded one." And Captain Maconochie, R.N., had observed[3] that "The severe coercive discipline [5] . . . is carried so far as to be at issue with every natural, and in many cases even laudable impulse of the human mind." Just the place for convicts to be "reformed" in ! And thither they were conveyed till they accumulated in thousands, entirely swamping the resources of the executive.

About this time a new method was to be put in force which was called the Probation System,[6] under which the convicted were to be made to pass through what Major Arthur Griffiths has termed " a species of crucible of discomfort." There were various stages to be gone through, the first being one of severe imprisonment.[7] The second consisted of the Government labour-gangs in various places.[8] The third gave them a pass to seek

---

[1] See Lord John Russell's Despatch, January 30, 1839.
[2] *Accounts and Papers British Museum*, vol. xxxviii. 1840.
Earl Grey, *Colonial Policy*, vol. ii. p. 4. London, 1853.
Braim, *Hist.* i. p. 260.
Coghlan and Ewing, p. 31.
" Hist. of the Australian Settlement," *Sydney Morning Herald*, p. 21. Sydney, 1888.
[3] *Report of* 1837, p. 285.
[4] *Report of Committee* 1838, p. xii.
[5] *Report of Van Diemen's Land*, p. 9, and see *Report of* 1838, p. 39.
[6] Braim, *Hist.* i. pp. 256, 258. Griffiths, *Millbank*, p. 315.
[7] Only those who had been reconvicted in the colony, or who had come out from England under life, or very long sentences, went to Norfolk Island, Griffiths, p. 316.
[8] Certain selected convicts with not greater than seven-year sentences were to pass the preliminary period, not exceeding eighteen months, in one of the English Penitentiaries, and were then upon their arrival placed either in a probation gang, or probation pass, or at once on ticket of leave.—DuCane, p. 141.

for possible work within narrow bounds. The fourth a wider range, with tickets of leave. And the fifth a conditional pardon and restored liberty.[1]

The new system was fully detailed in a despatch dated November 15, 1842, by Lord Stanley to Sir John Franklin,[2] the Lieutenant-Governor of Van Diemen's Land, and was put in force against all the convicts who were poured into that island by the year 1843.[3] Within three years there were some 25,000 collected there, besides 3,000 Pass-holders ;[4] the demand for their labour was quite inadequate, so that hiring gangs had to be established, in which the Pass men were maintained by the Government till they could find masters; meanwhile they were generally kept in a state of excessive idleness and stagnation,[5] with all the usual bad effects resulting therefrom.

The position of the Ticket-of-Leave men was indeed deplorable, " being thus thrown upon the world," [6] wrote the Lieutenant-Governor, " with nothing but their labour to support them, and no labour being in demand, either starve or steal." This was one way of creating Bush Rangers ; once again the community manufactured the criminals it deserved. So choked was Van Diemen's Land with its convict masses [7] that transportation there had to be suspended during 1847 and part of 1848, and a certain number of exiles were despatched, after having served through their punishment, to New South Wales and also Port Phillip. The Government even contemplated forming a penal colony in tropical North Australia,[8] but unhappily for the convicts the scheme fell through, and they began to build " separate " prisons in England.[9]

About 1847 we find a new or second Probation System[10]

[1] DuCane, p. 141.
Griffiths, p. 316.
[2] Griffiths, p. 315.
[3] W. B. Ullathorne, *Memoir of Bishop Willson*, p. 42. London, 1843.
[4] Griffiths, p. 411.
[5] DuCane, pp. 142, 143.
[6] See Grey, *Colonial Policy*, p. 9, and Griffiths, p. 413.
[7] DuCane, p. 144.
Grey, p. 35.
[8] DuCane, p. 144.
[9] Grey, p. 31.
[10] Earl Grey, ii. 17.

being prepared, mainly by Sir George Grey, and about 1848 the Government ordained [1] that the first part (six to eighteen months—as much as could be endured by the average man) of all sentences which involved transportation, should be passed in an English Penitentiary. Then was to come penal labour in a Home prison, or at Bermuda (up to 1862) or Gibraltar (up to 1875).[2] It was originally intended that after having got through their punishment the convicts should have been sent out to the colonies [3] on tickets of leave, and in 1848 the Order in Council [4] of 1840 by which New South Wales had been forbidden as a depot for convicts was revoked, and for the next two or three years (i.e. 1848–49–50) attempts were made to revive transportation and to send exiles to New South Wales, Van Diemen's Land,[5] and even the Cape of Good Hope.[6]

But it was soon found that the tide in the Colonies ran strong against such a course. The " respectable " part of the population had become touchy on the subject of convicts, and did not want what has sometimes been called (elegantly !) attenuated sewage poured in amongst them ; for, rightly enough, they did not believe, in practice, that any real reformation could arise through imprisonment. The working class likewise objected, as they dreaded cheap labour,[7] and the free immigrants did not wish to be mixed up with such company; so that when, on June 8, 1849, the convict ship *Hashemy* arrived before Sydney with a party of " exiles," public meetings were organized and vast numbers protested [8]—although there were other points of view in the upland stations. In the same year the Legislative Council voted an Address to the Queen against the revival of transportation. The

[1] Griffiths, p. 425.
Grey, p. 23.
[2] Griffiths, p. 426.
Royal Commission of 1879, *Report*, p. 10.
[3] Grey, p. 23.
DuCane, pp. 145, 146.
[4] Grey, p. 45.
[5] Committee of 1861, *Evidence*, p. 15.
[6] From Bermuda in September 1849: see Griffiths, *Millbank*, p. 437.
[7] Grey, p. 47.
[8] Henry Parkes, *Fifty Years of Australian Hist.*, p. 14. Lond., 1892.
Grey, p. 46.

opposition was so strong and well-organized that the Home Government had to give way.   Despatches were sent to Sir Charles Fitzroy [1]—November 10 and 16, 1849 —to say that no further contingents of convicts would be sent to the Colony, and the Order in Council already alluded to was altered again in the year 1852.[2]   In that year sailed the last convict ship for Van Diemen's Land.[3]

In 1850 Western Australia, a younger colony with a vast area, and a population [4] at that time of only 4,600, was found to be anxious to receive convict labourers,[5] and the first batch was landed there on June 2.[6]   The system to be carried out was that laid down in 1847–48, except that a certain number of prisoners passed about half their " public works " (*i.e.* penal servitude) period in the colony,[7] where a large cellular prison had been constructed at Fremantle.   It was claimed that the men (no women convicts were to be allowed to be sent to Western Australia) were well conducted, moral and orderly, and that life and property in the colony—which the officials hailed joyfully as being " a vast natural gaol "—were perfectly safe.

But, as we have seen, the real objections to transportation which had been made were based upon other grounds altogether, and these pursued the latest Settlement and prevailed.   So transportation to Western Australia also came to an end,[8] and no more shiploads were sent there after the year 1867.[9]

The Punishments for Transported Convicts

So far, the story of Transportation has shown, in my opinion, that it might have been, and to some extent actually was, the wisest way of dealing with long-sentence criminals.   It had removed a huge, if straggling army,

---

[1] Grey, p. 50.
[2] Parkes, p. 19.
[3] Griffiths, p. 436.
[4] Grey, *Colonial Policy*, p. 57.
[5] DuCane, p. 147.
[6] Grey, p. 62.
[7] DuCane, p. 149.
[8] *Ibid.* p. 154.
[9] *Ency. Brit.* ix. ed. art. " Pris. Dis." p. 754.

amounting to more than a hundred thousand prisoners [1] from the certainty of hopeless degradation and chronic misery, and it had afforded them a fresh start with real possibilities of being restored into the Commonwealth.[2] Left at home, those placed beneath the ban of Society would merely have occasioned the erection of prisons and workhouses ; as things were, they established new States, and developed a Continent. But there were stark and terrible abuses rooted round transportation ; we must remember that it was carried out in a brutal age and under the management, at its best, of rough men whose hands were hard and horny with wind and weather, and at its worst, of barbarous martinets and prison officials, long since become inhuman and butcherly, of " creatures that once were men."

The great prophylactic and social " remedy " of those rough times in which transportation took place was beating people in various ways. The children were beaten at home, the boys were flogged and birched in the schools; the servants were frequently thrashed in the country districts; the prisoners in the gaols, both men and women, were commonly whipped ; and all disciplined men of the fighting forces were knocked about until their skins became as red or blue as their jackets, and were sometimes even mammocked to death.[3]

---

[1] Sir Edmund DuCane says (p. 111) that the total number of convicts sent to Australia during the continuance of the system amounted to 134,308, but such totals as 137,161, 159,623, etc., can be made up from various authorities. The reader may refer to : *Committee of* 1838 *Report*, p. 37, and Appendix, p. 372.
Lang. *Hist.*, p. 12.
Coghlan and Ewing, pp. 31, 32.
Sydney Morning Herald Hist. p. 21.
Committee of 1861 *Report*, p. 16.
[2] Lord Grey ascertained that in the year 1850 there were 48,000 persons in the Australian colonies who had once been convicts, nearly all of whom were then maintaining themselves.—*Colonial Policy*, p. 76.
[3] For a few instances of fatal or tremendous floggings the reader is referred to :
F. R. Skrine, *Fontenoy*, pp. 253, 254, 303.
Samuel Romilly, *Memoirs*, vol. ii. p. 133.
The Globe, May 24, 1828.
Barton, *Hist.*, p. 229.
A. F. Tytler, *Military Law*, p. 328. Edin., 1800.
Horace Bleackley, *Distinguished Victims of the Scaffold*, p. 121, etc.
F. Myers, *Botany Bay*, p. 22.
Charles James Napier, *Remarks on Military Law*, p. 152. Lond., 1837.

Our forefathers made their punishments to be as public as possible. They were not over-sensitive about witnessing suffering, they believed firmly in the old deterrence theory, and did their best, or worst, to make the law's grim terrors tangible. Dr. Johnson observed in the well-known passage: " Tyburn itself is not safe from the fury of innovation. Executions are intended to draw spectators ; if they do not, they do not answer their purpose. The old method was most satisfactory to all parties ; the public was gratified by a procession, the criminal was supported by it. Why is all this to be swept away ? "

Keeping to facts, they found that pockets were being picked beneath the very gibbets on which thieves were being strangled. As the Act (8 Eliz. c. iv.) recites, they pilfered even " at the time of doing execution of such as had been attainted of any murder, felony or other criminal cause, ordained chiefly for terror and example of evil doers ; [the criminals] do without respect or regard of any time, place or person . . . take the goods of diverse good and honest subjects. . . ."

It was expressly ordered that convicts were to be whipped as publicly as possible.[1] Bentham desired that the " instructive ignomany " of prisoners should be witnessed by as many people as possible.[2]

Hence executions were public parades and prisoners were flogged through the open streets. In the earlier period they were not condemned to receive a definite number of strokes, but were ordered to be flogged throughout certain journeys—as from Newgate to Tyburn, which was close to the spot which is now Marble Arch— and in this way the victims must have received a truly prodigious number of lashes, although the actual severity of a flogging cannot be altogether estimated from this alone ; much would depend upon the instrument used, and also upon the arm of the operator, which was apt to grow tired. In the brutal military floggings [3]—where the number of lashes was regulated by the Court sen-

---

[1] See *Report Committee of* 1837, p. 348.
[2] Letter to Lord Pelham, p. 4.
[3] Something of the almost incredible enormity of these service sentences may be learned from the pages of General Sir Charles James

tencing, or by the interference of the surgeon when the life-limit was approached—the drummers [1] were supposed to be relieved after inflicting twenty-five cuts,[2] and often after every dozen lashes; they also practised upon inanimate objects to get their hands in.[3]

In such times as those we may be sure the convicts received their share of the flagellations. Under Governor Phillip we read of such punishments as one hundred lashes for going among the women convicts on shipboard;[4] two hundred lashes for a marine who endeavoured to pass bad coin. Two men, for a violent assault, were sentenced to no less than five hundred lashes each, but, says Surgeon-General White, " they could not endure the whole, as they were feeble with scurvy." In the rough and primitive life of the colony, the cat was the main thing resorted to in dealings with convicts. The " cat," as everybody knows, was a whip, usually with nine lashes or " tails," but it is not always easy to make out its quality. It was called a " cat " because it was said to " scratch " the backs of its victims; and indeed some of the mediæval whips had metallic claws.[5]

Historically, there must have been almost as many appliances for lashing the unfortunate human body as there were cutting weapons to make holes or stabs in it. Whips have been made with three, five, six and nine tails, and these have been heavy or light, flat, round, or triangu-

Napier. " In them often was the unhappy victim of such barbarous work brought out from the hospital three or four times to receive the remainder of his punishment, too severe to be borne without danger of death at one flogging; and sometimes I have witnessed this prolonged torture applied for the avowed purpose of adding to its severity. On these occasions it was terrible to see the new tender skin of the scarcely healed back again laid bare to receive the lash. I declare that, accustomed as I was to such scenes, I could not on these occasions bear to look at the first blows; the feeling of horror which ran through the ranks was evident, and all soldiers know the frequent faintings that take place among recruits when they first see a soldier flogged."—*Military Law*, p. 160.

[1] A. Somerville, *Autobiography of a Working Man*, p. 288, etc. Lond., 1848.

[2] *Committee of 1837*, Appendix, p. 94.

An Australian police superintendent declared that a man could not properly inflict more than 150 lashes a day. *Ibid.* p. 89.

[3] Somerville, pp. 289, 294.

[4] John White, *Journal of the Voyage*, pp. 50, 55, 159.

[5] The old Roman flagellum . . . had sometimes three thongs with bone or brass knots fastened to them. *Enc. Brit.* xi. ed. vol. v. p. 487.

lar, according to the time and places in which they were put together. Some of the most murderous whips invented,[1] such as the knout of Russia (employed up to 1845),[2] the korbash or sjambok of Africa, possessed but one deadly thong,[3] or were leathern rods or wands which could slice like swords and kill in comparatively few strokes whenever the death penalty was intended with them.

But keeping to the implements of our own place and period, we find cats were made of varying form and weight. The naval cat was perhaps the most formidable ; [4] it has been described as " being made out of a piece of rope thicker than a man's wrist,[5] 5 feet in length all over, three of which were stiff and solid stuff and the remaining two feet ravelled into hard twisted and knotted ends. Such was the old-fashioned cat ; but even when wooden handles were substituted for rope ones, it was generally heavier than the military instrument." Another account describes a cat employed on an English merchant ship as consisting of " a handle or stem made of a rope $3\frac{1}{2}$ inches in circumference and about 18 inches in length, at one end of which are fastened 9 branches or tails composed of log line with 3 or more knots upon each branch." [6]

The military cat has been described [7] as " a weapon about 18 inches in length, armed with 9 thongs of the same length, each thong bearing 5 or 6 knots compressed and hardened into sharp edges till each acquired the consistency of horn." [8]   Private Somerville [9] alludes to the cats employed in his regiment as having handles two feet in length and similar tails ;   the latter being

---

[1] W. M. Cooper, *History of the Rod*, ch. xxvi.

[2] The modern Siberian instrument is the plet, a whip with a very short handle and three thick thongs : *vide* J. Y. Simpson, *Side-Lights on Siberia*, p. 218.   London, 1898.

[3] Leonard Willoughby, *Pall Mall Magazine*, April 1912.

[4] *Royal Commission of* 1863, p. 108.

[5] Cooper, *Hist. Rod*, p. 369.

[6] Alexander Falconbridge, *An Account of the Slave Trade*, p. 40. London, 1788.

[7] Cooper, p. 357.

[8] The condition of the whip appears to have been considered important and was carefully attended to.   *Vide Committee of* 1837, p. 94, etc.

[9] Somerville, *Autobiography*, p. 294.

twice or perhaps three times the thickness of whip-cord.[1] Each tail contained six hard knots, and as there were nine of them, and as each knot made an abrasion, he calculated upon receiving fifty-four stinging cuts at every stroke. We also hear of the Double or Thief's cat being employed [2] at some of the penal stations ; it is stated to have been both larger and heavier than the ordinary, and to have had a double twist in the whip-cord ; it bore nine tails and as many knots in each one. But besides all these there were doubtless a number of fancy whips used for flogging, and we may well believe that they served their purpose, for it has always been easy to hurt although hard to heal, since the world began. At last, about 1833, Sir Richard Bourke, who was Governor, compelled the officials, at any rate, to keep to one kind of cat.[3] This is described as having been made with a two-foot handle, to which were attached five lashes of whip-cord, each having six knots in them.[4]

The authorities were allowed great powers of punishing : a police superintendent and justice could summarily order the infliction of fifty lashes on convicts [5]—freemen had to be tried by a bench and could appeal to the governor [6]—a Bench of three justices could give up to three hundred ; [7] away in the country a single magistrate could officiate as a Bench.[8]

We have been talking so much about the instruments used to flagellate that we may now endeavour to find out what effects they had.

Writing of things he beheld in the year 1829, Sir Roger Therry says in his *Thirty Years' Residence in New South*

---

[1] Dr. Quinton, a prison Governor, remarks that knots in the modern cats have now been abolished, though he had seen them in use.—*Crime and Criminals*, p. 34.

[2] *Committee of* 1838, p. 38.
G. E. Boxall, *History of Australian Bushrangers*, p. 4. London, 1908.

[3] Charles White, p. 504.

[4] This standard instrument is said to have been prepared by Superintendent Slade. *Vide* John West, *History of Tasmania*, p. 256.

[5] Macquarie to Bathurst, June 28, 1813. Sec. 13, Record Office C.O. 201, 67.

[6] Phillips, pp. 70, 78.

[7] *Report of* 1812, p. 11.

[8] Donnelly, p. 78.

Wales: " As I passed along the road about eleven in the morning there issued out of the prisoners' barracks a party of four men who bore on their shoulders (two supporting the head and two the feet), a miserable convict writhing in an agony of pain—his voice piercing the air with terrific screams." [1]

He was informed that it was " only a prisoner who had been flogged, on his way to the hospital." Once there he would be a week or ten days under treatment,[2] but if the flogging [3] was a severe one or had been inflicted with the heavy,[4] or thief's cat, he might easily be a month or two in the doctor's hands,[5] and occasionally died from inflammation or shock.

Another truly ghastly description is given in an Australian book previously quoted.[6] At a convict station of the interior a witness on his way to the Court had to pass the triangles which had been in use that day. " I saw," he observes, " a man walk across the yard with the blood that had run from his lacerated flesh squashing out of his shoes at every step he took. A dog was licking the blood off the triangles, and the ants were carrying away great pieces of human flesh that the lash had scattered about the ground. . . . The scourger's feet had worn a deep hole in the ground by the violence with which he whirled himself round on it so as to strike the quivering and wealed back, out of which stuck the sinews, white, ragged and swollen. The infliction was one hundred lashes at about half-minute time, so as to extend the punishment through nearly an hour [7] . . . they had a pair of scourgers [8] who gave each other spell and spell about, and they were bespattered with blood like a couple of butchers."

At length, about 1833, the Governor, who was Sir

---

[1] P. 42.
[2] Therry, p. 42.
[3] Somerville, p. 293.
[4] C. White, p. 355.
[5] *Committee of* 1838 :   Evidence of Dr. Barnes, p. 38.
[6] Charles White, *Convict Life*, p. 499.   Compare also Somerville's account.
[7] The hideous knout is said to have usually taken one hour to inflict twenty stripes.—Simpson, *Siberia*, p. 219, note.
[8] *Ibid.* p. 499.   C. White (quoted p. 123).
See also Gibb, p. 28.

Richard Bourke, secured the passing of what has been called the Quarter Sessions or the Fifty Lashes Act,[1] by which a magistrate could not order the infliction of above fifty lashes (with the new standard cat), in lieu of one hundred and fifty which had been frequently given in three distinct floggings. This, says the Rev. Dr. Lang,[2] " naturally gave offence to the adherents of General Darling's policy—the colonial Tories, and a mighty outcry was accordingly raised." Two petitions were presented to the Legislative Council stating that the amount of punishment which the justices could award under the Colonial Act, 3 W. IV. No. 3, was too small,[3] and that the instrument, *i.e.* the new cat, was too weak.[4] Thereupon Sir Richard Bourke caused a Circular Letter to be sent by Mr. Alexander McLeay [5] from the Colonial Secretary's Office on August 21, 1833, addressed to the police magistrates, directing them to superintend the forthcoming floggings personally.[6] They presently reported that the new cat was severe enough, and sent in returns [7] from which we may extract a few instances.[8] September 30, 1833, D. McDonald, fifty lashes; much lacerated, bled after twentieth stroke. J. Denison, twenty-five lashes; bled much. John Orr, a boy, twelve lashes; cried out much.

Another official gives cases [9] from September 1 to October 1, 1833. J. Green, fifty lashes; fainted after. T. Holdsworth, blood at fifth lash. J. Kenneth, blood at eighteenth lash. E. Davis, continued crying after flogging was over.[10] Other cases showed : blood at fourth stroke, blood at twelfth, blood at twentieth, etc., etc.[11] Several boys received twenty-five lashes for feigning (?)

[1] *Report of Select Com. on Trans. of* 1838, p. **xxxix**.
Lang, *Transportation*, p. 94.
Charles White, p. 500.
[2] *Transportation*, p. 94.
[3] Flanagan, *Hist.*, vol. i. p. 417.
[4] *Vide* Circular Letter of May 18, 1833.
[5] *Colonial Law Tracts*, B. M. Cat. 6605. b. 17 (1) p. 13.
[6] Flanagan, *Hist.* vol. i. p. 417.
[7] *Report Committee of* 1837, Appendix, p. 87.
[8] *Ibid.* p. 87.
[9] *Report of* 1837, p. 88.
[10] *Ibid.* p. 90.
[11] *Ibid.* pp. 92, 93.

154   A HISTORY OF PENAL METHODS

sickness : [1] many of those were from Carter's Barracks, which was one of Mudie's places.[2] So much for the effects of the fifty lashes, which the magistrates had thought quite inadequate ![3] It may be interesting to learn that a quick flogging to give this number took up four minutes,[4] but if it was administered— as it frequently was—in half-minute strokes,[5] it would occupy twenty-five, and one hundred lashes would prolong the torture into nearly an hour. And what did it all feel like to the victims who were tied up ? Most probably, as with all punishments, the effects were unequal.[6] I would much rather be flogged than imprisoned, but in the old days the flagellated must have endured most terrible sufferings.

Private Somerville, from whom we have quoted, has conveyed his experience. " At the first blow," he writes, " I felt an astonishing sensation between the shoulders under my neck, which went to my toenails in one direction, my finger-nails in another, and stung me to the heart as if a knife had gone through my body. The Serjeant-Major called in a loud voice, ' One ' . . . The voice called ' Four,' I felt my flesh quiver in every nerve from the scalp of my head to my toenails. The time between each stroke seemed so long as to be agonizing, and yet the next came too soon." [7]

General Sir Charles Napier says with reference to the most severe forms of this punishment : " I have seen hundreds of men flogged, and have always observed that when the skin is thoroughly cut up or flayed off the great pain subsides. Men are frequently convulsed and screaming during the time they receive from one lash to three hundred lashes, and then they bear the remainder, even to eight hundred or a thousand lashes, without a groan ;

---

[1] C. White, p. 502.
[2] See also Flanagan, *Hist.* p. 479.
[3] The English Committee of 1837–8, however, considered that Sir Richard Bourke had " acted with wisdom, justice and humanity." *Report*, p. 39.
[4] *Report of* 1837, p. 96.
[5] C. White, p. 502.
[6] See Sir Charles Napier's remarks in his *Military Law*, p. 151.
[7] *Autobiography*, pp. 288, 289.
See also Joseph Collinson, *Facts about Flogging*, ch. iii. Lond., 1905.

they will often lie as if without life, and the drummers appear to be flogging a lump of dead raw flesh."[1] It is probably the surface nerves which convey the pain, and after a time these may be numbed or partly destroyed; also, it would appear that there is only a certain amount of pain that nerves can convey, and that nature thus circumscribes and limits the devilish deeds of men. But when we think on such scenes as those just described, we can only endorse the words of the stern old warrior, when he wrote that in the course of these floggings it seemed as though " the culprit had disappeared and the martyr had taken his place."[2] In these days, when certain ignorant or forgetful people are seeking to reapply the lash for this act or that, I would remind them that such " remedies " have been tried of old.[3] Giving evidence before the Committee of 1838, Dr. Barnes observed, " I never knew a convict benefited by flagellation. I have always found him afterwards to be a more desperate character than before, and after the lash had been once inflicted he was generally among those who had it repeated."[4]

These rough and very sanguinary punishments with the cat were not, unhappily, the worst blots upon the British transportation system. Flogging was then so common and universal that, in the lesser doses,[5] it was regarded as a short and summary punishment for misdemeanours and breaches of discipline. Magistrates, as we have seen, could order terrific floggings to be inflicted, and, in the case of convicts, over whom they possessed powers almost unlimited,[6] could also impose other and more enduring punishments,[7] such as consignment to the ironed gangs

[1] *Military Law*, p. 163.

[2] *Ibid.* p. 164.

[3] *Vide* H. S. Salt, *The Case against Corporal Punishment*, p. 15, etc. London, 1912.

[4] *Report*, p. 38 (*Brit. Museum Rpts. of Committees*, vol. xxii.).

[5] " The fact is, flogging in this country is such a common thing that nobody takes any notice of it. I have seen young children practising on a tree as children in England play at horses." *Vide* Mary Carpenter, *Our Convicts*, vol. i. p. 234. London, 1864.

[6] An idea as to the extent and potency of the summary jurisdiction may be gathered from G. B. Barton's *History*, vol. i. p. 393.

[7] *Vide* 3 W. IV. No. 3.
Committee of 1837, App. p. 54.
Donnelly, p. 75, etc.

or the penal settlements, about which we shall come to speak presently.

For the graver offences men were tried and judged by a kind of court-martial, which was composed of the judge-advocate [1] and (generally) six naval or military commissioned officers.[2]

The establishment of civil juries of twelve men was prepared [3] for by the Constitution Act of 1828,[4] and by the year 1833 [5] we find them in action with the Emancipists [6] permitted to serve on them but not colonially-convicted citizens.[7] The Courts of course possessed the power of capital punishment ; [8] ropes and whips being the readiest, were therefore the commonest implements of repression in a nascent community.

But the Courts had two other penalties at command, which were mainly reserved for those previously convicted,[9] and these were the Ironed Gangs and the Penal Settlements.[10]

In a country where, for a long time, there were no regular prisons, fetters would be the obvious method of restraining the prisoners.   As we have seen, they were

[1] See 27 Geo. III. c. 2, 1787.
Barton, *Hist.* i. p. 213.
Phillips, *Colonial Autocracy*, p. 58.
[2] Sometimes there were only four officers (34 Geo. III. c. 45 and 35 Geo. III. c. 18), or five officers (4 and 5 W. IV. c. 65).
The Act 9 Geo. IV. c. 83 of 1828 provided that " until further provision be made as hereinafter directed for proceeding by juries, all offences should be tried before a judge and seven naval or military officers." J. Quick and R. Garran, *Australian Commonwealth*, p. 808, Sydney, 1901.
[3] 9 Geo. IV. c. 83.
[4] *Official History of N.S.W.*, p. 54.
[5] Accused persons could still claim to be tried before the military tribunal up to 1839.   Finney, *Hist.*, p. 96.
[6] Barton cites the act 4 W. IV. No. 12, in his *History*, vol. i. p. 390.
[7] Flanagan, i. p. 342.
[8] Braim, i. p. 279.
[9] Persons born, or coming free into the Colony, were not, for their first offences, sent to the Penal Settlements, but went to Tasmania. *Vide Committee of* 1837, App., p. 306.
R. Donnelly, *Acts of Council of New South Wales*, p. 70.   Sydney, 1841.
[10] Prisoners from England might be, and sometimes were, sentenced to commence their period of transportation in those terrible places, even to Norfolk Island.   *Vide Com. of* 1837, pp. 203, 282.
Griffiths, *Millbank*, p. 299.
James Backhouse, *Visit to the Australian Colonies*, Appendix J, No. 2.   London, 1843.

employed on board ship early in the voyage, and on land they served as a punishment for misconduct. Even Governor Macquarie, who always held out a friendly hand to well-behaved convicts, was sometimes severe with troublesome prisoners ; he had gaol-gangs formed in 1814 at Sydney,[1] Parramatta, Windsor and Liverpool (N.S.W.), to which a few convicts were sent for short periods ; they were to be clothed in parti-coloured garments of black and white. In the course of years the number of convicts sentenced to the chained gangs greatly augmented ;[2] they were scattered about chiefly up country in parties of eighty.[3]

The black and white attire, already referred to,[4] was altered to a dress of yellow and brown in the later times.[5] The prisoners had their hair closely cropped and were shaved twice weekly.[6] They were to work for at least ten hours a day,[7] and generally toiled on the road and quarries from six to six.[8] At night, when the sweat of the day was over, they were shut up in parties of twenty in four strong boxes or shanties built of thick timber ; at first these used to be within a stockade, but later on they relied on the sentries with their loaded guns.

So small was the cubic area of these places, that the inmates could not all stand or sit together at the same time, unless with their legs at right angles to their bodies ; often the width of floor on which each could lie was only 18 inches per prisoner.[9] But the most grievous part of

[1] Macquarie to Sidmouth, p. 90.
[2] The system was largely extended by Governor Bourke (Griffiths, *Millbank*, p. 300). In 1834 there were about 1,000 thus placed in N.S.W. (C. White, p. 265), and there were some 700 in Tasmania. (*Com. of* 1838, p. xiv.)
[3] *Committee of* 1838, p. 251.
[4] Griffiths, *Millbank*, p. 289.
  Committee of 1837, p. 29.
[5] In Tasmania the chain-gang men appear to have worn a yellow dress with the word Felon stamped over it in several places.
  Com. 1837, App. p. 54. Chained convicts in Sydney are said to have worn a costume of grey and yellow. *Vide* C. White, p. 245, and Therry, p. 41.
[6] *Com. of* 1837, App., p. 81.
  C. White, p. 259.
  Com. of 1837–8, p. 252.
[7] Griffiths, *Millbank*, p. 300.
[8] C. White, p. 137.
[9] *Committee of* 1837–8 (British Museum, *Reports of Committees*, vol. xxii. p. 14).

158 A HISTORY OF PENAL METHODS

the chain-gang punishment consisted of the fetters which the men wore.[1] The chains weighed from 6 to 7 and sometimes 9 lb.[2] They were riveted on by blacksmiths, and were examined every morning and evening lest they should be tampered with.[3]

In these they lived throughout the length of their sentences,[4] which might be six months, twelve months, two years, in the ironed gangs. In chains they laboured like beasts of burden through the Australian heat, sometimes with legs chafed and galled by the iron clasp;[5] and fastened they lay at night, though it might be with torn backs and much-smarting tendons after having had fifty lashes at the hands of the scourger,[6] or twice that number if returned after flight. Even upon removal to hospital, although the parti-coloured clothing was given up[7] the chains were kept on, by official orders ; and convicts were often interred in them.

Well might Sir George Arthur declare in his evidence, " This description of punishment is a very severe one, as severe a one as could be inflicted on man."[8] The English Committee said it belonged to a barbarous age.

But there was a lower depth still—does not the abyss of misery always seem bottomless ?—and that we find in the prisons of the transported, the dreaded Penal Settlements. All prisons are mournful places, but these were among the worst that have ever been.

There were quite a number of these places of torment

[1] Griffiths, *Millbank*, p. 300.
[2] C. White, p. 83.
Additional fetters might be imposed as a punishment, or upon men who seemed likely to attempt to escape. *Report*, 1837, App., p. 81, and *Com.* 1838, p. 276 ; also, Griffiths, p. 398. Sometimes men wore a chain fastened to only one leg
[3] Griffiths, *Millbank*, p. 300.
C. White, p. 258.
Com. of 1837, App., p. 81.
[4] Donnelly, p. 75.
Com. of 1837–8, p. 239 ; Bourke to Glenelg, December 4, 1837.
[5] C. Whe, p. 373.
[6] A prisoner out of irons was attached to each camp to flog, for which service he received 1s. 9d. a day in addition to rations. *Com. of* 1838, App., p. 252.
Donnelly, p. 77.
[7] *Com. of* 1837–8 : Bourke to Glenelg, App., p. 252.
C. White, p. 260.
[8] *Com. of* 1837–8, p. 14.

scattered about, including Macquarie Harbour and the larger settlement of Port Arthur in Van Diemen's Land, and Norfolk Island in the Pacific Ocean, which was perhaps the deepest hell of all. There was a certain similarity in the prison settlements ; in all of them we read of brutes ill-treating the brutalised. Desperate ruffians as many of the prisoners had become, they certainly could not have surpassed some of their overseers in cruelty, and we can say nothing worse of the most dangerous convicts, than that, had they been in command themselves, they might have been as barbarous as their governors.

PORT MACQUARIE—a penal settlement from 1821 to 1833—was a deep inlet along the western coast of Van Diemen's Land,[1] about two hundred miles from Hobart Town. Access from the sea was extremely difficult : two small rivers empty into the bay, and across the narrow mouth of the entrance a bar had been formed, and the ocean rollers swept over it with resistless violence when the winds blew, or when a far-distant storm sent in a long ground swell.

Approach over land appears to have been impossible in those days ; the place was so shut in by marshes and mountains, that even of the goaded and desperate prisoners, only some eight or nine ever escaped except to perish of hardships, from what has been described by Marcus Clarke as a life of one continual agony.[2] The men worked at felling timber and dragging logs, they laboured in irons and were often chained together in gangs as well ; but it was not the work or even the place, so much as the brutal discipline that made life unbearable. " One man," says the Rev. John West,[3] " a convict overseer, delighted in human suffering—this was his qualification for office." The convicts were flogged again and again with the heaviest sort of whips,[4] and were also punished [5] by being compelled to sleep on wet rocks in

[1] West, *History of Tasmania*, ii. p. 182.
[2] *Stories of Australia in the Early Days*, p. 112. London, 1897.
[3] *History of Tasmania*, ii. p. 183.
[4] *Report of* 1838, p. 38.
[5] West, *Hist.*, vol. ii. p. 183.
Committee of 1838, p. 37.

damp clothes and fetters;[1] occasionally some of them drowned themselves. There were gloomy yards and thick-walled prison buildings on Sarah Island where the main body slept on return from toil, and there were not lacking solitary cells, to which a certain number were sentenced; for the authorities had learned the art of breaking the prisoners' minds as well as their bodies,[2] and the more refined nineteenth-century tortures of cells and tread-wheels[3] were added to the whips and fetters of the earlier periods.

Those who have passed in a ship, as I did, from Sydney along the eastern coast of Tasmania, making for Hobart, will, as they enter Storm Bay, wherein is the harbour, have rounded Tasman's Peninsula. Thereon, from 1830 to 1877, stood the Penal Settlement of PORT ARTHUR. Next to Norfolk Island it was the largest of the colonial prisons, having an average population of over a thousand prisoners.[4]

The settlement was cut off from the mainland, or rather from Forestier's Peninsula, by a sandy isthmus four or five hundred yards broad called Eagle Hawk's Neck. This pass was always guarded by sentries who were further assisted by savage dogs which were established in stages across the passage, and even into the shallows on either side,[5] while farther out, in the deep water, the sharks patrolled, ready to snap up an escaping convict, or, if a chance occurred, his pursuers, impartially. Yet men did attempt to get through occasionally, preferring to take their chance of being eaten by sharks, or even, under the stress of famine, by one another, when in the bush, to the slow, studied cruelty which prevailed at the settlement.

[1] Marcus Clarke, *Stories of Australia*, p. 113.
An offender at Sydney was sentenced to be fastened to a rock on Goat Island by a chain 26 feet long, his legs being also in trumpet-irons (*i.e.* those with very long links not unlike a trombone); he was sent away later on to Macquarie Harbour. See *Meliora*, vol. iv. p. 12. London, 1862.
[2] Backhouse, *Australian Colonies*, p. 49.
[3] They had treadmills at Hobart—*vide* Backhouse, p. 33, and *Committee of* 1837, p. 304; at Port Arthur—see Griffiths, *Millbank*, p. 323; at Norfolk Island—see *Com. of* 1837, p. 69; in Australia—see *Com. of* 1837, App., p. 309, and 3 W. IV. No. 3.
[4] In the year 1835 there were 1,172.—*Report of* 1838, p. xiv.
[5] Marcus Clarke, *Stories of Australia*, p. 197.

It is worth observing that there appears to be no doubt that many if not most of the dreaded bandits and highwaymen were driven into desperate courses by the cruelties to which they were subjected. Bushranging, we may read, was not common in Van Diemen's Land until the arrival of the " disciplinarian " Governor Arthur.[1] Speaking of New South Wales, Sir Roger Therry remarks about bushrangers,[2] " Of some hundreds of them who passed through our criminal courts I do not remember to have met with one who had not been over and over again flogged before he took to the bush." " Many," says the Rev. John West, " fled to the bush to avoid flagellation." [3] " Bad masters," says a Tasmanian writer, " and severe dishonest magistrates,[4] have devoted more men to live as bushrangers and die on the scaffold than any inherent depravity of their victims."

The deeds and exploits of these wandering bandits have occupied many volumes, in which will be found the romantic and often almost incredible accounts of their depredations. I am glad, for the credit of human nature (always making for good in the individual and always at its very worst when acting in corporate bodies of any sort), that it would appear that few of these desperate quick-shooting banditti were unredeemed by acts of generosity and even humanity ; whilst nearly all displayed a valour worthy of better usage and happier circumstances. In fact, from the evidence it would really seem that, once again, the communities obtained the criminals they deserved. Port Arthur, as the name of the place implies, was generally approached from the ocean, and at its harbour large and extensive quays and solid stone structures had been built by the convicts. It was a massive prison,[5] with walls and buildings containing all the nineteenth-century accessories for degrading the inmates and crushing life out of them.

---

[1] *Report of* 1838, p. 41.
Gibb, p. 90.
[2] *Thirty Years' Residence*, p. 43.
[3] *History of Tasmania*, ii. p. 130.
[4] W. B. Dean (Cabby), *Notorious Bushrangers of Tasmania*, p. 8.
[5] " The walls are like those of a Bastille, the air is damp and heavy . . . a sort of yellow darkness."—Clarke, *Stories of Australia*, p. 194.

The prisoners wore a dress of yellow (sometimes yellow and black), with strong leather caps on which were marked the word "Felon" at back and front.[1] Most of them were in irons, which were usually of about 7 lb. weight,[2] and they were occasionally made fast to a log of wood [3] by a chain about 3 feet long attached to their leg-irons, and consequently they were obliged to drag it about with them wherever they went. Some of them were even chained to the wall.

There was a chapel built at Port Arthur, but it has been described as having been little better than an additional place of punishment.[4] The convicts had to half stand or crouch in separate boxes, and at one period their heads were muffled up in helmets of cloth which were pierced with eye-holes.[5] Perhaps the best idea we can get of the penal settlement is to be found in Marcus Clarke's account of a visit made to it in the year 1870. It had faded then, but enough remained for a lasting picture when portrayed by a master hand.

"I know," he wrote, "that the prisoners seemed all alike in feature, and that I could no more distinguish the one from the other than I could swear to a Chinaman or a two-toothed wether. I know that a general scowl of depression seemed to be in the fellows' faces, and that the noise of the irons made my unaccustomed ears tingle. I know that I thought to myself that I should go mad were I condemned to such a life . . . I know that there seemed to me to hang over the whole place a sort of horrible gloom, as though the sunlight had been withdrawn from it. . . . How many sighs had gone up to heaven from among those trim trees, how many tears had moistened those neatly chiselled flag-stones! The scene upon which we gazed had been the loathed lifelong prospect of many a poor scoundrel who perhaps was not so much worse than I."[6]

[1] Gibb, p. 103.
  Martin Cash, *Adventures*, ed. by J. L. Burke, p. 57. Hobart Town, 1870.
  Clarke, *Stories of Australia*, p. 191.
[2] Cash, p. 64.
[3] *Ibid.* p. 61.
[4] Gibb, p. 107.
[5] Clarke, *Stories of Australia*, p. 194.
[6] *Ibid.* p. 193.

And then he speaks of those who were, or had been, made mad. " The criminal lunatics were of but two descriptions ; [1] they cowered and crawled like whipped foxhounds to the feet of their keepers, or they raged howling blasphemies and hideous imprecations upon their gaolers." The worst man whom the authorities claimed to have on their books was a certain Mooney— he had been transported about the age of thirteen for stealing a hare.[2] He had become, in time, a raging, desperate convict ; he had been flogged, he had been in a mutiny, he had been a bushranger, and a whole list of things. " And where is he now ? " the visitor asked. "Oh," said the genial official, with a calm self-satisfaction (so it seemed to the questioner) at the excellence of the system which he administered, " he's all right now ; we've got him all right now. He's a lunatic in Port Arthur *now*." [3]

" I was eager," continues the writer, " to see my poacher of thirteen years. The warder drew aside a peep-hole in the barred door, and I saw a grizzled, gaunt, and half-naked old man coiled up in a corner. The peculiar wild-beast smell which belongs to some forms of furious madness exhaled from the cell. The gibbering animal within turned, and his malignant eyes met mine. ' Take care,' said the gaoler ; ' he has a habit of sticking his finger through the peep-hole to try and poke someone's eyes out.' I drew back, and a nail-bitten hairy finger like the toe of an ape was thrust with rapid and simian neatness through the aperture. ' This is how he amuses himself,' said the good warder, forcing-to the iron slot ; ' he had best be dead, I'm thinking.' " [4] This was the last stage of a prison product seen in the recent and Christian year marked 1870. Less than a decade after Marcus Clarke's visit Port Arthur had happily ceased to be a penitentiary.

NORFOLK ISLAND, 1788–1856

Far away, about a thousand miles in the Pacific Ocean, stood Norfolk Island, E.N.E. of Sydney. It was first

[1] *Stories of Australia*, p. 195. [2] *Ibid.* p. 194.
[3] *Ibid.*   [4] *Ibid.* p. 195.

colonised as long ago as 1788,[1] when nine male and half a dozen female convicts were sent from the parent party newly come to Port Jackson. But those were the early days, when transportation meant mainly deportation and colonisation ;[2] about 1806 it ceased, for a time, to be a penal settlement. In 1826 the place was reoccupied with fifty convicts and a guard of as many soldiers,[3] and it was during the second quarter of that wicked nineteenth century [4] that it became the largest and the vilest of the ghastly penal settlements.

Most of the convicts there were kept in fetters, of course, but these were often of the heaviest kind : irons are mentioned as weighing 14, 36, even 47 lb. [5]—those on the mainland being usually from about 6 to 9. Martin Cash describes having been placed in chains the basils of which were as thick as a man's arm,[6] and the links of which appear to have been thicker [7] than the safety chains of a railway train. A spirit of wrath and insupportable oppression appeared to animate and possess the officials upon the island,[8] and several times the goaded and maddened convicts rose in short and sanguinary rebellion, only to be beaten back by bullets and bayonets and have their leaders ruthlessly hanged for them—which was perhaps the happiest termination that the malcontents could expect. In 1834, after one of these outbreaks, the condemned cells were visited by Dr. (afterwards Archbishop) Ullathorne. "And now," he writes,[9] " I have to record the most heart-breaking scene that I ever witnessed. The prison was in the form of a square, on one side of which stood a row of low cells covered with a roof

---

[1] *Dict. Nat. Biography*, art. " P. G. King."
[2] J. J. Spruson, *Norfolk Island*, p. 13. Sydney, 1885.
[3] *Ibid.* p. 13.
[4] C. White, p. 276.
[5] W. B. Ullathorne, *Memoir of Bishop Willson*, p. 55. London, 1887. West, *Hist. Tas.*, p. 301.
[6] *Adventures*, p. 134.
[7] Captain Maconochie found 1,400 doubly ironed convicts when he arrived at the island, March 6, 1840.—Mary Carpenter, p. 97.
[8] The convicts were dressed in brown and yellow clothing of frieze. Ullathorne, *Autobiography*, p. 92. They were required to cap each private soldier whom they met, and even each empty sentry-box that they passed. They tore their food with their fingers and teeth, and drank for the most part out of water buckets.—Mary Carpenter, p. 97, and see also *Meliora*, vol. iv. p. 10.
[9] *Autobiography*, p. 100. London, 1891.

of shingles. The turnkey unlocked the first door and said, ' Stand aside, sir.' Then came forth a yellow exhalation, the product of the bodies of the men confined therein. The exhalation cleared off, and I entered and found five men chained to a traversing bar. I spoke to them from my heart, and after preparing them and obtaining their names, I announced to them who were reprieved from death, and which of them were to die after five days had passed. I thus went from cell to cell until I had seen them all. It is a literal fact that each man who learned his reprieve wept bitterly, and that each man who heard of his condemnation to death went down on his knees with dry eyes and thanked God. Night had now fallen, and I proceeded to Government House, where I found a brilliant assembly, in strange contrast with the human miseries in which my soul had just been steeped."

There certainly *were* brutal people upon the island, and some of the worst of them were not prisoners ! Now and then a voice of protest was raised, as in later times by the Rev. T. Rogers, and a coxswain, James Weir.[1] But the clergy were generally much more shocked at the sensuality of the convicts than by the hideous cruelties which were inflicted upon them,[2] and their urgent protests on the former account [3] really intensified the degree of their sufferings,[4] by causing solitary cells and separation to be yet added to the sum of misery.[5]

[1] Cash, *Adventures*, pp. 141, 142. West, *Hist. Tas.*, p. 300.

[2] For some amazing details as to the prevalence of innate and substitutional sexual inversion, disease, etc., etc., the reader can make reference to *Com. of 1837*, p. 67. The ordinary punishment was 50 or 100 lashes (p. 68).
Select Com. on Trans. 1837-8, British Museum : Reports from Committees, xxii. (16) p. 42.
Sir E. Eardley Wilmot to Lord Stanley, March 17, 1846. *Accounts and Papers*, vol. xlviii. p. 33, etc.

[3] Rev. T. B. Naylor to Lord Stanley, *Accounts and Papers*, vol. xlviii. (15) p. 67, 1847.

[4] " I scarcely ever went into the Comptroller's room but the first thing he said to me before I came to the table was : 'Bishop, there are fifty cells for you, or twenty cells for you ; knowing that that would be the first thing I should mention and which would please me most to hear."—Bishop Willson. *Vide* W. B. Ullathorne's *Memoir*, p. 49.

[5] At one period there was severe separate imprisonment at Norfolk Island as a preliminary punishment. See *Meliora*, vol. iv. p. 7.
There were thirty-three cells for solitary confinement at Norfolk.—Stewart's *Report*, p. 83.

We have seen what the island was under that barbarous martinet Major Anderson. In 1840 the reins were in the hands of an altogether different person, Alexander Maconochie, who was a Captain in the Royal Navy.[1] He was a man with many reasonable and enlightened views, but somewhat of a crank,[2] and a merciless moralist. However, in spite of his puritanism, his methods were considered by the authorities to be quite out of keeping with their views on punishment, and he was succeeded in 1844 by Major Joseph Childs.

To this officer was assigned the task—apparently an uncongenial and unwelcome one to him—of revoking all Maconochie's concessions to prisoners, and making the prison to be a prison, in all the bad old nineteenth-century sense, again. A sad and difficult task it was sure to be, certain to arouse ill-feeling in all concerned, and bitter resentment on the side of the prisoners, who especially felt the loss of tobacco [3]—in such a place no small item of consolation to them. The convicts became sulky and angry, and Major Childs, though a man who had led a forlorn hope in earlier life,[4] appears to have been somewhat tactless and vacillating in managing men, although the mere task of rebarbarising the settlement would almost certainly have led to catastrophe.

Now the turbulent and threatening condition of the convicts at Norfolk Island had come to the ears of the authorities in Tasmania, and Mr. R. P. Stewart, a magistrate, was sent out to investigate.[5] Amongst other things, he impressed upon Major Childs the need for greater severity on his part,[6] and a short time afterwards these orders bore fruit, and gaolers seized upon the prisoners' pots and pans, in which they were wont to do their own private cooking, thereby making many much-prized

[1] Spruson, p. 14.
[2] Gibb, p. 74.
Capt. Maconochie to Mr. Hawes, M.P.—British Museum, *Accounts and Papers*, vol. xlviii. (15) pp. 104, 105. London, 1847.
[3] Stewart's *Report*, p. 84. *Accounts and Papers*, vol. xlviii. Ullathorne, *Memoir of Bishop Willson*, p. 60.
[4] Cash, *Adventures*, p. 124.
[5] Eardley Wilmot to W. E. Gladstone, September 3, 1846.
[6] Yet he found twenty-one prisoners there awaiting trial who had been eleven months shut up in seven small cells wearing heavy irons. —Stewart's *Report*, p. 83.

additions to the hard, stinted and unhealthy fare officially
given (out of scraps, fruits, vegetables, and in fact any
odds and ends that came ready to hand upon the semi-
tropical island), and doing small kindnesses to messmates
and favourites.[1]
They were taken away at night and put under lock
and key, and when the convicts missed the things in the
morning they broke out in another mutiny, in which
some warders were killed and a number of mutineers were
shot down by the military ; the leaders of the revolt
being afterwards tried and executed. Major Childs was
removed from his governorship by the Hobart authorities.
They wanted a man who would stamp out rebelliousness,
and they selected a well-known disciplinarian, Mr. John
Price, who had been police magistrate.[2]   In some respects
he was a man of good parts : he had a light, easy way with
him, and an eyeglass ; he was a man of courage and quick
resolve ; but he was also one of those human tigers who,
if they cannot obtain some uniform to cover their crimes,
are apt to get hanged for them, or at any rate to come
to a violent end—and Mr. Price was ultimately assassi-
nated by some of his prisoners.   But not on the island :
he arrived there in 1846 armed with authority to execute
vengeance ; he was to put the prisoners back into convict
dress,[3] which, it would appear, they had laid aside ; he
was to rule the place with a rod of iron, and quench the
sparks of mutiny in blood.

It would be hard to conceive a worse place than Port
Macquarie, or a more dismal convict settlement than
Port Arthur ; men dragged out their days in chains
and gloom, and often died and were put away underground
in fetters unfreed ; things can't be much worse than that.
But Norfolk Island was the worst place of all in several
ways.   The sentences were generally longest ; a number
were there for life[4] (especially in the latter days), and
the Colonially-convicted were frequently sent out to
the settlements " for the remainder of their sentence " of

[1] C. White, p. 342.
[2] Wilmot to Gladstone, *Accounts and Papers*, xlviii. p. 77.
[3] *Accounts and Papers*, xlviii. p. 74.
[4] *Ibid.* pp. 118, 119.
C. White, p. 319.
West, *Hist.* ii. p. 294.

transportation,[1] which might easily involve them in a life doom (or sometimes for a comparatively short term, for much the same sort of crime).[2] The sentences, too, were often increased in the penal settlements at Norfolk Island; many of the prisoners never returned till the place broke up[3] (most of them were taken away in the year 1855), and one writer states that two-thirds of them perished there.[4]

Moreover, at Norfolk Island especially, but not exclusively under Price,[5] they employed gags, bridles or head-stalls,[6] and a veritable engine of torture known as the Stretcher, which has been described as an iron frame some six feet by three, not unlike a bedstead, the sides being kept in position by round iron bars twelve inches apart.[7] Upon this frame the victim was fastened, the head extending over the edge and without support. One man is said to have been placed upon the instrument in a dark cell and left in this fashion for the space of twelve hours; he was found to be dead when ultimately they came to him.[8]

Another mediæval method was to suspend chained prisoners by one hand;[9] and one of the most dreaded penalties sometimes resorted to, was to sentence a man to work—often with unhealed wounds from quite recent flogging—in the Cayenne pepper mill, the fine stinging dust from which was especially maddening.[10]

But the hellish conditions prevailing in all those inhuman prisons for colonial penal servitude can best be conceived from side-lights thrown upon them by the behaviour of the wretched prisoners.

[1] West, *Hist.*, ii. 181.
[2] Cash, *Adventures*, p. 138.
[3] T. B. Murray, *Pitcairn*, p. 277. London, 1885.
[4] C. White, p. 328.
[5] Stewart's *Report*, p. 83. Ullathorne, *Memoir*, p. 57. Gibb, pp. 31, 139.
[6] Cash, p. 135. West, *Hist.* p. 301.
[7] Cash, p. 141. Gibb, p. 69.
[8] Cash, p. 141.
[9] Gibb, pp. 65, 66.
Hanging by the thumbs was a military punishment, and has been awarded on the other side of the Atlantic within the last twenty years or so (1912).
[10] Gibb, pp. 71, 77.
Cash, p. 137.
Compare also Falconbridge, *Account of the Slave Trade*, p. 41.

As we shall find them doing at English convict prisons many years afterwards, the prisoners would injure and mutilate themselves [1]—as for instance by putting lime in their eyes—to get in the hospital. I will reproduce an official description of all they had upon Norfolk Island for the care of two thousand men. "The hospital," [2] observes Mr. Stewart, " is a low building containing three wards, two of them accommodating five beds each, the other ten. The mode of ventilation is objectionable, as a thorough draught cannot be avoided ; the wards are exceedingly hot in summer and cold and damp in winter. They open upon a narrow verandah into an enclosed yard about 80 feet by 20 ; this is the only place in which the patients can take exercise. . . . The smell is always offensive in consequence of the want of a proper sewer, but during the hot season the stench is excessive.[3] Twenty beds, and a detached cold convalescent ward are the extent of hospital accommodation."

Likewise, at each and all of the penal settlements, the prisoners committed desperate assaults, often upon each other by pre-arrangement,[4] " from absolute weariness of their lives," in order to get away from those dreadful places, if only as witnesses, or even as persons accused of murder.[5] At Macquarie Harbour, on one occasion, three prisoners tossed : one was to be slain, another was to strike the fatal blow, the third was to be the witness [6] of the planned deed ; so they would get a respite—a grim " holiday." At Port Arthur one man murdered his own particular friend and companion, that both might get free from it.[7]

The same hideous tragedies took place also at Norfolk Island ;[8] crimes were committed to obtain the journey to Sydney, even if it were to be upon a capital charge.

---

[1] C. White, p. 335.
[2] *Accounts and Papers*, xlviii. p. 83 (of vol. 179).
[3] Martin Cash, who had been a convict there, also alludes to the odour from the festering wounds of those who had been flogged at Norfolk Island.—*Adventures*, p. 141.
[4] Sir George Arthur, *Com. of* 1837, p. 310.
[5] *Report of* 1838, p. xv.
    Braim, *Hist.* p. 286.
[6] Marcus Clarke, *Stories of Australia*, p. 113.
    Vide also Charles White, pp. 353, 357, 363.
[7] *Com. of* 1837, p. 310.
[8] *Report of* 1837, p. 17.

There too the " parts " to be taken were often decided by lot,[1] and they always tried to furnish the greatest possible number of witnesses. The appearance of these has been described by Sir Roger Therry, who at that time was Attorney-General. They had been two or three years upon Norfolk Island, and "Their sunken, glazed eyes, deadly pale faces, hollow fleshless cheeks, and once manly limbs shrivelled and withered up as if by premature old age, created a thrill of horror amongst the bystanders.[2] They were all under thirty-five years of age." The authorities met this terrible state of things in a manner typical of nineteenth-century Prison Boards. In 1834[3] the New South Wales Governor was empowered to convene a Criminal Court upon Norfolk Island, to be composed of a barrister and five officers. Henceforth these desired journeys to the trials at Sydney would be denied ; the abuses they let alone, and the outrages might continue, but all was to be settled out at the prison ; and the gallows would swing men there.

It is however necessary to bear in mind that all the horrors we have been reading of, the cruelties which can be better felt than adequately denounced in language, belong more to penal servitude than to transportation. These colonial prisons began thirty and forty years after the original convict settlers founded Sydney, and after the enlightened rule of Colonel Macquarie. They flourished in times when transportation had lost its first character, and had become more of a punishment ; when freemen, rather than convicts, were looked for as settlers, and when the Home Government wanted prisons rather than lands and colonies for its criminals.

Thus we need not altogether blame transportation for the fell deeds which prison officials did far away from freedom. There was much that was good and healthy in transportation, but the guilt and stain round the rocks of those dreadful prisons will hang and linger in the memory of mankind till the ocean of time, which is vaster than the Pacific, engulfs them, and sweeps them, and us, away.

[1] Therry, p. 19.
[2] *Thirty Years' Residence*, p 21.
[3] 4 and 5 W. IV. c. 65.

CHAPTER V

THE ORIGIN OF THE CELL PRISONS

For it drives back my thoughts
Upon their spring
By a strange introversion, and perforce
I now begin to feed upon myself
Because I have nought else to feed upon.
Dream of Gerontius.

THE end of the eighteenth century opened up an eventful period in the theory and practice of all prison management. John Howard (1726–90) had been exploring the gaols and lazarettos of England and Europe; Elizabeth Fry (1780–1845) was visiting the women in Newgate; and Romilly (1757–1818) was striving to reduce the number of capital offences, of which, as we have seen, there were over two hundred. In fact, a little band of earnest men and women, zealous reformers, had at length compelled the ruling classes to look into the state of the prisons. What was revealed there, we already know. They found simply dustbins of demoralisation and pest-houses from which all kinds of evil sprang, and it was this well-intentioned, no doubt necessary, protest against the old order of things that set on foot a series of experiments on living animals—the prisoners—which, while they removed a good many of the then existing scandals and cruelties, yet inaugurated a machine for the infliction of suffering, compared with which the old barbarities were short and relatively merciful.

The old prisons were crowded, squalid, germ-laden, and filthy; the new were to be clean and sanitary. In the old buildings debauchery and open vice were coarse and rampant; amidst the damp and miasmatic darkness would be heard the oaths and obscenities of the most abandoned of both sexes, along with the jingle of their

171

heavy fetters, which sound might be checked from time to time by the sharp slashing of the gaoler's whip. The new prisons were collected cells ; they were huge tiers of tombs, in each of which a solitary inmate lingered and often died. Deep silence reigned, but sometimes ghostly figures, ever-guarded, and wearing masks,[1] lest they should possibly recognise one another, were hurried through the cellar-like passages, not daring to turn their heads to look around them, and scarcely to lift their eyes for a covert glance if another mask should shuffle swiftly by. As the more sanguinary and violent penalties began to shock the public conscience, imprisonment became the general punishment, and prisons passed from the detention-dens they had been into places actually for tormenting their inmates by a variety of ways and means concealed under the name of discipline. With primitive notions and little understanding of the real, various, and complex nature of all the many acts that are called criminal, the reformers classed all offences as being the outcome of mere " sinfulness," and, as a corollary to this view, they diagnosed the broad and simple remedy for crime to be " repentance " artificially produced.

Very much as the religious zealots of the dark ages strove to make heretics conform to their views by the infliction of torture, so these eighteenth- and nineteenth-century prison managers endeavoured to force the captives to reform by suffering. They attacked " Crime " as a concrete entity in the person of the offender, but left untouched those deeper and far-reaching causes from which it must inevitably have sprung.

The penitentiary system is said to have been begun in Rome. " It is the fashion,"[2] wrote Archbishop Ullathorne, " to ascribe the origin of the solitary and the silent system to the Americans, as having developed the experiment begun by Howard at Gloucester. But allow me to quote Monsignor Cerfbear, who was sent by the French Government to examine and report on the Italian

---

[1] For numerous illustrations of prisoners wearing these see Mayhew and Binny, *Criminal Prisons of London* ; also J. Field, *Prison Discipline*, ii. pp. 99, 215, 239 (London, 1848).

[2] M. F. Glancey, *Characteristics*. From the writings of Archbishop Ullathorne, p. 218. London, 1889.

prisons in 1839. ' I feel it to be a duty,' he says, ' to establish the truth. The correctional system is Christian, it is Catholic, it is no new system. It had its birth in the monasteries, and a Pope gave it its baptismal name when it came into the world.' " Pope Clement XI. (1700–1721) as early as 1703 erected the prison of San Michele on cellular principles, causing the following inscription to be placed over its door : " Parum est coercere improbos poena, nisi probos efficias disciplina." [1]

The idea was subsequently taken up in Milan, where a prison was built upon the San Michele model, and it has been claimed that the experiments which were tried in Belgium, at the Ghent Maison de Force, and spread thence over the United States, owed their initial inspiration to the prison begun at Rome. But in all probability the then untried solitary system—a phase in the prison management in many parts of the world through the last century—was the natural reaction against the indiscriminate herding together which had lately been exposed. In England, Howard had a good deal to do with its introduction ; and apart from other evidence, this point is borne out by the following inscription, which was cut deep on the foundation stone of the New Baily, Manchester, one of the many prisons which were the outcome of his revelations. " That there may remain to posterity," it ran, " a monument of the affection and gratitude of this country to that most excellent person, who hath so fully proved the wisdom and humanity of the separate and solitary confinement of offenders, this prison is inscribed with the name of ' John Howard.' " Under his advice and direction the Duke of Richmond built a "separate" gaol at Horsham, Sussex, in 1776. In 1778 an Act was passed (19 Geo. III. c. 74), for the erection of Penitentiary Houses ; and " solitary " prisons at Gloucester (1791), Glasgow, Southwell, and, in the course of time, at many other places, followed accordingly.

The isolation movement was also active in America. The Quakers of Pennsylvania succeeded in abolishing capital punishment in 1786.[2] At first they substituted

[1] W. Tallack, *Penological and Preventive Principles*, p. 157.
[2] Griffiths, *Millbank*, pp. 9 and 141.

gang labour along the public ways;[1] the convicts were chained by fetters and iron collars, they wore a distinctive dress and had their heads shaved—the latter being a common punishment in Siberia for attempted prison-breaking. Naturally this sort of public employment was soon strongly objected to, and was given up largely through the exertions of the Society for alleviating the miseries of Public Prisons. But its efforts, as we have often seen, only set up evils far worse than were remedied; about 1790 the famous Walnut Street Prison, which had been used for the captured British prisoners of war, was utilized for criminals. Here thirty solitary cells were added, with the idea which was expressed in the Act, "that the addition of unremitted solitude to laborious employment as far as it can be effected will contribute as much to reform as to deter." Thus the new torture was begun; but the "reformers" reached a deeper level of horror when in 1818 the legislature of Pennsylvania resolved to construct a penitentiary for enforcing solitary confinement without even work! At another prison a trial of solitary confinement was made upon eighty convicts. In 1822 they were shut up for ten months each in a little cell 7 feet long by 3½ feet broad,[2] and were not allowed to leave it at any time or for any purpose.

In various States these hideous experiments were carried out, with such variations as may from time to time have dawned upon the minds of the "philanthropists" in power. In Maine the prisoners were kept alone in underground cells,[3] which were veritable pits entered only by a ladder through a trap-door two feet square. These dungeons had a "Baronial castle" aspect, except that we read that besides the trap-door just alluded to "the only other orifice is one at the bottom, about an inch and a half in diameter, for the admission of warm air," which has a touch of dismal science and the nineteenth century. In Virginia the same sort of system had a trial,[4] and the cells were more

---

[1] W. Crawford, *Penitentiaries of the United States*, p. 8. London, 1834.
[2] *Ibid.* p. 15.
L. Gordon Rylands, *Crime*, Appendix 2. London, 1889.
W L. Clay, *The Prison Chaplain*, ch. v. Cambridge, 1861.
[3] W. Crawford, *Report*, p. 15.   [4] *Ibid.* p. 16.

"Baronial" still, for the walls would drip with water and they were quite unwarmed, so that one prisoner was found with his feet frozen. The cells were dark, and lamps had to be taken in when they were visited. But the new torture, solitary confinement, was never meant to be applied that way, and never was by the skilled tormentors. In the experiments just glanced at, the zeal of the too ardent disciples of "discipline" defeated their object. Death and insanity were so wholesale and universal that no amount of figures and "philanthropy" could explain staring facts out of the way. We shall see how the new school erected their masterpiece later on, but meanwhile we may consider what had been doing in the Old Country.

CHAPTER VI

"As he went through Cold Bath Fields he saw
A solitary cell,
And the devil was pleased, for it gave him a hint
For improving his prisons in hell."
The Devil's Walk.

As we have said, one of the consequences of Howard's revelations had been the erection of quite a number of gaols on the cellular system in different parts of England. The reformation-by-solitude theory was then hailed on all sides as the Magna Charta of prison management. Once make prisoners think, and they will forthwith see the error of their ways. The broken-down, the cretinous, the neurotic, the unbalanced, once made to think, were somehow to solve all the terrific problems of disease and environment ; repent, and so save themselves.

That the governing classes, the sound, the privileged and prosperous, should pause and reflect—that they should really consider the root-causes of crime, and seriously try and mean to make an end of them—was a remedy too revolutionary and uncomfortable to be even dreamed of throughout those selfish drunken decades of the nineteenth century ! To give effect to the new theories a vast and special Penitentiary was to be built, and Millbank was duly commenced about 1812. For ages there had lain a marshy flat along the river side, which had many a time been shot over for snipe, and may have been once a field for chase and falconry ; but upon which the toadstools of the great city had begun to extend, in the shape of a pest-house and a bridewell. About 1821 there stood upon this spot on the Mill Bank a huge and gloomy many-towered prison, large enough to be clearly seen upon the Metropolitan maps in the form of a thick-spoked wheel, which fancy might have rendered into a human spider's web to catch unwary flies, which in truth it was. This black, forbidding-looking "reformation engine" is reckoned to have possessed three miles of corridors.[1] "Hidden amongst its hundreds of cells,"[2] writes its learned historian, "its length of corridor and passage, beneath its acres of roof, are, without exaggeration, miles of lead piping . . . flagstones without end, shiploads of timber, millions of bricks." It had cost nearly half a million of money.

We can make but a very brief survey of that long record of dreary cruelties and bungling experiments which for a good many years were carried out at Millbank.

At first it was very much a plaything for Society, and often visited from the outside ; the prisoners were well treated, though from the beginning the construction of the buildings aimed at solitude and separation, the full effects of which were to come out by-and-by.

But the place lost its novelty, and soon lapsed into the hands of a regular committee and the salaried officials, and thenceforward the System began to be worked out with the thoroughness which is usually exhibited to the full when one class inflicts what another class alone must feel !

As we should now expect in a cell prison, we read of a great and increasing number of attempts at suicide. Again, as might be expected, these were nearly always classed by the official mind as being "feigned" when unsuccessful ; and generally as having been "accidental" whenever death ensued. At one period the dietary was suddenly lowered to some theoretical standard, no doubt fully approved of by the powers that were. But in this case it resulted in a serious epidemic (scurvy) of a somewhat peculiar character,[3] and which proved so obstinate and deadly that the entire building had to be abandoned for a while, and all the prisoners removed elsewhere.[4]

From the quality of the human material within the Penitentiary, and still more from the nature of the.ex-

---

[1] W. Hepworth Dixon, *The London Prisons*, p. 132. London, 1850.
[2] Griffiths, *Millbank*, p. 37.
[3] P. M. Latham, *An Account of the Disease*, London, 1825.
[4] Griffiths, *Millbank*, chaps. iv. and v.

periments constantly practised upon them, especially in the direction of dark cells and separate confinement, it was only to be looked for, that much friction should follow, and barbarous repression come in consequence.

The favourite mode of punishment was the dark cell, strangely enough, a terrible one for most natures. Of this we have the graphic account in Charles Reade's deathless tale,[1] which however relates to a period about a generation later on ; so tenaciously do prison horrors last, so hard are all secreted things to sweep away !

But the committee looked for further powers, and then obtained the right to inflict corporal punishment.[2]

About this time the Governor was a Captain Chapman, of whom the able author of the *Memorials of Millbank* tells us a good deal. He is described as having been a man of courage and action, as no doubt he was. But it is really curious to notice that we find, over and over again, that his " good nature " is insisted upon, and indeed almost alleged against him : he was, we read, "amiable to a fault, etc."

But it is often a little difficult to fathom the official view of things, and after reading the above, the lay mind may begin to wonder at the continued consignment of prisoners to the dark cells, and still more to find this too merciful man superintending the infliction of a hundred lashes from the " cat." But the historian just quoted calls this " a highly necessary chastisement," and appears astonished that some feeling was aroused about it in the unofficial mind outside, especially as about 1830 " soldiers, for purely military offences, were flogged within an inch of their lives."[3]

Some time later another prisoner was sentenced by a local magistrate to no less than three hundred lashes, of which one hundred were laid on in the presence of this soft-hearted governor and a crowd of the convicts. None of these spoke a word, though many were in tears.

What this ghastly exhibition meant will be best realised to-day when we remember that the greatest number of lashes it is now legal and possible to inflict upon a prisoner is thirty-six ![4]

---

[1] *It is Never too Late to Mend.* [2] 7 and 8 Geo. IV. [3] *Millbank*, p. 130.
[4] *Departmental Committee on Prisons*, 1895. Appendix VI., p. 573.

In 1837 the Rev. Daniel Nihil was given the office of governor in addition to that which he already held of chaplain. That he was hard-working is undoubted, and that in his narrow wooden way he was sincere, is very possible, but, like most prison officials, he had become well hardened to the sight of suffering. One lad of only eighteen he got sentenced to three hundred lashes with the cat, seventy-five of which were laid on, the boy expiring some years afterwards, whilst still immured in the Penitentiary.

The dreaded dark cells appear to have been in constant requisition, and it is sickening to trace the long-continued, cruel, useless struggle which was carried on with the tormented and the mad. In short, Mr. Nihil was what the great Charles Reade would have called commonplace ; he was a man with no depth of understanding as to human needs, and a token of his character may be clearly made out from the fact that he opposed with all his might the subsequent appointment of a Roman Catholic chaplain who was to minister to prisoners belonging to that faith.[1]

In 1838 the Penitentiary [2] was furiously attacked in the House of Lords on the ground that three little girls and two young men had been kept in cellular confinement for over a year and had completely broken down.

But this apparently noble onslaught is described by Major Griffiths as a party move,[3] since " The attack made upon the Penitentiary was really directed against the Government," for Millbank was controlled, or should have been, by the Home Office. And there is reason to fear that this view is largely correct, for though we may make a little allowance for the common instincts of humanity which are possessed even by legislators, yet it was a brutal and callous age, in which prisoners, old or young, were of absolutely no account, and all the weak were kept within the wall.

So that the statements on both sides must be looked upon with caution ; but the admitted facts are bad enough. After gaining information, Lord Melbourne (true to his creed of " Can't you let it alone ? " of course knowing

---

[1] *Millbank*, p. 172.
[3] *Ibid.* p. 224.
[2] *Ibid.* p. 225.

nothing of it personally), proceeded to defend the institution.

The little girls, he said, were all very profligate children, and their ages had been understated—they were each at least *ten* years old. These hardened sinners took exercise twice a day together, although in silence ; they went to school twice a week, to chapel on Sunday, and they were visited by Mrs. Fry and her associates.

Of the young men, both had been left for death at the Old Bailey, but their sentences had been commuted to one year at Millbank. They would appear to have spent most of their lives in Marylebone workhouse, to which they were ultimately sent back, none the worse, so the investigators said.

One was a lad of only seventeen, the other was of weak intellect ; but it was contended that he had always been so.

Such are the admitted facts, and the breeze passed over, as it would not do to-day. It is quite clear that those little children, who tried to crumple up their sheets into the semblance of dolls, to mitigate their heavy loneliness, and whose only consolations were the reproving lectures of official visitors, were subjected to a much longer spell of separate cell confinement than is to-day awarded to the adult convict as a prelude to penal servitude.

But the imprisonment of children has been by no means limited to Millbank, and it extended far beyond the " thirties." In his interesting work, published in 1850,[1] Mr. Hepworth Dixon cites some cases that had come under his personal notice, such as " a child of eleven then undergoing his second sentence of six months' imprisonment," fourth time in gaol ; a boy aged fifteen " under sentence of transportation for seven years, this being his tenth time of recommitment."

We shall have more than once to refer again to these sort of outrages upon the very young, and they form indeed one of the darkest stains upon our dreadful prison history.[2]

But public opinion seems to have been as apathetic as it was ignorant in those evil times, and not only was Mr. Chaplain-Governor Nihil allowed to continue his work,

[1] *The London Prisons*, p. 21.
[2] *Vide* J. W. Horsley, *Prisons and Prisoners*, p. 126. London, 1898.

but even to push the system to far greater lengths than
heretofore.

We have seen that his main idea was to prevent communication between the solitary prisoners; and they,
alone in their cells, spent weary and unprofitable hours
thinking out all conceivable and inconceivable ways of
gaining the eye or ear of their companions in calamity.
To find out what minds sharpened by solitude and
hungry from mental starvation might have contrived,
the Governor took counsel with one of the prisoners, for
he easily found (as when have those in power not done?)—
some wretched creature ready to add betrayal to his
other and lesser crimes.[1]

By the help of this man's comprehensive suggestions
the discipline was made more and more solitary, until the
prisoners' minds began to break under the ordeal. No
doubt certain natures had given way all along, but they
had been too few to attract attention ; now the mental
cases rapidly increased, until even the Committee inter-
fered. With the crass ignorance and blundering barbarity
well worthy of the scientific knowledge of that age, the
offenders against morality were to be left in their living
graves, their numbers being too few to bring discredit
on the system with the public ; but for the rest of the
prisoners, the " discipline " was to be somewhat easier,
lest the whole place should grow tenanted with the insane.

But the supposed panacea of solitude was still widely
believed in at the time. A new and " model " prison was
just being built: whether separation could be long continued with sanity is, said the Committee, " a subject of
much controversy, and can only be determined by actual
experiment."

And so more " philanthropists " of various grades and
professions continued shutting people up, starving them
in body, mind and soul, and then expecting reformation
to arise out of the cell. And the world waited a generation
or so with all the patience and the insight of a deluded
fowl, that vainly warms and tries to hatch an artificial
egg.

[1] *Millbank*, p. 232.

CHAPTER VII

THE " MODEL " SYSTEM

" Dark cells, dim lamp,
A stone floor, one may
Writhe on like a worm."
BROWNING.

IN 1832 a Mr. William Crawford (1788–1847) [1] was sent over to examine and report upon the prisons of America ; for which he is said to have received £5,000.[2] This gentleman has earned for himself a brief notice by J. W. " from personal knowledge " in the *Dictionary of National Biography*, where he is described as a philanthropist. He had been secretary to the London Prison Discipline Society, and was afterwards, with Mr. Whitworth Russell, who had been chaplain at Millbank, appointed an inspector of prisons by the Government.

The two systems which divided the United States Penitentiaries between them at that time, were the Silent-Associated and the Separate, or solitary.

When we read his description of them we appear to be confronted by that proverbial choice between the devil and the deep sea, or, as Robert Ingersoll might have put it, between Pestilence and Famine.

In the Association system the prisoners slept in single cells, but laboured together, no one however being allowed to speak or even to glance round. They were watched by visible and hidden warders, there were spy-holes in the very walls, and any breach of discipline was forthwith visited by a flogging from the warders, who were all armed with heavy cowhide cutting whips ; [3] they could

---

[1] Dixon, *London Prisons*, p. 146.
[2] F. H. Wines, *Punishment and Reformation*, p. 154.
[3] Crawford, *Penitentiaries of the United States* [1834], p. 17.

inflict what amount of stripes they chose, only making to the superintendent afterwards such a report as they saw fit themselves.

In this way one woman was practically flogged to death, and prisoners were continually being taken to the hospital as the result of blows. The men sat together in the workshops, but by the savage rules all were compelled to work with ever downcast eyes, and " if a convict is caught looking off his work . . . he is flogged by the overseer." [1]

Such was the evil atmosphere of the place, but yet these sort of " workshops " are but too common in prisons—indeed they are often held up as examples of what such places ought to be. Speaking of Preston a good many years back, the late Rev. John Clay took pride in the belief that no prisoner there would look up even if visitors and ladies came into the room.[2]

Referring to certain prisons in the Old Country, Mr. Crawford observes : " When labour is imposed, its corrective influence is lost from the absence of constant inspection and means of restraint. Silence, although nominally enjoined, is not scrupulously maintained, and prisoners are not, as they ought invariably to be, prohibited from looking off their work and gazing at various objects in the wards and yards." [3]

This sort of " discipline " has found much favour up to very recent times, and I recollect an eminent divine relating with some surprise, that once at Dartmoor, when a prisoner had a fit during chapel, not a convict moved or dared even look round to see what was the matter. We may suppose and hope, for the sake of his soul, that Mr. Crawford, of the Prison Discipline Society, was a commonplace man with little imagination. No punishment appears to have come home to him, and then but feebly, that was not physical, acute, and obvious.

Yet the most fearful of all punishments—solitary confinement—is one that leaves no trace and makes no sound.

In order to inflict this penalty, it must be said, at that time, little understood, a new and very special prison had

[1] Crawford, *Penitentiaries of the United States* [1834], p. 17.
[2] Dixon, *London Prisons*, p. 338.
[3] Crawford, *Report*, p. 30.

been erected about four years before, and Mr. Crawford hailed it as the promised—gaol. This was the Eastern Penitentiary. The story of this dreadful place reads like a chapter from the Spanish Inquisition. A prisoner on being received passed through three rooms. In the first he was undressed ; in the second he was cleaned by a warm bath ; in the third he was attired in the prison garb and his face was covered by a hood.

Thus blindfolded, he was led into the presence of the warden,[1] who gave him a talking to ; he was then taken to his cell, and left there. For the first few days he had neither books nor occupation of any kind, till he was thoroughly crushed and humbled by the awful solitude. The cells were 11 ft. 9 in. by 7 ft. 6 in. ; and 16 ft. high to the top of the vaulted ceiling aloft, lest he should look out on earth or into the infinite space of heaven, was the window. Means of sanitation were provided in each cell, and there were the usual ventilators and hot-air pipes, for it was to be quite a *modern* place of torment. A small aperture, closed by an iron door, allowed the daily food to be passed in, without a human being to be seen or heard ; he had no (private) visitors or letters, his isolation was complete, and he was buried in a veritable tomb.

From the ground-floor cells, thick double doors led out into a sort of stone tank which was called a yard, but which was only 18 ft. by 8, and surrounded by walls 11 ft. high ; even then, prisoners might not exercise in adjoining yards at the same time. The victims in the cells of the upper stories never went out at all. It has been estimated from returns that out of every 1,000 prisoners who passed the gate from 90 to 100 did not live to finish their sentence or feel the open air again.[2]

Such was the inferno which had been created under the craze about " contamination " and the mockery of reformation. Indeed it was a grisly pretension in this case, for in this precious penitentiary, with all its utter empty loneliness, there was at that time no regular religious service, and there was no chaplain there ![3]

---

[1] Crawford, *Report*. Appendix I.
[2] Sir J. Jebb, Purveyor-General of Prisons, *Report of* 1847, p. 59.
[3] Crawford, *Report*. Appendix.

If anything yet were wanting to fill up this measure of cruelty, it would be the fact that, there being then no State lunatic asylum in Pennsylvania, admitted lunatics were not infrequently consigned to the mercies of the Penitentiary.[1] Yet this was the institution which impressed the older school of " philanthropists," and of which Mr. Crawford wrote saying that, " with the addition of moral and religious instruction, in which this prison is eminently deficient, solitary imprisonment, thus enforced, might be made permanently efficient not only in deterring but in reforming the offenders."[2]

It may be argued in his defence that the penitentiary had then only been about four years in partial operation (in prisons Time seems almost shut in too ; but glacier-like it does move and take the stones and buildings on with it), and that his " ideal " system which *might* lead to good results was somewhat different from the one he actually found in action.

But Mr. Crawford had shown himself to have been a man without imagination, and, perhaps consequently, without heart.

Even John Howard, to whom many cruelties as well as reforms were undoubtedly due, possessed all the hardness as well as the strength of the Puritan character, and an admiring biographer is still constrained to say of him that " No man ever lived who was less a creature of impulse. He had no sentiment, scarcely any ideality—he was simple and grand like an iron column in a rock of granite,"[3] and from our present knowledge of his domestic life and of his religious views, I can well believe that he was more shocked at the flagrant irregularities which he discovered behind prison walls, than at the actual human misery which they entailed.

But few indeed can picture what they have not seen, or suffer what they have not felt. So Mr. Crawford returned to London full of admiration for the new system in its extreme form, which was to be productive of reformation if moral and religious instruction were only added.

[1] Crawford, *Report*. Appendix.
[2] *Report*, p. 14.
[3] W. Hepworth Dixon, *Life of Howard*, p. 30.

This was, as Mr. Hepworth Dixon has keenly pointed out,[1] simply a theory of what he thought would or should happen, under future conditions. Many State cruelties have been set on foot in the same manner, and the idea had great influence with the Home Secretary of that day, who introduced a Bill in 1839, advancing separate confinement. The next step was to erect a "model" prison—at Pentonville—which was finished in 1842.[2] So convinced were people of that period that they were definitely on the right road, that within the next six years fifty-four new prisons were built in England after this precious "model,"[3] and the new doctrines spread far and wide.

At Pentonville the isolation theory was carried out with all the ardour of a new religion under the personal watchfulness of Mr. Crawford, who had become an inspector of prisons, and who died suddenly within the prison he was regulating, in 1847.

The ruling notion of this school has always been that prisoners meeting, under any circumstances, was about as much to be avoided as a confluence of the small-pox spots ; so for long periods, for two years at the beginning,[4] and later for eighteen months, every man was kept in isolation.

Up to 1853 the prisoners wore masks along the passages,[5] they sat in separated pigeon-holes in chapel,[6] even on the treadwheel they were partitioned off, and the newly-invented crank was ground in solitary weariness within the cell ; where each took an hour's exercise a day, in what has been called a "triangular den," surrounded by high gloomy walls.[7]

The convicts to be subjected to the "model" discipline were specially selected as being likely and promising subjects to endure it.[8] The sickly and those supposed

---

1 *The London Prisons*, ch. vi. [1850].
2 *Ibid.*, p. 151.
3 Griffiths, *Secrets of the Prison-House.*
4 Tallack, p. 139.
  Griffiths, *Millbank*, p. 146.
5 Clay, p. 193.
6 Dixon, p. 175.
7 Clay, p. 192.
8 Griffiths, *Millbank*, p. 338.

to have a tendency towards insanity [1] were carefully weeded out ; for a sound mind—so far as was compatible with criminality—in a sound body,[2] was naturally regarded as the very best material [3] on which to make experiments.

But in defiance of " model " theories it became manifest, as time went on, that the prisoners were giving way under the stress of solitude. For a long while the officials would not hear of it, and accounted for morbid symptoms in all sorts of ingenious ways. A story is related that, at one period, they even attributed them to the somewhat sulphurous earnestness of a too-vehement chaplain : discourses that could be calmly borne in the prospective smell of roast mutton and onion sauce, were brain-shaking upon solitude and skilly. A milder man is said to have been procured, but the mental wreckage still continued ; it was the experience of Millbank all over again.

The first batches of convicts on their way from Pentonville to the antipodes,[4] were discovered to be quite unable to take care of themselves. The sudden inrush of the outer world was too great a shock for the enfeebled, crushed-out creatures they had become. Some had convulsions, others fainting-fits, yet more were idiotic, and nearly all were described as thoughtful, subdued and languid in their ways. Clearly some subtle mischief had been working upon them. In the decade from '42 to '52 the discipline had to be continually modified ; in the end, the " solitary " was brought down to nine months, that being, it was then considered, the most that could be safely borne ;[5] yet when ordinary instead of selected prisoners began to be received at Pentonville [6] the rate of insanity flew up fivefold and some even say eightfold, under the " discipline " in its modified form.[7]

[1] *London Prisons*, p. 156.
[2] Jebb, *Report*, 1847, p. 20.
[3] W. L. Clay, *The Prison Chaplain*, 190 and 246.
[4] Dixon, p. 163.
[5] Clay, p. 225.
[6] *Ibid.* p. 246.
[7] Tallack, p. 139.

CHAPTER VIII

"MODEL" LABOUR

THE influence of the "shallow dreamers" who had evolved the cell system, and had mapped out human nature straight from their dull imaginings, was yet by no means spent. And as certain eruptions attack the limbs and extremities after they have left the centre of the body, so the new " discipline " spread into the country, and even, in some degree, to distant lands and far-off colonies, long after it had been modified and altered at its prime centre of invasion.

Nay more : as time went on, the cell began to relinquish even its original pretensions towards effecting reformation, and to be chiefly relied upon as a sure if subtle means of systematic torment ; which has always been termed " discipline " in modern parlance ; just as little wars, where the loss is all on one side and the loot on the other, are often called in Europe, " military operations."

Now in the old days men, women and children were " pitchforked " into prison all together. Nobody thought about them or their needs ; nobody wanted to reform them ; and no brood of " philanthropists " had yet begun to worry and increase their sufferings.

But the prisoners idled about without work, order, or classification : to employ people well and wisely within narrow walls would have required far more effort and intelligence than is generally directed upon criminals. One day it happened that Sir William Cubitt (1785–1861), the eminent engineer, was appealed to ; and, in an evil hour, though very likely with the best intentions—for it is said that he did not at first contemplate the machine [1] being used as a means of punishment—he devised the Treadwheel.[2] This was in 1818.

[1] Cubitt, *Dictionary of National Biography.*
[2] See third and fourth Reports, Society for the Improvement of Prison Discipline (1821, 1822).

Its ordinary form [1] was something like that of a very wide mill-wheel such as is turned by water power, containing twenty-four steps.[2] Each prisoner held on to a wooden bar or ladder-rung, above his head, and kept on treading as the steps went round. The body, or barrel, of the wheel, was mostly about 5 ft. in diameter, but in early days there appear to have existed several varieties ; as for instance at Leicester, where it was 20 feet across, and the prisoners worked from the inside ; but after having had two fatal accidents—of course, according to the official report, " from the perverseness and wilful misconduct of the men "—this inside-scramble style was given up.[3]

But the ordinary wheel was not, it would seem, without its dangers : in the official correspondence just quoted we are told that a man was killed upon the mill in Suffolk,[4] while from Northallerton came an account of a prisoner having his arm torn off by the machine, in each case from that most deadly of all offences against the " model " system—attempting to speak to an adjacent fellow-toiler who was a human being and not an official. Usually little stalls were built upon the wheel, so each man had, as it were, a little box all to himself. Hard and brutalising as of course this kind of " labour " always was, women were set to do it. In a letter written by the Clerk to the Justices of Middlesex [5] to the Secretary of State in 1824 mention is made of a woman who was with child, having recently been set to work upon the wheel, which was followed by the medical results that might have been expected, the next day ; but it was pleaded that her condition was not known at the time. From the same correspondence we learn that at Guildford a woman was sentenced to three months' hard labour and the treadmill for the curious offence of being delivered of an illegitimate child—her third—which became chargeable to the parish of Godalming.[6] This too was made the task of un-

---

[1] Some views of the wheels and of that still more ghastly instrument the crank are given in *Reports from Committees*, British Museum, vol. xii. 1835, also Mayhew & Binny, *Criminal Prisons of London*.
[2] *Accounts and Papers*, 1824, vol. xix.
[3] Letter from Leicester officials to Home Secretary in above.
[4] *Accounts and Papers*, 1824 (British Museum).
[5] *Ibid.* p. 153.   [6] *Ibid.* p. 161.

convicted prisoners in those days, and so wearying is the monotony of prison life that they are said sometimes to have desired even such employment.[1]

The tasks set for the treadmill varied very much : at first prisoners had to ascend a number of steps, ranging from 5,000 to 14,000 feet ; [2] in later times the regulation task was 8,640 feet for the day's work.[3] Sometimes the wheel was employed in pumping or grinding, sometimes it was achieving nothing, but going round like a " damnation mill."

The Crank, a still more " model " instrument for the cell-theorist, dates from a later period, having been first invented by one Gibbs at Pentonville, probably about 1846.[4] Sir J. Jebb, writing in 1847, says that " it was brought forward in consequence of certain objections having been urged against the treadwheel," and speaks of it as a new thing. Like so many nineteenth-century prison " improvements," the crank was far worse than anything of the kind yet invented, and, next to the cell itself, it soon became the chief " reforming engine " of the " model " system.

The newest monster might be compared to a churn in appearance, or to a chaff-cutter, or twenty other things, made up of a case and a handle ; it was just a metal box raised to a convenient height by a support. It had a handle to be turned and a little clock-like face upon one side to count the revolutions made. The requisite amount of resistance was secured by a metal band, which could be tightened with varying force pressing inside, upon the axle ; it might perhaps be compared to the band-brake sometimes seen upon the back wheel of a bicycle. The ordinary resistance was nominally from 4 to 11 lb.[5]

The usual number of revolutions [6] required was 14,400 a day, being at the rate of 1,800 an hour.[7] Soon other prisons which had sprung into existence out of the parent penitentiary at Pentonville adopted the crank and drove

---

[1] Letter from Norfolk Prison in above.
[2] Crawford, *Report*, p. 33.
[3] E. F. DuCane, *Punishment and Prevention of Crime*, p. 97.
[4] *Report of the Surveyor-General of Prisons*, 1847, p. 17.
[5] *Ibid.* Appendix K.
[6] *Royal Commission of* 1863, p. 415.
[7] Jebb, *Report* 1847. Appendix K.

it for all it was worth ; more correct would it be to say, that they made the prisoners do the working while the officials moralised—which was much pleasanter. At first it had been intended only for vagrants and short-sentence men, but after 1848 it tended more and more to oust other labour altogether : a noble model for the admiration of God and the imitation of men.

The instrument was improved upon in various ways, and a sort of exhibition of Cranks was held at which the various devices were examined—amongst them one machine which was a kind of sand-churn ; but the *Appold* crank ¹ appears to have been the one that met with the official sanction.²

It was in 1851 that the murderous tyrant who has been lifted into the lasting pillory of shame in Charles Reade's story,³ was made Governor of the gaol at Birmingham. In this modern hell upon earth the cell was the reforming force, the crank its worthy minister ; and a merciless martinet was urged to carry out the model system to the very utmost ; and he did. One is naturally apt to fancy that the great novelist over-coloured his tale ; but the whole terrible story is preserved in an official record, and stands a lasting stain upon our comfortable self-complacency.⁴

Ten thousand revolutions a day of the crank were then required, at a nominal resistance of 5 lb. for boys and 10 lb. for grown men. If the work was not done, even the scanty prison food would be withheld, and the prisoners were crushed and squeezed and strapped into that modern variety of the " Scavenger's daughter " of the Tower—the punishment jacket.

The cranks were in cells round a yard, and the victims who had not completed their task were often left there, turning the machine desperately for their very lives—turning and turning after darkness had set in, when the dial of the indicator could no longer be read ; so that sometimes, even after the heavy official task was really

---

¹ *Royal Commission on Birmingham Prison,* 1854.
  Accounts and Papers, vol. xxxvii.
² See also fifteenth *Report of the Inspector of Prisons, Home District.*
³ *It is Never Too Late to Mend.*
⁴ *Report of the Royal Commission on Birmingham Prison,* 1854.
  Accounts and Papers, vol. **xxxvii.**

done, they would work on and on, as never slaves worked at the Pyramids of Egypt, making many more revolutions even than they had to do ; yet next day these were not counted to them, but all the long ten thousand had to be done anew.

Even this was not all, for it was found that these cranks, which were of an old pattern, were faulty in construction and false in registration, for whenever they grew heated from the friction of the working, it was estimated that the resistance would increase threefold ; and it was found that half-starved lads were set to go through tasks requiring one-quarter of the power of a dray horse to accomplish, which of course could not be done ; and then the victim was pronounced refractory ! [1] Thus " Josephs " (really, Edward Andrews), a fifteen-year-old boy—a quiet, neglected, inoffensive creature, who had stolen a piece of meat and was in for three months—was put on a " 5-lb. crank," which is said to have been equal in resistance to one of 20 lb.[2] And because he could never do the impossible task he was starved and jacketed,[3] and put in the black cell and punished, till the miserable boy broke down and hanged himself in his lonely cell and was found dead.

Then at last some tardy retribution came ; there are times when the silence of the wall is broken down, and when the people gain a passing glimpse of what tormentors do.

The city was moved to anger : the governor, the prison surgeon (a jackal-minded scoundrel, who had abetted everything), and the visiting justices who had morally become accessories to wilful murder, were shown up to general hatred and loathing, and a special Government Commission sat upon the gaol.

The arch-devil is said to have been condemned to prison for three months,[4] which seems almost too good to be true, for there have been many people very like

---

[1] *Report*, p. vii.
[2] *Minutes of Evidence*, p. 275.
[3] A somewhat similar punishment jacket, contracting the members and organs with extreme suffering, was in use in Italy, I understand, until the present reign.
[4] M. D. Hill, *Repression of Crime*, p. 232. London, 1857. *Daily Express*, Sept. 15, 1900.

him in the prison service who have never had even that ;
nor any foretaste of their just reward, within the little
mist-bounded span of life the eyes of men have been
allowed to see. The same Royal Commission then went on to Leicester
prison. Things there they found nearly as bad, though
the cruelty was more of the ordinary systematic kind,
which is much harder to bring personally home. The
solitary cells had been added in 1846, and there was no
infirmary, for, says the official report,[1] " At that period
the opinion seems to have been entertained by many
of the early founders of the system, that prisoners when
sick could be treated without any disadvantage in their
separate cells, and that the integrity of the system need
not be infringed even in cases of serious disease." [2]

The crank, of course, was going strong, the maximum
task being 14,400 turns for an adult and 12,000 for
juveniles. Daily food had to be turned for ; thus 1,800
revolutions were necessary to gain breakfast—such as it
was ; dinner took 4,500 more ; supper another 5,400,
leaving 2,700 turns to be done afterwards if not completed
earlier. The effect of this sort of thing was that many
of the prisoners were nearly starved to death, and of
course the continued loss of food rendered them less and
less able to do the heavy tasks before them. One man
is confidently believed by the Commission to have had
only nine meals in three weeks of working days ; on the
Sundays they were all fed. The tasks were performed,
or attempted, in the cells, which were stuffy and ill
ventilated for this violent kind of labour where men were
bathed in perspiration. Besides semi-starvation the
prisoners might be flogged with the light cat up to three
dozen lashes ; but the punishments just alluded to were
probably worse than this, as we shall subsequently find.

Within these kind of prisons were to be found two or
three children aged nine,[3] and a good many of eleven,
twelve, and thirteen ; all carefully isolated and all utterly
desolate.

[1] *Report of Royal Commission on Leicester Prison*, 1854, p. x.
Accounts and Papers, vol. xxxiv., British Museum.
[2] " The Infirmary was a spot on the sun,"—Charles Reade
[3] *Birmingham Pris. Comm. Min. of Ev.*, p. 260.

Then prisoners might be ill in their cells, and even die—three had so died at Birmingham—with no one near for any sort of help or human consolation. And in the morning, at the regulation hour, the turnkey came, as to the dead child " Josephs," to find that while the Home Office had procrastinated, while the patrols went round and all the heavy gates and doors were locked and barred, a Messenger had come through the caverned silence, taking the trial to the King of kings.

CHAPTER IX

THE BREAK-UP OF THE MODEL

THE separate system, that disastrous fad which wrecked so many lives and long created untold misery, can claim but few adherents now.

But once this cell-salvation was a veritable creed ; [1] many a savage crimson-stained idolatry has done less harm, and not been more inhuman and grotesque.

But all *beliefs* die hard, and none the less so when they are most monstrous ; the cell was once the very emblem of prison progress. "The officials like it," wrote Mr. Hepworth Dixon in the middle of last century ; " it gives them very little trouble, so, without pretending to understand its complicated effects, moral or mental, they almost all swear by it." [2] It was looked up to as a counsel of perfection ! Even now there still remain some pious but dull-minded " philanthropists," who keep on muttering the shallow shibboleths of empirical penology, but they have grown rather numb and impotent in these latter days, like blood-sucking mosquitos left out in the cold.

But there are backward countries more important than retarded individuals ; there are distinct stages of prison management, just as there appear to be in the progress of civilisation. Thus Morocco may be said to be (remember for good as well as for evil !) in the middle-ages of prison development. Italian penal servitude is probably much worse, and more resembling that of the earlier nineteenth century. For prisons have always been the stagnant backwaters of life, but little corresponding to the genius of a nation.

[1] Ferri has called it one of the " greatest aberrations of the nineteenth century."—*Vide* C. B. de Quiros, *Modern Theories of Criminality*, p. 181. London, 1911.
[2] *London Prisons*, p. 154.

We must do our best, and earnestly hope and strive that those other lands may not also have to pass through that dreary, desolate period of the cell-sepulchre system, which crept in on us under the guise of progress.

We have ourselves been great transgressors in the past, but it is something to know that we have ultimately shaken off this snare, and that the " model " discipline has disappeared for ever.

We have seen that Archbishop Ullathorne claimed that the cell system was first brought into use by the Catholic Church. But the penitentiary begun by Pope Clement seems to have differed widely from those afterwards tried in England and America.

It would appear that what the Pope had in his mind was to employ the monastic discipline of meditation as a potent moral agent ; the prisoners were employed in work, and were assembled together for instruction. What he purposed that the penitentiary should be, is pretty well explained in the Latin inscription which Howard translated " For the Correction and Instruction of profligate Youth : That they who when idle were injurious ; when instructed, might be useful to, the State. 1704." [1] We are told that " The silence was not enforced so unmercifully but that the prisoners could talk quietly together in recreation for half an hour on Sundays and holidays." [2]

No doubt there were yet many dangers inherent to the system, but the effects of solitude were not appreciated then ; there is also evidence that the Papal plans were afterwards allowed to fall into neglect, as has mostly been the case with prison matters everywhere.[3]

But while claiming the " correctional " system for his Church, the Catholic prelate denounced the mere empty barren solitude of the later penitentiaries in most unsparing terms.

" The Solitaries of the East," he wrote, " were usually trained in monasteries or under recluses ; and when they petitioned to go and converse with God alone in the silent desert, they carried this admonition with them, that a

[1] Howard, *State of the Prisons*, 1780.
[2] Glancey, *Characteristics*, p. 219.
[3] Howard, *Account of the Foreign Prisons, etc.*, 1789.

solitary man is either an angel or a devil. Still they had occasional visits from the brethren and from other solitaries and from pious or afflicted persons who sought counsel or comfort from them. To quote but one experienced authority, St. John Climacus says, 'Few are the persons who lead the eremitical life led by the light and wisdom of the Holy Ghost.' What then must it be to shut up one of our godless and reckless criminals, strong in animal instincts and void of spiritual or mental resources, within the four white walls of a contracted cell, without even a window low enough for him to look through ? It is like shutting up a living body within a dead one. It is the Carthusian's life without his grace, without his vocation, without his contempt of the world, without his soul open to heaven, and, not to forget the material part, without his rooms and little garden, and without the long chanting of his brethren in the choir." [1]

" Even the anchoret," the Archbishop continues, " had the open desert and his work for the poor of the cities. But the criminal is thrown upon his own denuded and sterile nature, such as vice and profligacy have left him ; and the question that remains is, how long will he go without breaking down or sinking into imbecility ? " [2]

Perhaps the chief reason why the punishment of solitude received so much support and endured so persistently, is that its effects require some experience to perceive and the gift of imagination to estimate. In this respect the cell resembles some of the worst tortures of the middle ages. One of these is said to have consisted in letting water fall drip by drip upon the victim's head—a process that looks as innocent as a morning bath, but which, we are told—for torture was a fine art then—resulted in convulsions, madness, and death in horrible anguish. Another torture very commonly employed consisted simply in pouring a large quantity of fluid down the prisoner's throat, which soon set up acute compression of the tightly-packed internal organs, cramps, spasms, and great suffering ; this was the torture to which, in the ordinary course of business, the beautiful but infamous Marquise de Brinvilliers was subjected just before her execution in 1676. [3]

---

[1] Glancey, p. 284.   [2] *Management of Criminals*, p. 25.
[3] F. Funck-Brentano, *Princes and Poisoners*.

" What the eye sees not the heart feels not," runs the proverb; but the converse is also true, that what the heart does not appreciate the eye does not really convey : it is the soul that sees.[1]

Who shall ever say how much the heavenly gift of sympathy depends upon the possession of imagination ? An official faddist like Mr. Crawford, when he looked upon the dumb, dreary, unbroken, hopeless misery of the Eastern penitentiary, is quite pleased and content at " the mild and subdued spirit which seemed to pervade the temper of the convicts, and which is essentially promoted by reflection and solitude and the absence of corporal punishment. The only offences in the Eastern penitentiary which a man can commit are idleness and wilful damage to the materials on which he is at work."[2] No corporal punishment indeed ! but minds were tortured there ; the prisoners " universally concurred in the conviction that solitude was of all punishments the most fearful," yet nothing less than the puffed and purple furrows of the lash came home to the official mind, or troubled it much then.

Speaking of the prisoners whom he had visited, Mr. Crawford wrote : " Although generally serious, they were not depressed, and several talked with a cheerfulness which I did not expect to find in men thus situated."[3] Again this shallow-minded person mistook the signs he saw. Looking over an old report by Sir J. Jebb, Surveyor-General of Prisons, I came upon the following explanatory passage : "The appearance of cheerfulness is more probably due to the excitement of their solitude being broken in upon than to any abiding feeling of the kind when alone."[4] Mr. Crawford could not understand, but happily Dickens could. A great man *does* sometimes pass through the gates of woe—not always as a free and honoured guest, I hold. It is a relief to turn from that official husk of humanity to read the burning words of one whose body lies with the old Abbey's dead. Of that same place, the Eastern Penitentiary, a few years later,

[1] I believe it was William Blake who said that men see through, rather than with, their eyes.
[2] *Report*, 12.
[3] Crawford, *Report*, p. 10.
[4] Jebb, *Report for* 1847.

he wrote in ever memorable words : " In its intention I am well convinced that it is kind, humane, and meant for reformation ; but I am persuaded that those who devised this system of prison discipline and those benevolent gentlemen who carry it into execution do not know what they are doing.

" I believe very few men are capable of estimating the immense amount of torture and agony which this dreadful punishment, prolonged for years, inflicts upon the sufferers. I hesitated once, debating with myself whether if I had the power of saying yes or no, I would allow it to be tried in certain cases where the terms of imprisonment were short ; but now I solemnly declare, that with no rewards or honours could I walk a happy man beneath the open sky or lie me down upon my bed at night with the consciousness that one human creature lay suffering this unknown punishment in his lonely cell, and I the cause or I consenting to it in the least degree." [1]

It is not at first very obvious why mere solitude should be such a real and dreadful punishment.[2] That it is a waste of life, dreary, useless and unprofitable, might well be pretty clear to anybody who was not steeped in that fool's philosophy which has been hit off in the saying " Confine the leopards in separate cages, the cages will take their spots out while ye're sleeping." Dickens expressed the great heart of the people when he wrote : " It seems to me that the objection that nothing wholesome or good has ever had its growth in such unnatural solitude, and that even a dog or any of the more intelligent among beasts would pine and mope and rust away beneath its influence, would be in itself a sufficient argument against this system." But the effects of solitude are definitely known now. If we do not kill time, then time kills us. It required experience and a long series of hideous experiments in vivi-sepulture, to make us realise that the human brain—and more especially a thinking one—has that strange quality of self-

---

[1] *American Notes*.

[2] " It has pleased the Creator to implant in man that feeling of attachment to society, that to be withdrawn from his fellow creatures was a punishment compared to which the torture, the rack or the stake were vulgar and inefficient."—A Recorder of Birmingham, quoted by Field, *Prison Discipline*, vol. i. p. 328.

consumption. The process is slow but certain ; other punishments might be " mercifully " put aside ; the cell would do its work. " We know," wrote Major Arthur Griffiths, " by the light of our modern experience, that solitary imprisonment prolonged beyond certain limits is impossible except at a terrible cost. The price is that the prison becomes the antechamber to the madhouse, or leads even to the tomb. It has taken years to establish this now incontrovertible conclusion, but it is now so distinctly known that argument seems superfluous." [1] Oh, but it has been hard to bring this home to those in power ! That the prisoners dreaded it beyond description, was held to be one more argument, if any were needed, in the system's favour.

It required the genius of Dickens, the minute and vivid accuracy of Charles Reade, to gain a hearing with the multitude and shake the system to its dungeon depths. Even then it required years of continued failure, deaths and outbreaks of mania, with constant recommittals and crimes ever continued, which things could not be always shelved and put away, to bring the system to an everlasting end.

[1] *Millbank*, p. 145.
See also *Secrets of the Prison-House*, i. p. 265. *Re* Belgium.
Departmental Committee, 1895, p. 508. *Re* Italy.
Jebb, *Report for* 1847, p. 103.
Evidence of Captain Groves. Gordon Ryland's *Crime*, p. 200.

CHAPTER X

PENAL SERVITUDE: THE PANIC COMMISSION

"Deprived of hope and freedom at a blow,
What has he left that he can yet forego?
Yes, to deep sadness sullenly resigned,
He feels his body's bondage in his mind,
Puts off his generous nature, and to suit
His actions to his fate, puts on the brute."

COWPER.

THE refusal on the part of our colonies to receive any more convicts compelled the Government to abandon the old-time transportation which might have been made such a mighty agency for good, and which, in spite of all its actual infamies and cruelties, has left some worthy monuments.

There had always been a certain number of poor creatures left behind, probably cripples, half-mad people, and more or less medical cases, whom it was considered inadvisable to dispatch with the more fortunate majority across the seas.

They were mostly kept upon the floating prisons or hulks, which lasted from 1778 till the remaining one was destroyed by fire in 1857; and which were, in fact, the first prisons employed for convicts who were neither executed nor transported. A few are said to have lingered in the local prisons—there were no others—and their condition was presumably very pitiable.

But the time came when nearly eight thousand convicts had to be disposed of upon English ground, and special prisons were then erected to carry out the latest form of punishment.

The first of these was opened at Portland in 1848; the next was Dartmoor,[1] which had once held some

---

[1] For some astounding stories about that place, the reader is referred to Basil Thomson, *The Story of Dartmoor Prison*. London, 1907.

thousands of French and American prisoners of war, and which was repaired and reoccupied by convicts in 1850 ; Chatham came later about 1856.

The first Penal Servitude Act was passed in 1855.[1] It abolished all sentences of transportation of less than fourteen years' duration, and, recognising that the new punishment was to be far more penal, it made four years of it to correspond with seven years beyond the seas, and other sentences in like proportion.

As usual, one State decree is soon amended or superseded by another, and in 1857 came the second Penal Servitude Act, which did away with transportation altogether ; made the sentences of the new punishment to be as lengthy as those of the milder one, but fixed the minimum sentence at three years.

The general scheme of the new system was that there should be three stages : firstly, twelve months of strict cellular confinement ; secondly, associated and chiefly out-door labour on the public works ; thirdly, conditional release for the period of remission earned by hard work and good conduct, upon ticket of leave, which was always liable to revocation.

Without going into minute details, we may say that the remission which could be earned consisted in one-fourth of the public works period for men,[2] and one-third of the whole sentence passed on women. Life sentences had no remission, but were reconsidered in those days at the end of twelve years.[3]

A word must be said in passing about this preliminary term of separate confinement. It was originated in 1842 by the then Home Secretary, Sir James Graham, and was intended to be purely reformatory. Later on, says the official report, " The original intention [4] . . . appears (fifteen years after) to have been lost sight of," and " the main object of the separate confinement had come to be deterrence." [5] It would not be too much to say that the whole design of the prison system " had come to be

---

[1] *Report Royal Commission of* 1879, p. vii.
[2] *Ibid.* p. xvii.
[3] *Report Commission of* 1863, p. 69.
[4] Committee of 1895, *Report*, p. 27.
[5] *Ibid.* p. 28.

deterrence," until within two years of the conclusion of the nineteenth century, as we shall see.

From the many experiments already made it was discovered that twelve months in a solitary cell was more than could be borne by men who had the dismal outlook of a long subsequent sentence to reflect and brood upon. It was therefore reduced to nine months in 1853, that being thought to be about the longest period that the average convict—(and all through the prison system the head was forced to fit the cap, and if it didn't, so much the worse *for the head*)—could safely endure, although this was considered harmful by some of the officials, and even by a severe governor like Captain Groves ; [1] but nine months it remained for nearly half a century.

The next stage was to be that of labour on the public works : at Portland the convicts built the mighty breakwater, at Dartmoor they reclaimed land from the bogs, at Chatham they dug huge docks out of the mud of the Medway. All this was good and useful work ; but the spirit of fear, not the spirit of progress, hung over the place—every day and every task was all along subordinated to the grim purposes of punishment.

But in 1862 occurred events which were to set back the clock of penal reform for five-and-thirty years, and were to make our convict prisons a worse doom than Siberia.

According to the official return there were, in the latter half of the year 1861,[2] seventeen cases of robbery with violence, which was a bit below the average. But in the corresponding six months of 1862 a dangerous gang of criminals hung about the streets of the Metropolis, and the figures rose, that half, to eighty-two.

A number of brutal assaults, and especially an attack upon a member of the House of Commons, created a kind of panic and a newspaper campaign. At the November Sessions for 1862 a whole batch of these offenders were convicted before Mr. Baron Bramwell.[3] A Return of December 4 of that year gives the names of twenty-four prisoners, only two of whom were over thirty ; fifteen

---

[1] Gordon Rylands, *Crime*, p. 202.
[2] *Report Commission of* 1863. Appendix, p. 180.
[3] *Ibid.* p. 136.

were more than twenty years of age, the rest being probably what we should now call Hooligans, and of the worst sort too.

It is instructive to notice that nearly all the garrotters of 1862 were fitting and worthy products of one or other of the monstrous " model " systems which we have been examining. A few had been shut up in Millbank [1] under Mr. Nihil, the clerical faddist ; one of the men convicted had been a warder there. They all received tremendous sentences, and that particular gang and outbreak were made an end of. But not, unhappily, the panic which was produced, for in July of the following year, 1863, a Bill was passed to punish all such outrages with the cat.[2] Mr. Wharton naïvely expressed the position when he was trying to get another flogging Bill through the Commons, in the year 1909 : " A member of the House was garrotted at the Duke of York's Column on his way down to Westminster, and upon this the House, he would not say passed —rushed the Bill through." [3]

Nothing has been more widely misconceived than this unfortunate Garrotters Act of 1863, for the fact somehow got loose into print and parlance, that the threat and use of the cat alone had actually put down robbery with violence. I read the statement of a bishop a few days back ; this may have been faith, or it might have been hope on his part, but it certainly was not accuracy ; for it did not. That particular gang was clearly captured and broken up before the Act in question became law. That these crimes are not stopped can be easily perceived in the newspapers any day. It is true that, for the moment, the victims are not generally choked by mufflers, any more than they are now throttled by fashion with a stiff stock, or, if women, inflated by crinolines. But such details relate to the manner and not to the matter of the offence. Localities have their peculiarities : the sand-bag is the usual mode in America ; the lasso was employed in the south of France, where I used to live years ago ; last week, as I was revising these pages, a man had paper

[1] Griffiths, *Millbank*, p. 432.
" Some were ticket-of-leave men."—Therry, *N.S.W.*, p. 503.
[2] H. B. Bonner, *The Gallows and the Lash*, p. 37.
Chitty's Statutes, vol. iii. p. 286. London, 1912.
[3] *The Times*, March 29, 1900.

covered with treacle placed over his face, while the robbers captured his bag. All these are local details, which alter with times and places where crimes occur ; but the real offence has never been stopped, and never will be, merely by punishments. For strife and evil have their roots in bad social systems, and are not to be removed by anything so simple as cruelty : *that* was tried first of all, hundreds of years ago.

But much more followed : in 1863 a Royal Commission, breathing fire and brimstone, was appointed to look into the state of the prisons, and the effects of its report were bitterly experienced by the convicts through many, many long and hopeless years.

It is well to remember that the system which it found to be in force was by no means a humane one. Said the Report :

" A very general impression appears to prevail that the system pursued in these prisons is not of a sufficiently penal character . . . we consider that, upon the whole, this impression is erroneous. The life of the prisoners is extremely monotonous. Having been used in most cases to constant change and excitement, they are debarred from all pleasures, they are compelled to pass their time in dull unvarying routine of distasteful labour, and at the close of each day's work they return to the cheerless solitude of their cells." [1]

Yet, working on the old and untenable hypotheses as to human conduct, the Commission considered that penal servitude could not be sufficiently dreaded, because persons who had been through it were " not effectually deterred from pursuing a course of crime by the fear of incurring this punishment again, which is shown by the fact that a large percentage of those discharged from convict prisons are known to be reconvicted." [2]

So the Commission proceeded to make prison life harder and more dreary than ever ; and, as it is one of the grim truths of life, that while it requires greatness and wisdom to do good, yet even the smallest and meanest creature can give pain, this purpose was effectually accomplished. They tried to make seven years the minimum sentence

[1] *Report*, 1863, p. 41.
[2] *Ibid.* p. 23.

(it was fixed, however, at five years), and finding that after long terms of years convicts had been able to earn what may be called " deferred pay," amounting sometimes to £30 or £40, even, it is said, to £80,[1] they determined to make his restart in honest life more " probable," by limiting his money to £3, or, as an utmost limit, for specially good conduct, to £6.

After the Penal Servitude Act of 1864 a mass of cast-iron, mostly senseless and barbarous rules, were drawn up and fixed by Act of Parliament, and the great world-flow of crime, disease and misery went steadily on, and was about as much affected by these crude and barbarous regulations as were the Channel tides.

[1] *Enc. Brit.*

CHAPTER XI

THE MILITARY DESPOTISM

"A hell to love unknown, a whited tomb
Where hearts may break and wither and fever burn
Gnawing unsoothed, and pining atrophy
Sap reason slowly from its citadel."
Book of Chains.

THE Prisons Act occasioned by the last Commission riveted the new system together ; bound it in red tape and iron ; made it, in fact, a terrible machine that slowly ground its prisoners to pieces.

And Crime, having so little to do with prison systems, continued very much the same. Some fifteen years later, in 1878, another Royal Commission sat to see how things were going on. It certainly accomplished little that was good, and when we review the horrors unmasked before it, and consider the criticisms that it left behind, we can only say that in sheer hide-bound brutality it was extremely like its predecessor !

Such a description applied to the sovereign's "Right trusty and well beloved" may sound exaggerated, but nothing that we could say would prove so damning as the admitted facts ; and to these then let us go !

In 1872 a Russian nobleman and a member of the Howard Association went down to Chatham Prison, and were much impressed with what they saw : " it is magnificent," they said. The prisoners had warm jerseys and good boots, and an official remarked, " These men are in many respects better off than the honest labourers outside," with much more of the same sort.

Now it was really a somewhat unfortunate time and place for these gentlemen to go into ecstasies, because in that very prison, about the 'seventies and maybe for a

¹ *Royal Commission* of 1879, p. 208.

few years before, occurred some of the worst atrocities in the whole convict service.

The labour there consisted in the excellent and useful work of digging out the huge dock basins, and the wet and stodgy clay was carried off in waggons drawn by an engine. But if the task was good, the spirit of the place was evil, for it had grown to be quite a common practice for men to cast themselves beneath the wheels, so fearful was the discipline, so absolutely unendurable became their lives !

What the true character of the place was, will easily be perceived when we consider what was done to meet these actions, which were prompted by despair.

In a Blue Book of 1872, besides the usual minor mutilations so common in the cruel convict prisons, there were reported no less than seventeen cases of prisoners wilfully fracturing their arms and legs under the engine.

The prison surgeon reported that they " were of so severe a character, that amputation was immediately necessary in most cases, as the limbs were so mangled as to preclude any hope of recovery." Before the Commission of 1879 the then governor was asked if any measures had been taken to prevent these fearful mutilations, upon which he replied : " Yes, we took very severe measures ; a great many men were flogged, and we took precautions. We did not allow them to be near the engines when they passed. A great many of the men who mutilated themselves were afterwards flogged." [1] And then Major Farquharson adds a sentence which well reveals the spirit of the place, and of the man. " There was no reason why they should not be flogged because they had only mutilated an arm or a leg." [2] Can the harsh records of any other time or place upon the poor outraged earth go much further than this in glaring inhumanity ?

Besides the ghastly atmosphere of that " grim joyless silence "[3] which has often been spoken of as a special feature in English convict life, there is abundant evidence that the prisoners at Chatham were very insufficiently fed to perform the heavy kind of work they had to do.[4]

---

[1] *Roy. Com.* 1879, p. 210.   [2] *Ibid..* p. 627.
[3] George Griffith, *In an Unknown Prison Land,* p. 130.
[4] See Evidence of Dr. Campbell, *Royal Com.* 1879, p. 578

The result of this was the horrible practice of eating
candles, and even refuse,[1] which has been a not infrequent
custom in all the convict prisons. A former Governor
of Portland says: " At Dartmoor and other prisons, the
practice of eating candles is extremely common ; the
prisoners stir their gruel or cocoa with a candle, and
they then drink the compound . . . they have an idea
that it is more savoury,[2] it produces a fatty coagulation
on the top, which in winter they think palatable."   The
Commission, it appears, considered that this candle or
refuse eating did not arise from want of food [3]—a conclusion which, as Dickens said of the workhouse Board, could
not have been arrived at by people of merely common
intelligence ; but that the prisoners desired to eat more fat
than the dietary afforded.   The truth is that the system
struck a rough average as to how much could be endured
and how little could be eaten, so that nearly all were in a
state of perpetual hunger, and some were very nearly
starved to death.

But while a state of semi-starvation (allowing for a
certain amount of bulimia, morbid appetites, etc.), was
quite the normal condition of the mass of the prisoners,
Chatham had been particularly inhuman in all respects.[4]
The remedy employed there for candle eating was to
place each one in a sort of wooden measuring-box,[5] and
if the candle vanished too fast, the convict had to stay
in the dark until his turn came for another.   But the
military martinet who was then governor possessed at
least one virtue amidst his crimes—he was so very frank
and outspoken.   The average prisoner, if he were sane
and moderately wise, knew better than to make complaints
to the authorities, for they had little chance of any
impartial hearing, and were very likely to be termed
frivolous, and therefore to entail fresh punishment.   But
the half-mad and weak-minded were generally full of real
or self-imagined grievances ; they were continually breaking the rules—and in a place where almost everything
seemed to be expressly prohibited, this was not difficult—

[1] *Royal Commission of* 1879, p. 355.
[2] *Ibid.* p. 680.
[3] *Ibid.* p. xxxviii.
[4] See *Committee of* 1895 ; Evidence, pp. 330, 571.
[5] *Commission of* 1879, p. 622.

and must have had an awful time of it, for they were being
continually punished for the sake of the " discipline." [1]
　To appeal to most governors appears to have been both
useless and decidedly dangerous for the appellant ; but the
Major put the case with bluntness that rather astonished
the official committee. " I always show the prisoner,"
he said, " that I take the warder's part,[1] but if I am at
all doubtful about the matter, I only admonish the
prisoner." The word of a warder, he admitted, was absolutely decisive in every case ; it was not this circumstance,
however, but only the major's manner of stating it, that
seems to have been unusual. The Governor of Strangeways
Prison, examined before the Committee of 1894–5, gave
it as his opinion that whenever a prisoner brought a
complaint before the visiting justices, he usually received
punishment under all circumstances.[1]
　But the practical impossibility of obtaining redress for
anything may be realized from the statement of a former
inspector of prisons, that he had invited complaints from
some 5,000 prisoners every month for fifteen years, and
though hearing many petitions, he has left us this record :
" I cannot call to mind a single case of well-founded complaint of ill-usage of any of the gaol officials." [1] Thus
we see that out of no less than 900,000 possible cases
(5,000 × 12 × 15), necessarily involving a large number
of officers, who were presumably not all quite admirable,
no single complaint was held to have been well-founded.
Hum !
　There was another grievance which, repellent as it is
to discuss, yet caused too much unspeakable distress to
be quite passed over. In the earlier cells there used
to be a complete system of sanitation ; but later on, the
closets were all removed, partly on the ground of health,
but also because the drain-pipes sometimes occasioned
the awful prison sin of " communicating." The change
was approved by the commissioners in 1870,[1] and in
certain ways it was good, because it took the men out of
their cells. But it is horrible to find that very often

[1] See, for instance, evidence of Capt. Harris : *Com. of* 1879, p. 675.
[2] *Royal Commission of* 1879, p. 630.
[3] *Committee of* 1895, p. 260.
[4] Arthur Griffiths, *Secrets of the Prison-House*, p. 452.
[5] *Report* 1870, paragraph 29.

they were *not* let out ; [1] even the placid commissioners who sat in 1878-9 drew special attention to this monstrous evil, and thought that there was real cause of complaint.[2] At night the state of things became even worse ; [3] some Governors and certain prison Doctors had ordered that the cell utensils should not be used without special leave, on pain of report and probable punishment ! Thus, from locking-up time, 6.30 at the latest, to 5 a.m. an action of the bowels became an offence,[4] and no prisoner could be let out of his cell till unlocking time in the morning, for the warder on night duty had no key. At one prison the function was allowed once a day ; [5] at another there was an appointed hour.[6] The pretext given for these inconceivable prohibitions was that the prisoners often tried to annoy their neighbours and the officials by making use of certain vessels at night ; but this story is rebutted by other prison authorities.[7] When we remember the reported difficulties of the convicts in finding opportunities during the daytime, we can perhaps understand the degree of suffering and sickness, fear and punishment, that such a monstrous forbidding of the natural needs must have entailed upon the inmates of the cells.[8]

[1] *Royal Commission of 1879*, vol. ii. p. 341.
[2] *R. C.* 1879, *Report*, p. xliv.
[3] *Royal Commission of 1879*, vol. ii. p. 146.
[4] *Ibid.* p. 178.
[5] *R.C.* 1879 ; Colvill's evidence.
[6] *Ibid* : Question 1726 in vol. ii.
[7] See *R. C.* 1879, Evidence, vol. iii. pp. 817, 877.
[8] See also the more recent criticism by Oscar Wilde : " The Case of Warder Martin," written in 1897 and given in *De Profundis*, p. 179. London, 1908.

CHAPTER XII

THE SILENT SYSTEM

Just as about fifteen years intervened between the Commission of 1863 and that of 1879, so there was destined to be a somewhat similar interval between the latter and the last Commission, which sat in 1895.

The first two never for a moment seem to have remembered that they had to determine the fearful afterfate of men and women ! The brotherhood of man and the great all-embracing fatherhood of God were notions which lay dead within their hearts ; and the elegant terms " criminal sewage " and " human refuse " expressed their attitude towards the fallen. The last Commission was composed of different men, and throughout acted altogether in another spirit. At last a really independent body was granted powers to survey the system, which had been spared so long because its secret working was not open to the world ; and many of its recommendations were made law by the new Act of 1898, which marks at once an end, and a beginning of the long-withholden dawn of better days.

Beyond doubt during the last decade or so, that is, up to 1898, the penal machinery had been rendered more and more severe. Every screw was tightened, every time-discovered crack, through which, perchance, a little stray illegal light had penetrated, was very soon stopped up by some new red-tape rule.[1]

There was a brisk revival of that very old " contamination " craze which had before produced the horrible cell-prisons in America, and given us the so-called " model system " here.

About 1877 [2] even the Sunday conversation at

[1] For instance, " To leave one's bed and pace the cell at night is a breach of discipline."—J. S. Balfour, *My Prison Life*, p. 44.
[2] *R. C.* 1879, pp. 165, 435.   *D. C.* 1895, p. 341

exercise was stopped for all male prisoners, and the Dantesque walk round ring paths and in single file was introduced instead.

People outside the wall, who know nothing of prison ways, will with difficulty realise to the full extent the misery this monstrous prohibition inflicted for some twenty doleful years. The House of Commons, where they talk too much, never really weighed and thoughtfully considered what it must cost to penalize a precious human faculty. Indeed, one of " Our trusty and well beloved," mentally looking down through the inverted glasses of officialdom upon the lower orders, expressed surprise when a convict witness asserted that he would prefer to have the company of any human creature with a soul and shape, to trotting round and round a ring all by himself ! It was this same sapient legislator who imagined that those who had been many times convicted and held for lengthy periods in bondage would scarcely care, or ultimately notice, whether they were in or out of prison.[1]

This cutting off of all communication, although of course it fell with very different effects upon various natures—the lowest and the more debased always suffering least—came as a cruel hardship to the prisoners. Not so much, doubtless, to those in the local prisons, where the sentences were comparatively short (the outside limit being two years,[2] a period which has been generally condemned),[3] as the men passed nearly twenty-three hours out of the twenty-four within their cells.[4] But in the convict prisons the least term was five years (three after 1891),[5] and the unfortunate creatures, debarred from human influence for long stretches of time, strove hard, especially upon the public works, to snatch exemption from this ghastly regulation.

There is no doubt that they did succeed in breaking the rule more or less, especially when under a lenient and good-tempered warder ; it is probable also that the enforced secrecy of the unlawful conversations promoted

[1] R. C. 1879, p. 188.
[2] R. C. 1863, Report, p. 75.
[3] D. C. 1895, p. 331 (Capt. W.).
[4] Ibid. p. 304 (Dr. L.).
R. C. 1879, p. 78 (Capt. H.).
[5] D. C. 1895, p. 228 (Col. G.).

a good deal of coarse and undesirable whispering. But most certainly a huge number of prison punishments continually arose from this barbarous ukase; the hungry were deprived of their scanty food, and those already captives were shut up close in isolated cells, prisons within the prison !

The speech-ban placed an appalling power in the warders' hands, and that it was sometimes abused appears to be too certain, for in every considerable body of men there will be found those who are hasty, those who are bad-tempered, and those who must be spiteful and malicious. Woe then to the prisoner who ever, rightly or wrongly, had once incurred this sort of warder's hatred, or who happened to be placed under a bully's charge! That special sin, attempting to communicate, stood ready like a loaded stick within the warder's grasp; against his word there could be no defence, and the prisoner's abject position had been vividly portrayed by the late invalid lady " E. Livingston Prescott " (Miss Edith Spicer-Jay) in her book *Scarlet and Steel*.

Bad men there have no doubt been in the prison service, indeed the villainy and cruelty of some of them would be impossible to surpass and not easy to equal anywhere, in prison or outside. At the same time, a warder's life was an extremely trying one, the hours were exceedingly long, the surroundings depressing and dreary, and there must often have smouldered in the minds of the more thoughtful and discerning officers a feeling of revolt and detestation against that huge remorseless mill of man, which ground so slowly and so small, and left but wreckage, broken hearts and tears !

Moreover, besides the sullen, the desperate, and the half-mad, there were always a certain number of admittedly weak-minded prisoners, classed under what had become a very common formula as being deficient of intellect but not insane. It has been granted on all hands that these poor creatures were not as the others were, and it is said that they were sometimes encouraged and set on by other convicts of the vilest sort,[1] so as to be deliberately brought into collision with the ruling power.

[1] R. C. 1879, *Report*, p. xliii.

And sure enough the military martinets, following their
habitual methods of indiscriminate brutality,[1] duly
punished the weak-minded ones for the sake of example ;[2]
those who became more demented, used to be sent to
Millbank and retained there under observation sometimes for three or four months without any employment.[3]
Mr. Hepworth Dixon gives a short account of where they
were sometimes placed.[4] " The dark cells at Millbank,"
he wrote, " are fearful places . . . You descend about
twenty steps from the ground-floor into a very dark
passage . . . on one side of which the cells, small, dark,
ill-ventilated, and doubly barred, are ranged. . . . On a
former visit to Millbank some months ago, I was told
there was a person in one of these cells. ' He is touched,
poor fellow,' said the warder, ' in his intellect. . . .' They
put him in darkness to enlighten his understanding . . .
he was frightened with his solitude and howled fearfully.'
I shall never forget his wail as we passed the door of his
horrid dungeon. The tones were quite unearthly and
caused an involuntary shudder."
    It is only fair to state that these black cells were given
up about 1876.[5]
    But there still remained a number of prisoners who
were not considered mad enough to be sent away, who
were perpetually in hot water, and who gave the officials
a great deal of annoyance. Some of these unhappy
creatures were almost always under punishment, and
their previous condition became worse and worse from
semi-starvation under long-continued bread-and-water
diet and a variety of other torments.[6] Many were, or
became in time, perfectly mad (the case is mentioned of
a prisoner being made to wear a protective skull-cap of
iron to save the head from being dashed against the
wall !),[7] and some were no doubt very troublesome.

---

[1] R. C. 1879, Report, p. xliii.
[2] Ibid., Evidence, p. 243.
[3] Ibid., Report, p. xlii.
[4] Dixon, London Prisons, p. 143.
[5] R. C. 1879, Report, p. xlviii.
[6] Ibid., p. 126.
[7] Millbank, p. 207. Driven to frenzy by the solitary cells, prisoners
would often " break out " and destroy everything around them, for
which they were placed in jackets of canvas. One man at Millbank
tore the very nails off his toes. See Griffiths, p. 388.

But, all things considered, we shall generally find that the individual officers were far less cruel than the law. A great number of warders have often done their best to be humane in the face of that relentless and immovable machine in which they all were but as wheels. I have heard of many acts of care and kindness on the part of people in whom one would little expect ever to find them, and I am glad to know that even within the shadow of a prison there still lie hidden springs of charity which regulations do not always dry !

We may naturally wonder why the superior officers in the prison service, and especially the chaplains, made in the course of years little effective effort in the cause of humanity and reform. But it must be remembered that they were very much in the position of junior officers under a hard and self-willed colonel ; their protests, even if made, would probably be ignored, their reports could with the greatest ease be expurgated or suppressed ; pay and promotion rested absolutely with the ruling ring, which could not be defied.

The governors and deputy governors were appointed by the Prisons Board,[1] and all the other officers, including chaplains and doctors, appear to have been chosen by the Chairman at his absolute discretion.[2] There was practically neither examination nor outside control ; the central authority could select any military or naval man to be a governor, and any clergyman or surgeon to act in those capacities.

Naturally, the management chose its own friends ; naturally again, those friends would be very unwilling to oppose the system planned out by their chief. And so it came to pass that all these went their way, and acquiesced ; performing their dreary duties and retiring, or dying, highly respected ; while men went mad or drooped and died around them, and many humble homes were rendered desolate !

But at least one prison chaplain did his duty, choosing that better part which has a higher and more urgent mandate than the commission of an earthly king. For many years the Rev. Dr. W. D. Morrison [3] assailed the

---

[1] *R. C.* 1879, p. 248.   [2] *D. C.* 1895, p. 356.
[3] Now Rector of St. Marylebone Parish Church.

cruel and senseless prison machinery which callous and amateur legislators had devised, and then entrusted to more amateurs, to put in motion. Largely to his exertions we owe the appointment of Mr. Herbert Gladstone's committee by Mr. Asquith ; largely to that committee we owe Sir M. W. Ridley's Bill of 1898.

And now we have embarked on a new road, which will lead us a long way on.

CHAPTER XIII

THE VISITATION OF THE SICK

In all that dreary world within the wall there was one man to whom the prisoners might go for consolation, and that man was the Chaplain. But he too was an official appointed like the rest, he too was constantly surrounded by the familiar sight of systematic suffering, and had in the nature of things long since grown entirely accustomed to it.

The Rev. Dr. Morrison [1] drew special attention to the danger of the hardening effect of this on any nature ; and to expect the real and unfeigned heart-sympathy (suffering with !) from a seasoned prison chaplain would be like looking for emotion in an undertaker over an ordinary client's funeral.

The medical student generally faints on witnessing his first bad operation, but he cannot go on fainting ! Soon all personal compassion will surely pass away and he will become absorbed with scientific interest. We all must follow that merciful law—which has been said to reach even the prisoners after about six years [2]—by which we grow acclimatized to our surroundings in the course of time.[3]

No man, however conscientious, can go through the same salaried duties, month after month and year after year, without becoming more or less professional, and drifting to some extent into a set routine. But, apart from what was unavoidable under the system, which

[1] D. C. 1895, p. 118.
[2] DuCane, *Punishment and Prevention of Crime*, p. 7.
[3] " It is to be observed," says General Sir Charles Napier, " that when men are charged with the infliction of any punishment (no matter how revolting it may be in its nature) they generally become desirous of adding to its severity ; their minds grow hardened to seeing such punishments inflicted, and they erroneously believe that the bodies of their fellow creatures grow equally indurated."—*Military Law*, p. 146.

made the clergy prison officials holding permanent appointments, actual conditions rendered the chaplain of very little value towards the consolation of his closely-tethered flock, even supposing that he was always really worthy of his calling. For he was practically unapproachable. In the small local prisons he generally increased his stipend by taking duty in the adjacent town ; in the larger gaols the chaplain, with one assistant, might have to look after a passing population averaging about a thousand prisoners ; [1] ten or eleven thousand thus drifting through the establishment in the course of a single year.[2]

Consequently the captives in their separate cells could hold but little personal communication with the prison priest. This is clearly admitted in various reports the clergy have made out. For instance, we find the chaplain at one large prison explaining that, having eight hundred men to supervise, it was extremely difficult to visit them all, but still he tried to see each of them once a month.[3] Another chaplain somewhat similarly situated expresses the same intention, and adds that the schoolmaster has also paid a monthly visit of ten minutes to each prisoner.[4] At the public works the convicts saw even less of the chaplain, and many had to go from one year's end to another without a solitary visit from him.[5]

Even in a recent report the chaplain at a convict prison tells us that he endeavoured to see each man twice in the course of the year, but found that with the pressure of his many other duties it could not be managed.[6] But if the prisoners saw nothing of their chaplain as a man, they appear to have had a great deal too much of him in the light of a preacher.[7]

For years together—while lads developed into manhood

[1] R. C. 1879, p. 264.
[2] D. C. 1895, p. 122.
[3] R. C. 1879, p. 436.
[4] Ibid. p. 496.
[5] D. C. 1895, p. 297.
Five Years' Penal Servitude, ch. ii. London, 1882.
[6] Report, 1901, p. 562.
[7] See also H. J. B. Montgomery, Nineteenth Century, Feb. 1904 ; Adolf Beck, Evening News, August 11, 1904; and Harold Begbie, Broken Earthenware.

and adult convicts became bowed and grey— the same clergyman would drone forth the unchanging chapel service ; and through the period of prayer, as at all other times, armed warders would be ever watching lest any head should turn, or lest some miserable convict might convey by whispered word or secret signal some sign or greeting to a fellow prisoner, or send some human, meaning-laden message that was not stamped upon official forms !

The Christian Church has long since given up its ancient claim to right of sanctuary, and seems somehow to be no longer able really to forgive. It is not easy to restore the erring, or, in the midst of wide dishonesty, to rehabilitate the weaker few who have been once found out.

Over the prison service the evil spirit of punishment hung always heavy like a pall ; and the black blur of the broad arrow, the wrathful talon-mark of the avenging State, is deeply stamped upon those books which elsewhere bear the cross.

There remained one real oasis in the great whitewashed desert of negations forming the penal system ; and that was the infirmary, which has been well termed the gaol paradise. To gain admission there—even though, in those days, it entailed a lower number of obtainable remission-marks—all manner of desperate devices were continually resorted to. Irritating coloured matter, such as bits of wool or stitches from a garment, were often introduced beneath the skin to set up artificial sores. Powdered glass was sometimes swallowed, so as to bring on blood spitting ; and not only would the convicts maim and horribly mutilate themselves in all manner of ghastly ways (one poor creature once sewed up his lips and eyelids with needle and thread),[1] but it is stated that men would often inflict grave injuries on fellow prisoners upon the latter's urgent supplication ! [2]

From what we have already seen of the spirit regulating prison matters in the nineteenth century, we shall not surely be surprised to find that the oasis was not looked upon with favour by the grim governing powers. In Charles Reade's day the infirmary was the " spot in the

[1] Griffiths, *Secrets of the Prison-House*, p. 195.
[2] *D. C.* 1895, p. 326.

sun," a blemish to the perfect—cell! The Commission of 1879 reported that at that time some prisons were having separate infirmary cells built,[1] so that, except in very special cases, even the sick and dying should be left alone!

"By this means," said the Commissioners, "convicts are cut off from opportunities of communicating with each other, which are liable to be much abused. This improvement should be extended to all prisons!"[2] One of this select body—it was that same legislator who in 1878 imagined out of some comfortable inner consciousness that the many-times-convicted prisoners must have become indifferent to pain and punishment—even asked if *all* the sick in hospital might not be kept alone! And although this truly infamous idea—worthy of crass and heartless ignorance of human needs and feelings— was not carried out in its entirety, a good many separate hospital cells were no doubt subsequently built and occupied. The author of *Five Years' Penal Servitude*[3] says just a passing word about these dreary cells, into which he once peeped through fastened iron gates, wherein the invalids were isolated, locked and left. But even when the prisoners were not in single cells the fear of some extraordinary contamination would seem to have been ever haunting the official mind—at least if the sad scene described some few years back by an eminent Queen's Counsel and M.P. may be considered as a fair example. The food and raiment Mr. Richards considered to be satisfactory, but he wrote that he felt "for one poor dying prisoner who lay in his bed alongside a less sick companion, with a warder on guard to prevent any speech—a punishment which surely is greater than any crime deserves."[4]

Whatever may have been the circumstances surrounding the case just alluded to, it is quite clear that even the conversation of those prisoners who were seriously ill—and only such would be passed into the infirmary by the suspicious, ever-watchful prison surgeon—was held to be

---

[1] See also *Punishment and Prevention of Crime*, p. 161.
[2] *R. C.* 1879, *Report*, p. xliv.
[3] Ch. ii.
[4] *The Sun*, Sept. 5, 1896.

corrupting in its influence, a view which to my mind [1]
stands as a vile and unjust slander against human nature, [2]
monstrous in theory and unwarranted by facts.

And yet this veritable blasphemy against the soul still
has effect in some parts of the world. I was once visiting
a Continental prison in the year 19— : it was much like
ours used to be—so clean, bare of all dirt as of all sympathy, a whited sepulchre ; and the sick were alone in
cells. One of them was an old man whose face was
puckered with weeping. " Cheer up," said the Chaplain,
a particularly healthy-looking man with a fat red face ;
" it's not so bad after all ! " And the old man lay in
bed mumbling, as I looked into his eyes to show him that
I was at least a stranger and not a prison official ; he
had been there over eighteen months, and was to be
out again in six weeks (many in that dreary place were
not to leave their cells for as many years), but the chaplain
told me that they believed that his mind was giving way. I
told them what *I* thought of their System—but not exactly
in the way I should have liked to bring truths home !

Although, as I have said previously, the individuals
working the penal system of any land are mostly better
than the State which they serve, yet there are men who
seem to grow hardened by their horrible employment.
(I am told that many of the kindlier prison people throw
up their posts and take to more human work.) One
such case is mentioned by Major Griffiths. There was
a hospital warder of the old school, who is described as
having been " tied and bound to red tape, ever insisting
upon the punctilious observance of the rules for tidiness.
Woe to the patient, however ill, who allowed his bed-
clothes to be untidy, or failed to arrange his sheet in a
perfectly straight line under his chin ! " [2] He must be

---

[1] See Dostoevsky, *Souvenirs de la Maison des Morts*. Paris, 1886.
F. Scougal, *Scenes from a Silent World*. Edinburgh, 1889.
" The only really humanising influence in prison is the influence
of the prisoners."—Oscar Wilde, *De Profundis*, p. 181.
" All the vices of the old gaol system are nothing compared with
the diabolical effects of solitude on a heart smarting with daily wrongs."
It is Never too Late to Mend, chap. xii.
" . . . Our model and modern penitentiaries being a hundred times
more corrupting than the dungeons of the middle ages."—P. Kropotkin,
Paroles d'un Révolté, p. 243. Paris, 1885.
[2] *Fifty Years of Public Service*, p. 179.

long dead now, and will torment nobody any more. I remember, a few years back, an inquest upon a soldier who had been committed for trial and had died of pneumonia. The jury added a rider saying that the wards ought to be made more comfortable for unconvicted prisoners. Only the unconvicted? Surely there can be few such monstrous crimes in all the records of this world of woe, as firing on the wounded or as punishing the sick.[1]

[1] I was rejoiced to read in the *Report of the Prison Commissioners* for 1906, that the opaque glass was being removed from out of the windows of the convict prison hospital: but imagine the minds of the " old gang " who put it in!

CHAPTER XIV

MONOTONY

> "But neither milk-white rose nor red
>   May bloom in prison air;
> The shard, the pebble and the flint
>   Are what they give us there;
> For flowers have been known to heal
>   A common man's despair."
>
> *The Ballad of Reading Gaol.*

BUSY people, full of health and action, have sometimes gone over a convict prison, noted the clean cells and the well-kept corridors, and have then compared the place to a very dull country house! You must not make things too comfortable, is a very common observation; and off go the critics through the kaleidoscopic scenes of life's great ever-shifting pageant with just a faint sort of impression of having had a glimpse of everlasting Sunday! But these kind of comments only emphasize once more the unfortunate fact that sympathy depends upon the power of imagination. It is this same want of insight and of understanding that draws forth laughter at the lunatic, and childish glee before the pain-imparted antics of performing animals.

Monotony: the free world lightly uses words that only slaves can feel. "There are elements in the agony of life," wrote a prison visitor of many years' experience, "as it is meted out to the inmates of a prison which have no place in the sorrows, cruel as they often are, of the poor and helpless without its walls." [1] Such terms as "dull" and "uncomfortable" may be applicable to the occupied and the free, under their various circumstances, but they are shallow sounds to express what prison means to all but the most brutalized; we might

---

[1] *Scenes from a Silent World*, p. x.

as reasonably talk about the "discomfort" of cancer,
or of the dullness of the grave !

Those bright and breezy birds-of-passage visitors who
talked about the "dull country house" would have
noted the grey-clad arrow-spotted groups at work in
sullen silence. Did they at all realize that every one of
the scarecrow figures that may have shuffled shyly by,
or been halted like a beast, or put face to the wall like
an ill-managed school kid, had been consigned there
for at least three years (five, before 1891), and that not
a few were surely doomed to that most dreary place for
ten, fifteen, even for twenty years ? Did they remember
that some of the prisoners they saw before them, from the
stern stress of all-etiolating time, would never more be
free to walk the earth, or look again in liberty upon those
faces they had loved and known ? But besides these
long-apportioned periods there yet remained one sentence
in which no remission marks could be obtained, and to
which no definite extent had been assigned by law ;
that was the term for Life. A long while ago such cases
used to come up for consideration at the end of a dozen
years ; but this was later reckoned as too short an interval of time by busy and ambitious men in power, and
outside![1] The Commission of 1879 discovered, and of
course approved, that at that time life sentences were not
again brought under examination till after no less than
twenty years had come and died away.

Even this doom did not appear to be sufficient punishment to "Our trusty and well beloved," who would
willingly have introduced those hideous sentences of
actual lifelong penal servitude which are unhappily in
force in certain foreign countries to-day. Our country
stands free from this reproach, and a life sentence generally
means in practice about twenty years. And although
there still remain too many fatal illnesses and deaths
which take place in the course of unremitted years in
convict prisons, sentences are now looked over (though
not necessarily altered) at the end of every five years.[2]

Monotony : that is the harmless-looking word, which,
with that other one, accumulation, means so much in

---

[1] *R. C.* 1879, *Report,* p. xxxiii.
[2] On the highest authority.

prison life.[1] Yet there is nothing so hard to bring home
to the multitudes outside the wall, for they have never
known it ! Some time ago a brilliant journalist and
war correspondent went over a gaol, and wrote that a
plain man who sees the warm, airy, light (*sic*), clean cells
of a British prison, is apt to ask himself wherein, but for
the necessary loss of liberty, the hardship of imprisonment
consists.[2] This sounds very like the tale of the Irishman
who is said to have observed, after an accident, that it
was not the fall which had injured him but the sudden
stop at the end of it ! The writer, who had led a very
active, strenuous, successful life, did not pause to realize
what was expressed the other day by a first-class prisoner
who had served three months (which is not a long sentence,
and first-class prisoners are very well treated) : " You
have nothing to think of, nothing to begin, nothing to
finish all day long. It was very wearying. . . ." [3]
So terrible is prolonged Negation that the panic Commission of 1863 recommended that certain special isolated
cells should be constructed in the convict prisons, so that
men should no longer have to be brought to London for
trial (as was then the custom) for prison offences, because
" The journey is considered a relief from the monotony
of prison life and takes off much of the fear of being
remanded to separate imprisonment." [4] What need we
further to reveal what penal servitude has meant than
this official statement that so unendurable was the existence, that being taken to be flogged was yet considered
a relief ! But there are thousands of well-meaning
people who recoil from the red suppurating furrows of
the obvious cat, and who are shocked at the idea of
chains, who seem entirely unable to realize the meaning
of a mind torture ! Yet I believe that the latter is in
reality far worse, and men who ought to know have said
so too. The late Dr. Guy of the Prison Service, whom
no one familiar with his evidence would suspect of
humane sentiments—being of course familiar with all
the ordinary prison punishments, such as the black cell

[1] See *Never Too Late to Mend*, ch. xviii.
[2] See *Humane Review*, April 1902.
[3] A speech by Earl Russell.
[4] *R. C.* 1863, *Report*, p. 44.

and long-continued bread-and-water, etc., which were
enforced with merciless severity in those evil days—has
said, "I wish to express my deliberate opinion, and I
have no objection to anybody knowing it, that flogging
[which he advocated for both sexes] is the most merciful
punishment we have." [1]

Again, Colonel Baker of the Salvation Army tells us
that he found that some prisoners "would rather go to
the lash than into solitary confinement," [2] from which
they would often beg upon their knees to be let off ; and
when the present writer was in an Australian prison the
Governor told him that one rather troublesome convict,
whom he had placed by himself to keep him away from
the rest, had petitioned that he might receive a flogging
if only he might then rejoin them !

So much do prison punishments, like many other things,
differ from what they seem !

The chasm which gaped between the free without, and
the condemned of that contracted world within the wall,
was year-long wide and generation deep. All that
might reach the prisoners over the gulf would be the
three-monthly visit of half an hour (always supposing
distance and expense permitted) or the quarterly and
much-inspected letter—if these rare privileges were not
to be forfeited for some prison offence. And while the
great distance at which the convict prisons were situated
from the Metropolis and the Midland towns, etc., made
it frequently impossible for poor people to reach them,
no token or photograph of either relatives or friends was
at that time allowed to be placed in the cell. In fact, no
touch of nature ever might intrude into that artificial
whitewashed hell the cruel State had made.

It is curious also to note that *any* outside visitors were
looked upon as being evil influences, and consequently to
be kept away from the prisoners as carefully as the worst
criminals. No vivisectors could more object to the
intrusion of the public into their operating sheds than the
officials did to the entry within the gates of anybody
whatsoever not belonging to the sworn prison service.
" There is a great deal of sentiment in some people, and

[1] R. C. 1863, *Report*, p. 247.
[2] D. C. 1895, p. 279.

they, as visitors, might overdo their duty," [1] said an inspector of prisons who is now dead, and whom I gather to have been a man of kindly feelings. And yet it is just this divine " sentiment " which is the only hope of reformation and stands the holiest possession of all our suffering humanity ! The effect of being long shut up is felt even by the picked and iron-nerved sailors who have to man and tend the lone-rock lighthouses. I have read that it has been found absolutely necessary to give them long and fairly frequent spells of work on the mainland. Yet they have surely nothing on their minds ; they have companionship, pay, and tobacco, and are surrounded by the ever-changing open sky and sea. But the prisoner is shut up without any solace, beset by racking thoughts of sorrow and shame, sealed fast in a little cell which " differs from every other sort of apartment designed for human habitation, in that all view of external nature, such as might soothe and possibly elevate the mind, is with elaborate care excluded." [2]

The ground-glass windows, here alluded to, were mentioned before the Commission of 1878,[3] and are among the many horrible " improvements " of the nineteenth century. I am sorry to learn that they have been introduced to some extent into the new French prisons also, but they are absolutely indefensible.

The plea of security which was advanced about twenty years ago is no justification, as we shall perceive when we remember that clear glass is used to confine the largest snakes, and also to guard ships' portholes from the beating of the waves. I am glad to know that this malignant piece of cruelty does not meet with the approval of the present executive, and that blind windows will be removed and altered as soon as circumstances will permit of it. The cell has not infrequently been eulogised on various grounds by people who have never tenanted one ! Fortunately the late chief of the Detective Department, Sir Robert Anderson, whom we have just quoted, once had occasion to cause himself to be locked up for a few hours

---

[1] See article by J. M. Price, *English Illustrated Magazine* (1893–4), p. 1225.
[2] Sir Robert Anderson, *Nineteenth Century*, March, 1902.
[3] *R. C.* 1879, p. 190.

with a political offender, and he has left us his impressions of that time. " I seemed," he wrote, " to be in a pit. There was no want of air, and yet I felt smothered. My nerves would not have long stood the strain of it." He was not a convicted prisoner, he was not alone, his mission had been successful ; " and notwithstanding all this I suffered from a feeling of depression which deepened as time went on, and which in my case would ultimately have become unbearable." [1]

The foregoing account affords a striking illustration of the cell's terrible influence upon a prisoner of nervous temperament. And as modern punishments have been mostly mental, they have always fallen heavily upon those who had a mind that could be worked upon. The combined effects of solitude, brutalizing labour, and general starvation of body and mind, have been set forth by one who had no small share in framing the English system. " To men of any intelligence," he wrote, " it is irritating and debasing to the mental faculties : to those already of a low type of intelligence it is too comfortable a state of mind, out of which it is most desirable that they should be raised." [2]

It is sometimes put forward that prisoners are a people apart, with neither nerves nor feelings ; and that, consequently, no harm comes to them : a very comfortable arm-chair argument, by no means new in the long course of history.

But in actual fact, almost every variety of human being may be found within a prison ; though, as the main-stream of criminality consists of offences against property, the grip of the law is not felt by the governing and respectable classes as it is among the struggling and inarticulate.

Again, from the nature of things, prisoners always constitute but an extremely small minority in the midst of the whole healthy community : it has been reckoned that, in England, about 1 person in every 1,764 forfeits his or her liberty, while only 1 in every 10,000 persons is kept in penal servitude. [3] For these reasons, and

[1] *Nineteenth Century*, March 1902.
[2] *The Punishment and Prevention of Crime*, p. 175.
[3] *Report by the Chairman of the Commissioners of Prisons*, 1899. Appendix A, p. 26.

because the prisoners have been potentially a voiceless, voteless multitude, they have all along been grievously misjudged and wronged. Small minorities have seldom had fair treatment in a democratic land, and the weak and ill-equipped are nearly always abused everywhere; hence huge neglect and the hiding away of difficulties, ignorance almost beyond redemption by a doubt, and all its consequences.

The long-sentence man of popular imagination still remains represented by Bill Sikes; and people picture the wife-beating and garrotting sort of ruffian. But though of course the lowest types are to be found in penal servitude, I should like to point out that the long sentences are seldom passed upon the sort of man whose cruelty makes home a hell, and women and children tremble at his savagery. Unless he throws a lighted lamp or commits some special act of violence which ends in the actual death of the victim, and brings him to his right place, which in many such cases really seems to me to be the gallows, he is let off with terms which are expressed in weeks, if not indeed with fines. Speaking generally, the long " stretches " appear to be reserved for (1) the more or less medical cases involving ungovernable assaults of various kinds; (2) the continued repetition of offences often not very heinous taken by themselves, but which incur accumulating consequences; (3) serious offences against property, for which there is less excuse, since they are often deliberate, and will occasion widespread misery and dislocation—but which are seldom committed by people of low mental type, and often require no small amount of perverse ingenuity to carry through.

Amongst all those contained in the great body of people confined in local prisons, have been, and are, a number of nervous, emotional, often well-meaning, but unbalanced prisoners, upon whom the cell and the discipline soon told with murderous effect.[1] The rate of insanity was terribly high, and in the midst of conflicting and misleading estimates [2] and much " explained," euphemized facts,[3] we can at least assume that either

---

[1] See Evidence before the Departmental Committee of 1895.
[2] *Insanity in Prison*, by Bernard Molloy, M.P. London, Reeves.
[3] Rev. W. D. Morrison, in *Fortnightly Review*.

a great number of prisoners were previously mad, and therefore not proper subjects for punishment of any sort, or else that they went mad within the gaols. Much the same may be said of the extraordinary precautions that were taken against suicide. For though I do not think that self-destruction is, *per se*, any evidence of insanity in certain circumstances,[1] yet its extensive prevalence argues either mental derangement or a terrible distress of mind.

While the number of actual suicides has all along been inconsiderable, the attempts at self-destruction—which in the bad old days were always classed as "feigned" when unsuccessful, and often as "unintentional" even where death ensued—were very much more numerous. The suicide rate is said to have fallen somewhat towards the latter days of the old régime, but the insanity rate flew up meanwhile, and the decrease has been attributed[2] to nothing else than more elaborate precautions having been taken on the part of the authorities.

Prisoners have always been continually searched and watched in every possible way to prevent them from secreting anything about their persons, which they would very often try to do; and in 1895 wire netting was carefully placed along the corridors of some fifty prisons, lest men should try to dash themselves upon the stones beneath. In fact, so minute were the precautions taken against suicide that the real wonder is that it could ever be successfully accomplished.

In this world we shall never know how many perished by the prison system in all that guilt-stained nineteenth century. Deaths were so easily tabulated; madness could always be accounted for. Far from being set down to the system, it was mostly classed among the ordinary sequelæ of earlier criminal tendencies. In 1894 no single case of insanity was attributed to imprisonment—by the selected surgeons.[3] Even certain physical excesses occasioned largely by the solitary cell, and tenfold aggravated in their consequences by semi-starvation, were held up by a governor who must now be dead, in

---

[1] See, for instance, Dr. Strahan's thoughtful work on this subject.
[2] See *Evidence before the D. C.* 1895, p. 104.
[3] *Report,* 1894, p. 89.

his shocking evidence before the Commission of 1878, not as showing the monstrous and maddening conditions then prevailing in the prisons, but as indicating individual vice.[1]

In 1896 the country, which had been disturbed by the exposures in the *Daily Chronicle* some two years before, was startled and amazed at the condition of the Irish " politicals " who were about that time released from prison.[2] Their liberation was stated on the highest authority to have been absolutely necessary on medical grounds; and some of them came out in that crushed and pitiable condition in which so many prisoners have been returned to freedom. One, I believe, has permanently lost his reason, and is still confined in an American asylum. But the most remarkable feature in the case is the fact that they were released after all! " . . . What is the natural inference ? " wrote the *Westminster Gazette* : " why, that their case is typical of the whole prison system, and that there are probably hundreds of men convicted for other crimes in the same condition. . . ."

" I may tell you," said an inspector of prisons, now (1902) holding a very high appointment, " that there is nothing so unequal as the punishment of imprisonment, and nothing can be so unequal. . . . An educated gentleman commits an offence against the law. . . . The treatment which that man receives, and which the law lays down shall be the same for all convicted prisoners, is to him a million times more punishment than it is to an habitual criminal. . . . It is too dreadful to contemplate." And then, official-like, he added, " But I fail to see how you can alter it."[3]

Colonel Baker of the Salvation Army, when examined before the Committee which sat in 1894, said in his evidence : " As to convicts on discharge, I should like to say that we find a great number of them incapable of pursuing any ordinary occupation. They are mentally weak and wasted, requiring careful treatment for months after they have been received by us. In several cases they are men who are only fit to be sent off home or to a hospital."[4]

[1] *R. C.* 1879, p. 178.
[2] September 1896.
[3] *D. C.* 1895, p. 222.
[4] *D. C.* 1895, Ev. p. 279.

Mr. Thomas Holmes, in that grand " human " book, which feels like the saving grip from the hand of a strong man, says of a certain newly-returned convict: " His eyes betrayed him, his high cheek-bones and hollow cheeks betrayed him . . . but most of all his voice betrayed him. How he talked ! There was no stopping, he ran on and on ; and though I wanted to tell him much, I had to sit and listen to his queer voice as the words came tumbling over each other. . . . But he begged to be allowed to hear his own voice once more—he had had no one to talk to for a period of years." [1]

But the effects of the cell upon the nervous and the young was not by any means confined to convict prisons.

In 1895 a lad named C. H. F., aged eighteen, was sent to serve two months in Wandsworth Gaol. He was reported twice, and punished on seven occasions, for prison offences. And he never got through those two months, for having a wounded hand he unwound the bandage and hanged himself to the detestable crank, which was still in use at that time, and was fixed inside his cell. A pathetic case of the same sort occurred in 1898. On September 8,[2] C. R., an emotional nervous lad of only seventeen—and God help such within a modern prison !—was sentenced to twelve months' hard labour. Taken to Wormwood Scrubs, he became depressed and cried for his mother.[3] Two days after admission he was found in his cell again crying, bleeding from a wound in his head, supposed to have been caused by his having knocked himself against the wall. He was then taken to the infirmary and placed by himself in an observation cell. When a warder did look in, the boy was found in a half-sitting posture, hanging by a large handkerchief at the foot of his bed, and one more broken spirit had been released by that great warrant which respects no rule. This case exemplifies the worst side of our prisons as they stood before the operation of the Asquith-Ridley

---

[1] *Pictures and Problems from London Police Courts*, ch. ix.
A morbid, sickening sort of indifference distempers the long-punished convict. Though liberated at last, the objects round him have lost their hue—life itself is without relish.—Dr. James Ross, *Essay on Prison Discipline*, p. 12.
[2] See *Daily Telegraph*, Oct. 1, 1898.
[3] Mr. Davitt's letter in *Daily Chronicle*.

Bill of 1898, and too much of which remains even to-day.

A hand on that boy's shoulder would have saved him. One touch of nature, the pity and solace of any other human spirit of man or woman, would perhaps have restored him afterwards to his mother, reformed and chastened. But they gave him only the bare walls and the blurred windows, and barred out all the earth and the expanse of heaven, till He who moveth beneath all foundations stood near and set him free.

I do not like to think of such a scene ; there are some things which so astound our judgment that we can only feel that they must rest with God, and leave all there

These are but isolated cases that I happen to have come across in connection with a good many years' work on prison subjects; they are but typical of the greater mass of misery, living and dead, which prisons have occasioned. Major White, who was one of the Raid prisoners, wrote after his release : " It is no exaggeration to say that very few nights were spent in prison without our hearing the sobbing of children who were passing many hours in the gloom and confinement of the prison cell." [1]

We do not realize the misery of Nothingness until we go apart and think, or suffer it ourselves. The day which breaks out of the east upon the million-moving world is all so full ; we do not recognise how many subtle sounds are merged and blended to make up our so-called silences. A " Lady Deadlock " dreads the demon of boredom ; I remember in a recent play " Mrs. Daventry " spoke of the days coming up as enemies to be lived down somehow ; yet only prisoners know real monotony.

How we all try to kill time, even in the very midst of life and social happiness ! I have seen men reading while having their hair cut ; taking bundles of papers for a journey measured by hours in the midst of passing scenery. I have been on the great ocean for days and days out of sight of shore and shipping ; and we were all very glad to touch a port again, though games and a hundred other

---

[1] Hon. Robert White, *Nineteenth Century*, August 1897.
On this subject see also *Daily Chronicle* and *Westminster Gazette*, May 28, 1897.

pleasant things, besides unlimited companionship, filled up the spaces between land and land.

Nature is mostly kinder than we know, and many lives that now appear so hard have many mitigations ; often quite unperceived and unappreciated till they are removed. There are few spots upon the great round globe that are not sometimes sanctified by tears of human sympathy. I have seen people in the wards of hospitals made bright and happy in the midst of pain, drawn together by their common need.

And in the times of heavy stress and storm, most men possess (but yet, alas, not *all*, for some seem so self-centred as to have no souls, and move upright but spiritually dead) the safe and precious harbours of their homes, as refuges against the rough winds of the world, and feel a few will always stand fast friends.

But unto those who dwell apart within the walls—the most distressed—comes neither break nor balm. Each memory bears its own load of sorrow, even as the west wind weeps in rain ; and home, the refuge of the wanderer, becomes perhaps the saddest thought of all. The heart withers in sombre silence, the brain broods in dull despair ; even the eyes can find no sight of rest, but only rectilineal angles of the hard, forbidding buildings, high walls of yellow brick (as though the very clay were driven to jaundice from its horrible employment), or llnes of grim and frowning granite. And so the long years break, like waves upon the rough unyielding rocks, and the prison gate appears never to open, so long as the living tomb retains its own !

And then, maybe, after a generation, steals forth a shadow that was once a man ; to find that while he stood in decaying stillness the world had somehow moved and slipped beyond him. Parents are dead, and friends scattered and gone ; landmarks have shifted; he has now no place. It is Peter Kraus, it is Rip van Winkle in actual life. And the forlorn creature creeps like an unshriven soul, avoided and homeless.

For him rest, pardon, and salvation can be attained only beyond the grave.

CHAPTER XV

THE CONVENTIONAL VIEW

To vilify and distort the image of the thing we fear or hate has been an ancient and most precious prejudice extending through all times and populations. Thus, to our forefathers in the Middle Ages, the " Devil " was represented to be black or red in colour, while among savage races " he " is just as frequently conceived as being white; in either case, sufficiently human to be popularly execrated, and sufficiently apart and monstrous to make acute appeal to the imagination. The fallacies of the ages have clung close around that great and apotheosized offender—for instance that most mischievous idea of the innate attractiveness of evil, and " his " perverse delight in its pursuit.

Built on the model of the deity of Darkness, we find the villain of the novels and plays, in which either the authors have not followed human nature's strange and many-motived workings,[1] or, as is much more probable, they have exaggerated for effect and contrast. Thus the conventional villain is of course utterly bad, loves sin for sweet sin's sake with fine disinterestedness, and is consigned to utter damnation, to the intense and very natural satisfaction of the indignant audience, and the great credit of the play or story.

Next to what we may call the petty devil of the melodrama stands out the " Criminal " of popular imagination, who is largely the creation of people who generalised without knowledge and imagined without thought; and he is almost as much a scarecrow of the fancy as was

---

[1] " The good are not so good as they think themselves ; the wicked are not so bad as the good think them."—Mandell Creighton, Bishop of London.

that other most unpleasant individual the " Economic Man." This quite imaginary sort of person, one who should or would go about always contriving crimes and villanies, if he were not " deterred " therefrom by the terrific penalties that were attached to them, all the grim working of which was to be kept before him by their infliction on detected people. And every crimson tragedy the Law set forth, and every consignment of its captives, though to a doom far worse than death itself, was always justified upon its day of doing, by one well-worn, all-extenuating plea : that though such sights were sad yet they were salutary, because " the criminal " was then looking on, and he would slink away and be deterred.[1]

Doubtless, at first sight, it would appear as though he ought to be : prisons had been made hard as they could be made, our forefathers had no wish but to make them so, and had gone in for everything—the lash, thick chains, and solitude, worst of all ; and they had killed, maddened and broken down bodies and minds with the weight of torments. But they had never prevented the repetition of crimes ; they had not deterred ; even to Port Arthur and to Norfolk Island, many prisoners were sent back after fresh convictions.[2]

How came this ?   Why was the criminal moth, although maimed and singed, continually drawn back to the penal candle, often to perish miserably against the flame ? Because he was drawn back by the force of circumstances ; because in most of the cases his will was weak and the force was strong, and he could not help it. No one will deny that the punishments decreed, and possibly awaiting, were dreaded beyond expression, but they had (evidently) been established on crude false theories by

---

[1] The statute 8 Eliz. c. iv. sets forth that while the crowds stood watching the executions, the pickpockets were busy at robbing people under the very gallows-posts ; and it proceeded to deprive them of all benefit of clergy.

[2] Notwithstanding the severity of the punishment at the penal settlements, offenders are not infrequently sent a second time to Norfolk Island or Port Arthur.—*Vide Report of* 1838, p. xxii.   Prisoners were frequently recommitted to Port Arthur in spite of its being " constantly exhibited as a place of profound misery ; it carried the vengeance of the law to the utmost limits of human endurance."—John West. *Hist. Tas.*, ii. 244.

Et vide C. H. Hopwood, *A Plea for Mercy to Offenders.* London, 1894. " Appellant," *Crimes and Punishments*, Romilly Society.

men who did not know (or care) about human nature, and so, when dealing with living people, they did not work. And what of " The Criminal," the real man (or woman), with all his most complex ties and tendencies ; the living victim of deterrence fallacies ? Why, he gambled in chances, trusted to luck, to charms, to pieces of coal, horseshoes, or even relics ; through which he hoped to escape detection (and then there would, of course, be no unpleasant penalties to consider), and seldom bothered much about consequences (they were too dreadful possibilities to reflect upon ; they were the anticipations of suffering, they were the thoughts to drown in a good long drink !), or all the frightful penalties the State might inflict on him ; until he felt the handcuffs on his wrists, or lay awake remanded in his prison cell ; then it was too late.

So much for our survey of the theoretical (and if we are right, of the actual) position. It will also be found that the importance of punishment is far more insisted upon by those who have never looked into the matter seriously (or any other : I remember hearing some blood-thirsty sentiments from a newly-married woman at a big dinner party as she sat toying with her recent rings) than by those persons who have dealt with facts. " The criminal," says the Select Committee in its *Report* of 1838 (p. xxxiii), " only dreads punishment and is acted upon by it, when he sees the lash at hand and suspended over his head ; and prospective punishment has no effect in deterring from the immediate gratification of his desires when exposed to temptation." [1]

Even the " Panic " Commission of the year 1863 stated in its *Report*, p. 23, that " The number of crimes committed . . . is probably less affected by the system of punishment which may be in use than by various other circumstances, such as the greater or lesser welfare of the population," and the demand for work, etc., etc.[2]

When Major Arthur Griffiths, for many years a Governor and afterwards an Inspector of prisons, was examined

[1] De non apparentibus et non existentibus eadem est ratio. " A convict will sell for a pint of spirits the necessaries which should serve him for months."—Evidence: *Historical Records of N.S.W.*, vol. i. part ii. p. 556.
[2] See also Rylands, *Crime*. Appendix II.

before the Commission which sat in 1878–9, his verdict was that " Anything like punishment does not, as a rule, prevent their (the prisoners') committing themselves again when they go out " (Evidence, p. 271). Asked upon what ground he based a punishment at all, he replied, " Simply to keep them out of harm's way and to prevent them as long as possible from committing depredations upon the public." " But," expostulated Lord Kimberley, who was in the chair, " we must have some general principle upon which to base our system of punishment." And so they still adhered to the old rough, ready, erroneous one, and Parliament has continued to muddle along upon its false and cruel premises.[1]

Let us now turn to the evidence given before a very different sort of Committee, which was appointed by Mr. Asquith when he was Home Secretary in the year 1894. Major Knox, then Governor of Leeds Prison, gave his opinion, saying, " I do not think that a man who is going to commit a theft or a burglary looks to the sentence a bit." [2] (If this be so in the case of such deliberate crimes, how far will any sentence be kept in mind in the case of impulsive acts ?) Captain H. K. Wilson (an Inspector of Prisons), also examined, was asked by Mr. Herbert Gladstone : " In fact, then, do you think any sentence is more or less useless except for the purpose of keeping him [the criminal] away from doing harm ? " To which the reply was : " You keep him away—that is all." [3]

Lastly, Mr. H. M. Boies, a man of many years' experience as a prison officer in America, sums up the results of what he has seen, in the affirmation that Scientific Penology proclaims it as a law " that the fear of punishment does not restrain crime." [4]

This, then, is the verdict of all these representative prison officials, whose sympathies would certainly have been in favour of ascribing the best results to the huge institutions over which they presided. They had yet

[1] Whiteway, *Penal Science*, p. 48.
[2] *Departmental Committee of* 1895, Evidence, p. 265.
[3] *Ibid*. Evidence, p. 332.
[4] *The Science of Penology*, p. 77, New York, Putnams, 1901.
" . . . il est connu que la peur de la punition n'a jamais arrêté un seul assassin."—P. Kropotkin, *Paroles d'un Révolté*, p. 242.

to admit, with Holtzendorff, that, in so far as deterrence went, the prison systems had indeed made shipwreck. Belief in " luck " and " chance," in fact, the gambling spirit generally, is very strong and deep in human nature. Vainly will Andrew Carnegie affirm that, according to all the teachings of experience, the gamester who counts on Fortune shall perish poor (for the Jay Goulds of the world have been men of great, if misdirected, mental power who knew their game). Thousands of fools who could not pass in ordinary mathematics will invent " systems " which shall break the bank, and all the while the tables make their vast and steady profits for the various casinos, year after year. Also, to any one who watches current events, it is clear that the multitude is largely composed of weak, uneducated, foolish people. The newspapers are filled with advertisements proclaiming " competitions," percentages, and all sorts of bargains which every business man knows must be fraudulent or impossible. But the best bait to capture human gulls with, is to pretend to give them some unheard-of advantage and to appear to be making a sacrifice ; and these wild statements must bring in clients or they would not be paid for.

The fortune tellers, living and automatic, do a brisk trade, and there are also pernicious pseudo-medical quacks who make a monstrous living out of the shame and ignorance of their victims, who fear to consult a qualified practitioner. How many scatter-brained citizens are really about, may well be sampled from the post office returns. In 1900 there were no less than 2,767 letters containing valuables posted without any address. From these undelivered epistles the authorities took £136 in notes and money, and as much as £9,628 in other securities. And yet the State, having these thousands of haphazard people to deal with (and surely the criminals will be likely to be among the most unbalanced of all), pays them the somewhat cruel compliment of assuming in them the power of sober forethought, and of estimating more or less problematical consequences and pains.

So judges and magistrates, with serious faces, mete out so many months for this offence, so many lashes for that, and so many years' penal servitude for the other, as if offences and punishments were really commensurable,[1] and almost as if prospective offenders might ponder the penalties or look them up like stations printed in the A.B.C. Now in reality the Law can never excite more than a vague, fog-looming, distant terror in the average mind. The dull dark wall of prison *may* lie ahead—a submerged rock before the drifting, rudderless ship on its tragic course. Something sharp and ruinous, expressed in months ; something long-drawn and dreadful, expressed, but yet unrealized, in terms of years, *may* be in store. The actual or prospective offender will seldom be able to appreciate more than that, if he thinks thus far. And neither he *nor any one else* can tell what sentence will be dealt out for a given offence ; it will depend entirely on the judge, perhaps on how his lordship feels that day ; in fact nobody knows. Somewhere near, you may say ? Not at all : if sentences were blindly drawn out of a bag full of numbered tickets, there would not be much greater uncertainty, and perhaps often not much greater injustice.[2]

The inequality of sentences has furnished innumerable columns of adverse press-criticism—often, I fear, prompted merely by political motives—and I shall only select a few instances out of my case books, in which, for a good many years, I have been sorting and collecting evidence. About 1886 one George O., a boy of sixteen (or just seventeen), was convicted of the very serious offence of trying to obtain money by menaces, and he was sent away to penal servitude for life. I cannot conceive a crime which will be more universally condemned, but he was so very young ; think of it—an infant in the eye of the Law, and a schoolboy still under his mother's care in the sight of common sense, getting the doom which one does not like to read of as being passed upon adult and desperate criminals. There was some hostile comment at the time, but such " small " matters are soon forgotten, the fatal door had quietly closed, and there was no appeal, except for matters of money, then.

[1] Cf. Edward Carpenter, *Prisons*, p. 12.
[2] For the varying penalties prescribed by the laws of different American States for similar offences see Griffith J. Griffith, *Crime and Criminals*. Los Angeles, 1910.

Some ten years later a similar case occurred. The prisoner was about the same age, his crime was a still bolder variety of the same offence, and had he been more moderate in his terms, the blackmailed person would, as the evidence showed, undoubtedly have paid up, and kept discreet silence, as well-placed people generally do in these sort of circumstances. But it fell out that young J. D. was prosecuted and convicted, and he got twenty— years you might anticipate, after the earlier sentence passed by that judge, who was sometimes alluded to as the " English Torquemada "—no, twenty *months*, on account of his youth, and the newspapers the next morning called *that* a tough sentence. Two other notorious trials occur to me as I write, though I can only relate these from memory. In the West of England, a good many years ago, a certain man was taken by two others to be a poacher—which he was not—and was forthwith pursued and quite illegally chased by them on the Queen's highway. Being apparently a very nervous individual, in a great state of alarm, and having a revolver upon him, he suddenly turned and shot the two men who were overtaking him. Although this was admittedly done in his own defence under the influence of an access of terror, he yet received a twenty years' sentence for manslaughter. A great outcry was raised at the time, and numerous petitions were signed by all sorts of people, including my father ; and the sentence was afterwards altered to one of eight months' imprisonment.

The other trial which I remember was for a murder upon the high seas. Their ship having gone down far away from land, part of the crew went off in an open boat, and were afterwards reduced to the last extremity for want of food and drinking-water. Omitting to cast lots for the needed victim, they slew a lad who was nearly dead from exhaustion, and (as has been described from life in Captain Marryat's stories) they proceeded to drink his blood.[1] The half-eaten body was found in the boat when the survivors were ultimately rescued and brought to land by a passing vessel. They were then tried

---

[1] Such terrible tragedies are well known, and are always liable to occur ; see for another instance J. H. Lefroy, *History of the Bermudas*, p. 65.

for the (legal) murder, though popular sympathy was largely extended to them on account of their having been actuated by such unendurable sufferings, and although formally convicted, it was expected that they would be immediately pardoned. However, as they had not drawn lots, the then Home Secretary only commuted the sentence to one of six months' imprisonment.

Another trial was cited by the late Lord Russell of Killowen as an example in severity, which I have in a case book. A woman had been convicted before the late Mr. Justice Manisty on a charge of stealing some blankets, and was sentenced by him to no less than twenty years' penal servitude ; the judge afterwards found that he had exceeded the legal maximum, and was compelled to reduce the sentence to fourteen years, although he expressed regret at having to take that course.[1] So far as one is in a position to determine, I believe that there were (*temp*. Ed. VII.) only two living judges who would have given the unfortunate woman as much as half that number of years for what she had done. So are lives and liberties tossed about in the machinery of the courts of justice.

Sentences, then, cannot be estimated beforehand, and are very often cruel and capricious in character. But this is not sufficient to explain why the hard facts of experience have all along confuted the old theories as to the possibility of deterring by punishment. For even if penalties could be made fixed and invariable for each proved offence, all circumstances being henceforth ignored, and if every schoolboy were taught to know what would be done to him for each kind of transgression, the current theory would still not stand, for it assumes the *certainty* of retribution. And every offender, in so far as he or she may be said to calculate at all, counts on not being caught. This fact it is which really nullifies the force and truth of the deterrence theory. If states could achieve the *certainty* of conviction, and could ensure the restitution of stolen property, I believe that all the crimes which can be deterred by anything (*i.e.* the deliberate, as distinct from the passionate) would be

[1] *Daily Chronicle*, March 21, 1900.

quite met by, say six months' imprisonment, and most likely by some lesser penalty.[1]

But as this certainty of conviction is absolutely impossible to arrive at, we shall not deter by terrible threats and occasional victim-making ;[2] and crime remains what it always was, " a statistical average ; a little less at times, a little more at others," as Hopwood said, depending upon all sorts of complicated causes, and disregarding the penal system almost as completely as accidents ignore the state of hospital accommodation.

The average offender always thinks he will escape, not as a result of any hard or laborious reasoning, but principally because he *hopes* he will, and because he has a sort of general idea—if he is an habitual criminal, a very practical and soothing experience—that a great number of people do remain uncaught and at liberty. For while he may know that the ill-starred Brown is going through a long and dreary sentence, away out of sight and, consequently, largely out of mind, he may take comfort in the fact that Jones and Robinson, and any number he may think besides, did the same things and yet continue to be very much at large. And when we come to look into the question, we shall find that the criminal has much more solid reason for the hope which is in him than most of us would readily suppose.

Murder, at any rate, is popularly imagined to be nearly always followed by most certain retribution.[3] But looking at the last available Report of the Metropolitan Police, we shall find that in the year 1900 there were sixteen *discovered* murders in London.[4] For these

---

[1] " Wilful acts are the only ones that can be prevented by the fear of punishment."—Archbishop Whately, *Thoughts on Secondary Punishment*, p. 26.

[2] The deterring power of punishment is undoubtedly subject to what is known in political economy as the Law of Diminishing Return, which is found to apply to the producing capacity of the soil, the speed attainable in ships, and many other matters which we have not time or space to discuss here.

[3] That able writer Mrs. Bradlaugh-Bonner worked out that a murderer has 9 chances to 1 that he will escape the death penalty, and (which is more important) 5 to 1 that he will escape punishment altogether.—*Humane Review*, July 1903, p. 133.

[4] For instance, in that same year 1900, open verdicts were returned in 2,396 inquests, the juries not being able to determine the causes of death. See *Judicial Statistics, England and Wales*, p. 19.

only eight persons were actually convicted, although it is only reasonable to add, that five assailants executed themselves, doubtless from fear and horror at what they had done and what was in store for them. But in the other cases (and in how many more that were never heard of !) no one was caught ; and figures for other years give somewhat similar results.

Much more pronounced are the statistics with regard to housebreaking,[1] for which in London the returns gave 1,416 cases and only 117 convictions, so that the ratio of crime to conviction stood about 12 to 1. I do not say that the conviction-rate is as low as that for the majority of offences ; but adding together the principal detected crimes (and these alone do we know about) for that average year in London, we get 18,088 cases and 9,429 convictions.[2] The proportion of prosecutions to known crimes in England was given at 77 per cent., ranging from below 50 to over 100.[3]

But figures are frequently made to prove or disprove almost anything, and do not always count for much till we know the bearings ;[4] in this instance, we may accept the words of the official report that they do not afford any index to the number of unpunished crimes,[5] or to the efficiency of the police action. The late Mr. Whiteway, in his excellent work,[6] held that from one-half to two-thirds of our criminals evade punishment, while from judicial statistics made in the 'seventies,'[7] Mr. Farrer placed the immunity for indictable offences at no less than 77 per cent.

Much the same state of things will prevail in other civilised countries[8] where social and economic conditions approximate to our own. " In the United States," says

[1] *Report of the Metropolitan Police for* 1900, p. 62.
[2] *Ibid.* p. 62.
[3] *Judicial Statistics, England and Wales, for* 1900, p. 16.
[4] The late Sir Wilfrid Lawson once gave an amusing illustration of this. It had been stated that at a certain station in India 50 per cent. of the teetotallers had died off. This was quite true in a way, but there happened to have been only two of them, and one of these two was picked up by a tiger.
[5] *Judicial Statistics*, p. 18.
[6] *Recent Object-Lessons in Penal Science*, pp. 47, 122.
[7] *Crimes and Punishments*, pp. 94, 100.
W. M. Gallichan in *Free Review*, vol. v. p. 142.
[8] See for instance Professor Ferri's *Criminal Sociology*.

Dr. Hall, "comparatively few men are executed or imprisoned for the many murders committed,[1] but the average citizen, not called upon to investigate closely, does not realize this. . . ." "The total number of convictions during 1899,"[2] says Mr. Boies, "was only 1 out of every 33·1 of the total arrests"; and again : scarcely 1 in 3 even of those arrested for serious crimes is convicted. We must bear in mind that all these figures relate to crimes which have been discovered. Many others, and an incalculable number of illegal acts, are never recorded, and find no column in the criminal tables of any country.

Offences such as infanticide [3] (and this I fear will very likely increase somewhat since incest was made a punishable offence by an Act passed in 1908 : the true remedy for this particular evil would have been to improve the housing accommodation, but to make a new crime was much cheaper, much easier), illegal operations,[4] and frauds upon insurance companies, etc., are no doubt committed with no small impunity ; and as to offences against current morality, in which there has been collusion and consent, the law becomes a veritable booby-trap merely to catch the foolish or unfortunate.

It seems evident, then, that punishment, although not actually a negligible quantity as a deterrent to deliberate crimes, has yet been greatly overrated in value. I shall endeavour to prove that it is not by any means the thought-out product of modern science, but is in reality a survival from savagery. To establish this we must go back to history.

[1] *Crime in its relation to Social Progress*, p. 19. Columbia University Press, 1902.
[2] *The Science of Penology*, pp. 75, 311.
[3] While engaged upon this chapter a case was reported in the press of a young woman who had been feeding her baby on ice cream, tinned salmon, and pickles. A great number of infants are overlain.
[4] Whilst Dr. C. was on his trial with respect to the death of Mrs.——, for which he received seven years' penal servitude, some correspondence came to light in which certain ladies declared that since the sudden removal of Dr. C. they had already "got another Man."

CHAPTER XVI

THE INSTINCT OF RETALIATION

PUNISHMENT OF THINGS, ANIMALS AND CORPSES

THROUGHOUT the records of the human race—of man, the victim of idealism, of him, the most irrational animal—we are continually beset by the degrading spectacle of people mentally and physically prostrate before some shapen image which they have set up. Almost anything will do : a bloated reptile shall receive children torn from a mother's arms or hurled by them in monstrous piety ; a stuffed figure, with which a farmer might scare away crows, and which a dealer in curiosities would hardly consider good enough to place in his window, may yet have human blood streaming before it, and be held up to dread and veneration. A time-worn tradition, a mere mythoplasm, some sanctified untruth ; such things have made whole communities miserable ; so low could sink the dormant minds of men. But why have such very mean and paltry objects ever received such worship all the world over ? Clearly this was not due to anything belonging to the carved and feathered idols themselves.

No, but they stood for the religious *instinct* of their places and periods. The votaries of the idols gave them their power through their belief ; they had, as it were, charged these grotesque " batteries," and they received back the current they had imparted, even to shocks resulting sometimes in death ; though it was all subjective —in their own minds.[1]

---

[1] Savages, says Sir Francis Galton, have been known to die at the very idea of having broken a Taboo. " The facts relating to taboo form a voluminous literature, the full effect of which cannot be covered by brief summaries. It shows how, in most parts of the world, acts which are apparently insignificant have been invested with an ideal import-ance, and how the doing of this or that has been followed by outlawry

Just as Idolatry derived its power from the Religious Instinct out of which it arose, so Punishment originated and grew out of the world-old instinct of Retaliation, and is instinctively retained for vengeance' sake.

" If there be one general law of life," says Guyau,[1] " it is the following : every animal (and we could extend the law even to vegetables) replies to an attack, by a defence which is itself often a repelling attack, a sort of answering shock : there is a primitive instinct which has its origin in a reflex movement, in the irritability of the living tissues, and without which life would be impossible : even animals deprived of their brains, do they not still endeavour to bite those who seize hold of them ? "

" The reflex instinct of defence," says Letourneau, " is the biological root of the ideas of law and justice, since it is evidently the basis of the first of laws, the law of retaliation."[2]

" The human being, like the animal," says Professor Hamon, " when struck, instinctively gives back blow for blow . . . the animal wounded by a stone or arrow seeks vengeance of the stone or arrow. It considers it responsible for its wound."[3]

Now Instinct is old while Reason is recent. Reason may go back thousands of years ; Instinct has millions of years behind it. So punishment, which is *cold* revenge, deferred or systematized, arising from instinct, is ancient and universal. And everywhere we find it existing, and all the various and conflicting reasons[4] which may be

or death, and how the mere terror of having unwittingly broken a taboo may suffice to kill the man who broke it."—*Sociological Papers*, vol. ii. p. 9. London, 1906. See also J. G. Frazer, *Psyche's Task*, p. 7. London, 1909.

[1] Quoted from the French by Dr. S. R. Steinmetz, in his *Ethnologische Studien zur ersten Entwicklung der Strafe*, p. 117. Leiden, 1894. J. M. Guyau has been translated into English by G. Kapteyn. London, 1898.

[2] *Evolution Juridique*, p. 10. Paris, 1885.

[3] " The Illusion of Free Will," *University Magazine*, vol. xi. London, 1899.

[4] I have alluded to some of the more complex ones that have been given, elsewhere ; but with respect to the more commonly accepted motives for punishing, Lord Justice Cherry has well observed : " The notion of an offence against the State is of entirely modern growth, and the theory that punishment is imposed for the sake of reforming the criminal and deterring others from following his example is even still more modern."—*Growth of Criminal Law in Ancient Communities*, p. 3. London, 1890.

assigned for it—when any are needed for a feeling so natural—are added on afterwards.[1]

But punishment, besides its antiquity and universality, shows further and stronger traces of its instinctive origin in that we find it resorted to and applied in ways and circumstances which serve no rational or objective purpose; in ways that could not, I should imagine, be defended as rational, by even the thickest-headed advocates of deterrence; in ways so manifestly childish and animistic that, I submit, we cannot account for them except as acts instinctive and concessory.

PUNISHMENT OF THINGS

Xerxes had made a floating bridge over the Hellespont; it was a narrow strait of sea, only about a mile in width, between Asia and Europe. But nevertheless a great storm shattered the work. " And when Xerxes heard of it he was deeply enraged and ordered that the Hellespont should be scourged with three hundred lashes and a pair of fetters thrown into it." [2]

True, this was animistic : seas and rivers were then Personalities; human qualities were imputed to them— the very words of the story indicate this. The scourgers were bidden by the furious king to address the strait in

[1] " In point of fact, nothing that can with any tolerable propriety assume the name of policy, not sober reason, not so much as reflection, appears at any time to have been an efficient cause of the use so abundantly made of it " [the death penalty, but we can say punishment]; " vengeance, passion, began the practice; prejudice, the result of habit, has persevered in it."—*Bentham to Lord Pelham*, p. 5.

" Penal law, like every other social phenomenon, is evolved according to the momentary exigencies of society; the evolution of an explaining theory always comes later and is dependent on the necessity of providing a satisfactory reason and a philosophic basis for that which was decided by the contingencies of the moment."—E. Lugaro, *Modern Problems in Psychiatry* (Orr & Rows's trans.), p. 281. Manchester, 1909.

" A very common phenomenon, and one very familiar to the student of history, is this. The customs, beliefs or needs of a primitive time establish a rule or a formula. In the course of centuries the custom, belief or necessity disappears, but the rule remains. The reason which gave rise to the rule has been forgotten, and ingenious minds set themselves to inquire how it is to be accounted for. Some ground of policy is thought of which seems to explain it and to reconcile it with the present state of things; and then the rule adapts itself to the new reasons which have been found for it, and enters on a new career."— O. W. Holmes, Jun., *The Common Law*, p. 5. London, 1882.

[2] Herodotus vii. 33, 34, 35.

these words : " Oh bitter water,[1] thy lord inflicts this punishment upon thee because thou hast wronged him although in no wise ever harmed by him." And the King, even Xerxes, will cross thee whether thou wilt or no, but to thee doth no man justly do sacrifice, for thou art a deceitful river of salt water."

But I think we may claim that this attempt at punishment was instinctive too.[2] The war-lord had been affronted and set at naught ; the notion of punishing was a relief to his feelings,[3] and though in those times it might have seemed reasonable to try and placate the seas and rivers with sacrifices, yet if the king had realized the futility of his orders, if he had seen his fetters swallowed up, and that the waves received his impotent strokes and moved no more than at the plashings of a shoal of young sardines, could any man deliberately have thought that he could do the waters injury ?

Cyrus must have derived somewhat more satisfaction [4] from diverting the river Gyndes into 360 channels. This tributary of the Tigris had drowned one of his sacred and precious white horses ; and though rivers—like the great human passions—cannot be stopped, he had at least the consolation of making it fordable.

The anger of the Sovereign, or State, often extended from the offender down to all his belongings.[5] So in the Decrees of Darius and of Nebuchadnezzar,[6] whosoever disobeyed was to be executed and was to have his homestead made into a dunghill.

Instincts are universal, although they may be manifested in many different forms ; and we are told of very

---

[1] *Ὦ πικρὸν ὕδωρ, δεσπότης τοι δίκην ἐπιτιθεῖ τήνδε, ὅτι μιν ἠδίκησας οὐδὲν πρὸς ἐκείνου ἄδικον παθόν.*—Herod. vii. 35.

[2] If any should doubt the existence of instinctive punishment, I would cite the almost universal fact that messengers who have brought *good* news are rewarded accordingly, whilst bearers of *evil* tidings, although equally loyal, have scarcely dared to enter a prince's presence—for instance Henry I. was told of the White Ship's loss by a weeping child. " The Devil damn thee black, thou cream-faced loon," is a typical attitude.

[3] Dr. Steinmetz has emphasised the immense importance of feeling in vengeance and punishment. See *Entwicklung der Strafe*, i. p. 361, etc., etc.

[4] Herodotus i. 189, 190.

[5] Ezra vi. 11.

[6] Daniel ii. 5, iii. 29.

similar decrees having been in force upon the continent of America in pre-Spanish times. Did a man seduce a Virgin of the Sun, then, " By the stern laws of the Incas she was to be buried alive,[1] her lover was to be strangled, and the town or village to which he belonged was to be razed to the ground and sowed with stones." This form of instinctive vengeance at one time formed part of the law of England.[2] If a layman had been convicted of a capital felony[3] the king had the right, " in detestation of the crime," to " prostrate the houses, to extirpate the gardens, to eradicate his woods, and to plough up the meadows of the felon, for saving whereof and *pro bono publico* the Lords of whom the lands were holden " (by the convict) " were contented to yield the lands to the King for a year and a day." " And therefore not only the Waste was justly omitted out of this chapter of Magna Charta,[4] but thereby it is enacted that after the year and day the land shall be rendered to the Lord of the fee, after which no Waste can be done."[5]

The original custom had been for the King to devastate the habitations of felons in a truly savage and primitive fashion. " But this custom tending greatly to the prejudice of the public, it was agreed in the reign of Henry the First in this kingdom, that the King should have the profit of the land for one year and a day in lieu of the destruction he was otherwise at liberty to commit."[6]

In later times the Crown used to claim Year-Day *and* Waste (17 Ed. II. c. 16), which many learned lawyers regarded as an encroachment on the royal prerogative. Blackstone, writing about the middle of the eighteenth

[1] W. H. Prescott, *History of the Conquest of Peru*, p. 53. London, 1878.

[2] J. Comyns, *Digest of the Laws of England*, vol. i. p. 378. London, 1762.

[3] Edward Coke, Second Part of the *Institutes*, cap. xxii. p. 38. London, 1669.

[4] *Vide* 9 Hen. III. c. 22. " We will not hold the lands of them that be convict of Felony, but one year and one day, and then those Lands shall be delivered to the Lords of the fee."

[5] Coke, *Second Inst.*, ch. xxii. p. 37. " The property was regarded as in some way under the King's ban, perhaps because it was regarded, like the deodand, as tainted with guilt."—Holdsworth, *Hist.* iii. p. 63.

[6] Blackstone's *Commentaries*, fifteenth Edition, bk. iv. p. 385. See also H. W. Challis, *Law of Real Property*, p. 30. London, 1885. Stephen, *Hist. Crim. Law*, i. p. 472. A. J. Horwood, *Year-Book of Edward I.*, 30–31, p. 538.

century, says, " This year, day and waste are now usually compounded for ; but otherwise they regularly belong to the crown, and after their expiration the land would have naturally descended to the heir, did not its feudal quality intercept such descent and give it by way of escheat to the Lord." Houses which had domiciled heretics were frequently broken up by the Inquisition,[1] and the abodes of offenders were sometimes pulled down in New England by the Puritan colonists in the seventeenth century.[2] At home, criminals' trees were pulled up in cases of perjury.[3] In Russia, in 1591, after a tumult arising from the death of the Czarewitch, who had been found fatally stabbed at Uglich, " many of the inhabitants were sent to Siberia, which was now beginning to be a convict settlement,[4] and thither also was sent the great bell of the town." The " Exile of Uglich " is said to have been first flogged[5] and deprived of its top ring, and remained in disgrace or neglect for three hundred years afterwards.

About the year 1685 the church bell at La Rochelle was also treated in a grotesquely animistic manner. " It was," says a contemporary historian, " the subject of a very singular comedy. It was whipped, as though to punish it for having assisted Heretics. It was buried and disinterred to show that it ought to be reborn on passing into the service of Catholics. To complete the farce of this rebirth, there came a lady of quality who undertook the office of midwife, and another whom they bestowed as nurse upon this newly-born infant. They questioned it. They compelled it to speak. They made it promise that it would never again return to the conventicle. It made *amende honorable*. Finally, it was reconciled, baptised, and bestowed upon the church which bears the name of St. Bartholomew."[6] Although the writer just quoted speaks of these strange proceedings

---

[1] Lea, *Hist. of the Inquisition in the Middle Ages*, i. p. 481. For an instance in Brussels see W. H. Prescott, *History of Philip II.*, vol. ii. p. 225. London, 1855.
[2] J. Winthrop, *History of New England*, p. 34.
[3] Besant, *Steuarts*, p. 345.
[4] W. R. Morfill, *Russia*, p. 92. London, 1904.
[5] *The Globe*, May 20, 1902.
[6] E. Benoit, *Histoire de l'édit de Nantes*. Tom. v. pp. 753, 754 (A.D. 1695).

in a surprised and evidently mocking vein, I fully imagine that the whole ritual was intended quite seriously at that time and place. Even in the twentieth century we still have the baptising of battleships, the blessing of the Neva, houses, etc. ; and also the reconsecration of churches where violent crimes or suicides have taken place within the walls or precincts of such edifices.

In ancient Greece [1] an object which killed a citizen was brought to trial at the Court of the Prytaneum, and if convicted,[2] cast beyond the borders. The introduction of this custom has been attributed to Draco, but Dr. Frazer observes that it was probably much older. " For such a custom based on the view that animals and things are endowed with a consciousness like that of man, goes back to the infancy of the human race." [3] The actions, as I think we have seen, were originally instinctive.

The same idea as to passing judgment upon things inanimate can be found nearer home, in the laws as to Deodands. Originally it appears to have been intended that whatsoever caused the death of a person should be delivered to the kinsmen of the deceased, as something they could be avenged upon.[4] The weapon,[5] or tool, or tree, might have been used

[1] Demosthenes, *Contra Aristocratem*, xxiii. 76.
[2] J. G. Frazer, *Pausanias*, vol. ii. p. 370. London, 1898. See also J. E. Harrison, *The Bouphonia* ; trial of the sacrificial axe or knife, which was condemned and thrown into the sea. *Prolegomena to the Study of Greek Religion*, p. 111. Cambridge, 1903.
[3] Pausanias ii. 371, and compare Plato, *Laws*, Bk. ix. c. xii.
[4] It was called the Bane, the slayer, and " In accordance with ancient ideas this bane, we take it, would have gone to the kinsmen of the slain ; the owner would have purchased his peace by the surrender of the noxal thing . . . In the past, they would have received the bane, not in compensation for the loss that they had suffered, but rather as an object upon which vengeance might be wreaked."—Pollock & Maitland, *H. E. L.* ii. 474.
" A consideration of the earliest instances will show, as might be expected, that vengeance, not compensation, and vengeance on the offending thing, was the original object."—Holmes, *Common Law*, p. 34.
" In England the inanimate murderer was to be given up to the kinsmen of the slain surely not as a compensation for the loss they had suffered, but as an object upon which their vengeance was to be wreaked. . . . It did not matter that its owner was innocent ; the punishment was not intended for him."—Westermarck, *Moral Ideas*, i. 263.
[5] Among many savages, " if a man was killed by a fall from a tree, his relatives would take their revenge by cutting the tree down and scattering it in chips."—Tylor, *Primitive Culture*, i. 286, ed. of 1903 ; and see Holmes, *C. L.*, p. 14.

ever so innocently, and have belonged to some absent person or the deceased himself,[1] yet *it* had done the mischief somehow or other, and had become at once the accursed thing, to be forthwith condemned and forfeited. As the State gradually superseded the kindred in the taking of vengeance,[2] the King, instead of the relatives, took the deodand ; it was wont to be sold, and the proceeds were then administered by the Church for some pious purpose,[3] often for securing services to be held for the dead man's soul. The old savage custom, in fact, came to be freshly interpreted. The deodand object had to be an active agent of Death.[4]

The age had outgrown the notion of taking vengeance upon a stone or tree that was stationary, but it was still sufficiently animistic to assume a kind of guilt and free will in unconscious things, and for a great lawyer, Coke, (1552–1634) to plead, in attempting to explain why a ship in *salt* water could not be deodand,[5] that " the ship or other vessel is subject to such dangers upon the raging waves in respect of the wind and tempest ; " implying that it was helpless and therefore exonerated. Stanford, J., also endeavoured to explain and justify the law as he found it, overlooking its origin, when he declared that, " If A killeth a man with the sword of B, the sword shall be forfeit to the King as a Deodand, because *movet ad mortem* and for default of safe keeping of the same by the owner."[6] Thus trying to make appear rational what had arisen instinctively. The law as to Deodands lingered on until the year 1846.[7]

PUNISHMENT OF ANIMALS

Since even inanimate things were once the objects of deliberate vengeance, much more would animals be

[1] " Even therefore when, as was commonly the case, the bane was a thing which belonged to the dead man, none the less it was deodand." Pollock & Maitland, *Hist.* ii. 474.

[2] Holmes, *Common Law*, p. 24.

[3] Sometimes the Justices in Eyre directed how the money derived from the sale of the deodand was to be spent.—P. & M., *Hist.* ii. 473.

[4] " Recte loquendo, res firma sicut domus vel arbor radicata quandoque non dant causam nec occasionem," etc.—Bracton, f. 136, b.

[5] Third Part of the *Institutes*, p. 58. London, 1680. Westermarck, *Moral Ideas*, i. p. 263, et seq.

[6] Quoted in Coke's *Third Inst.*, p. 58.

[7] Westermarck, *M. I.* i. 262.

certain to incur punishment.[1] By the Hebrew Law it was decreed that "If an ox gore a man or a woman that they die,[2] then the ox shall be surely stoned and his flesh shall not be eaten ; but the owner of the ox shall be quit." The animal having been punished, retribution was satisfied. The Laws of the Twelve Tables (B.C. 451) provided that if an animal had done damage,[3] either the animal was to be surrendered or the damage paid for.

In Plato's Laws,[4] if an animal killed a man, it was to be prosecuted for murder, and if found guilty, put to death and thrown beyond the borders. The main idea in dealing with an offending animal in the early periods,[5] was that the creature (or slave) should be surrendered to the person who had been injured, or if he had been killed should be delivered over to the vengeance of the relations. By certain Teutonic laws, half the usual Wer-geld,[6] or man-fine, was to be paid for an injury done by any domestic animal, and, for the other half, the beast would be handed over. We find the same injunction in Alfred's Laws : " If a neat wound a man let the neat be delivered up or compensated for."[7] And even as late as the sixteenth century, Sir Anthony Fitzherbert (1470–1538) could cite as a sound legal proposition the statement that " If my dog kills your sheep, and I immediately thereupon offer you the dog, you are without further claim against me."[8]

The primitive custom of the noxal surrender[9] of homi-

---

[1] "The animal had to suffer on account of the indignation it aroused." Westermarck, *Moral Ideas*, i. p. 257.

[2] Exodus xxi. 28.   [3] Holmes, *C. L.*, p. 8.

[4] *Laws*, ix. 12.   [5] Holmes, *C. L.*, pp. 17, 18.

[6] W. E. Wilda, *Strafrecht der Germanen*, p. 589. Halle, 1842. Holmes, *C. L.*, p. 17.

[7] *Laws of Alfred*, 24. See Thorpe, fol. ed. p. 35.

[8] *La Grande Abridgement* : " Barre ; " fol. 126. Sec. 290, Ed. of 1577. Noxal Surrender prevailed in Flanders up to the sixteenth century at least.

E. Jenks, *Law Quarterly Review*, vol. xix. p. 24 (January 1903).

[9] The fact that afterwards, in the later Middle Ages, this form of reprisal (*i.e.* giving up the wrong-doer to private avengers) " was in certain instances transformed into regular punishment, only implies that the principle according to which punishment succeeded vengeance in the case of human crime was, by way of analogy, extended to injuries committed by animals."—Westermarck, *Moral Ideas*, i. p. 256.

See also Hamon, " Illusion of Free Will," *University Magazine*, vol. xi London, 1899.—F. Puglia, *Evoluzione storica del Diritto*, Messina, 1882.

cides, etc., human and animal, was generally succeeded by legal vengeance carried out by the Courts, and, in a great number of instances, this was taken on animals. " On the continent of Europe down to a comparatively late period, the lower animals were in all respects considered amenable to the laws. Domestic animals were tried in the common criminal courts, and their punishment on conviction was death ; wild animals fell under the jurisdiction of the Ecclesiastical Courts, and their punishment was banishment and death by exorcism and excommunication. . . In every instance advocates were assigned to defend the animals, and the whole proceedings, trial, sentence, and execution, were conducted with all the strictest formalities of justice." [1]

They were,[2] from about the eleventh up to the eighteenth century,[3] placed in the penal mill just like human beings, and ground to pieces in its pitiless machinery.[4]

Understanding,[5] responsibility, malice prepense, and guilt, were fully imputed to the unreasoning creatures ; even speech on their part was not thought inconceivable, when they were brought into court as being the only available witnesses ;[6] their silence was construed

---

[1] Frazer, *Pausanias*, p. 371.

[2] Menabrea, *Soc. Roy. de Savoie*, xii. p. 401.

[3] The accused animals were kept in the ordinary prisons for human criminals.—E. P. Evans, *Punishment of Animals*, p. 142.

[4] Shakespeare, " who knew everything," alludes to the practice of punishing animals: see *Merchant of Venice*, Act. IV. Sc. i.

> " Thy currish spirit
> Govern'd a wolf, who, hanged for human slaughter,
> Even from the gallows did its fell soul fleet,
> And whilst thou lay'st in thy unhallowed dam
> Infused itself in thee ; for thy desires,
> Are wolfish, bloody, starved, and ravenous."

It is interesting to notice that a law of the Twelve Tables allowed a debtor, where there were several creditors, to be cut up in pieces and distributed amongst them (*vide* O. W. Holmes, *Common Law*, 14). If there were but a single creditor he might put the debtor to death or sell him as a slave. So that old Shylock's claim may not have been so whimsical as it would appear, though possibly out of date.

[5] " Das Thier wurde demnach als verbrecher ausgesehen. Es wurde ihm ein verbrecherischer Wille zugeschrieben."—Karl von Amira, *Thierstrafen*, p. 9. Innsbruck, 1891. See also Arthur Mangin, *L'Homme et la Bête*, p. 340. Paris, 1872.

[6] This idea presumably arose out of the then-believed legend of Balaam's ass ; at the same time, a demonstration on the part of, say, an intelligent house dog might afford valuable evidence.

as being to some extent favourable to the person suspected.[1] Accused animals are said to have been put to the torture [2]—doubtless on the principle of going through all the scenes of the usual criminal drama [3]—and their moans were then taken to be admissions of guilt. The ordinary penalty for any animal convicted was death ; often they would be strung up by their hind legs.[4] Occasionally they would receive a " poetic " punishment,[5] like the sow at Falaise, which, in the year 1386, was convicted of having bitten the face and leg of a child. She was dressed up in human clothing, and mutilated in the head and hind leg, before being hanged before the crowd in the market place. Amira alludes to an instance of a sentence of temporary imprisonment passed on a dog,[6] and strangely enough, I read in a modern newspaper [7] of a monkey having been given three months' solitary confinement in an animals' hospital to render it docile ; but this case had nothing to do with the criminal courts.

As might have been expected from what we found, animals were frequently involved in accusations of witchcraft and sorcery.[8] A typical example comes down

---

[1] R. Chambers, *Book of Days*, vol. i. p. 129.

[2] Mangin, *Homme et Bête*, p. 344.

[3] The common judicial tortures on the Continent varied somewhat in the different courts ; filling a person up with an enormous quantity of water, and thereby causing agonising cramp and compression of the internal organs, was a process very frequently employed. See for instance C. Berriat Saint-prix, *Tribunaux*. Paris, 1859.

[4] A sow was condemned at Savigny in 1457, " pour estre mise au dernier supplice et pendue par les pieds derrières à ung arbre."—Menabrea.

See also Evans, *Punishment of Animals*, p. 165.

[5] An engraving of this scene had been reproduced by Mangin, Carlo d'Addosio (" Bestie Delinquente ") and Evans. See also P. G. Langevin, *Recherches Historiques sur Falaise*, p. 146. Paris, 1814.

[6] *Thierstrafen*, p. 9.

[7] *Daily Mirror*. London, Nov. 22, 1907.

By the fifteenth-century laws of Sardinia, asses were condemned to lose one ear the first time they trespassed on a field not their master's, and their other ear for a second offence. See J. A. Farrer, *Crimes and Punishments*, p. 90. As to the trial of cattle by the Irish in the seventeenth century, as though they were human beings, and the alleged testing as to whether they might be able even to read, see Lecky's *Ireland in the Eighteenth Century*, vol. i. pp. 68, 69, footnotes. London, 1892.

[8] This is alluded to by the great Victor Hugo in his story of *Notre Dame*.

from Bâle, where in the year 1474 a cock was burnt upon the Kolenberg for having been accused and convicted of laying an egg.[1] These "cocks' eggs" were supposed to possess magical qualities.

Monsters,[2] such as the basilisk (cockatrice), were said to emerge from them,[3] and they were destroyed with great care.

Animals were also occasionally drawn into sexual offences by human beings which were then punished with hideous cruelty,[4] person and beast being often burnt or buried together.[5] So strong was the taboo placed upon all allusions to sexual aberrations that (in England) such cases were not to be tried before a judge in a court, even the hearing of them being forbidden.[6] And on the Continent the records were generally destroyed with the victims' bodies,[7] lest even the deeply

[1] J. Gross, *Kurtze Basler Chronick*, p. 120. Basel, 1624.
The cock was possibly an hermaphrodite or, more likely, a crowing hen (these are not very uncommon: I once possessed one. An old saying, well representing the common instinctive hatred of abnormality, used to run, "A whistling woman and a crowing hen are neither good for gods nor men).
Mr. Evans, p. 164, refers to the eighteenth-century experiments of Lapeyronie as showing that certain eggs were malformed through disease in the fowl, and often contained a small vermiform yolk, which may have given rise to the idea of a serpent.
See also S. Baring-Gould, *Curiosities of Olden Times*, p. 56.
[2] See interesting article in the *Penny Cyclopædia*, vol. vii. p. 310. London, 1837.
[3] These sort of popular misconceptions on physiological matters have many times been the cause of great cruelty. Thus among certain peoples a woman who gave birth to twins was considered for obvious, although quite erroneous reasons, to have been an adulterous wife. See Westermarck, *Moral Ideas*, i. p. 395, and R. Ligon, *Hist. of Barbadoes*, p. 47. London, 1657.
Monsters were (and in the country villages still are) thought to be born through the commission of bestiality; and perfectly innocent, though unfortunate mothers of malformed children, might become liable to their neighbours' suspicion and persecution.
[4] On one occasion, in 1585, the executioner cut off all four hoofs of a troublesome mule, before consigning it to the flames.—Mangin, p. 349.
[5] J. Döpler, *Theatrum Poenarum*, p. 574, *et seq.* Sonderhausen, 1693–97. Fleta, lib. i. c. 37.
A. Corre & P. Aubry, *Documents de Criminologie Retrospective*, p. 465. Lyons, 1895.
Among the Teutonic peoples in early periods, sorcerers, inverts and (sometimes) adulterers, might be burnt alive or smothered in marshes.
[6] See *Mirror*, ch. xiv: "The mortal sin of Laesa Majestas against the heavenly King," etc.
[7] "Car ils auraient souillé les archives des tribunaux."—Menabrea, p. 522. And see Evans, *Punishment of Animals*, p. 150.

blood-stained criminal torture-houses should in some way become contaminated by them. All through, the legal fiction of full responsibility was kept up. At Vanvres, in 1750, a she-ass was saved from a dreadful death by evidence of good character,[1] her master alone being sentenced for the offence. In the year 1457, at the trial of a sow with six little pigs, for killing a child, the sow was duly condemned for murder, but the piglets were acquitted on account of their youth and of the bad example set by their mother.[2]

I have not thought it needful to multiply instances, but the literature on the subject is very considerable, many of the authorities I have quoted giving a great number of references.[3]

The cursing of the mythical serpent in the Garden of Eden[4] furnished a precedent for future anathemas, and was accordingly followed both in isolated instances and with formal procedure. St. Bernard[5] denounced the flies which annoyed him when preaching at Foigny;[6] a Bishop of Trier rebuked the birds which were flying about the cathedral, and forbade future entrance upon pain of death; whilst St. Patrick and other saints banished reptiles, rats and leeches, etc., from different places.[7]

From time to time, however, the formal machinery of the Ecclesiastical Courts was set to work against the wild creatures, just as the penal processes of the criminal courts had been employed against the domestic animals. But with this difference, that while the animals which were individually charged with committing crimes incurred

---

[1] Evans, p. 150.
[2] Chambers' *Book of Days*, i. p. 128.
[3] Amongst books not already quoted are A. Chaboseau, *Procès contre les Animaux*. Emil Agnel, *Curiosités Judiciaires et Historiques*. Gaspard Bailly, *Traité des Monitoires, avec plaidoyer contre les Insects*. For further works see E. P. Evans' *Bibliography*.
[4] Genesis iii. 14.
[5] J. Eveillon, *Traité des Excommunications et Monitoires*, p. 520. Paris, 1672.
[6] Evans, p. 28.
[7] Baring Gould, *Curiosities*, pp. 59, 61, 62.
Evans, *Punishment of Animals*, pp. 29, 103.
Among the hills round the Mediterranean where I was brought up, it used to be believed by the peasants, that the processional caterpillars, which infest the wild pine trees, once preyed upon garden produce, until they were constrained by spiritual powers to take to the firs instead.

painful deaths and sometimes terrible torturings, the various species which were assailed with mere maledictions pursued their appointed ways and were apparently not even aware of them.

It was chiefly farmers' plagues,[1] such as rats and swarms of destructive insects of many kinds, against which the Church directed its fulminations.   It is clear, however, that the Bishops acted with caution and circumspection, not caring to risk disregard of their menaces. Pope Stephen V, when battling in the year 855 against an insect invasion,[2] offered rewards to the peasants for destroying the visitors, and subsequently had holy water sprinkled over the fields : practical efforts had to be resorted to first.   The Church was evidently reluctant to proceed to extremities against harvest pests ;[3] doubtless it had been taught by past experiences, that such conflicts were really against the mighty movements of nature, which knows no creeds, and it felt it must temporize.

But in times when the trees and the crops were being devoured, the villagers would turn in their great distress to the Church for help, and then the Ecclesiastical Courts would be set in motion.[4]   The proceedings resembled those which were taken when employed against heretics or moral offenders.   Three notices of the action had to be served, which if disregarded would establish contumacy.[5]

Summonses [6] were served by the officers of the court reading them at the places where the animals frequented, or leaving the notices near their holes ;[7] and

---

[1] Though individual animals might be exorcised, the devil was sometimes excommunicated while in the form of a beast.   See Baring Gould, *Curiosities*, p. 61.   Evans, p. 85.

[2] P. Lebrun, *Histoire Critique des Pratiques Superstitieuses*, tom. i. p. 244.   Amsterdam, 1733.

[3] Chambers, *Book of Days*, p. 127.

[4] *Vide* Evans, p. 95, etc.

[5] Ménabréa, p. 482.

[6] Chambers, p. 127.
Baring Gould, p. 60.

[7] Instinctive acts seem very similar all over the world ; thus Lord Avebury says : " The inhabitants of Lake Itasy are accustomed to make a yearly proclamation to the crocodiles, warning them that they will avenge the death of any of their friends by killing as many ' vaay ' in return, and warning the well-disposed crocodiles to keep out of the way, as they have no quarrel with them, but only with the evil-minded reptiles who have taken human life."—*Origin of Civilisation*, p. 282.
The same childish idea of confounding the *wish* to act with the *power*

plenty of time was accorded to rats, mice, locusts, caterpillars, or whatever the particular creatures then accused may have been, in which to appear. Naturally, they did not appear ; but able counsel were always assigned to them, who entered into elaborate forensic and more or less theological arguments on their part, besides raising all kinds of legal quibbles and quaint excuses for more delays,[1] which were usually granted them. The end generally was, that the plague abated, and the proceedings " ran into sand," as the Germans say. If not, then the curses went forth, and if the marauders vanished they were believed in, but if the creatures still lingered, it might well be alleged that the Devil was helping them, or that the people were being punished for their past sins.

It would appear that these spiritual penalties invoked on the lower animals, for fulfilling their instincts, were often demanded by popular clamour, and that they were disapproved of by numerous writers and clergy from the thirteenth to the seventeenth centuries.[2]

PUNISHMENT OF CORPSES

If men so tried to take revenge on what they hated, as to assail things and unreasoning animals, much more would they wreak vengeance on an enemy's body ; when living, if possible, by mutilation and torture ; and failing the living, then upon the dead. Maltreatment of the corpse of a fallen foe was just the ordinary instinctive

of accomplishing, finds expression in the letter which was addressed to the dead St. Martin and was laid on his tomb. See Hallam, *Middle Ages*, iii. 303.

A few years ago a little girl whom I know, addressed and sent a postcard to her dog, which I still possess. Innumerable letters were received at the Zoological Gardens for Jumbo the elephant, before he was taken away to America.

[1] Chambers, p. 127.

Evans, p. 95.

[2] See Philip de Beaumanoir (13th cent.) ; Leonard Vair (15th cent.) ; Martin of Arles and Pierre Ayrault (16th cent.) ; also, Cardinal Duperron and J. Eveillon (17th cent.), etc., etc.

Pierre le Brun is more critical of the criminal court, observing, " Mais il étoit ridicule que les officiaux prétendissent que leurs sentences juridiques devoient avoir le même effet sur les animaux que les paroles d'un Saint."—*Hist. Critique*, i. p. 249.

practice, universal in savage and in old-world warfare
generally. And this instinctive ferocity, when deferred
and elaborated, resulted in punishment. In the seventh
century before Christianity,[1] King Josiah dug up the
bones of priests of another creed and desecrated the rival
altars.[2]

In 506 B.C.[3] " Tse et Po p'i frappèrent de coups de
fouet le cadavre du Roi P'ing afin de donner vengeance
à leurs frères respectifs." Aristotle mentions a case of
sacrilege in which the bones of the guilty dead were dis-
entombed and cast beyond the borders of Attica.[4]

At Rome, about A.D. 898, Pope Stephen VI saw fit to
bring the body of his predecessor to trial.[5] The corpse
of Pope Formosus, then some months buried, was brought
before Pope Stephen and his council and placed, clad in
prelate's robes, in a chair of state. Having appointed
the corpse a deacon for counsel, they thus addressed it :
" Why didst thou, being bishop of Porto, prompted by
thy ambition, usurp the universal see of Rome ? " The
old man's body, like a monstrous doll, might nod and
bend while the attendants supported it, or collapse in a
ghastly bundle if they left it alone, but it made no sound ;
and the deacon would probably be wary in his defence,
for there were dark holes near by, other than sepulchres.
So they cut off its benedictory fingers and cast the corpse
into the yellow Tiber. After other adventures, it was
ultimately rehabilitated and put back in the tomb.

The corpse of King Manfred of Sicily [6] was also cast
out of that kingdom by order of the Archbishop of
Cosenea.

In 1126 the rebels having slain Enna, king of Leinster,[7]

---

[1] 2 Kings xxiii. 16.

[2] The ceremonial defilement of foreign sanctuaries may have been
the main object in that particular case, but the act was quoted as a
precedent before the Council of Constantinople held A.D. 553, when it
was desired to anathematize certain persons who had been dead for a
century ; the proposal was carried in spite of the opposition of Pope
Virgilius. Vide Lea, Hist. Inq., i. pp. 230, 231.

[3] E. Chavannes, Les Mémoires Historiques de Se-Ma Ts'ien, p. 23.
Paris, 1901.

[4] Westermarck, Moral Ideas, i. p. 46.

[5] A. Bower, History of the Popes, vol. v. p. 73. London, 1761.
Lea, Hist. Inq., i. p. 231.

[6] Oscar Browning, Guelphs and Ghibellines, p. 27.

[7] Dictionary of National Biography, art. "Macmurchada."

are said to have burned his body along with that of a dog, to show their contempt for him.

The bodies of criminals were not infrequently burned immediately after hanging,[1] and the ordinary penalty for treason in England was that the person convicted should be drawn feet foremost upon a hurdle to the place of execution,[2] where he was hanged from a noose to exhibit him as a felon, between heaven and earth as being worthy of neither.[3] He was promptly cut down and, whilst still living, mutilated, eviscerated, and had his heart cut out and thrown into a fire.[4] The head was then cut off and the body was quartered and carried away to be parboiled to preserve it ; afterwards the head and the members were distributed in different places and hung up to the public gaze.[5]

The Inquisition, when heretics had escaped its clutches while living, often proceeded against them though they were dead. There were many motives for this, since if the dead were condemned, their property would be seized upon by the State,[6] and the Church also got its share. Moreover, the sons and grandsons of heretics could not

---

[1] See for instance the case of that amazing sex-maniac and murderer, Gilles de Laval, Baron de Rais (or Retz), a marshal of France, whose crimes are believed to have been the origin of the legend of Bluebeard, and who was executed for heretical wickedness, after a trial before the Bishop of Nantes and the Vice-Inquisitor, October 26, 1440. *Vide* Michelet, *Hist. de France*, tom. v., and T. Wilson, *Bluebeard*, etc., etc.

See also an account of an eighteenth-century Puritan pogrom in Holland by Dr. von Römer in *Jahrbuch für sexuelle Zwischenstufen*, viii. Leipzig, Max Spohr, 1906.

[2] In the earliest times the victim was generally drawn by a horse upon the bare ground ; later, ox hides or sleighs were used, *Vide* Alfred Marks, *Tyburn Tree*, pp. 28, 90.

[3] Coke enters into an elaborate explanation in the Gunpowder Plot proceedings. See *State Trials*, ii. p. 184.

[4] See for instances *State Trials*, i. p. 1088, a case in 1570 ; same, vol. v. p. 1334, case in 1662.

[5] After the Monmouth rebellion " The pitch caldron was constantly boiling in the assize towns, and the heads and limbs preserved in it were distributed over the lovely western country, where, for years after, in spite of storms and crows and foxes, they frightened the village labourer as he passed to his cottage in the evening gloom."—Meiklejohn, *Hist.* ii. 157.

" The peasant who had consented to perform this hideous office afterwards returned to his plough. But a mark like that of Cain was upon him. He was known through his village by the horrible name of William Boilman."—Macaulay.

[6] Lea, *Hist. Inq.*, i. p. 507.
W. H. Prescott, *Ferdinand and Isabella*, i. p. 260. New York, 1845.

hold office except by special permission ;[1] so that none amongst whom there might be even traditions of heresy should hold place or power.

Also, the orthodox desired to free their cemeteries from what they would regard as contamination ; according to Dr. Lea, dead persons found guilty of offences,[2] involving imprisonment or some lighter punishment, would be merely dug up and cast out of church territory, whilst those whose misbelief had deserved the stake, were drawn —although but corpses or skeletons—through the streets, preceded by a trumpeter fore-announcing—" Who does so, shall perish so " ;[3] and were burned as objects accursed.

In this deliberate burning of mere remains we perceive the vengeful and instinctive nature of the proceedings. And this is made the more manifest when we find that suspected and accused persons who had contrived to flee, and were condemned in their absence for not appearing, were yet conveyed in effigy to the flames, the figures being dressed up in all the grotesque attire worn by the condemned.[4] These effigies often represented the dead in the great processions of the Autos da Fé, and carried their bones and dust in small chests. The names of the persons they represented were marked upon them, and they were borne aloft on poles in front of the prisoners, to be burned on the flaming pyres that were kindled for living men.

This practice of disinterring corpses was not by any means unknown in England :[5] in 1428 the bones of the preacher Wycliffe, who had died forty-five years before, were exhumed and burned ; in 1514 the body of Hunne was sent to the flames at Smithfield for heresy[6] ; and in 1532 the last act of the last free convocation of England[7] was to dig up and burn the bones of one Tracey,

[1] Lea, *Hist.* i. p. 499.
Nicolas Eymeric, *Directorium Inquisitorum* : Quaestio lxiii.
Prescott, *Ferdinand and Isabella*, i. 263.
Antonio Puigblanch, *Inquisition Unmasked*, vol. i. p. 281. London, 1816.
[2] *Hist. Inq.*, vol. i. p. 404.
[3] *Ibid.* i. p. 553.
[4] Puigblanch, *Inquisition*, i. pp. 196, 317.
[5] C. Oman, *Hist.*, p. 80.
[6] James Gairdner, *The English Church*, pp. 37, 38.
[7] Gairdner, p. 134.
H. A. L. Fisher, *Hist.*. p. 314.

who was found to have expressed heretical sentiments in his will. We may here allude to the story of Becket's tomb, although it is of very doubtful authority. When Henry VIII in 1538 resolved to lay hands upon the priceless treasure which pilgrims, in the course of four centuries, had heaped upon the shrine at Canterbury, he followed his usual practice of committing his crimes with all the show and pomp of a lawful process.

A formal citation to appear within thirty days is said to have been served on " the late Archbishop," to answer to grave charges of high treason. One would have given much to have beheld the lofty-minded and imperious prelate stand up before the burly ruffian then upon the throne : brave men must have been very rare in Henry's day, but doubtless they always are in every age. It was not to be, for neither in the allotted month, nor yet in thirty million times as many years as there were seconds in those thirty days, might the dead man attend to any earthly summoning ; and only a paid proctor set up a Dutch defence before the tyrant king. Becket was then of course immediately condemned, the gold and jewel-crusted plating of his tomb was torn away, and two great chests were filled with the stolen treasure. The ring of world renown placed there by Louis VII was placed upon the thumb of Henry, and the archbishop's body was disinterred, and what remained of him was burned to dust and ashes.

Although the story just related has been alluded to in a Bull of Pope Paul III, it is considered to have been a fabrication. Still such forgeries were founded upon possibilities, and as Mr. Froude observed,[1] " In the fact there is nothing absolutely improbable, for the form said to have been observed was one which was usual in the Church when dead men, as sometimes happened, were prosecuted for heresy." So that the mere existence of the legend gives us a side-light on instinctive punishment.

In 1558 Cardinal Pole burned a number of books and also some bodies ;[2] and in 1603 the corpse of Francis Mobray was duly produced at the legal bar and then

---

[1] *History of England*, vol. iii. p. 302.
See also H. S. Ward, *Canterbury Pilgrims*, p. 289.
[2] Meiklejohn, *Hist.* ii. 39.

received sentence; "to be dismembered as a traitor, his body to be hanged on a gibbet and afterwards quartered; his head and limbs stuck upon conspicuous places in the city of Edinburgh, and his whole estate to be forfeited."[1]

After the Restoration the bodies of Cromwell, Ireton and Bradshaw[2] were removed from the Abbey and, on January 30, 1661, the anniversary of King Charles's death, they were hanged at Tyburn and afterwards buried beneath the gallows.

Instinctive acts generally persist, and in 1902 there was another instance at Northenden. A man had murdered his master (a crime which once had been petty treason) and then killed himself, and his body had been locked up in a stable awaiting inquest. In the night some neighbours broke in and dragged out the lifeless body of the offender into a field, where it was kicked about and otherwise set upon.[3] The bodies of persons who have been executed are still so far deliberately dishonoured, that they are buried in quicklime within prison walls.[4]

Punishments as employed in the instances we have been examining will not now be defended as rational. But they were yet exceedingly natural as instinctive acts, and were evidently carried out for the pleasure of doing them. We have looked into the crude beginnings of punishment; which sprang from revenge—the notion that plenal responsibility could be extended even to things—the assumption that the attempted, or real, infliction of pain, was always needed to put things right or to satisfy "justice."

Punishments are not remedies which were devised by man's reason, but concessions to sub-human instincts which stir in him. Punishment is a survival of savagery.

[1] H. Arnot, *Criminal Trials*, p. 65.
[2] R. Lodge, *Hist.*, p. 9.
State Trials, vol. v. p. 1335.
[3] *Daily Chronicle*, Feb. 26, 1902.
[4] DuCane, *Punishment*, p. 26.

CHAPTER XVII

CLASSIFICATION OF CRIMES

FOR the sake of clearness in our line of reasoning I have already spoken of the " Criminal." But for a criminologist to leave it so, would be as for a doctor to describe an illness as " disease." What should we think of any hospital which placed all kinds of cases in its wards, mixing (as they used actually to do in some countries in the last century) [1] the ophthalmic cases with the surgical, and the infectious with the incommunicable ? Still more, what should we think if the said hospital possessed only one remedy—say blisters ? We take in a case involving perhaps a congested region or requiring a counter-irritation, and the blister does very well ; but we find another case perhaps presenting a broken or bruised limb—but again a blister is applied to the already sore and injured part ! What would be said of such an institution ? what would be done to those who managed it ?

And nothing reveals more clearly the state of stagnant putrifying neglect in which the treatment of crime has been allowed to lie, than the great damning fact, that for the thousand sins and sorrows that must come before the Courts we have all along had but one " remedy "—in various doses—and that one remedy was punishment.

Crime is divided into two great classes which have a totally different origin, and require, of course, different treatment. There are crimes of circumstances, and crimes of impulse. In other words, one great group of offences arises from the stress and pressure of environment ; the other from some defect or abnormality in the nerve-structure of the individual.

[1] See for instance John Conolly, *The Treatment of the Insane*, p. 7. London, 1856.

The former class comprises the offences which are set up by surroundings, and which perhaps the majority of people would fall into under a like environmental pressure. The latter arise from constitutional idiosyncrasies which lead to acts that may not even *tempt* the ordinary run of men and women. In my opinion the key to the ultimate solution of the whole crime-problem lies in the recognition of this great and absolute division. For though offences do sometimes appear to overlap the line of separation, yet I believe the existence of these two great groups is as exact and positive as any broad and classifying law ever laid down by science.

The group for which the criminal law really exists is for the former, or the Circumstantial crimes. In these, we deal with the main stream of temptation, with the jagged " narrows " caused by competition, and with the fearful race for wealth. In modern industrial states, money, or the want of it, fixes a gulf almost unbridgable between the rich and poor. The " dingy dumb millions " produce without enjoyment, and the ruling classes enjoy without proportionate production. There is a currency that can be coined, stolen, and forged to any extent, and those who obtain control of it by means however anti-social, which the law does not, or cannot, prosecute as criminal, are, *ipso facto*, rewarded as never noble deeds are recompensed. Human nature is thus confronted by the threefold impetus of want, desire, and ambition, and " as long as society bows and cringes before the great thieves, there will be little ones enough to fill the jails." [1] " Crime," says Dr. Nordau, " is human parasitism ; in this sense most men are criminals, in fact the germ of crime exists in all." [2]

Who then can wonder that this dazzling allurement proves too much for the knavish and lax-principled, and more especially (since the true calculating villains are not often caught) for those unbalanced and unstable people who frequently, for a brief spell of luxury and leisure, incur a lasting ruin and disgrace, and cast away from their weak lives for ever, any good prospects which they might have had ? Yes, the big cities and civilization

[1] Ingersoll, *Crimes against Criminals*, p. 28.
[2] *La Revue*, Paris, October 15, 1902.

give but too much occasion that the circumstantial crimes indeed should come. Mr. Troup, of the Home Office, stated in evidence that "the number of crimes against property is so large compared with other crimes that the variation in the total of indictable offences is completely dominated by the offence against property." [1] The same eminent authority tells us that larceny and one or two kindred offences make up about five-sixths of the whole volume of serious (indictable) crime. Thus, according to the compiler of our *Judicial Statistics*, we have only the little fraction of one-sixth left to express all other indictable crimes ! The majority of these will doubtless come under our second, or impulse division, and are often absolutely pathological. "There is an absolute distinction between crimes of passion and crimes properly described." [2] Compressed into this little fraction of the whole crime-current we shall find the assault cases, the homicidal and the sexual, in all their infinite variety and (apparent) degrees of moral responsibility and guilt ; all the more serious outbreaks of hatred, jealousy, and passion ; lastly, we shall find the would-be suicides and the sexual inverts, who, in the light of reason and modern scientific knowledge, should not be classed as criminals at all.

So vastly have human ideals and beliefs been changed and dislocated in the course of history that, in the telling words of J. S. Mill, " it often happens that the universal belief of one age of mankind—a belief from which no one was, nor without an extraordinary effort of genius and courage could, at that time, be free—becomes to a subsequent age so palpable an absurdity that the only difficulty then is to imagine how such a thing can ever have appeared credible." Hard has it ever proved for reason to pierce prejudice ; nay, truth has shone amongst us like the sun—the most tremendous obvious thing in all the world, and yet withal, in its meridian majesty, so very seldom faced and looked upon ! So different indeed have arguments appeared from widely opposing points of view that Montaigne even went the length of saying,

---

[1] Departmental Committee of 1895, *Evidence*, p. 407 ; and see diagram opposite p. 540 of the above.
[2] Nordau in *La Revue* just quoted.

" variety of opinion proves that things are only what we think them "—a thought which Kipling has popularised in his delicious satire about the dreams of Kew.

No doubt much, if not all, of the confusion which has prevailed in dealing with the hard world-problems has been due to the presence of those mighty, if often morbid, influences of which we can see traces in the wildest savage tribes ; to the influence of Demonolatry and the resultant forces of extra-rational sanction and condemnation. Had reason had full play the greater nations would long ago have attained to that degree of precision and spontaneous uniformity which has been won in the domain of the physical sciences ; we should not see whole groups, if not communities, engaged in bitter strife with one another on ethical and moral issues. But reason and treason were about equally dangerous offences in the Middle Ages, and there are few who dare be absolutely honest in all the many-interested world to-day ! People are indeed habitually unreasonable in the domain of morals. But ethical systems owe neither their inception nor their preservation to rational processes. For, in the words of Locke, the three great things that govern the world are reason, passion, and superstition : the first governs a few, the last share the bulk of mankind and possess them in their turns ; but superstition is the most powerful and produces the greatest mischief. Isolated epochs there have been—little oases in the vast deserts of Demonolatry—where pagan sanity, philosophic teaching, and even revolutionary zeal, established human happiness as an ideal and consequence, as the criterion of moral conduct. But taking a wide view of the past (and remembering that we in this present world are not permitted either to justify or to explain earth's mysteries) there seems but too much truth in Schopenhauer's saying, " wickedness has the upper hand, and folly the casting vote " ; or, as Ibsen expresses it in one of his plays, the majority is always wrong ! For reason, though indeed the highest, and the latest, of man's attributes, has been, so far, perhaps the least effective force directing human destinies.

The influence of standpoint upon human judgment is most amazingly revealed in the long history of suicide.

Even apart from frequent theological bias, the very military and paternal states of old might well look with misgiving on practices which might deprive them of their citizens and might also maintain open the door of that one sanctuary which all the despotisms and decrees of man have never been allowed to violate. We know that, once a Roman made appeal to Cæsar, the matter passed from the provincial courts, which then could neither pardon nor give sentence. But there was yet appeal beyond the seat of Cæsar ; and when the humblest reached the domain of Death, the grave-gate closed against all sound or siege, and barred men out for ever. It was this world-old thought that Seneca—the brother of Gallio, and the tutor of Nero—expressed in the fine passage that has come to us : " To death alone it is due that life is not a punishment, that erect beneath the frowns of fortune I can preserve my mind unshaken and master of itself. I have one to whom I can appeal. I see before me the crosses of many forms. . . . I see the rack and the scourge and the instruments of torture adapted to every limb and to every nerve ; but I also see Death . . . wherever you look there is the end of evils . . . the eternal law has decreed nothing better than this, that life should have but one entrance and many exits." [1]

Such proud defiance of all human power may have proved offensive to authority. Whom the king would he slew ; but whom he would he could *not* keep alive. The very thought of that unbroken subject's sanctuary might seem to have the trend of mutiny ! At any rate suicide was forbidden by the early laws of Athens [2] and Sparta.[3] In the former city the body was not allowed to be honourably cremated, and the right hand was severed from the corpse.[4]

Aristotle [5] called it a sin against the State, and Pythagoras forbade men to depart from their guard or station in life without an order from their commander [6] ; that is God.

[1] Lecky, *History of European Morals*, i. p. 217.
[2] Wynn Westcott, *Suicide*. London, 1885.
[3] Lisle, *Du Suicide*, p. 347. Paris, 1856.
[4] See Alexander Grant, *Ethics of Aristotle*, ii. p. 141, *note.*
[5] *Ethics*, V. xv.
[6] Cicero, *De Senectute*, xx. 73.

Plato allowed it occasionally in his *Laws*,[1] but forbade it in his *Phædon*.[2]

But with the rise of philosophy and intellectual scepticism, also perhaps with the increased assertion of the individual, the feeling towards suicide became quite changed. The practice grew to be defended not only as a right belonging to the citizen, but as a deed befitting men of lofty lives and aspirations. It was upheld by the great schools of classic teaching and advocated by Sophists, Cynics, Stoics, and Epicureans, although not always from a common standpoint. But Stoic pride and Epicurean calculation alike agreed that self-inflicted death was often the only course open to honour, the only path that led to peace and happiness.[3] At Ceos and at Massilia, about A.D. 31,[4] the municipality heard applications for permission to commit suicide,[5] and kept a public supply of prepared hemlock poison for the use of those to whom leave had been granted. A system very much like this was suggested by our own Sir Thomas More in his *Utopia*, in which he has been followed again by many modern writers.

This interesting custom is said to have been brought from Greece,[6] perhaps from Athens.[7] In fact, we may say that the ideal of death became accepted by the pagan world as part of its best life.[8] And, in the words of a great historian,[9] " when we remember how warmly it was applauded or how faintly it was condemned in the civilizations of Greece and Rome . . . we must realize the complete revolution which was effected in this sphere by the influence of Christianity." [10] But the acceptance of suicide as part of the social system, which in Greece and Rome was the outcome of scepticism and ratiocination,

---

[1] *Leges*, ix.
[2] For various views taken in Greece and Rome the reader may go to Lecky's *History of European Morals*. Professor Westermarck's chapter upon the subject (*Moral Ideas*, vol. ii. ch. xxxv.) is a veritable mine of information on the whole question.
[3] Strahan, p. 16.
[4] Lisle, *Suicide*, p. 312.
[5] Wynn Westcott, *Suicide*.
[6] Lecky, *Hist. Mor.* i. p. 218, note.
[7] O'Dea, ch. iv. p. 107.
[8] Dean Farrar, *Early Days of Christianity*, p. 15, note.
[9] Gibbon, Dr. W. Smith's edition, vol. v. p. 326.
[10] Lecky, *Hist. Mor.* ii. p. 54.

has been brought about and upheld in many other countries by the very religious spirit which has often proved so hostile to it. Religious suicide is said to be extensively recorded in the history of ancient Egypt.[1] It has been for ages a time-honoured tradition in China.[2] It was, however, criminal to kill a prisoner who had been left for death, even at his request. And if his son, grandson, slave, or hired servant should then despatch him, the slayer was to lose his head " for so great an offence against piety and subordination."[3]

But the universality of the practice is told by every traveller, while the death of the brave Admiral Ting was an important event in the late Chino-Japanese war. We may remember also that, in deference to Chinese custom, some of the leading " Boxers " were ordered to commit suicide by the allied powers of Europe.

Among the Japanese[4] suicide has been a very ancient, often a religious institution.[5] It is looked upon as a step in spiritual evolution by the Brahmans,[6] and is largely practised wherever Buddhism is the prevailing faith.[7] In India it was regarded by the Hindus in the light of a religious duty.[8] To be drowned in a sacred stream[9] was the best consecration of a pious pilgrimage.[10]

In the ancient *Laws of Manu* suicide is evidently provided for. " When the father of a family perceives his muscles becoming flaccid and his hair grey, and sees the child of his child, let him seek refuge in a forest "[11] (vi. 2). This is the old Eastern ideal, to go away into the wilderness, to be with nature and to dream and pray. But the Brahman was to cast off mortality ; he was to cease to

---

[1] Reference to the practice in the case of certain prisoners in Wilkinson's *Manners of the Ancient Egyptians*, edited by Dr. S. Birch, p. 307. London, 1878.
Strahan, p. 21.
Wynn Westcott.
The habit among the Ethiopians is alluded to by Diodorus Siculus.
[2] Strahan, p. 5.
[3] Sir George Staunton, *Penal Code of China*, p. 441. London, 1810.
[4] E. Lisle, *Du Suicide*, p. 332.
[5] Strahan, pp. 5 and 36.
[6] *Ibid*. ch. i.
[7] O'Dea, ch. iii.
[8] *Ibid*. p. 18.
[9] Le Tourneau, *Sociology*, ch. xiii. p. 243. London, 1893.
[10] Josephus, *The Jewish War*, bk. vii.
[11] Sir William Jones, *Institutions of Manu*. Madras, 1880.

harm, to rage, to fear, even to love (so different has been the ascetic from the classic view of inspiration). He was to be beyond all dread and all desire. " Let him not wish for death," says the text (vi. 31). " Let him not wish for life ; let him expect his appointed time as a hired servant expects his wages."[1] In the view of Schopenhauer suicide is not the negation of the will, but rather its strongest affirmation ; and the spirit seeking reunion with the Universe was to cast off feeling. Hence, it was better not to rush to death or to will anything, but to dissolve through maceration and be dried up into air ; but if perchance the Brahman had an incurable disease he might wander away towards the north-east, " feeding on water and air till his mortal frame totally decay, and his soul becomes united with the Supreme "[2] (vi. 45).

The Indian commentators say " that a man may undertake the Great Departure, on a journey which ends in death, when he is incurably diseased or meets with a great misfortune, and that because it is taught in the Sâstras it is not opposed to the Vedic rules which forbid suicide." " . . . a voluntary death by starvation was considered a befitting conclusion of a hermit's life."[3]

But in the beautiful idea expressed in the Laws (*Manu*, vi. 40), " To the Brahman, by whom not even the smallest dread has been occasioned by sentient creatures, there can be no dread from any quarter whatever when he obtains release from his mortal body."

The teaching of the Scandinavian religion was of a different character, yet it extolled suicide as a veritable passport into paradise. But the Northern nature was ever strong and fierce in face of man and myth ; and its religion—as usual, corresponding to the soil below from which it grew—contained neither the dread nor dreaminess of Oriental creeds. Of the Viking heaven it might indeed be said that " the violent bear it away." Odin, the divine warrior, received not those to feast with him who died in bed unscathed.[4] Valhalla was only for

[1] O'Dea, p. 104.
[2] Jones, *Manu*, p. 141.
[3] Bühler's *Laws of Manu* (*Sacred Books of the East*), edited by F. Max Müller, vol. xxv. p. 204 ; note on vi. 31 and 32. Oxford, 1886.
[4] The Goths held much the same belief. See E. Durkheim, *Le Suicide*, p. 234. Paris, 1897.

the battle-knights ; it was thus called " the hall of those who died by violence." [1] Hence the custom of bestowing the mark of the spear, by which the aged would " give themselves to Odin." [2] The ancient Sagas of the North [3] have handed down many time-honoured legends about the self-dealt death of kings and heroes. [4] The Jarl who could not die in the delight of battle, feeling the cold and numbing touch no valour could resist, scorned to decay, corrupted by disease. There exists more than one stately tale of an old king, out-worn, broken down, who sailed away in his funeral barque, with the fir-cones piled, and his armour on—and left the land for the dark-rimmed deep, " in a kingly way to meet King Death " ; and then in the silence of night and sea, he lighted the cones and the sky was red, and burned on his ship as a Viking should. Or else he lay down in his armour, and turned his faithful sword at last against its master. [5] (Was it not named, and loved, and ultimately buried with him ?)

A fine description of this state of mind is given in the following poem, which I select from the century-old work of a most ardent student and translator of the Northern Sagas. The hero feels his final hour is come, but he will face it, who had never feared.

> " Shall Oswald, then,
> Sink, tamely sink, to everlasting night ?
> Shall feeble age with lingering hand conduct him
> To the bleak region girt with stubborn frost,
> And bend this warlike heart in massy chains of folded ice ?
> What ! shall the holy bards, who sang my glorious deeds, thus
> End the song ? ' Alas ! he dared not snatch the joys of
> Heaven, but meanly fell the prey to age and sickness.' " [6]

And then the old chief sees Valhalla opened and Odin sitting at the feast, and his own golden chair unoccupied and waiting him ; and so he struck, to storm the hill of heaven.

The whole position of the Jews with regard to suicide

[1] Strahan, p. 21.
[2] Du Chaillu, *The Viking Age*, i. 373. London, 1889.
[3] *Ency. Brit.*
[4] Lady Gregory, *Cuchullin of Muirthemne*, ch. vii. p. 139. London, 1902.
[5] See Fouqué's *Theodolf the Icelander.*
[6] F. Sayers, *Poems*, p. 94. Norwich, 1803.

is strangely neutral, if indeed they did not rather favour it.[1] Although there are some few cases (four, I believe) of self-destruction mentioned in the Bible, they are described without remark. It has been alleged that the Rabbinical teaching was in the olden time distinctly hostile to the practice,[2] but that later on a regular philosophy of suicide arose.[3] In support of the view that it had been once condemned we have the well-known speech of Flavius Josephus, in which he declared that the Jews used not to bury the bodies of their suicides till after sunset. All sorts of strange superstitions always cling closely round the vast movements of Nature; thus people were popularly supposed in seaside places to be born only with the rising, and to die, or " go out," with the receding tide. Snakes, eels, etc., were affirmed to writhe and live until the setting of the sun. The practice of night-burial of suicides may well have had its origin in some such rustic notions.

The erudite Dean of St. Paul's, referring to this passage,[4] said that he knew not upon what law it was founded. Dr. Strahan[5] conceives it possible that Josephus may, in the desperate circumstances in which he found himself, have been confounding Jewish with Athenian law. But the more important fact is that, as Dr. Donne[6] points out, the Jewish leader at the time was pleading for his life. The circumstances surrounding his discourse are so remarkable that we must quote Josephus's own account of them.

In the thirteenth year of the Emperor Nero the siege of Jotapata had just ended, and one more Hebrew hiding-place had fallen before the legions of Rome, the terrible all-conqueror. Flavius Josephus, the commander of the Israelites, had, with a remnant of the garrison, sought refuge in a cavern. After quite vainly seeking for his body among the slain, the victors had discovered his retreat, and had then summoned him to yield in friendly terms. This he was willing to do,

---

[1] Strahan, p. 8.
[2] Lisle, *Du Suicide*, p. 341.
[3] O'Dea, p. 63.
[4] John Donne, ΒΙΑΘΑΝΑΤΟΣ, p. 96. London, 1648.
[5] *Suicide*, p. 12.
[6] ΒΙΑΘΑΝΑΤΟΣ, p. 96.

but the desperate soldiers "ran at him from all sides with drawn swords, upbraiding him for cowardice and manifesting a determination instantly to cut him down." [1]

It was under these circumstances that he made his speech against all suicide, but finding it of no avail, he had recourse to something like a stratagem. "'Since you are resolved to die,' he cried, 'let us commit our mutual slaughter to the lot, and let him to whom it falls die by the sword of him who comes next to him, and the same fate will thus pass through all.' To a proposal so apparently fair they readily assented, and having thus far prevailed he cast the lot. He to whom it fell bared his throat to the next, not doubting but the general would soon share his fate, for death with Josephus they deemed sweeter than life." But the wily general had no such intention, it seems ; being left with only one other, " and anxious neither to be condemned by the lot himself, nor, should he remain the last, to stain his hands with kindred blood, he persuaded him also, on a pledge given, to remain alive," and they surrendered to Vespasian. Josephus, then, can hardly be considered an impartial commentator, and, devout as the Jews have always been to their national law and religion, he very evidently failed to influence them.

Very different in tenor were the words of another Jewish leader at the tragic siege of Masada. "For of old," he said, "and from the first dawn of reason, have the national laws and the divine precepts, confirmed by the deeds and noble sentiments of our forefathers, continued to teach us that life, not death, is a misfortune to men ; for it is death that gives liberty to the soul and permits it to depart to its proper and pure abode, where it will be free from every calamity." [2] And so the gallant Eleazar perished, along with his devoted garrison of 960, men, women, and children ; and when the victorious Romans swarmed into the fortress they found but two or three who had hidden away from the sight of their desperate countrymen, and all the rest consumed by sword

---

[1] Josephus, *The Jewish War*, Dr. Traill's edition, bk. iii. p. 36. London, 1851.
[2] Traill's *Josephus*, vol. ii. p. 243.

and fire. Josephus spoke of this as having been a
" miserable necessity." Moreover, the Jews in all ages
have frequently resorted to this last extremity when
pressed by overwhelming enemies ; thus in 1095 a
multitude fell by their own hands in France to avoid
torture.[1] At York, in the time of Richard I., the Rabbi
Jocen repeated,[2] upon a somewhat smaller scale, the
doings of Masada, and the same happened at the siege of
the castle of Verdun in 1320.[3] Doubtless there are many
other instances. In the face of all the negative and
positive evidence, we cannot say that suicide was always
held accursed, or even ignoble, by the " People of the
Book."

As we have seen, the later pagan law permitted suicide,
which only entailed penal consequences if practised to
escape conviction for some anterior and actual crime.
This spirit of toleration continued long, for the old pagan
legislation remained unaltered in the Theodosian [4] and
Justinian [5] Codes. But meanwhile a fresh and fanatical
moral system was rapidly asserting its power over the
Western world, and the new system came with the
preaching of the new religion, Christianity. Having no
direct precepts in their sacred books, the Christians
appear to have been somewhat undecided as to suicide.
The practice, it has been said, persisted, " but the pleas
were altered to suit Christianity ; it was now to secure
from the danger of apostasy, to procure martyrdom, or
to preserve the crown of virginity," [6] etc. For this last
reason there were many suicides, perhaps the most remarkable being that of St. Pelagia, a girl of only fifteen,
whom the Church afterwards canonised, and whose
memory, says Donne, is celebrated on the 9th of June.[7]
Many other Christian suicides of the same character [8]
have been recorded.[9]

It is said that at the capture of Rome by the Goths in

[1] Lecky, *Hist. Mor.* ii. p. 50. [2] Dickens, *Hist. Eng.* p. 73.
[3] Strahan, p. 24.   [4] Lecky, *Hist. Mor.* vol. ii. p. 50.
[5] *Ency. Brit.*, art. " Suicide." [6] *Ibid.*
[7] Strahan, p. 20.   [8] Wynn Westcott, p. 16.
[9] Strahan, p. 20.

For the views of the early Fathers of the Church, and indeed for
the history of the whole subject, the reader is referred to Professor
Westermarck's *Origin and Development of the Moral Ideas*, vol. ii.
chap. xxxv.

410,[1] a great number of Christian women killed themselves[2] rather than fall into the power of the abandoned soldiery.[3] But suicide to preserve chastity has been upheld and defended by many of the early Fathers,[4] notably by St. Ambrose, St. Jerome, and St. Chrysostom. On those extreme occasions, such as when St. Pelagia cast herself over the parapet,[5] Catholics have claimed that there was special inspiration which impelled her act and gave permission for it. Slow sinking brought about by the long practice of intense asceticism, which may be said to have amounted to death, self-occasioned out of purely religious motives,[6] was looked upon as being worthy of the highest honour.[7] We saw something of religious maceration as a worthy life-end in the *Laws of Manu*, although there seemed to be a different ideal. It must, I think, be admitted, that with the Christian ascetics death was not the deliberate aim, although it was inevitably brought about by the strain and intensity of their religious exercises.

Like all intensely ascetic and spiritual religions, Christianity engendered more or less indifference towards this present life. Expecting the swift and sudden advent of the world-end, Christians despised its cares and shrank from its pursuits. Before the tremendous thought of the approaching Judgment Day, the so-called serious affairs of life became as trivial matters, and its best pleasures seemed intrusive snares. It was this overwhelming weight of expectation that caused them easily to be accused of " hatred to mankind " ; but what they did hate was mortality ; fully believing (and in a way we little understand, for faith grows cold when hardened into monuments) in the most swift and certain resurrection of the body, they longed to cast aside its limitations and corruption.[8] The very clouds on-drifting with the storm

---

[1] Gibbon's *Roman Empire*, ch. xxi.
[2] O'Dea, p. 75, note.
[3] Strahan, p. 21.
[4] Lecky, *Hist. Mor.* ii. 47.
[5] Wynn Westcott, p. 16.
[6] Lecky, *Hist. Mor.* ii. p. 48.
[7] Staeudlin, *Geschichte der Vorstellungen und Lehre vom Selbstmorde*, 1824.
[8] See M. Felix Bourquelot, *Bibliothèque de l'Ecole des Chartes*, tom. iv. p. 242. Paris, 1841.

stood forth as tokens of the wrath to come ; the far-breathed voices of the angry elements reminded them of the great final cataclysm. The pagan peoples still might shear and sow, and fill their minds with cares of flocks and fields. The early Christians listened for the breath that was to raise the harvest of dry bones, and looked to see them join and stand erect ; their hopes were set on high.

Thus while the dazzling dreams of real and heart-felt faith paled the dull work-day dress of actuality, they set alight the zeal of martyrdom. So sweet is human praise, so strong the call of the ideal in our natures, that there has never been a lack of sacrifice, given a really great occasioning. And the believers in the Way had absolutely all upon the issue of their fortitude : on earth, such veneration as no kings receive ; [1] beyond it, angel throngs, the ecstasy of close and present heaven. And if there could be yet further incentive, we must not lose sight of the other side of the question—disgrace in the sight of all believers, and the apostate's part in the abyss, in hell, which roared as close beneath as heaven shone above. No wonder, then, that martyrdom was sought,[2] in persecution periods, by provoking, almost compelling death at the hands of the pagan powers,[3] and later on, in snatching the martyr's crown,[4] even though it involved the soon-to-be-forbidden price of suicide.[5]

"The desire for martyrdom," says Lecky, "became at times a form of absolute madness, a kind of epidemic of suicide, and the leading minds of the Church found it necessary to exert all their authority to prevent their followers from thrusting themselves into the hands of their persecutors." [6] It is said that at the Council of Elvira, about A.D. 305,[7] a canon was passed denying the honours of martyrdom to deliberate provokers of punishment, such as the idol-breakers.[8] Mensurius, a bishop of

---

[1] See Renan, *Marc. Aurèle*, ch. xxix. p. 525.
[2] Charles Moore, *A Full Inquiry* . . . *Suicide*, vol. i. p. 288. London, 1790.
[3] See Gibbon, ch. xvi.   [4] Donne, ΒΙΑΘΑΝΑΤΟΣ, p. 186.
[5] Todd, *Life of St. Patrick*, p. 454.
[6] Lecky, *Hist. Mor.* vol. i. p. 390, etc.
[7] Moore, *A Full Inquiry*, vol. i. p. 291. He calls it a council of Illiberis.
[8] Conybeare, *Monuments of Early Christianity*, p. 13; London, 1894.

Carthage, early in the fourth century, and Cæcilian his successor (A.D. 311), also endeavoured to check the inordinate love for martyrdom at that time prevalent among the Christians of North Africa, amongst whom it was held to be " the becoming conclusion of the Christian life." [1] Somewhere about this period there arose in Africa [2] the formidable sect of the Donatists.[3]

With these, the death-longing (perhaps really what may be called the " other side " of those transcendent visions of the world to come, to which we have referred) was most intense ; the hesitating pagan powers, nay, even passers-by upon the highroads, were frequently compelled to grant them execution ; but failing this, they made end of themselves in all manner of ways, or leaped from cliffs as eagerly as those who " went to Odin." Petilian, a Donatist bishop of Cirta, about 395–400, " taught that whosoever killed himself as a magistrate to punish a crime committed before, was a martyr." [4] Although assailed and anathematised by councils, at Rome in 313, Arles in 314, and crushed by the Council of Carthage in 411,[5] the Donatists smouldered on for some three centuries,[6] till the whole Church of North Africa was swallowed up together in the rising flood of Islam. It is interesting to remark that, in spite of the pronouncements to which we shall immediately refer, the custom of death-hastening reappeared among the Christians in the sect of the Albigenses in the twelfth and thirteenth centuries.[7]

But now at length the time was coming when the Church was to denounce the practice which the excesses of the fanatics had forced on its consideration.

In the beginning of the fifth century, the fiery Bishop of Hippo sent forth his book [8] (written from 413–426), in which he most uncompromisingly condemned all suicide. " La réprobation," says Félix Bourquelot,

[1] Smith and Wace, *Dictionary of Christian Biography*, vol. i. p. 882. London, 1877.
[2] Gibbon, ch. xxi.
[3] Smith and Wace, art. " Donatism."
[4] Donne, ΒΙΑΘΑΝΑΤΟΣ, p. 69.
[5] Sir N. Harris Nicolas, *Chronology of History*.
[6] Gibbon.
[7] Lecky, *Hist. Mor.* vol. ii. p. 49.
[8] St. Augustine, *De Civitate Dei*, lib. i. c. xvi.

" manifestée par l'Eglise Chrétienne contre le suicide se trouve pour la première fois formulée d'une manière absolue et dogmatique dans les écrits de S. Augustin ; " [1] and, as M. Lisle observes, " C'est en effet quelques années seulement après la publication de la ' Cité de Dieu,' que nous voyons l'Eglise Chrétienne s'occuper pour la première fois de cette question délicate," and from this time, what even Christian writers have called " the dark shadow of Augustine " [2] spread over the Catholic world for many centuries. We shall find presently that his influence, increased no doubt by the reaction against the frenzied sects of which we have just spoken, led the Church far into the opposite extremes, notions that will now appear to many scarcely more sane and sensible than the wild ravings of the Circumcelliones !

A case involving the suicide of a woman appeared before the Synod of Ancyra as early as A.D. 314, since " A certain person who had betrothed himself to a girl, had connection with her sister so that she became pregnant ; he then married his betrothed, and his sister-in-law hanged herself. . . . All parties were condemned to long periods of penance, but nothing would seem to have been said about suicide specially."[3]

Lecky has told us that " a council of Arles in the fifth century [4] . . . pronounced suicide to be the effect of diabolical inspiration," and Lisle also refers to that Council's proceedings.[5]

But the 53rd Canon [6] dealt only with those cases where servants had been provoked to slay themselves in order to bring trouble upon their masters, a method of reprisal well known in China and all the East.

More definite condemnation was to come later. In 533 a Council of Orleans (15th Canon) forbade the ac-

---

[1] *Bibliothèque de l'Ecole des Chartes*, tom. iii. and iv.
[2] Dean Farrar, *Eternal Hope*, p. 167, and see his remarks, p. 65.
[3] *Vide* the 25th Canon, and Bishop Hefele, *History of Christian Councils*, vol. i. p. 222, W. R. Clark's ed. Edin., 1871.
[4] *Hist. Mor.* ii. p. 50.
[5] E. Lisle, *Du Suicide*, p. 396.
[6] *Vide* Concilium Arelatense, ii : " Si quis famulorum cujuslibet conditionis aut generis, quasi ad exacerbandam domini distinctionem, se diabolo repletus furore percusserit ipse tantum sanguinis sui reus erit, neque ad dominum sceleris alieni pertinebit invidia,"—Mansi, tom. vii. p. 884.

ceptance of oblations for suicides, while permitting them for those killed in the commission of crimes.[1] But in A.D. 563 the Council of Braga refused to allow religious services over the body, and ordered that no masses should be said for the soul of a suicide.[2] This Canon, depriving the dead of funeral rites, was a direct and emphatic condemnation of self-willed death.

The Council of Auxerre[3] in 578 again forbade the acceptance of the oblations of suicides, but still the condemnation of self-destruction appears to have been temperate in those early times, for we find the 4th Canon of the Council of Toledo[4] (A.D. 693) punishing the attempt with only two months' exclusion from fellowship. But later the Church's attitude became more severe ; in 878 the Council of Troyes[5] ordered that the bodies of excommunicated persons, suicides, etc., should not be granted Christian burial.

In 866 Pope Nicholas, in his reply made to the newly Christianised Bulgarians, prescribed that the body of a suicide was indeed to be buried, lest it injured the living ; but no sacrifice was to be offered—for who, he asked, had more fully committed that sin unto death which was not to be prayed for, than he who imitated Judas, and, with all approbation of the Devil his master, became his own murderer?[6]

Towards the end of his reign, St. Louis, king of France (A.D. 1215–1270),[7] ordered the confiscation of the property

---

[1] C. Aurelianse, ii : " Oblationes defunctorum, qui in aliquo crimine fuerint interempti recipi debere censemus. si tamen non ipsi sibi mortem probentur propriis manibus intulisse."—Mansi, tom. viii. p. 837. Florence, 1762.

[2] C. Bracarense, 16th Canon : " Item placuit, ut hi qui sibiipsis aut per ferrum, aut per venenum, aut per præcipitium, aut suspendium, vel quolibet modo violentiam inferunt mortem, nulla pro illisin oblatione commemoratio fiat, neque cum psalmis ad sepulturam eorum cadavera deducantur : multi enim sibi hoc per ignorantiam usurpaverunt. Similiter et de his placuit, qui pro suis sceleribus puniuntur."—Mansi, tom. ix. p. 779. Florence, 1763.

[3] C. Autisiodorense, 17th Canon. Vide Mansi, tom. ix. p. 913.

[4] C. Toletanum : Mansi, tom. xii. p. 71 ; and see Hefele, vol. v. p. 245.

[5] C. Tricassinum : Mansi, tom. xvii. p. 349 ; also Bourquelot, p. 554.

[6] Vide Migne, Patrologiæ, tom. cix. p. 1013. Ad Consulta Bulgarorum, Bourquelot, p. 555.

A. Legoyt, Le Suicide, p. 104. Paris, 1881.

Moore, vol. i. p. 301.

[7] F. H. Perry-Coste, The Ethics of Suicide, p. 31. London, 1898.

of suicides [1] in addition to the ecclesiastical penalties already imposed.[2] But by this cruel edict he was only applying and extending to them the truly barbarous criminal laws of the olden time, by which the goods of convicted prisoners—and in some cases the lives and limbs of their relations too—were declared forfeited to the avenging State.[3] The Church confirmed the canons as to refusing burial, etc.,[4] at the Synod of Nîmes in the year 1284.[5] But other and non-Christian creeds had turned their thunders against self-destruction.

Ages before the period of which we have just been speaking, the Magi, or priests of Persia, had forbidden it, and suicide is, according to the Zoroastrian religion,[6] one of the most horrible crimes, belonging to the class of *marg-arzan* or deadly sins. And when,[7] in the seventh century, the soldiers of Mahomet broke up the Persian power and drove the remnant of the Zoroastrians headlong into India, they continued to hold the sinfulness of suicide, already formally condemned by the new creed, straitly forbidden in the book of the Koran.[8]

Thus from the seventh century onwards suicide had come to be condemned by the religious systems of the West and East, and besides the terrors threatened in the world to come, the most cruel and revolting penalties were laid upon the senseless body, and, what was more important, also on the nearest relatives. But suicide, being an instinct in man's nature, could not be put down by fear. It is indeed asserted to have become comparatively rare, or at any rate to have become concealed and shameful.[9] But it did not cease, and was well known even in the monasteries as the result of intense melan-

[1] See Abbé de St. Martin, *Etablissements de Saint-Louis*, ch. lxxxviii. Paris, 1786.
[2] Lisle, *Du Suicide*, p. 403.
[3] For the Roman law see Dr. W. Smith's *Gibbon*, vol. v. p. 326.
[4] For some English cases previous to the passing of the Forfeiture Act, 1870, see Mews' *Harrison's Digest*, vol. ii. p. 1798. London, 1884.
[5] Mansi, *Sacrorum Conciliorum*, tom. xxiv. p. 546. Venice, 1780.
[6] Haug, *Religion of the Parsis*, edited by E. W. West, p. 313, note. London, 1884.
[7] For their strange notions as to the pollution of the elements by the disposal of dead bodies, etc., see G. Rawlinson's *Religions of the Ancient World*, p. 116. London, 1882.
[8] See Rodwell's translation of Sura, iv. 33, on p. 534. London, 1861.
[9] Bourquelot, tom. iii. p. 555.

choly,[1] which was called acedia, which was the frequent outcome of ascetic life.

The probability is that, like all passion-actions thought to be " stamped out," it was merely driven under the surface, hushed up in the great families where possible, smoothed over and explained away (although the bitter hostility of the priest in *Hamlet* doubtless reflects the spirit of the time), and Legoyt remarks that many bodies were constantly come upon who left no trace of their identity or means of death,[2] showing that the more sane and deliberate of these unhappy people wandered away and died in secret, risking their souls, according to theology, but saving their homes and kindred from ruin and from persecution.[3] The Continental Canons are said to have been extended into England in 673 at the Council of Hertford.[4] A little later in the seventh century we find the rules for the interment of suicides laid down, with more charity and discrimination than was usual, in Theodore's *Penitential,* under the heading " De Vexatis a Diabulo."[5] The possessed (or madman) was to be prayed for after death if he had previously been religious. If he had killed himself from desperation, fear, or from some cause unknown, the matter was, said the archbishop, to be left in the hands of God—they dare not pray for such an one.

Egbert, Archbishop of York (734–766), is said also to have decreed that if any one killed himself at the instigation of the devil, no masses should be said for him, etc.[6] In 963 we find that in the Penitential Canons attributed to Dunstan it was ordered " that if a man wilfully kill himself with a weapon, or through the instigation of the devil "—that old and ready way of accounting for things !—" it was not allowed to sing masses for such an one, nor that his body be committed to the earth with psalmody, nor that it be buried in a holy place ; the same doom belongs to him that loseth his life as a punishment

---

[1] Bourquelot, tom. iv. p. 250.
[2] *Le Suicide*, p. 111.   Paris, 1881.
[3] Moore, *A Full Inquiry*, i. p. 307.
[4] O'Dea, p. 124.
[5] Haddon and Stubbs, *Councils and Documents*, vol. iii. p. 197. Oxford, 1871.
[6] Moore, *A Full Inquiry*, i. p. 307, etc.

for his crimes ; that is the thief, and murderer, and traitor to his lord." [1] In the reign of King Edgar [2] the suicides were classed at law with criminals. [3]

According to Bracton, [4] who wrote in the thirteenth century, those who committed suicide to escape conviction were considered, as by the Roman law, to have been guilty of the previous offence. In the case of ordinary suicide the movable goods were confiscated to the Crown, but not so in the case of the insane. For centuries the unreasoning and exaggerated attitude adopted by the Church from the time of Augustine prevailed in England and throughout Europe ; and though in the fourth century St. Martin of Tours is related to have restored a suicide to life, [5] yet, in the latter Middle Ages, it seems to have been regarded as a very special and unpardonable sin when dealt with from the Christian standpoint. The spirit of the period was well exemplified at the trial of the Marquise de Brinvilliers in 1676, when the presiding judge said to the prisoner " that the greatest of all her crimes, horrible as they were, was not the poisoning of her father and brother, but her attempt to poison herself." [6]

Indeed, it would really seem as if the anger of men against one who sought death equalled the extent of their absolute powerlessness in the matter ! Yet the body at least was left behind to be abused and mutilated, and was mauled and disfigured with a degree of wanton barbarity no naked savages could ever have surpassed. And when, in time, burial of any sort came to be allowed for the convenience of the living, it evolved into a ceremony

[1] J. Johnson, *Laws and Canons of the Church of England*, vol. i. p. 433. Oxford, 1850.
[2] O'Dea, p. 124.
[3] Strahan, p. 198.
[4] *De Legibus*, edited by Sir T. Twiss, vol. ii. p. 507. London, 1879.
[5] Sulpicius Severus, *De Vita S. Martini*, ch. vi.
[6] Funck-Brentano, *Princes and Poisoners*, p. 75, edited by G. Maidment. London, 1901.
" . . . The experience of all ages and nations shows that the immaterial motives are frequently far stronger than the material ones, the relative power of the two being well illustrated by the tyranny of taboo in many instances, called as it is by different names in different places. It shows how, in most parts of the world, acts that are apparently insignificant have been invested with ideal importance, and how the doing of this or that has been followed by outlawry or death."
Francis Galton in *Sociological Papers*, vol. ii. p. 9. London, 1906.

even more horrible in its official form than the excesses of the brutal rabble. All reverence for the presence of death, all compassion for the feelings of the mourners, all sense of justice for the absolutely innocent, appears to have been set at nought before the ghoulish orgies that ensued. The Church, as we have seen, refused to receive the body within its pale ; the corpse was buried at the junction of four roads.[1] An entire chapter, if not a separate volume, could well be written about this strange and very obscure custom of cross-road burial. I have a mass of notes upon the subject, but am content to follow Professor Westermarck,[2] who suggests that it was due to the superstition that, at these places, the malign influence exercised by such bodies would be diffused abroad and so rendered harmless. As possibly throwing some further light upon the origin of this notion, we may remember that persons who had perished by sudden violence have always been alleged and expected to occasion all sorts of mysterious and terrifying phenomena. We cannot, I fancy, altogether disregard the world-wide evidence which has accumulated for centuries in support of the existence of ghosts, or what pass for them. But what the things seen or imagined, actually are—whether they are objective, subjective, self-conscious, or mere impressions that have been in some way fixed round the localities where events took place—cannot be discussed here.

To such a place the corpse was brought and shot into a hole, and then a stake was driven through the body to pin it down and keep its ghost from " walking " ! This was the form of burial for our dear brothers and sisters departed, prescribed in civilized England as late as 1823.[3] In that year it was enacted that the body of a suicide should be buried privately between the hours of nine and twelve at night, without religious rites. This remained law till 1882, when it was decreed that the body might be buried at any time and with such service as the person in charge of the funeral might think fit and could procure.[4] As regards interment, therefore, there now remains no longer any grievance. But even worse than the dese-

---

[1] *Suicide*, p. 199.
[2] *Moral Ideas,* vol. ii. p. 256.
[3] Strahan, p. 199.
[4] Strahan, p. 200.

cration of the dead was the monstrous spoliation of the innocent relations. In this we possess yet another instance of the instinctive nature of all punishment : the body, so stiff and rigid in its mute defiance, was too removed to receive cruelty ; the blow descended better on the wife and children.

Mr. Moore, the eighteenth-century clergyman from whom I have already quoted, with that perversity which we so often notice when reason strikes against prevailing prejudice, and, in such natures, crumples up before it, quiets his conscience with the following remarks : " It is not the law," he says, " which in this case acts unjustly to the family of a suicide . . . but the self-murderer himself who is thus atrocious and cruel to his nearest connections."[1] I have met with this sort of argument in much more recent times, but I prefer the spirit of Voltaire's scathing commentary when he said that they punished " the son for having lost his father, and the widow for being deprived of her husband." " They take away," he wrote, " the goods of the departed, which is practically to snatch away the means of the survivors to whom they belong."[2]

A notable historical instance of the Crown confiscation of goods is left us in the case of Sir James Hales. Being committed to prison for having, as a judge, taken action against some Catholics in the beginning of Queen Mary's reign, he lost, apparently, his mental balance, and very nearly took his life in prison by opening his veins. However, he was not treated badly by the Government, but, being presently released, he went and drowned himself in a shallow stream near his estate in Kent in 1554.[3] A jury having found that he had voluntarily destroyed himself at the instigation of the devil—for he was unpopular at court just then, and they were not likely to allow him the benefit of a verdict of insanity—the Crown made claim on all his goods and chattels. But it was held that neither his wife's dower nor yet freehold lands were liable to forfeiture, nor was the blood to be corrupted,[4] as there was no attainder, and there could be none since

---

[1] *A Full Inquiry*, p. 321, note.
[2] Bourquelot, iv. p. 474.
[3] Holinshed, *Chronicles*, vol. iii. p. 1092. London, 1587.
[4] Plowden's *Commentaries*, " Hales *v.* Petit." London, 1578. Edition of 1816, pp. 260, 261a.

the man was dead. The various possessions, amongst
which were some leasehold lands, were handed over to
one Cyriac Petit, against whom Margaret, Lady Hales,
brought an unsuccessful action early in the succeeding
reign. A variety of legal subtleties, dear to a lawyer's
mind, were then advanced by counsel on both sides, and
the whole trial may be read with interest.

The king, it seems, had claim to compensation for the
loss of a subject, and for the breach of his peace.[1] In
those Protestant times we hear less of the Church ; but
the act was classed as being murder, and not homicide
or manslaughter, and Lord Dyer stigmatised it as " an
offence against nature, against God, and against the
king . . ." The same idea is to be found at a much later
period in Blackstone, who speaks of the double offence—
one spiritual, as evading the prerogative of the Almighty ;
the other temporal, against the king, who hath an interest
in the preservation of his subjects, etc.[2]

But the people, who are always, as individuals, better
than the law, shrank all along from beggaring the manifestly innocent, and avoided a verdict of *felo de se* whenever
it was possible for them to do so ; and even to-day what
has been called the " amiable perjury " of " temporary
insanity " is continued in cases where the same twelve
men would undoubtedly convict had the deceased, in life,
been guilty of some serious offence.

Actual confiscation had been a sort of defunct legal
monstrosity long before the passing of the Act (33 &
34 Vict. c. 23), in 1870, by which all forfeitures were done
away with ; henceforth no felon's property could be
escheated to the Crown. The stake, the cross-roads
burials, and the vampire superstition, have passed away
into the horrors lumber-room of history ; but the harsh
law against attempted suicide is still in force in 1903,
and remains one of those semi-theological anachronisms
which make the Continental nations wonder at our ways.
Less than a generation ago a prison chaplain referred in a
monthly review to " this form of murder, which is often
more cowardly and less frequently followed by real
penitence than those forms of the offence which are
expiated on the scaffold," and advocated the then utterly

---

[1] Plowden's *Commentaries*, pt. i. p. 261.   [2] Bk. iv. ch. xiv.

brutalising punishment of hard labour for the miserable creatures to whom the world already seemed unbearable. And in a work on suicide from which I have quoted, and which was written a few years later, there occurs the amazing statement that "to murder a mother or a daughter is as much repugnant to a sensible man as to murder himself." It is difficult to imagine how in any age absurdity could go further than to present the matter in this diseased and much-distorted way.

In practice, it is probable that this law does but little harm ; no resolved mind fixed on the desperate end of self-destruction would for a moment care what men might say or do. And in spite of the many cranks who swarm about at large, and band themselves into societies,[1] attempted suicide is not regarded even by the laws as an attempted murder,[2] and in the great majority of cases the unfortunate people, though placed in the dock, are taken care of, and are handed over to their friends or to some institution, and are not looked upon by most of us as being really criminals at all.[3] But this is not always the case, for there are cranks and cruel people in high offices, and we occasionally find severe sentences, such as are (or, rather, very often are *not*) inflicted for brutal assaults and deliberate cruelty, passed upon people who have injured no one nor violated any living thing's consent. Thus an unfortunate woman who had previously been insane received (according to the official tables [4]) the maximum sentence of two years for attempted suicide, and was some time later removed again to an asylum from the gaol in 1898.

This case was absolutely scandalous ; but sentences of from six to twelve months, for failure to accomplish an act which is not punishable when completed, are by no means unfamiliar to those who read and study the reports of circuits. And though such sentences are of rare occurrence (yet not one whit the less unfair for that), we hear almost day by day of some unhappy brokenhearted creature, whom the rough world has driven to despair, rescued, perchance, from what seemed certain death, dragged

---

[1] Strahan, p. 201.   [2] Mews' *Harrison's Digest*, vol. ii p. 2065.
[3] See article, *Spectator*, March 16, 1889.
[4] *Report of the Commissioners of Prisons for* 1899, p. 124.

to a felon's cell, locked up and caged, as though accused of theft or cruelty. The principle of these sort of laws is *unjust*; they are an outrage upon personal liberty, and, as such, were overthrown at the great French Revolution.[1]

I have devoted so large a portion of this chapter to the story of suicide chiefly because a principle of *justice* seemed to be involved,[2] and also hoping it may teach us certain things. It appears evident that peoples could not reason, that local circumstances and the twists of teaching have given extraneous colours to men's thoughts, even as tinted glass imparts them to the sunlight. I think it may be admitted without prejudice that suicide has been looked up to as a crowning virtue, loathed and denounced as if the worst of crimes. Many people will hold that it may indeed sometimes be cowardly, often rash and foolish, always a desperate and most irrevocable step. But to all those who believe in liberty, it must remain a personal and self-regarding act, a matter for each one's conscience, not for courts of law.[3] The solemn passage of a human soul from this world to Eternity is not a scene on which we should intrude.

The world-old phenomenon of what is now known as sexual inversion is difficult to discuss, but obviously impossible to omit in any work on criminology in the present state of the law in England.

Mr. Stead, whose zeal for militant morality has had so much effect on legislation, justly expressed the problem when he wrote : " It may be alleged that such problems should not be discussed, and that the whole question should be buried in impenetrable silence. The answer to this is, that if the legislator makes one theory of the psychology of sex the basis for passing a law which sends citizens to penal servitude, it is impossible to shut out such a theory from public discussion." Impossible, of course, in the long-run.

---

[1] O'Dea, p. 280.

[2] For that the ethical, like the legal code of a people, stands in need of revision will hardly be disputed by any attentive or dispassionate observer. The old view that the principles of right and wrong are immutable and eternal is no longer tenable."—J. G. Fraser, *Taboo, and the Perils of the Soul*, p. vi. London, 1911.

[3] See F. H. Perry-Coste's thoughtful essay, *The Ethics of Suicide.* London, 1898.

The sexual inverts may be compared to the left-handed. They are indeed always a minority in every population, but an *eternal* minority which neither laws nor even religious systems have ever altogether swept away.[1] And as in the case of the illegitimate, whom the State has also refused to recognise, the names of some of them are written for all time in the world's history.[2]

But even as we saw in the case of suicide, the perplexing but primordial homogenic instinct has had a most amazing history, ranging in the course of centuries from a religious cult and form of consecration[3]

[1] See Lecky, *Hist. Mor.* ii. 329. The curious writings of St. Peter Damiani in Migne, *Patrologiae*, tom. cxlv. p. 159. H. C. Lea, *Sacerdotal Celibacy*, p. 86, etc. **W. L. Mathieson**, *Politics and Religion in Scotland*, i. 189. J. L. A. Huillard-Breholles, *Hist. Dip.*: Frederici Secundi, p. cxci. Paris, 1859. J. McCabe, *The Bible in Europe*, p. 203. London, 1907. J. Cotter Morison, *The Kingdom of Man*. ch. vi., "**Morality in the Ages of Faith**." J. Bingham, *Antiquities of the Christian Church*, vol. vi. p. 432, etc. J. Janssen, *Hist. of the German People at the Close of the Middle Ages*, A. M. Christie trans. vols. v. and vi. F. M. Nichol's *Epistles of Erasmus*, p. 44. Casper Wirz, *De Uraniër voor Kerk en H. Schrift*, Dutch trans. by A. P. Tierie. Amsterdam, 1904. E. R. K. Geestelijke, *Bibel und Uranismus*.

[2] Many accounts of the lives and eccentricities of great men are given in *L'Intermédiaire des Chercheurs et Curieux*, W. C. Rivers, *Walt Whitman*, Letters of Michael Angelo, etc. Döllinger, ii. p. 274. Albert Moll, *Etude*, ch. ii.

[3] (1) See St. Jerome's *Commentary on Hosea*, iv. 14, in Migne, *Patrologiae*, tom. xxv. p. 851. Paris, 1845. (2) The Bible. See F. C. Cook's *Commentary* on 1 Kings xiv. 24, vol. ii. p. 571. London, 1872. The same on Hosea iv. 14 in vol. vi. p. 435. London, 1876. (3) Alexander's *Kitto's Cyclopaedia of Biblical Literature*, vol. iii. p. 865, London, 1846. (4) Hackett's *Smith's Dictionary of the Bible*, vol. iv. p. 3073. New York, 1870. (5) W. Wilson's *Clement of Alexandria*, ch. ii. p. 40. *Ante-Nicene Library*, vol. iv. Edinburgh, 1867. (6) R. Payne Knight, *The Symbolical Language of Ancient Art*, p. 174. New York, 1876. (7) Pierre Dufour, *Histoire de la Prostitution*, tom. i. p. 71. Brussels, 1851. (8) J. A. Dulaure, *Hist. Abrégé de Différens Cultes*, tom. i. p. 419, etc. Paris, 1825. (9) L. Maury, *Hist. des Religions de la Grèce Antique*, tom. iii. Paris, 1857. (10) J. McCabe, *St. Augustine*, p. 26. London, 1902. (11) J. F. MacLennan, *Studies in Ancient History*, ch. vii. p. 101. London, 1896. (12) C. R. Markham, *Trans. of Royal Commentary of the Yncas*, i. p. 59. (13) H. H. Bancroft, *Native Races of the Pacific*, ii. p. 677. (14) J. G. R. Forlong, *Rivers of Life*, i. ch. iii. London, 1883. (15) *The Open Court* (Chicago), March 1901. (16) J. Bonwick, *Egyptian Belief*, p. 255, etc. London, 1878. (17) J. Rosenbaum, *The Plague of Lust in Classical Antiquity*, Paris, 1901. (18) Jabelon, *Origin of Religion*. London, 1902. (19) Hodder M. Westropp, *Primitive Symbolism*. London, 1885. (20) Pocock's *Grotius*, lib. ii. Oxford, 1660. (21) E. B. Pusey, *Letters of St. Ambrose*, p. 411. A few of the above have been included as bearing on the larger subject of Phallic worship, but about half refer expressly to the Galli, or Effeminati, frequenting the ancient temples.

to a crime which mankind refused almost to recognise as being possible.[1] It has been present in all ages and places throughout the Old World [2] and the New.[3]

[1] The origin of this has often been ascribed to the influence of Christianity: see Paley, *Evidences*, Part iii. ch. vii. ; Lecky, *Hist. Mor.* ii. p. 331. "All Christian legislation on this subject is simply an application and amplification of the Mosaic Law as recorded in Exodus xxii. 19 and Leviticus xx 13–16, just as the cruel persecutions and prosecutions for witchcraft in mediæval and modern times derive their authority and justification from the succinct and peremptory command Thou shalt not suffer a witch to live."—E. P. Evans, *Punishment of Animals*. But there have been from time to time also non-Christian measures of attempted repression—as, for instance, by Solon (B.C. 638–559) as regarded the slaves only, and by the Roman Scantinian Law of the third century B.C., which imposed a fine in the case of free men (see Darnell's *Döllinger*, ii. 274. Giles's *Lemprière's Clas. Dict.* p. 864, and W. Smith's *Dict. Greek and Roman Biography*). In the third century A.D. Alexander Severus made some severe laws (Lecky, *Hist. Mor.* ii. 311). The offenders were, at least legally, liable to strokes of the bamboo under the Chinese code. But no distinction as to sexes is made, Mr. Alabaster observes : "such offences are regarded as, in fact being less hurtful to the community than ordinary immorality" (*Notes and Commentaries on the Chinese Criminal Code*, p. 369. London, 1899), and were condemned by the Zoroastrians. They are said to have been savagely punished by the Incas before their overthrowal at the Spanish conquest.

[2] This statement might be supported indefinitely, but see, for instance : *Albania*. J. G. von Hahn's *Albanesische Studien*, vol. i. *Arabia*. R. F. Burton, *Arabian Nights*, vol. x. *Asia*. Döllinger, *The Gentile and the Jew*, ii. p. 238 ; Darnell's trans. London, 1862. F. Karsch-Haack, *Gleichgeschlechtliche Leben der Ostasiaten*. München, 1906. *Australia*. E. T. Hardman, *Proceedings of the Royal Irish Academy*, third series, vol. i. p. 74. Dublin, 1889–91. *China*. J. F. MacLennan, *Studies in Ancient History*, ch. vii. A Krauss, *Die Psychologie des Verbrechens*, Tübingen, 1884. P. Mantegazza, *Gli Amori degli Uomini*, eleventh edition, i. 277. *Huns*. Th. Ribot, *The Psychology of the Emotions*, p. 259. London, 1897. *Japan*. A. Moll, *Etude sur l'Inversion Sexuelle*, French trans. from the German by Pactet and Romme, p. 58. Paris, Carré, 1893. *Kamschatka*. Said to be alluded to in G. Klemm's *Cultur-Geschichte*, ii. 207. *Madagascar*. *Zeitschrift für Ethnologie*, i. 1869. *New Caledonia*. M Foley, *Bultn. Soc. d'Anthrop. de Paris*, 1879. *Normans*. E. A. Freeman, *Hist. of William Rufus*, i. p. 159. Oxford, 1882. *North American Indians*. G. Catlin, ii. p. 214. London, 1876. *Persia*. J. S. Buckingham's *Travels*. *Samarkand*. Emperor Bâber's *Memoirs*, J. Leyden's translation, p. 26, etc. London, 1826. *South Sea Islands*. John Turnbull, *A Voyage Round the World*, p. 382. London, 1813. James Wilson, *A Missionary Voyage*, p. 361. London, 1799. *Tchukchis*. E. Demidoff, *A Shooting Trip in Kamchatka*, p. 74. London, 1904. *Turkey*. W. Eton, *Turkish Empire*. London, 1799. B. Stern, *Geschlechtsleben in der Türkei*. Berlin, 1903. S. Purchas, *His Pilgrimes*. London, 1625.

[3] This is instructive, for neither Classical nor Oriental influences

But apart from this direct evidence, which does not, of course, pretend to be in any way exhaustive or complete, we may feel certain that this passion has to some extent always been present, however much discountenanced and driven under ground. Travellers, and especially missionaries and their publishers, are very reticent, besides, as Lubbock [1] has shown, often falling into excessive errors in their struggles with the languages. But in the absence of positive accounts, and even in the face of absolute denial, we may feel as sure of the existence of the homogenic attraction as of the presence of disease in every community, from *a priori* reasoning.

Because it is an innate instinct, and every real instinct is older than the pyramids.[2]

And while it was strangely systematised in many of the mightiest civilisations of the past into an institution,[3]

can have reached the indigenous peoples and civilisations of America before the advent of the Spanish conquerors.

See Garcilasso (or Lasso) de la Vega, *Royal Commentaries of the Yncas.* C. R. Marckham's trans. of the seventeenth-century Spanish. London, 1869.

H. H. Bancroft, *The Native Races of the Pacific*, i. 585, 635, 773 ; ii. 337, and as regards even the pre-Toltec period, v. 198. New York, Appletons, 1875.

J. F. MacLennan, *Studies*, ch. vii.

P. Mantegazza, *Gli Amori degli Uomini.* Milan, 1892.

Bernal Diaz, *Hist. de la Conquête de la Nouvelle Espagne*, trans. into French by D. Jourdanet, first edition, ii. 594.

Langsdorf, *Voyages and Travels*, pt. ii. 47, 1814.

J. F. Lafitau, *Mœurs des Sauvages*, tom. i. p. 603, etc. Paris, 1724.

[1] *Origin of Civilization.*
[2] See Herbert Spencer, *Contemp. Rev.* February 1893.
[3] (1) C. O. Müller, *History and Antiquities of the Doric Race*, Tufnell and Lewis's ed., book iv. p. 306. Oxford, 1830. (2) G. Cox, *General History of Greece*, p. 574. London, 1876. (3) W. Mure, *Language and Literature of Ancient Greece*, vol. iii. p. 315. London, 1850. (4) J. A. Froude, *Lives of the Saints*, p. 222. (5) G. Grote, *Plato*, ch. xxvi. Phaedrus-Symposium. (6) J. A. Symonds, *In the Key of Blue*, p. 55. London, 1893. (7) E. F. M. Benecke, *Women in Greek Poetry.* London, 1896. (8) J. A. Symonds, *A Problem in Greek Ethics.* (9) G. L. Dickinson, *The Greek View of Life.* (10) Edward Carpenter, *Civilisation.* (11) C. H. Pearson, *National Life and Character*, p. 186. London, 1893. (12) Döllinger, Darnell's trans. ii. p. 275. (13) J. A. Symonds, *Contemp. Rev.* September, 1890. (14) Bishop Thirlwall, *Greece*, i. 176. (15) Edward Carpenter, *Ioläus.* London, 1902. (16) E. von Kupffer, *Lieblingminne und Freundesliebe in der Weltlitteratur.* Eberswalde, 1900. (17) P. van L. Bouwer, *Histoire de la Civilisation des Grecs*, 1833–42. (18) M. H. E. Meier, in *Ersch and Gruber's Encyclopaedie*, art. "Päderastie." Leipzig, 1837. (19) J. W. Mackail, *Greek Antho-*

and continually confronts us throughout almost the entire range of Greek and Roman literature,[1] it is to be found in rude and primitive communities [2] where Rome and Athens are unknown names.[3]

A deep, inevitable impulse could never, of course, be penalised out of existence, but it is remarkable that an instinct which, at first sight, seems unfunctional and self-destructive should have persisted from the beginning, apparently regardless of the laws of natural selection and elimination. At the same time it appears as though only the more extreme examples of hermaphroditism were really incapable of affecting the birth-rate, and in the insect kingdom [4]—we find remarkable instances of the perpetuation of creatures not individually sexual and reproductive.[5]

Still it is evident that we do not yet know much about the cause of these sort of phenomena, for while the manifestations of passionate attraction, both of the true homosexual instinct [6] and of the venal, substitutional, and acquired vices which have often gathered round it, have been visible from the beginning, it is only within

---

logy, p. 36. London, 1890. (20) E. Bethe in Buecheler and Brinkmann, *Rheinisches Museum für Philologie*, Band 62. Frankfort, 1907.

[1] See for instance :—
1. Plutarch, *Morals*, ed. by A. R. Shilleto.   London, 1888.
2. *Athenaeus*, ed. by C. D. Yonge, vol. iii.   London, 1854.
3. Xenophon, *Minor Works*, ed. by J. S. Watson, Government of Lacedaemon, ch. ii.   London, 1884.
4. Lucian, *Amores*, The Athenian Society, 1895.
5. *Maximus Tyrius*, T. Taylor, trans.   London, 1804.
6. *Commentary on Catullus*, by Robinson Ellis.   Oxford, 1889.

[2] The learned theologian, Dr. Döllinger, observed that the degree of civilisation a people had attained to, might qualify the form but not the substance of the matter.—*The Gentile and the Jew*, ii. 238.   London, 1862.

[3] See Letourneau, *Sociology*, H. M. Trollope's trans. ch. iv. p. 71. London, 1893.
A. Bastian, *Der Mensch in der Geschichte*.   Leipzig, 1860.
Edward Carpenter, *Die Homogene Liebe*.   German trans. by H. B. Fischer.
Edward Carpenter, *An Unknown People*.   London, 1897.
F. Karsch, *Uranismus bei den Naturvölkern*.
H. Ploss, *Das Weib*.   Leipzig, 1884.

[4] See J. Lubbock, *Ants, Bees, and Wasps*.   London, 1872.

[5] M. Maeterlinck, *The Life of the Bee*.   London, 1901.

[6] Speaking of which Professor Mantegazza says " non è un vizio, ma una passione," *Gli Uomini*, i. 5.   And see William James, *The Principles of Psychology*, vol. ii. p. 439.   London, 1890.

very recent times that the strong achromatic lens of Science has been turned upon them. Only towards the end of the century we have just left has it been possible to let in light upon this melancholy subject, so that we may hope some day to make a real advance in dealing with the question. " Where you meet a social problem," said Henry George, " there you will find a social wrong at the bottom of it." We have yet far to travel towards truth, and, as Vesalius found in the sixteenth century, there are indeed many obstacles, both natural and artificial, placed in the way of new lines of research which criticise the treatment of a tabooed subject, and one " round which superstition, myth, and pseudo-morality have entwined themselves closer, perhaps, than round any other." [1]

All through the periods of ignorance the mad were placed within the province of the priest ; equally hopelessly, the unfortunate inverts have been left to the policeman. Not till the last part of the nineteenth century did Science dare to look into the question. Professor Westphal [2] of Berlin is claimed as the first medical authority to undertake the work. But probably better known is Dr. R. Von Krafft-Ebing, whose *Psychopathia Sexualis* has gone into some ten editions [3] and has been read all over Europe. Another important work is that of Dr. Albert Moll. [4]

Much has been lately written, [5] and in many languages.

[1] E. Belfort Bax, *Outspoken Essays*, p. vi. London, 1897.
Iwan Bloch, *The Sexual Life of Our Time*, Dr. M. E. Paul's trans. London, 1909.
[2] In the *Archiv für Psychiatrie*, 1870.
[3] A translation for medical readers has been made into English (F. J. Rebman. London, 1905), and an Italian version has been published by Drs. Sterz and Waldhart. Turin, 1889, etc., etc.
[4] *Etude sur l'Inversion Sexuelle*, translated into French from the German by Drs. Pactet and Romme. Paris, Carré, 1893.
[5] For instance :
Dr. James Burnet in *Med. Times and Hosp. Gazette*, Feb. 3, 1906.
Dr. C. G. Chaddock in F. Peterson and W. S. Haines, *Text-Book of Legal Medicine and Toxicology*, Philadelphia, 1903.
Dr. R. A. Gordon in *University Magazine*, Jan. 1898.
Dr. J. S. Kiernan in *Detroit Lancet*, 1884 ; *Alienist and Neurologist*, 1891.
Dr. J. Roux, *Psychology of the Sexual Instinct*. London, 1900.
Dr. C. F. Lydston in *Philad. Med. and Surg. Reporter*, Sept. 7, 1889.
Dr. B. Tarnowsky, *The Sexual Instinct*, Costello and Allinson, trans. Paris, 1898.

But the most important volumes printed on the subject are the studies of Havelock Ellis,[1] for he has not abused his technical knowledge of bones and bowels by attempting to " explain " emotions which we do not understand in terms of pathology which we *do* understand, but which have nothing to do with the real problems at issue. A vast similitude underlies all. The words of the American seer are being verified in these latter days. More than anything else, recent scientific researches have emphasised the oneness of creation. We are realising the fundamental unity and the possible transmutability of all varieties of matter, the intense inter-relationship between the various organs,[2] and the enormous

Prof. C. Féré, *Pathology of the Emotions.* Dr. Robert Park's trans.
Prof. A. Forel, *The Sexual Question,* C. F. Marshall's trans.
John Addington Symonds, *A Problem in Modern Ethics.* London, 1896.
The Continental literature on the subject is too extensive to exhibit in detail; the inquirer can consult the catalogues of Max Spohr of Leipzig ; Sauerländer of Frankfort ; Carré of Paris ; or the Wissenschaftlich-humanitären Komitee of Berlin. I may however allude to a few works picked out almost at random from many others.
La Rousse, *Dict. Universelle du xixe Siècle,* under " Péderastie."
Lacassagne, *Dict. Enc. des Sciences Médicales.*
Dr. G. Merzbach, *Die krankhaften Erscheinungen des Geschlechtssinnes.*
Dr. L. von Römer, *Die erbliche Belastung des Centralnervensystems bei Uranien.*
Dr. P. J. Moebius, *Die Wirkung der Kastration.*
R. Gerling, *Das dritte Geschlecht.*
Dr. Legrain, *Des Anomalies de l'Instinct Sexuelle.*
E. Mühsam, *Die Homosexualität.*
J. von Wilpert, *Das Recht des dritten Geschlecht.*
F. Carlier, *Les Deux Prostitutions.*
E. Bab, *Die Gleichgeschlechtliche Liebe.*
L. Frey, *Die Männer des Rätsels.*
Dr. B. Friedländer, *Die Renaissance des Eros Uranos.*
Dr. M. Grohe, *Der Urning vor Gericht.*
M. Hirschfeld, *Geschlechtsübergänge.*
H. Hoessli, *Die Unzuferlassigkeit des Geschlechtszeichen,* 1836.
F. von Ramdohr, *Ueber die Natur.* 1798.
M. Hirschfeld, *Sappho und Sokrates.* Leipzig, 1902.
H. Kaan, *Psychopathia Sexualis.* 1844.
Dr. F. Chevalier, *L'Inversion Sexuelle,* 1893.
Dr. P. Penta, *L'Origine è la Patogenesi della Inversione Sessuale,* 1896.
Dr. Letamendi, *La Criminalidad ante la Ciencia.* Madrid, 1883.
Max Dessoir, *Zur Psychologie Zeitschrift für Psychiatrie,* 1883.
André Raffalovich, *Uranisme et Unisexualité.* Lyons, 1896.
And the celebrated *Jahrbuch für sexuelle Zwischenstufen,* edited by Dr. Magnus Hirschfeld and published in many volumes by Max Spohr.
[1] The F. A. Davis Med. Pub. Co. Philadelphia, 1901.
[2] The functions of which, as K. H. Ulrichs profoundly pointed out

power of the will and the imagination [1] (which, in my opinion, represents that which is true in Christian science) over the nerves and members of the body. And this same unity extends to sex. The division indeed represents specialisation of function, which nature had carried out in numerous directions,[2] but not the gulf impassable it may appear to be.[3] " Males and females," says Professor Hertwig,[4] " whether they be more or less unlike, arise from the same germinal material.[5] The germinal material itself is sexless, that is to say, there is not a male and female germinal material," and elsewhere we read : " Every organism . . . (apart from asexual

(see his *Memnon*, new edition, 1898, Spohr. Leipzig), and other works ; also under *Numa Numantius*, are often dual or multiplex in action, as, for instance, in the case of the trunk or nose-hand of the elephant, etc., etc. The same thing might be said of the members in certain other perfectly normal human and animal relationships. " An organ," said **Darwin,** " may become rudimentary for its proper purpose and be used for a distinct one ; in certain fishes the swim-bladder seems to be rudimentary for its proper function of giving buoyancy, but has become converted into a nascent breathing organ or lung."—*Origin of Species.* London, 1888. Also the " artificial " method of swimming adopted by the sole and other flat-fish—see for instance J. T. Cunningham, *Treatise on the Common Sole.* London, 1890. And see *Quarterly Review,* July 1902.

[1] How very close is the affinity between different organs and senses is illustrated by the effect of an injury to one eye by "sympathy" upon the other ; and in the little-known phenomenon of colour-hearing, where sound conveys also a colour-image, varying according to the pitch. This is alluded to by Havelock Ellis, *Studies,* also by H. Croft Hiller, *Heresies,* ii. 301, **and** Ribot, *Psychology of the Emotions,* p. 181, London, 1897. **Suarez de** Mendoza, *L'Audition Colorée,* Paris, 1890. T. Flournoy, *Des Phénomènes de Synopsie,* Geneva, 1893. Dr. W. S. Colman, *Lancet,* March 31, etc., 1894. C. S. Wake, *Musical Tone and Colour-Music,* 1896.

[2] See, for instance, Demoor and Massart, *Evolution by Atrophy.* London, 1899.

[3] " The mammary glands are the same at birth in both sexes." Thomas Bryant, *Diseases of the Breast,* p. 6. London, 1887.

[4] *The Biological Problem of To-day,* P. C. Mitchell's trans. p. 123. London, 1896.

[5] " It is coming to be more or less widely accepted, and indeed it is little more than an obvious fact, that differences of sex have grown with growing civilisation. Beginning with a more or less undifferentiated savage masculine type of woman, who, except for primary sex differences, closely resembled man in her bodily form and mental character, and a savage type of man with many womanly features, the modern womanly and manly individualities have been slowly evolved." Dr. J. Lionel Tayler, *Sociological Papers,* vol. iii. p. 125. London, 1906. See also J. T. Cunningham, *Sexual Dimorphism in the Animal Kingdom,* p. 39. D. S. Jordan, *The Study of Fishes,* vol. i. ch. ix. London, 1905.

and parthenogenetic reproduction) [1] develops from a fertilised egg-cell. This material, which in one case develops into a male, in another into a female, is, so far as our experience can go, always the same."

Moreover, we must bear in mind that beyond asexual reproduction,[2] and parthenogenesis,[3] and quite apart from freaks and malformations [4] such as " free-martins " [5] and mules,[6] yet many creatures [7] (ranging, for instance, as high as the sea perch) are perfectly bisexual and quite normally hermaphroditic,[8] some even changing functions (or we might say sexes) with the seasons of the year.[9] (See Protandrism.)

Once having seen their absolutely common origin, we might expect to find what indeed really exists, a " latent bisexuality in each sex."[10] In the human race the similarity [11] is far greater than we mostly realise.[11] Custom, education, costume, and maternity [12] have all tended to accentuate the difference and obliterate the likeness of the two sexes, but, in reality, both in outline

---

[1] Geddes and Thomson, *Evolution of Sex*, p. 32.
[2] See Sir R. Owen, *Parthenogenesis*, p. 24, etc. London, 1849. Weissmann, *Heredity*, ii. 91 and 110. Oxford, 1891.
[3] C. T. von Siebold, *Wahre Parthenogenesis*. Leipzig, 1856.
[4] R. Leuckart, *Generationswehels*. Frankfort, 1858.
[5] *Evolution of Sex*, p. 39.
[6] W. D. Whitney, *Cent. Dict.* " Freemartins." J. Hunter, " Account of a Freemartin," *Philosophical Translations*, 1779.
[7] P. Broca, *Phenomena of Hybridity*, C. C. Blake trans. pp. 26, 65, etc. London, 1863.
[8] E. Haeckel, E. Ray Lankester's trans.; *Hist. of Creation*, vol. i. pp. 148, 275, etc. London, 1876.
[9] See, for instance, Otto Weininger, *Sex and Character*, p. 19. London, 1906.
A. F. Guenther, *Commentatio de Hermaphroditismo* [and bibliography]. Leipzig, 1846.
F. von Neugebauer, *Zusammenstellung der Literatur über Hermaphroditismus beim Menschen*, Jahrbuch vii. p. 471. Leipzig, Max Spohr, 1905.
Hermaphrodite Fishes. See *Camb. Nat. Hist.*, vol. vii. p. 420. London, 1904.
[10] Havelock Ellis, *Psychology of Sex*, p. 132. Darwin, *Animals and Plants*, ch. xiii. London, 1868.
Edward Clodd, *The Story of Creation*, pp. 84, 190, etc. London, 1901.
[11] A paper on " Panhermaphroditism," by Dr. de Letamendi of Madrid, was read before the International Medical Congress at Rome in 1894.
[12] See Dr. Harry Campbell, *Differences in the Nervous Organisation of Man and Woman*. London, 1891.
[13] Dr. M. Good, " Lactation in the Male," *Humanitarian*, December 1892. New York,.

of form [1] and in physiological potentialities,[2] they stand
extremely close together.[3]   They are, in fact, as a brain
specialist once said to me, opposite poles of the same
thing. Between these poles come all varieties of temperament, from the ultra-masculine to the infra-feminine.
We may conceive them spread out like a spectrum, the
colours (temperaments) blending into one another. For,
psychically, there is no great gap between the sexes,
which may indeed be said to overlap, on the emotional
plane, and, in mankind, the power of idealism often
appears to dominate and transform the working of the
whole material body.[4]

The main, or normal, attraction-forces, are at the two
extremes of the emotional scale, but there are evidently
others also, and thus among the infinite kinds of combination we also find the homogenic union.[5]

[1] Professor E. Metchnikoff, *The Nature of Man*, pp. 59, 78, 298, etc.
London, 1903.

[2] Dr. W. R. Williams thinks that many strange phenomena may be
rendered intelligible " if we bear in mind the principle of correlated
variability and the doctrine of the latent hermaphroditism of every
human being."—*Diseases of the Breast*, p. 112, London, 1894.   For male
lactation see p. 16, and A. M. Sheild's *Diseases of the Breast*, p. 17,
London, 1898 ; and L. Hermann's *Physiology*, p. 158, London, 1878 ;
and again, Dr. Thomas Bryant, *Diseases of the Breast*, p. 89, London,
1897.   Ernst Haeckel, *History of Creation*, p. 290. London, 1876.

[3] And more especially in adolescence. The young are apt to bear
the impress of the Past, and carry indications of primordial types.
[An instance of this is said to be shown in the extraordinary strength of
an infant's hand-grip.] Thus certain organisms are hermaphrodite
in their early stages though unisexual in their adult life, and, " according to some, most higher animals pass through a stage of embryonic
hermaphroditism " (Geddes and Thomson, *Evolution of Sex*, p. 65 ;
and H. Ellis, i. chap. vi.). See also Professor F. Karsch, *Päderastie und
Triebadie bei den Tieren*; and Dr. Norbert Grabowsky, *Die Mann-
weibliche Natur des Menschen*. For remarks on the alleged homosexual
habits of the partridge see for instance *Batman uppon Bartholome*
[*Bartholomaeus Anglicus*], lib. x. ch. xxx. p. 187. London, 1582.

[4] Some curious speculations on this point are advanced by H. Croft
Hiller, *Heresies*, vol. ii. chap. iii. London, 1900. Also by C. G.
Leland, *The Alternate Sex*. London, 1904, and by Frances Swiney,
"The Evolution of the Male," *Westminster Review*, March and April,
1905. White's *Selborne*, Letter vi.

[5] If we inquire the first cause of passionate attraction, we can
receive our answer in the words of Professor Owen : " It is plainly
denied to finite understandings . . . to comprehend the nature of the
operation of the First Cause of anything . . . the ablest endeavours
here to penetrate to the beginning of things do but carry us, when most
successful, a few steps nearer that beginning, and then leave us on the
verge of a boundless ocean of the unknown truth, dividing the secondary
or subordinate phenomena in the chain of creation from the great First

It may be that the gamut of the emotions is really wider and more comprehensive than we knew ; [1] in the light-spectrum it has been discovered that there are potent rays at either end which are invisible to human eyes. It may be nature has more needs and purposes than were dreamt of in our philosophy. But it is not within the sphere, or indeed within the power of criminology to *explain* the emotions.[2]

Nor does it help us much to moralise and ask why such an instinct should have been created, or to reflect what an amount of misery would have been saved if it had never been. We have, unhappily, a very present and practical problem to deal with, which it is useless to deny, and most immoral to ignore,[3] since the first principles of *justice* are involved. It is that we may rightly understand the nature of the phenomena, and not continue merely to beat about the shuttlecocks of convention in an atmosphere of lies, that I have tried to show what the facts really are.

So far we have not dealt with the drink question. Nor shall we have to dwell for any length upon it, because this fundamental problem has been already treated by many specialists whose work is comprehensive and accessible.

One dare not—with any hope of finishing this book, which has already taken years beyond the estimated time—touch upon the *history* of alcohol ; enough that it costs us 189 millions a year ; [4] how much it has cost

Cause " (*Parthenogenesis*, iii.). It is easy enough to discuss what takes place on the physical plane, but the problem is, what set up the *desire* ; what is ultimately sought and accomplished ? Perhaps with problems in idealism we must accept the keen saying of Herbert Spencer, that " a thing cannot at the same instant be both subject and object of thought ; and yet the substance of the mind must be this before it can be known."

[1] See *Sociological Papers*, vol. ii. p. 21. London, 1905.

[2] This has indeed been many times attempted, notably by Grant Allen in his *Physiological Æsthetics*, but all such efforts appear to me to resolve themselves into merely explaining one emotion in terms of another, both being equally unknowable. To express one sensation by another is very like " defining night by darkness," or running round in a circle in order to arrive somewhere.

[3] See remarks by Dr. Charles W. Allen in *Twentieth-Century Practice*, edited by T. L. Stedman, vol. vii. pp. 595, 596. London, 1896.

[4] T. P. Whittaker, *The Economic Aspect of the Drink Problem*, p. 11. London, 1902.

mankind, how much it has retarded human progress cannot be even estimated.[1] But keeping severely to our own subject, there is no doubt that the effects of drink on criminality are very great indeed, and many eminent authorities[2] have charged it with causing directly and indirectly three-fourths of the total of crime.[3] It should, perhaps, be added that this extreme statement has been questioned, or at least qualified. Captain Nott Bower, when Chief Constable of Liverpool, considered that fifty per cent. would be a fair calculation of the amount of crime set up by drink.[4] And Mr. W. D. Morrison thinks " the effect of drink has been exaggerated,"[5] pointing out that offences, and especially murderous affrays,[6] are very prevalent in the more

[1] See the views of John Bright and W. E. Gladstone quoted by Dean Farrar, *Fortnightly Review*, vol. liii. [1893].

[2] See Gordon Ryland's *Crime*, p. 22.

Francis Peek, *Social Wreckage*, Appendix.

Lord Chancellor Cairns said : " I believe it is scarcely possible to exaggerate the blessings that would come down upon this country from the practice of temperance. *It would empty our gaols.*"

[3] Cardinal Manning : " . . . According to the testimony of many of the magistrates it is the source, directly or indirectly, of 75 per cent. of the crimes committed."

Rev. J. W. Horsley : " Intemperance, which by a moderate estimate fills, directly or indirectly, three-fourths of our prison cells " (*Prisons and Prisoners*, p. 49).

Sir Robert Anderson : " Some of the ablest and most experienced of our judges, indeed, have publicly declared their conviction that most of the crimes which come before the criminal courts may be traced, directly or indirectly, to the one vice of drunkenness " (*Nineteenth Century*, March 1903, p. 499).

Judge Pattison (to a jury in 1844) : " If it were not for drinking, you or I would have nothing to do." (*Fortnightly Review*, vol. liii. p. 791).

Mr. Stipendiary Wright : " If you were to take away the effect of drink in my district " (Potteries), " I do not think I should have practically any work whatever to do " (*R. C. Licensing Laws Report*, p. 81).

General Booth : " Nine-tenths of our poverty, squalor, vice, and crime spring from this poisonous tap-root " (*Darkest England*, p. 47. London, 1890).

Mr. Stipendiary Cluer (to a prisoner): " You need not tell me that it began in a public-house. If there were no public-houses I should not be here, and nine-tenths of the policemen would not be needed."

[4] *Royal Commission on Licensing Report*, p. 80.

[5] *Mind*, New Series, vol. i. p. 514.

[6] But I should like to know how many of the crimes of violence drink may still be accountable for. A man may not be absolutely drunk, but yet have taken sufficient alcohol to lose his mental balance. Many of the rows along the Mediterranean coast take place over gambling games, such as Mora. One of the heroes of *The Iliad*, if I remember rightly, committed manslaughter on being angered over dice.

temperate countries of the south of Europe. But while their people are undoubtedly given to almost maniacal outbreaks of fury when provoked to anger, they are also very poor and often terribly taxed out there. But while I cannot affirm that the removal of alcohol would abolish crime under the present conditions of Western civilisation, where the struggle for wealth—not for bread and subsistence alone, but for all the honours and alleviations which that one little word implies— causes five-sixths of the more serious offences,[1] yet alcohol remains a huge demoralising force, and just as gambling gnaws at the tap-root of industry, so drink decays the very bones of character.

The bar is the curse of every ship afloat that carries one, and nearly all the brawls and outrages which keep the police busy have staggered out into the street hot from the public-house. There is enough of the wild beast in human nature to make it always very dangerous to cloud restraining reason. What the results are may be seen all round. But again I would repeat the words of Henry George, that where we find a social problem there is a social *wrong* at the bottom of it. Reform will never come by negative repression ;[2] only he can destroy who can replace. In the wicked old days it was by drink alone our soldiers whiled away the hours in Indian heat and in English rain ; off duty there was nothing else to do. " Boozing," says the *Royal Commission Report*,[3] " was at one time almost the only excitement open to the working man." [4]

We have allowed the degrading public-house to remain the poor man's only club, his centre of enjoyment, his refuge from squalor and crowding at home, his palace of light and warmth out of the fog and cold.[5] And all this

---

[1] See W. Bevon Lewis, "Origins of Crime," *Fortnightly Review,* vol. liv. p. 329.

[2] See criticism of Mr. Charles Booth's work, *Saturday Review,* vol. xcvi. p. 333.

[3] *Licensing Laws*, p. 2.

[4] On the failure of the Anti-gin Legislation of 1736 see W. Besant, *London in the Eighteenth Century,* p. 297. London, 1902.

[5] "Many a man takes to beer not from love of beer, but from a natural craving for the light, warmth, company, and comfort which is thrown in along with the beer, and which he cannot get except by buying beer."—General Booth, *In Darkest England,* p. 48. London, 1890.

is kept up out of the sale of drink, and the selling is in the hands of the man who has to make his living by it, who has to keep his wife and children by it. It is only common human nature that he should wish as much as possible consumed—the more the better—and that the would-be temperate customer should feel he was not wanted there, should feel that he was mean and shabby if he did not keep on drinking, for the good of the house and the bad in the home.

Moreover, throughout all classes exists the excellently-meant but yet destructive form of " have-a-drinking " hospitality, ranging from the half-pint of the very poorest to the mess of the " Black Tyrones " [1] described by Rudyard Kipling, who, in the entertainment of their guest " individually and collectively . . . had striven in all hospitality to make him drunk." It may, I think, be said without exaggeration that the common and criminal assaults which do not take their origin in drink are very few in number, and nearly always pathological in character.

[1] *Life's Handicap*, p. 85.

CHAPTER XVIII

CLASSIFICATION : OFFENDERS

"Learn what is True in order to do what is right."
HUXLEY on **Descartes**.

IN the last chapter we examined the nature and classification of offences: we have now to try and understand the nature of the offender—of the criminal. It may seem strange that I should find it necessary to point out that the criminal is a human being, and not, as many foolish people really seem to imagine, a creature with incipient horns and an elementary tail! And all men have "organs, dimensions, senses, affections, passions." [1] Shylock's defence of his down-trodden race is true of all mankind, both free and bound.

It is time, in the twentieth century, to be quite clear in our minds that devils do not exist ; we have to deal only with men and women, and they can be cruel enough as they are. " The criminal," it has been said, " is always the man we do not know, or the man we hate, the man we see through the bitterness of our hearts." [2] Let us try to come very near, to make him confess without fear or deceit, and, with a knowledge of our own frailty, let us try to understand what manner of man he is.

Just as there are two great groups of crimes (the circumstantial and impulsive), so also the criminals fall naturally into two great classes: those who commit crimes from the stress of circumstances, and those who transgress the law from some defect or abnormality existing in themselves. There are indeed cases that overlap ; there are persons who, at first sight, appear to belong to one class, when they should really be placed

[1] *Merchant of Venice*, III. i.
[2] Clarence S. Darrow, *Resist not Evil*. London, 1903.

305

in the other ; and there are complicated cases where a number of evil conditions act and react upon the individual. But when we look close enough the dividing line between the circumstantial and the impulse prisoners is nearly always clear and obvious. And the gulf fixed between the groups is very great indeed.

The root of all real crime is selfishness. Not that the successful are necessarily altruistic, or the failures necessarily the more selfish. There is, in our present society, a direct incentive towards anti-social conduct, in that it is founded upon competition. Competition may, or may not, be a necessary process in the grim life-struggle, but it is most distinctly civil war.

To conquer in that war, to overcome their fellow citizens, is the supreme object of most men. For those who fail is reserved everything that is hard and unpleasant. To such as succeed all enjoyments are open ; the golden key once grasped unlocks all doors, few care how it was got ; people are not punished for being mean and parasitic, but for being aggressive in an illegal way.

The sword of justice descends not for breaches of honesty and honour, but for such delicts as are outside the rules of civilised (social) warfare, and which are so clumsily perpetrated as to be practically punishable. It may be said that this has been the theme of all the sermons since civilisation, and that our plaint is against fixed conditions red-written in the world-wide laws of life. But these points are beside the question and have no bearing on immediate facts.

Under competitive conditions it must needs be that offences come. The presence of crime is part of the price we have to pay for what is often called free competition. Some say it is the price of invention and progress ; others, that it is the penalty imposed for the lack of social organisation. It is sufficient for the criminologist to point out that the toll is taken, and that the sacrificed are in our midst.

The thing we have to fight is selfishness; and while there are no " devils " who delight in evil for its own sake (why *should* they ?) there are more people than one cares to reckon up devoid of all commiseration for their kind. These are the real criminals of the world, although they do not always occupy the dock [1] and may sometimes preside upon the bench or govern kingdoms from the place of power.

The true criminal, by whom I mean the man who will deliberately sacrifice others for his own advantage, is found in all ranks of society. He may never have occasion to transgress the law, and his true character may be disguised in rich apparel, showing forth only to the keen observer, in a number of actions which no law can punish and may even be made to support, but in which the brutal nature of the man comes out. [2]

We will not pause at this place to discuss how far he has been set up by surroundings, or whether he must really be born again—and born different! The anti-social man has been a persistent type from time immemorial in all competitive communities.

Methods and opportunities may vary with the centuries, [3] but through all kinds of clothes and customs we find the egoist ever emerging, the parasite (often in the worst cases, apparently unconscious of being one) preying on other people ; the traitor, the " friendly native," and the " sworn tormentor," waiting to be hired, and ever ready for the vilest tasks. I have wished to begin with what I may call the criminally-selfish class, because it may be placed at the opposite extreme from those which we shall presently examine ; and if prisons—as distinct

---

[1] When I read the story of the notorious murderer Lacenaire, I could not help thinking what high offices he might have filled had he been able to complete his legal studies. What a " strong " judge this man might have become if the paternal purse had not run short ! Brave, temperate, moral, and merciless, he might so easily have risen to be robed in red and ermine, and to be damned beneath a marble monument, instead of ending by the common guillotine. See H. B. Irving's *Studies of French Criminals*, etc.

[2] For instance, in an article entitled " The Passing of the Circuits," I read the following : " It is related of a member of the Western Circuit who afterwards attained great eminence, that, being as a young man too poor to drive and too lazy to walk, he more than once, at the beginning of a circuit, induced some unsuspecting dealer to let him have a horse on approval, and after riding it hard and feeding it badly for six weeks, would return it to the owner with the remark that it was but a sorry jade."—*Pall Mall Gazette*, Sept. 7, 1899.

[3] For instance, the witch-finder of the olden days has now evolved into the " sex " blackmailer. Popular ignorance of natural phenomena, fear, cowardice, and the scent of scandal can be always counted on. The justices did (and do) the rest in providing the tools.

from asylums—continue to be necessary in the future, for this class only will such structures stand.

I am not referring particularly to the "habitual criminal," of whom just now we hear so much, but to the deliberate wrong-doer ; the man who intentionally sacrifices others ; not, of course, from diabolical malice, but from cold-blooded insouciance. Also, I am referring not so much to the man actually behind the bars (for the calculating criminal frequently escapes, although he does get caught from time to time) as to the kind of man whom we should wish to see secured.

The presence of the inhuman parasitic type raises the complex question of responsibility. People talk very vaguely on the subject, making it monstrous with theology and foggy with metaphysics. Some will maintain that to question full freedom of choice, under all circumstances, is to make meaningless such terms as " good " and " evil " ; a doctrine which, in its extreme outcome, would surely place all Bedlam in the dock. Others have spoken of all crime as hereditary disease, which sounds about as sensible as saying that all disease is an hereditary crime !

We must distinguish, using common sense. I do not say that ALL have not excuse, even perhaps to ultimate exculpation, if the conflicting forces of temptation and resistance came to be balanced where all thoughts are known. I would repeat the saying of Thomas à Kempis, " In judging others a man labours to no purpose, commonly errs, and frequently sins; but in examining and judging himself he is always wisely and usefully employed." But while the absolute nature and quality of any one is a thing that can never be truly established on this side of the grave, we may not, in our diagnosis of criminality, assert that a man is mad merely because he is bad.[1]

Insanity means a definite state of disease or impairment of the mental machinery, and unfortunately the absence of altruism does not by any means imply the innocence of irresponsibility. Want of heart (the only real evil) does not unhappily always show want of head.

There are indeed people who will exploit (for the

[1] Or, if a man will be contentious, we can express it ; guilty of aggressive conduct, which, for practical reasons, we assume to be so.

deliberate crimes have nearly always to do with the destructive wealth-struggle) and sacrifice others to any extent, people who are reasonably responsible for their acts, people who are at war against the Commonweal. I have laid stress upon the practical responsibility of a certain class of criminal the more to emphasise, later on, how many qualifying circumstances we must in justice make allowance for.

" Good " people and " bad " people represent groups of tendencies, altruism or selfishness preponderating, as the case may be ; but in the extreme complexity of human nature, men can never be divided sharply into " sheep " and " goats," for none attain absolute virtue, any more than any descend into unmitigated villainy.[1] There is no hard and fast line drawn between the types—much as they differ—any more than there is a sudden and violent change in climate from the tropics to the arctic zone ; atmosphere alters but in infinite gradations, the one same heaven is overhead, the one same ocean sweeps from pole to pole. So a character is made up of long-accumulated qualities, some subtly inherited, but most of them acquired along life's road, the needs of nature underlying all.

We began our survey with the deliberate criminal (that is, the selfish-inhuman type, when it happens to transgress the law and to be found out doing so) because beyond doubt such a type exists ; but I think it will be found that the vast majority of offenders go wrong, not so much from having what is called a bad character, as from not having been morally strong enough to gain and hold a good one.

Even the Circumstantial criminal is mostly a warped, stunted, and ill-balanced being. Said that able criminologist the late Mr. A. R. Whiteway, " the equilibrium of the professional criminal is by nature so unstable that if he is hungry he steals almost automatically because he has no self-control " ; and elsewhere,[2] " the innate criminal is a poor creature in mind, body and estate.[3]

[1] " There is some good in every man," wrote the eminent criminal lawyer, Serjeant E. W. Cox, "if only we rightly search for it."—*Principles of Punishment*, p. 229. London, 1877.
[2] *Recent Object-Lessons in Penal Science*, p. 44. London, 1898.
[3] In his larger work of the same title, p. 67. London, 1902.

"Deficiencies in memory, imagination, reason," says the Rev. Dr. Morrison, "are three undoubted characteristics of the ordinary criminal intellect."[1]

Even that strong exponent of the hardest officialism, the late Sir F. DuCane, was so far in agreement when he admitted that "a large number of prisoners are persons who are absolutely unable, or find it extremely difficult, through mental or physical incapacity, to earn their livelihood even under favourable circumstances."[2] And Mr. J. B. Manning, late governor of Pentonville, declared of a certain class of the "habituals," that he had "those half-witted creatures coming again and again to prison."[3] Dr. Bevan Lewis, superintendent of Wakefield Asylum, said in his evidence,[4] "I should say that both insanity and crime are simply morbid branches of the same stock. Given a certain environment, you will have crime; given a more favourable environment and you will have simply insanity." And Dr. T. C. Shaw, of Banstead, said,[5] "According to my view, the moral demonstration depends on the perfection of the physical structure."

We have then conclusive evidence as to the habitually diseased and defective constitution of the common or Circumstantial criminal; and, as regards his physical condition at any rate, he is but typical of a very large class. Thus we read that out of 12,000 recruits examined for the army,[6] over 31 per cent. had to be rejected for diseases or defects; and elsewhere we are told that nearly 80 per cent. of the children in industrial schools had diseased and decaying teeth,[7] a state of things which, said the lecturer, brought thousands to the hospitals every year with all sorts of complaints. The housing problem and the nourishment problem do not lie within the compass of this book, but it is obvious that dirt,

---

[1] *Crime and its Causes*, p. 195. London, 1891.
See also Albert Wilson, *Unfinished Man*, p. 40, etc. London, 1910.
[2] *The Punishment and Prevention of Crime*, p. 171.
[3] *Departmental Committee*, 1895, Ev. p. 35.
[4] *Ibid.* p. 303.
[5] *Departmental Committee*, 1895, Ev., p. 197.
The whole evidence of these two eminent doctors may be studied with advantage.
[6] *R. Com. on Physical Training Report*, p. 22. Edinburgh, 1903.
[7] An address to the students of the Middlesex Hospital by Mr. Hern, *Brit. Med. Journ.*, Oct. 3, 1903, p. 796.

malnutrition, and especially drink, are mighty and active agents of degeneration, and when all these are present to aggravate the fierce and overwhelming competition struggle,[1] who can wonder that crime and misery are rife on all sides around ?

But besides the selfishly inhuman, besidesthe stampeded herd on-driven over the abyss of crime by bad social conditions, there remain those varied and often most perplexing people, whose qualities and defects arise within themselves, and who may all be roughly classed under Group II.

The Criminally-impulsive temperament, like the Selfishly-inhuman, may, or may not, bring the possessor into the iron clutches of the Law. But when the impulse-criminal escapes conviction, it is from good luck or some saving circumstance, rather than from deliberate design. He may indeed sail " somehow " through life like a badly-laden vessel, and may keep free from storms or be taken in tow. But under different conditions, our lop-sided ship may get bad weather right away, and, listing hopelessly at the first squall, plunge down for ever in the trough of crime. In other words, the weak-minded, fatally impulsive person, just simply from lack of " grit " and " grip," may easily become, and end, a hopeless and habitual criminal. For in the fierce contention of the crowd, when once a man of this sort is pushed over, he does not often have a chance to rise, and if he could not face life's battle when free, much less will he be able to do so afterwards, when weighted down by the additional hardship of having once been put away in prison, but rather, sinking under the increasing load, he will let things slide, abandoning all effort, until, as Mr. Whiteway expressed it, " his existence becomes a life of omitting to stand upright in any relation where it may appear to him, for the moment, to be an easier matter to lie down." [2]

But it must not be imagined that the impulse-offender is always a mere drifting degenerate: often indeed he is his own and only enemy—a man who may show real,

[1] It has been estimated that in 1901 the various undertakings by land or water in the United Kingdom cost the lives of 4,627 workers and wounded 107,290. See article by W. J. Gordon, *Leisure Hour*, Sept. 1903.

[2] *Object-Lessons*, p. 45. London, 1898.

though generally capricious, genius, and who may be
capable on great occasions of noble impulses and deeds
of daring, which ordinary respectable and selfish citizens
have not imagined even in their dreams ! The impulse-
offender is mostly unbalanced rather than bad, and
always far more to be pitied than condemned. A typical
illustration of the kind of man I mean will be familiar
to the reader, though perhaps not in that precise aspect,
in Dickens' character of Sydney Carton.[1] But in spite of
being frequently endowed with fine and even brilliant
qualities, the man of perilously-impulsive tendencies has
usually the hardest lot in life. The selfishly-inhuman
may batten monstrously upon others and quite escape
the censure of this world, but the unhappy victim of
a temperamental " twist " may have his very virtues
turned to elements of danger ; may easily trip up and be
caught and drawn [2] into the unrailed engine of the Law,
and then, with our present primitive and indiscriminating
methods, only a given act is to be dwelt upon in court, and
not the nature of the offending person, often the only
thing which truly indicates its kind.[3]

A word may now be said on " overlapping " crimes ;
offences which apparently belong to one class, but which
are really " mixed," or in the other—acts which may
appear to be in Group I (the Circumstantial offences),
but which, from the manner of their commission, should
be placed in Group II (Impulse-acts). Thus offences
against property, which constitute the overwhelming
bulk of serious crime, are set up by bad social conditions,
or by the deliberate conduct of parasitic people. But
this is not always so. In every rank of life, incredible as
it may appear, there are occasionally men and women who
steal : it may be some particular thing on which their
minds are morbidly intent, or it may be any object which
they can conveniently lay hands upon.

Such a person was the late Lord X, a territorial magnate
and a cabinet minister in the late reign,[4] who is alleged
to have been followed about by an agent or secretary,

---

[1] *Tale of Two Cities.*
[2] See also Blagg and Wilson in one of the Fabian Society's Essays.
[3] See Sir Robert Anderson's strong views upon this point. *Nineteenth
Century*, February and July, 1901.
[4] Of Queen Victoria.

who often settled and smoothed over the great man's eccentricities. Such a person was a former Lady C,[1] who was well known to pocket any small silver articles or knick-knacks she might fancy, and whose friends would often send round the next day requesting Lady C to return such and such a thing, that she had lately—borrowed ! It is sad to reflect that if these two, and others like them (and the same passion has been alleged against a man of still higher rank who died a decade or so ago), had been but people in a humble station, they would undoubtedly have passed their lives perpetually in prison. This has occurred over and over again ; looking back over my case books, I find a great number of instances of accumulating sentences amounting in their aggregate to twenty and thirty years, and even more, of penal servitude.

A typical trial of this nature took place at the Dorset Assizes a few years ago, when a man is stated to have been five times convicted of petty thefts, together not amounting to two pounds. For these he had endured sentences amounting to five-and-thirty years' imprisonment. The judge, in this instance, gave him but four months' imprisonment, and promised to write to the then Home Secretary about his ticket-of-leave, which of course threatened to be forfeited. Unhappily in the case of the poor and necessitous it is often a most difficult matter to distinguish between incorrigible roguery and genuine kleptomania ; but the clumsy commission of repeated offences, after having incurred severe and accumulating penalties (*i.e.* sentences increasing for the same kind of offence on account of the previous convictions) should make the court look very carefully into the prisoner's state of mind.

There are indeed a number of odd, eccentric offences, even against property, puzzling, overlapping, and Group II cases, which argue loss of mental equilibrium. An example of this kind is furnished in the conduct of J. W., who managed to forge cheques to the extent of £1,434. Part of the money he spent in betting transactions, so commonly the origin of a clerk's downfall ; so far, this seems an ordinary Group I crime. But it looks more

---

[1] I was told of this case by a lady now (1912) over eighty, who knew all the circumstances.

like an overlapping offence when we read that he would aimlessly indulge in special trains, frequently ordering this wild piece of extravagance a few minutes before the starting of the orthodox express. He received three years' penal servitude. Here is another story. G. B. had just come out of prison for defrauding the G.E.R. ; on his release from Ipswich gaol he again travelled without a ticket, for which, of course, he incurred certain trouble. It was subsequently stated that he had spent some fifteen years in prison, and had been many times convicted of this particular kind of offence.

A person who, on the reported evidence, might well have been placed in our Second Group was J. B. W. His mania was sacrilege, and he had torn up the books and fittings of a certain church and rifled the offertory box. But after he had done some thirty pounds' worth of this wanton damage, he wrote a note full of obscene expressions and addressed it to the rector. This letter he actually signed with his right name, through which he came to be arrested. In spite of this, the court apparently considered him responsible, and it awarded him twelve months' hard labour.

Mr. Thomas Holmes, the police court missionary, has given us some rare glimpses of human nature in that great-hearted record of his work.[1] " To my knowledge," he writes, " there are large numbers of criminals who commit but one sort of offence and are in every other direction honest and decent citizens."

And of such he gives many anecdotes written from personal knowledge. One poor woman had a craze for boots—stole always boots, and never anything else. She could have had no need of them, having been well supplied by one who knew her failing ; she was risking ruin and a return to long imprisonment, but she withstood the spell in vain and was dragged down. Another person took nothing but watches, urged forward by a similar obsession ; severely punished again and again, he forfeited his liberty and the decent comfort he could win by labour ; pulled under by the small metallic " hands " ! I too, have, in the course of time,

---

[1] *Pictures and Problems from London Police Courts*, p. 207. London, 1900.

collected a fair number of cases of all sorts—alas! but a small percentage of those that have occurred throughout the land.

In Paris they found a man who stole nothing but books ; he neither read nor sold them, but the police found his room piled with volumes of all sizes and prices ; the leaves had not been cut, and they acquitted him of theft. Another near-home case was of a girl who stole—but only bassinettes—perhaps in some vague groping way providing for that child unborn she dreamed of, whose image had turned her brain ?

But it is when we pass away from acquisition-crimes that we get more clearly and indisputably into the Second Group. Impulse-acts—altogether representing but about one-sixth of the whole volume of serious crime—can be subdivided into the normal and the abnormal. That somewhat arbitrarily-imagined being, the " average man," has in the centuries of civilisation slowly and painfully acquired some small degree of necessary self-control. It is an uncertain and a varying stay, built up only by careful training, sustained only by inward effort ; often undermined by alcohol, more rarely swept aside by overwhelming passion.

As the world stands to-day, and as things will remain within the practical and immediate outlook with which this book has to deal, all people must needs pass through terrible temptations. And it seems reasonable to assume that those who succumb are either beset with trials above the lot of ordinary mortals, or that they lack normal resisting-power.

That there is practically a breaking-point in the resisting strength of nearly every soul living, is fully apparent both from history and practice. Out of history it may be deduced, from the extraordinary criminality ever evinced by statesmen in all ages ; which after much puzzled consideration, I can only account for by the assumption that they must be far more tempted than are private people, from the great magnitude of the issues at stake. And in practical experience we continually find that a sudden, or an exceptionally strong temptation, will overthrow people of character.

Even the Law has sometimes allowed this, and actions

which are ordinarily considered to be highly criminal have been from time to time condoned as justifiable from overwhelming antecedent provocation.

Thus only a few years ago a judge who had been always looked upon as being most severe, gave a man nothing but a day's imprisonment for having shot another whom he had discovered with his wife under most flagrant circumstances. Some of my readers may likewise remember two much more recent cases in which sentences of six, and eighteen, months were given, for what seemed assassination ; and a good many years ago the survivors of a boat's crew, who had been tossed about for days till driven to delirium from thirst, received a sentence of six months' hard labour for cannibalism and murder. Instances involving all kinds of crimes and illegal acts might here be cited, but it will be sufficient for me to say that, whether admitted by the Law or otherwise, people of normal health and decent character may, at the many turnings of life's road, come to be struck by some wild passion-wind ; or find a whirlpool of allurement open, where seemed to be a safe and shallow ford ; before which ordinary and unaided nature will mostly turn and strive to fly in vain.

But the kind of cases which originate from the sudden stress of phenomenal temptation overcoming the resisting-power of an approximately normal citizen, are nearer to the Circumstantial, or Group I, offences, than those which are entirely due to some abnormal or diseased condition in the nerve-structure of an individual.

Thus there are certain offences which, I have noticed, most people commit, such as—to put it mildly—trying to get the better of a railway company by travelling in a superior class, etc. ; also evading customs duties and all manner of taxation—the Conscience money which is, from time to time, acknowledged by the Chancellor of the Exchequer, being, I should imagine, but a small percentage of the money withheld. Besides these, we find the common acceptance of secret commissions and the thousand-and-one acts of " Dodson & Fogg " equity, so plentiful in horse-dealing and in the fluctuating forms of business.

Differing vastly from the legal, but perhaps only in degree from the moral point of view, are the plainly punishable acts arising from immense temptation. Many a man has taken what he thought only an unauthorised loan, "borrowed" from his employer, as he might imagine, from some supremely pressing call, or in the mad idea of quietly repaying it.

Here we have obviously crossed the barrier of what is called common honesty, but all the same, these things have been too often done by weak-principled persons, who yet never intended to be systematic parasites. Similarly, I have no doubt that young men have been led into the commission of rape from the more criminal conduct of one or two of a party, who in the ordinary course of life were normal people of average impulses.

Even the clever and systematic swindler—a very different person from the man who keeps on committing small and easily-detected thefts—though a true criminal, is acting along normal lines. We need only to find utter selfishness—which is unfortunately all too common—and a combination of circumstances, to start a perfectly normal man on this pernicious path.

But there are other offences which the multitude would never commit—acts which no approximately normal and well-balanced being would attempt, even away in the solitude of the great Sahara, a thousand miles from any possible police station ! For at the extreme end of the Second Group, furthest removed from common causation, ordinary motives, and therefore, of course, from criminal responsibility, we reach the sphere of abnormality, the domain of disease, the borderland of insanity, and, ultimately, obvious mania. The various offenders within this category are often physically, and therefore mentally, incapable of ordinary self-control, sometimes as regards all the affairs of life, or it may be, only in certain directions, in which they become the victims of abnormal cravings and intense desires, *which the majority of people have never experienced.*[1]

[1] I endeavoured to express this when addressing the seventh International Congress at Cologne : " One great and absolute distinction can always be made in the classification of crime. And that is between the Normal and the Abnormal . . . predatory crimes then are generally normal ones. . . . But there are certain passions and desires which do not tempt the ordinary man or woman, and which are sometimes amazing and inconceivable," etc. *Vide Bericht*, p. 430. Heidelberg, 1912.

If the old bugbear of Free Will is here brought forward, I must reply that there is neither time nor space for purely philosophical discussions in these pages. Many indeed have dabbled in the doctrine to justify vicarious revenge, who yet refuse to face all it implies. But we are in nowise called upon to deal with abstract speculations as to what may be the precise relationship of Man to Mystery.

When metaphysicians and schoolmen have wrangled for thousands of years over Existence-problems, and have, in all that time, made no apparent progress with them, it will be wise for practical criminology to leave them alone. Therefore I refuse to discuss Freedom or Predestination, the Omnipotence of God, or the far-fallen state of Man, and also the theoretical responsibility of the sound and sane.

But I must most unhesitatingly assert that many unhappy people have not got Free Will, at any rate along temptation-lines. If such as they were ever in condition to claim it, a stage is reached when it is long-since lost. They are as rudderless boats whirled round in eddies where the current leads them, though it were through the mutilating mill ; they are as reckless riders of brakeless wheels, hill-drawn down the steepening danger-dip, and carried onward helplessly and hopelessly !

Punishment imparts nothing to such as these ; the boldest believers in the power of pain always assume the presence of a Will (on which alone their penalties could act, even if we ignored the complicated conditions, already examined, which render them so ineffective actually). In these pathetic people there is no will ; only a need that rises like necessity—an inward fiat urging on like Fate.

Whatever the mind's relation to the body may really be (and let us above all things keep away from metaphysics or theology), each of us must have painfully experienced, and have perceived or read in the case of others, how a derangement of the brain, or body, renders the clearest intellect unworkable. Who can contend against the dull weight of sick headache, or resist long-continued spells of sleeplessness, or retain reason during delirium, or command consciousness in the face of com-

pression ? And have not the greatest and the best gone
down before those subtle and intangible brain troubles,
which, if they come, can steal away men's minds, and
leave them mute or bellowing like beasts ?

" It is to the leaders of medicine," Dr. Poore is reported
to have said,[1] " that we owe the recognition of the fact
that conduct which we once regarded as sin, calling for
cruel and revengeful punishment, is in reality disease,
which must indeed be controlled with firmness, but
firmness tempered with mercy rather than vengeance.
There can be no doubt that one of the causes which has
led to the decrease in our prison population and the
increase in our asylum population has been the gradual
appreciation by the educated public that much disorderly
conduct is in reality disease. Not even a Jeffreys would
now be permitted to prescribe hard labour or a flogging
for a poor wretch with optic neuritis whose real need was
iodide of potassium."

The words of the Harveian Lecturer do indeed indicate
the ever-augmenting tendency of educated thought.

But the mass moves more slowly than the individual,
and the law—which Mr. Bumble so immortally criticised
when it came home to *him*—lags long behind popular
sentiment.

We do not now whip people to drive " devils " out of
them ; but yet the law, to every appearance, assumes
their continual presence *in* the prisoner, though we are
somewhat less crudely anthropomorphic nowadays, talk
only of the seductions of the devil in obsolete treason-
trials, and clothe what once were frankly " evil spirits "
beneath a metaphysical drapery, calling them sins,
depravity, etc.)[2] by obstinately presupposing mere
malignity of motive, in cases obviously due to innate
abnormality or organic disease.

In the more palpable and glaring cases, the victim is

---

[1] *Harveian Oration*, Oct. 18, 1899.

[2] See for instance Sir Robert Anderson's quotations from Sir Edward
Fry and others, *Nineteenth Century*, Jan. 1904, p. 125; and also some
of the views expressed by W. S. Lilly in his *Right and Wrong*, p. 124.
London, 1891.

The ready way in which brutal ignorance has always accounted for
anything it did not take the time or pains to understand ! Let us remember Mrs. Squeer's remarks on infectious disorders ; she said they
were all obstinacy !

handed over to the care of the asylums (or at any rate to Broadmoor), where his, or her, ailment is attended to on therapeutic principles; but in the subtle and in specialised cases, when we have to deal with the abnormal, monopathic, or half-mad, there is but small change from grotesque old times; the criminal courts seem to have slumbered on in all their medieval barbarism.

Acting upon erroneous premises, the penal law has been of course foredoomed to failure. The moral " Fetish " followed in olden times was the idea of " possession "; but while the " devils " disappeared before the rise of scientific daylight, a new crime-creed rose up and deceived many, which was to prove at least as powerful a plea for cruelty—the Fetish of Free Will.

CHAPTER XIX

THE DIRECTION OF REFORM

THE Criminal is ever present with us ; was it not always so ? He came, descending through the centuries ; he stands to-day in the deep shadows of Civilization ; and not in our own land only, but throughout all competitive communities. People have long since come to acquiesce in that to which they are accustomed, looking on crime as part of life's hard burden, ordained and fixed in the Nature of Things. They have indeed, from very force of habit, come to prepare for " ordinary " criminality, just as they look for crops in their due season. The perpetual presence of the " common " criminal is accepted much as the rats are amongst all ship's cargoes, as being a great, but perfectly unavoidable nuisance permitted by Providence. Both the robbers and the rats are always being pursued and chivied about in a desultory sort of way, but neither are traced home to their cause and origin, and so are never seriously met and stayed.

When we next observe a dog spin round and round, in frantic efforts after its own tail, we shall be witnessing conduct not much more irrational than police methods of dealing with men. Now in the Future there will be no ordinary crime. This I predict with quiet confidence. Calamities indeed will ever come ; the great world-doom of death, the deep soul-pain of parting ; a certain amount of madness and disease, and perhaps smouldering Berserk outbreaks of individual jealousy and hatred. These will be with us to the end of time, but prison populations will have passed away !

Utopian as this opinion may now appear, it is advanced through sober reasoning. Rousseau was doubtless right when he declared that it required much philosophy for

321

the correct observing of the things before our eyes. For it is never an easy matter to look ahead over local surroundings. I mean perhaps, rather, to think ahead. The great majority of people imagine that the precise conditions of their place and period form the real bed-rock of the universe, merely suspended by somatic dissolution, to be resumed "up-stairs" for all eternity. And the remaining minority is for the most part quite made up of dreamers who try to "think" those things for which they hope.

But all the admitted evidence of the Past appears to me to point to two plain facts. The terrible changelessness of human nature, which rises above the tiger and the ape through periods of almost geological immensity; and the responsiveness of people to environment, whereby the strongest customs and conventions are swayed about almost beyond belief. But the unchanging quality of human nature enables us, to some extent, to tell how it will act. We learn by history, and through experience, what has been done upon Mankind's long march. From this, as regards the main stream of the multitude, we can predict responsion to surroundings. Nothing occurs by miracle or malice.[1] If we can forecast the social conditions, it will be easy to map out the crimes.

It has been well remarked by Herbert Spencer that we best notice how the clock moves round, by recollecting where the hands had previously pointed ; constant and universal[2] as crime now may seem to be, we have but to look back a little way, to notice other customs also set up by surroundings, which, all through their prodigious periods of operation, must have appeared at least as ineradicable.

---

[1] Criminals "are neither accidents nor anomalies in the Universe, but come by laws and testify to causality, and it is the business of science to find out what the causes are, and by what laws they work." H. Maudsley, *Responsibility in Mental Disease*, p. 28. London, 1874.

[2] But only where creating conditions prevail. There are many primitive communities scattered over the world which possess no penal machinery, and which are practically crimeless.

The true curse of the savage is never lawlessness, but superstition. On the island of Minnikoy, to give but a single instance, some four thousand people manage to live in peace without police or prisons of any kind, although they are not free from disease. *Vide* A. Alcock, *A Naturalist in Indian Seas*, p. 189. There exist innumerable references much to the same effect, but they are far too general and scattered to find inclusion in the present work.

Thus among many tribes of savages, war is the natural and usual state.[1] It was so once even in England, where every village stood within ditch and rampart, and when a stranger coming across the forest mark, or border, had then to blow a horn to give note of his presence,[2] on pain of being shot down as an enemy.[2] A law of King Wihtraed, for instance, was that "if a man come from afar or a stranger go out of the highway, and he then neither shout nor blow a horn, he is to be accounted a thief either to be slain or to be redeemed." [4] Later the whole wide land was filled with fortresses; perched on the hills or cinctured with deep dykes, their drawbridges were raised every night, and casques of iron glittered from the battlements. The chiefs and all the free men carried arms, whether the *seax* of the invading bands, the lengthy rapier of the cavaliers, or the elegant " small sword " of the eighteenth century. Had men not always worn weapons about them? could people then conceive that this would cease? Yet but a turn of the great social wheel was wanted, for the whole habit to be laid aside. The city gates are now nothing but names, and it may sound superfluous to say, that the rich towns and open villages have ceased to dream of organised attack, while Norman keeps are ivy-covered ruins and moated castles quiet homes of peace. The swords and bucklers which our forbears carried were tokens of those restless tribal times. The stately, many-towered, feudal strongholds tell of rough ravine and baronial faction-fights; and those blind prison walls that stand to-day bleakly bear witness to a silent strife, and indicate an economic war. And who can wonder they must needs be there, while the wild scramble for the coinage lasts, while the successful gambler grows rich, and success waits upon ungenerosity? Prisons will stand while unrestricted " competition is the foundation of our social order." [5]

The regulations that were once enforced by many mediæval laws and customs, to mitigate the ruthlessness

---

1 Meiklejohn, *Hist.*, vol. i. p. 87.
2 J. R. Green, *Hist. English People*, vol. i. p. 6. London, 1894.
J. Finnemore, *Social Life in England*, p. 3. London, 1902.
3 G. Allen, *Anglo-Saxon Britain*. London, 1881.
4 T. Wright, *Hist. of Domestic Manners*, p. 78. London, 1862.
5 R. T. Ely, *Evolution of Industrial Society*, p. 97. New York, 1903.

of the possession-struggle, were dead and buried centuries ago. In 1539 the monasteries were suppressed, in the succeeding reign (Ed. VI.) the Lord Protector, Somerset, seized on the Guilds. The common lands were more and more enclosed. Gradually manor and farmstead ceased to be self-sufficing, and each man's avocation became specialized.

Times of transition must entail displacement, and in such periods of dislocation workers suffer. One of the greatest changes that ever came over the whole wide world was set up at the harnessing of steam.[1] When Adam Smith used the word "manufacturers," he was referring to a number of small craftsmen, who were individual workers. But with the advent of machinery the term soon came to mean employers of labour, hirers of hundreds and maybe thousands of men and women, who worked in droves amidst the plant of vast establishments. For then indeed a new Power had come; the Genius of the Lamp appeared to be man's slave, and falling into bad hands, it was to prove, at first, a frightful source of evil.

What may be called the old parochial barriers were henceforth to be swept away. The master lived no longer near his men; his " human " side was lived apart elsewhere, and sometimes blossomed in far-off philanthropy, but he would drive his slaves by deputy, and know them only as the numbered " hands." [2]

All obligation, duty, citizenship was set aside in the first rush for gain.[3] The industrial life of the home and the village had come to an end : the corporate life of the Nation had not yet begun !

But we have moved in very many ways far from those early and most evil times, of the " free " contract and the enslaved man ; and if the old homestead-ties had to be broken in the on-rush of the railways, some most pernicious artificial barriers were levelled down as well. For towns

[1] Ely, *Industrial Society*, p. 19.

[2] *Ibid.* p. 18.

[3] What would these mean and grasping men of business have thought of the rule of Aquinas ?—" Negotiare propter res necessarias vitae consequendas omnibus licet ; propter lucrum vero, nisi id sit ordinatum ad aliquem honestum finem, negotiare ex se est turpe,"—*Summa Theologica, Secunda Secundae*, quaestio 77, art. 4, quoted by P. Houghton Brown, " Trade Regulations in the Middle Ages," *Law Mag. and Rev.*, Feb. 1904.

and shires have been linked up together; [1] we scarcely realize that Squire Western swore in " Zomerzet," and rival counties which were formerly hostile are drawn close within the commonwealth. Even the classes tend to fraternize : the London Tube, for instance, has no class. The old discreditable Town-Gown brawls have grown harmless as a Guy Fawkes day, on which most aggravating anniversary all that is left of them still fizzles forth.

And though the population is not yet free from anti-social groupings,[2] yet such antipatriotic toasts as " Bloody wars and quick promotion " and " Our best Client, the man who makes his own Will," have, I am told, been quietly abandoned. These little things are straws upon the stream, and for the progress-current augur well. But yet the stern and unavoidable problem which science and machinery have set before civilization—the *just* producing and distributing of wealth—has to be solved for crime to disappear.

Vast and most controversial acts of State become involved in such a supreme question, and lie outside the scope of criminology. At the same time we must clearly remember that no possible prison system will ever make an end of wrong-doing while crime-creating causes operate outside. It may be urged that conduct will depend on character ; that Man is a moral being able to choose, and that he ought to be above environment. But abstract theories on imaginary " Man " break down before humiliating facts ; and while in all times isolated individuals have achieved greatness, both for good and evil, we never find heroic *populations* ; average people are but creatures of conditions, and will be moulded as surroundings shape them.

[1] How isolated they once were, may be perceived in the strange dialects and in the varied weights and measures which linger on into the present time (1904) ; and also in the truly savage notion that once prevailed in remote provinces, that the words " enemy " and " stranger " meant the same thing ; hence the old skit on the subject of brickbat throwing.

[2] The presence of Group-Parasitism has ever been an incubus on all the great civilizations. For some English instances see Lecky's *Map of Life*, p. 118.

Corrupting classes, such as detectives and prostitutes, are called into existence by the deplorable conditions under which we still live ; both offshoots of vast economic problems

In fact, the tendency of modern teaching has been to shift the seat of criminal responsibility ; and, passing by the " Devil " and " depravity," to fix it heavily on States and laws.

" Il delitto," says an Italian authority, " come tutti le altre manifestazione di patologia sociale, è il portato del sistema sociale presente." [1]

Quite as emphatic on this point is Dr. Maudsley : " It is certain, however," he says, " that lunatics and criminals are as much manufactured articles as are steam engines and calico-printing machines, only the processes of the organic manufactory are so complex that we are not able to follow them." [2]

Well may we say then, " Lead us not into temptation ! " because in practice it is clearly shown that, whenever the stress rises above, or the resisting-power of the individual sinks below the normal, commonplace people will most certainly succumb.

Heroes and martyrs are a race apart ; they have always existed ; they will be sent for ever from the Unknown, to lift life's burden and endure all things. Likewise the greater criminals of the world belong to Nature's aristocracy of strength.[3]   But the mere multitude are not of these ; they do not reach superlatives in any-thing ; they may float, but not swim ; they may sink, but do not dive ; they may wish, but cannot *will*.   Goaded by competition, they have been made selfish, dull of imagina-tion, they are often cruel ; groping for good through labyrinthine error, the people mean well, but have no strength in them.

But let us take some illustrative instances to show our theories have been forged from facts.   The Post Office forbids us to send coin in letters.   Why ?   Because its hundred thousand averagely-honest workers will keep

---

[1] E. Ferri, *Socialismo è Criminalità*, p. 9.   Turin, 1883.

[2] H. Maudsley, *Responsibility in Mental Disease*, p. 28.   London, 1874.   And see also J. von Kan, *Les Causes économiques de la Crimi-nalité*.   Paris, 1903.

[3] For Nature is most hopelessly unmoral ; she looks to the end, but cares nought for the means.   The world rewards according to success, thus many men of somewhat similar qualities, are very differently niched in history.   Take away trappings and the pomp of power, and through the course of ages men might wonder which was the criminal and which the king.

from stealing with pre-planned design, who yet might prove unable to withstand the chink and pressure of unguarded gold. But if the seductions of civilization threaten, in this and many other instances, to overcome men's common honesty, much more intense and terrible are organic desires. How many boats' crews of good British sailors have drifted days over the pathless deep, consumed with hunger, rendered wild with thirst! And to what have these sane and typical Europeans been repeatedly driven under the stress of such intolerable sufferings? To nothing less than cannibalism and murder. So weak is human nature, or so strong is human need! In truth, most criminals are made rather than born. Leaving out leaders, thinking in big numbers, we may assert that the great mass are made : the rest are the afflicted. This view is summed up in the celebrated saying: "Society has just those criminals that it deserves."

One clear and obvious example of circumstantial crime created by Society is furnished by the " Resurrectionists." Those very unpleasant products of eighteenth and early nineteenth-century social conditions, have now become so utterly extinct that the name sounds like that of some religious sect. But once their calling was a grim reality,[1] and body-snatchers formed a section of the criminal community, just as the far more parasitic coiners and receivers did. Nor were the exertions of this pariah class always confined to dealings with the dead. The medical profession set such store by carcasses, that criminals resolved to come by them : failing the ordinary " tradesmen's " methods—which although largely winked at, were yet most felonious—they did not hesitate at times to strike and kill. Thus those uncommon scoundrels Burke and Hare traded in bodies about 1828,[2] and more than sixteen murders were ascribed to them in Edinburgh. And Bishop, whose work lay round London just a few years later, owned to having furnished full five hundred corpses to the surgeons, and when condemned to death confessed to perpetrating sixty murders.[3] Thus

---

[1] See T. B. Bailey, *The Diary of a Resurrectionist*. London, 1896.

[2] See for instance, G. MacGregor, *The History of Burke and Hare*. Glasgow, 1884.

[3] Arthur Griffiths, *Mysteries of Police and Crime*, i. p. 304. London, 1898.

it is clear that many a dark deed was done because the surgeons needed bodies. The time had passed in which the practice of dissection was thought a ghoulish act of sacrilege ; but the day had not dawned (nor has it yet approached, for everything) in which unpleasant problems were to be met and wrestled with in honesty and reason. The ruling classes knew corpses must come, and let them be raised by stealth out of the darkness : limp packages were hurried through doors, and whispered of as " something for the Doctor." Thus a repulsive but a *necessary* undertaking was left to outcasts and made criminal.

But this particular form of crime should teach us much, since it has been suppressed. The penalty was death, and yet the practice flourished uncommonly upon that punishment. What then was done to bring those crimes to end, we ought to mark, for such events are rare ! Was there some special terror invented ? Had there been found, what no dark, dripping cell ever contained, or inquisition forged, at last the penalty which *would* deter ? By no means ; but for once the State attacked the root and so dug up the evil. What set men on to violate the tombs ? A keen and strong demand, seductive gold. Demand creates supply ; the economic drive, that modern lash, draws sables from the snows, orchids from deadly swamps, men into poison-fumes, young girls from home, bodies alive or dead ! And this impelled the diggers from their beds to steal abroad and grope among the graves. It could not be, nor was it, punishment that banished body-snatching from our midst. *Constructive* legislation wrought the change. The need for the supply, so long tacitly known, was recognised and satisfied. By the Anatomy Act of 1832, bodies thenceforth were got by lawful means. And so the crime society had created quite vanished, and the dead were left in peace.

It is, then, to the social forces of reconstruction and organization, and not to the barren negation of unprofitable punishment, that we must look to cleanse the land from crime. This is no smooth and comforting conclusion ; it has been always so much easier to gild and garnish pinnacle and spire, than to dig down and look to the foundations—that slow and costly underpinning work which all householders dread, but which must yet be done. There should indeed be penitence and reformation, and not the least in *us*, the whole Community ! For " in our haste to manufacture ' things ' we have forgotten the manufacture of men." [1] Rather, it might be said, that the competitive countries have come to look upon the population as a factory-made product ; mere units turned out wholesale, like machinery-made articles ; mites to be moved *en bloc* by government or demagogues. Thus in the conflict for control and power, no one remembers that the masses are *men* ; it were an empty mockery to maintain that they are looked upon as being equal fellow-citizens and brethren.

But there is nothing *new* in this—the Assyrians and Egyptians raised some tremendous monuments with *their* slave labour—except the extent and centralization of modern industry, set up, and for the first time rendered possible, by the employment of machinery. All the great Empires, all the great Republics, all human communities which had outgrown the immediate tie of the Clan-bond and the parochial sense of common causes and union ; all states and tribes in which the play of individual human feelings and affections became no longer geographically possible—and most particularly those huge steel-clad nations distraught by hunger-driven internecine competition—have ever been unmindful of their People ; indeed a really altruistic State remains utopian, and has yet to come.

Much has been done ; far more than yet has been approached; remains to do. It is not in my present place, or power, to summarize the evils of our social system, of all this anti-social chaos called civilization. Twelve millions on the verge of starvation.[2] Thirty thousand tramps and vagrants.[3] Over a hundred thousand people shut up as insane; [4] besides the wide-extending

---

[1] Ernest Crosby, *Tolstoy as a Schoolmaster*, p. 89. London, 1904.

[2] See quotation from the speech of a distinguished statesman, *Saturday Review*, Jan. 16, 1904.

[3] Statement by President of Local Government Board. See *Daily Chronicle*, Feb. 24, 1904.

[4] Officially certified 117, 199. See *Report of the Commissioners in Lunacy for E. and W.*, p. 4. London, 1904.

outer ring of half-mad and deranged. Truly it must fare indeed but ill with this vast body of our fellow-citizens.

And what of the young ? Neither the burden of crime nor the curse of drink can be laid to *their* charge ; where do these precious young "plantations" grow? how is the nation starting them upon the way ? It has been said that in London alone there are some sixty thousand children ill fed and defective.[1] But besides there are a neglected multitude, living in dirt and incubating maladies. " In many cases," says an official Report, " the children's clothes and bodies are infected, vermin being concealed in every seam and clinging to their skin, and there is little doubt that houses and furniture must also be affected."[2]

With a large section of the population brought up amidst such horrible surroundings, we need not wonder at degeneration and deformity. True, there are splendid hospitals for the " completed " patients, but the mischief has been done long before. Thus, out of 12,292 would-be recruits examined at St. George's Barracks, London, 3,908, or over 31 per cent., had to be turned away for various infirmities. Six hundred and seven were found deficient in chest measurement, 600 in weight, 457 in eyesight, 369 in the veins, and 322 in the teeth. The remainder of the rejected were suffering from various other troubles, which can be seen set forth in the official document.[3]

With these kind of conditions more or less chronic among the lower strata of the towns (and 77 per cent. of the population is said to be urban now)[4] we cannot be surprised that there are steps still downward. Dark ways indeed, whence hardly any return ; branching amidst

---

[1] Quotation from Sir William Anson, *Daily Chronicle*, Jan. 6, 1905.
[2] *Annual Report of the Medical Officer of the late School Board for London*, p. 11., L.C.C., March, 1904.
On this point see also Honnor Morten, *Consider the Children*, p. 7. London, 1904.
Also Charles Booth, *Life and Labour of the People of London*, final volume, p. 89.
[3] See *Royal Commission on Physical Training Report* Appendix iv. London, 1903.
See also article by Sir Frederick Maurice, "National Health," *Contemporary Review*, January 1902.
[4] A. Watt Smyth, *Physical Deterioration*, p. 55. London, 1904.

the sewers of the sub-stage, into the blurred blind alleys of despair. I have some such records in my case books.[1]
A man is taken out of the police cells to the magistrate, who is too horribly filthy even for the dock, and so is tried out in the open yard. Only last summer a number of more or less degraded and verminous people were turned out of the parks: the press rejoiced as if some reformative scheme had really been evolved. Nobody knew, or cared, where they were driven to, but the human dust was shaken up and shifted, as by a careless housemaid in a room ; and fell down somewhere else ! And this measure is typical of all those negative and superficial processes and " crusades " which Herbert Spencer has so well compared to the mere kicking in of a brass pot, on which it bulges out the other side ! We see again the " moving on " system, which Dickens pictured with his master hand. " 'Where can I move to ?' Jo cries out in desperation. 'My instructions don't go to that,' replies the constable. 'My instructions are that this boy is to move on ' . . . and pointing generally to the setting sun, as a likely place to move on to, the constable . . . walks away." [2]
The State has acted just like its dull minion ; has walked away and left the problem lying—truly a masterpiece of " brass pot " policy ! The State would not admit that there was a problem, it simply preached " self-help " —the only sort of help it understood—and " save yourselves." This is the last cry in catastrophe ! How should the weaker individual units solve social questions the community recoiled from ?

They did not, and in dumb response there spreads before our eyes the battle-field of ruin. One winter's night (Jan. 29, 1904), the L.C.C. officials found nearly two thousand wanderers, trudging the streets or crouched in nooks and archways.[3] And there is yet a colder habitation—all of us know about the Morgue in Paris ; many a time I speculated there, upon an awful silent company collected : poor derelicts, who, in the sea of shams, had foundered on that grim rock of reality. There

[1] For instance, *Private Case Book*, iii. p. 37.
[2] *Bleak House*, chap. xix.
[3] See *Daily Chronicle*, Feb. 29, 1904.

are some thirty mortuaries in London ; we do not talk about or show such things, but they are there, like all else good and evil, in this vast centre of the works of man. Thence, and from wards and workhouses, there come the nameless bodies for the hospitals, whose histories and troubles none can know.   Many so outcast in the hurrying world as to have had no value till they died : only the searching knives of the dissecting rooms proclaimed their kinship with humanity.

Yes, there is much to do.   For we must grapple with four potent crime-causes : want, waste, competition, and drink.   These evils act, and react, on each other. Poverty may be honest ; wealth, once acquired, may be honourable ; but whenever poverty and wealth dwell side by side, crime is as sure and certain to evolve as are the two parts of a seidlitz powder to effervesce and fizz when they are poured together.

Competition is war, and worse—it is a fight within the nation-fold.   Drink degrades all.   It may be said that these statements are truisms.   I would reply that they express the truth !   Prison reform really means social reform ; it would be strange indeed if our regeneration came from the weak and wayward inmates of our prisons. No, it is not the " failures " who will solve the profound problems of civilization, but the best intellects of Europe and America.   All these long years we preached to the poor prisoners, bidding *them* bear the burden and walk straight : we might have known that to be impossible ! The State alone, by strong and sustained efforts, can lift the load of long neglectful years.   A tremendous task : yes, even for the State, because it means that we should bring to use, burn, cleanse, repair, put right, set in its place, the litter and the deep decay of centuries.

" The evil that men do lives after them."   And we inherit from the inhuman past social as well as physical diseases, that men have made, which never need have been.   Thus those slave ships, conveying their living cargo, carried the curse of " colour " to America, setting up slavery and civil war, leaving a problem which is yet unsolved.   So the mean slum indifference allowed, grows to a complex vested interest that may cost millions to posterity.   These are but large examples out of many

None need invoke religion to perceive that fathers' sins are visited on children. This is not (appreciably) a moral law, but a physical fact.

Besides that piled-up burden of taxation, which is expressed in silver and in gold, there is a deeper, more destructive debt, which, like the smoke-fog or miasma from corruption, rolls an impenetrable blight over civilization. An old account, our forefathers incurred, but which stern Nature sends in to the Nations, and will exact through glacier-grinding power, with unremitted age-old interest. Of many items, but yet all expressed in that one word which bars men out of Eden, and builds up a blind blank wall between us and Utopia : and that one all-comprising word is, " Selfishness ! "

We cannot indeed expect to alter human nature ; but we *can* alter the eliciting surroundings. That there are depths of wickedness in men, we ought to know, since our civilization urges to effort, not to altruism. But there is untold goodness in them too, which even competition has not killed. All possibilities of love and hate lay hid and sleeping in the children's souls ; what has Society invoked and stirred up into action ? Decidedly the anti-social qualities ! Our life, as Herbert Spencer pointed out, involves the continual searing of the sympathies. In practice we have penalized compassion, we have imperilled generosity, we have exalted exploitation, we have rewarded gambling and greed. And after this shall we rail at results ?

But we must do something more than raise a jeremiad. If I have dwelt so much upon social surroundings, it is because they underlie our problem. To apply prison systems to the criminals, and leave at large the terrible temptations which beset people struggling in competition, is, as it were, to stop an uncleansed tooth. To treat the captured, yet neglect crime-causes, is just as if, in an eruptive fever, we spent our efforts in anointing spots ! The surface rash is not the cause of illness, but an effect of the internal poison. Likewise the prisoners are but outward signs of inward troubles which torment the State.

Once again, the criminal is the outcome of causes : he is mythologically the offspring of Ignorance and Injustice, and, practically, the worst kind of waste-product. But the especial feature of the age of science has been precisely the employment of all wastage. It was from heaps of disregarded rubbish, the very flotsam of a factory, for which the owners were surprised to get the offer of a halfpenny a pound, that Lister made his fabrics and his fortune. It is from dust ·destructors, burning filth and refuse, that electricity is being generated,[1] while from the remnant clinker they get bricks and concrete. In the great manufactories, especially in Germany, chemists are kept continually experimenting, to turn all débris to the best account. The fate of a whole business may hang on how the by-products are put to use ; in fact, no process is considered satisfactory where anything is wasted, cast aside. If then so much lay hid in the very refuse, if men have made the silk-waste into wealth, and turned the offensive dust-heaps into light and power, can we do nothing better with our brethren than shut them up to pine away in cells ? In very truth we can ; we have not really tried. When, in the Future, a criminal has been convicted, and is set aside for treatment, we shall have thought out what we aim at doing, because the State will either mend or end the prisoner. We must, upon the very watershed of ways, clearly determine on the answer given to one great question : Do we intend to replace this man, or this woman, back into society and citizenship ? Is he, or she, amenable to treatment at all ? can we, in fact, ever *forgive* the prisoner ? Now we must face this question honestly, because all hangs upon the answer we shall make to it. Say we will never pardon ; what remains ? Nothing for us to do, but only death. The old proverb is wise, " we can but hang the dog with the bad name." But if we conceive a new name can be earned, if we attempt a therapeutic process, let us be thorough and conduct it well. For reason would that we should either end or mend a man.

At present we do neither of these things—we only brutalise and maim the criminal. Magistrates mete out measured punishments ; but all the nations have divergent laws, and individual judges sentence differently for

[1] See for instance W. P. Adams, Paper read before the Institute of Electrical Engineers, Dec. 1904.

the same crime, urging all sorts of reasons for the penalties which they impose.[1] And while the theories advanced in support of punishment (always put forward in the later periods, since punishments arose from the revenge-instinct) have been so numerous and so entirely conflicting,[2] we cannot wonder that, in our rough-and-ready, hasty, wholesale application of them, we do not definitely aim at anything, and seldom or never amend anybody. For I repeat we do not end or mend, we merely maim and mutilate a man.

But in the Future, when the Courts convict a prisoner, he will not merely disappear from view, to undergo a senseless, indiscriminating punishment. He will not, in fact, be punished more than any other patient; but he may have to undergo a course of treatment varied according to his special need, which may, or may not, be painful in its operation.[3] The difference between the cut of the surgeon and the stab of the assassin lies mainly in the motive which made the wound. They will inflict no moment of unnecessary suffering ; if they have to give any pain, there will be purpose in it, and a friendly purpose.[4]

The Courts may have settled what the prisoner has done ; but the State will find out wherefore he acted so.

---

[1] See for instances:
A. R. Whiteway, *Penal Science*, pp. 15 and 19. London, 1902.
Edward Carpenter, *Prisons*, p. 12. London, 1905.
H. B. Bonner, *The Gallows and the Lash*, p. 14. London, 1897.
C. S. Darrow, *Resist not Evil*, ch. xi. London, 1904.
[2] Compare—
Lord Auckland, *Principles of Penal Law*, p. 7. London, 1771.
Sir J. Stephen, *Criminal Law*, p. 39.
W. S. Lilly, *Right and Wrong*, chap. v.
St. Luke vi. 37.
Sir W. Kennedy, *Law Mag.*, Nov. 1899.
Chief Justice Cockburn, *Royal Commission*, p. 86. London, 1863.
E. Westermarck, *The Origin and Development of the Moral Ideas.* vol. i., ch. iii. London, 1906.
C. Mercier, *Criminal Responsibility*, p. 13. Oxford, 1905.
R. M. McConnell, *Criminal Responsibility and Social Constraint.*
[3] " To a diversity of ills we must apply a diversity of remedies."— Dumesnil, quoted by Ferri, *Crim. Soc.*, Morrison's trans., p. 222.
And see Whitway, quoting Prins, Ferri, and Garofalo. " Social evils require social cures." *Penal Science*, p. 49.
[4] " There is a great difference between Society protecting *itself*, and Society punishing the *criminal*. The whole attitude is different." —Edward Carpenter, *Prisons, Police and Punishment.*

We shall ponder the *man*, reviewing all his past—even, as far as may be, his heredity and upbringing,[1] and we shall do our best to classify his case along the lines alluded to elsewhere.[2] For this the nature of the crime committed offers the plainest prima-facie clue, although, as we have previously seen, there may be complex " overlapping " instances.

First, it will be asked if the offence was *comprehensible*: that is to say, whether the act was one which would have *tempted* ordinary people to have done likewise in a similar position. This really is a most important point, as it may alter the whole aspect of a case.[3]

Next, was the act a *deliberate* one ? There is a great distinction to be made, between sudden lapses due to temptation accidentally coming in the prisoner's path, and deeds which he plans and sets himself to perpetrate. The coiner working with elaborate plans, in what might be a fitted laboratory, the burglar using scientific tools, the swindler laying carefully hatched plots, are much more dangerous, as well as (apparently) culpable, than ordinary law breakers. The third question arises from the foregoing, and it will be a crucial one for our prisoner's future. Did he commit a *parasitic* act ? Does this man live and prey on the community ? And if the reply be " Yes," to these three questions, how will the State then deal with such a man, when it is fortunate enough to have really secured him ? Now such a prisoner is a true

[1] On this point Sir Robert Anderson has written : " In our day it is not the disease the physician considers, so much as the patient. . . . The question should be, not what the prisoner did on the date specified, *but what he is.*"—*Nineteenth Century*, Feb. 1901, p. 278.
Mrs. Ballington Booth also observes, " It is the man we are dealing with, and not the crime " (*After Prison What?* p. 272). And see Whiteway, *Penal Science*, p. 52.

[2] See Chapters XVII. and XVIII.

[3] Some few years back a servant was dismissed, on which he ran a pitchfork through the horse under his charge. The man was a criminal, acting on a cruel, mean, and yet conceivable motive : to be revenged upon his mistress.
But in another case a horse was found, wounded and bleeding, in its owner's field. No quarrel, no revenge, no rational motive. Some person had been engaged in these horrible practices all round the neighbourhood for the mere lust of blood. Yet here was no criminal ; the worst ruffian in England would not have committed these outrages, because he could not possibly have wanted to. The offender was the victim of a monstrous overmastering passion ; most likely he was sexually insane.

criminal ; that is, he is a human parasite. I do not say he is the worst of men, for we are not concerned with moral judgments ; there may be viler lives no laws can reach ; we, the Community, may be responsible. But he is, to a certain extent, a *coercible* [1] criminal, and therefore of great importance to the criminologist. To hold, or imply, that any one goes wrong for the mere sake and joy of evil-doing, is to show little knowledge of our nature, and also most absurdly to endow the criminal with a disinterested singleness of purpose, the like of which never occurred to him. But no one can go through life with open eyes, and not be weighted with the sad conviction that men abound with no care for their kind, with little love except for sordid self, ready to batten upon anything.

The man we have just imagined was one of these. He acted *Comprehensibly*—he did what the average person might have been tempted to do ; some wishes all of us *would* gratify, if we were not restrained by conscience or the consequence.

He acted *Deliberately*. Only the scheming rogues can be deterred, and only they should be severely dealt with.

He acted *Parasitically*—thus sacrificing others for the benefit of self.

In all such cases the State will endeavour to put self-interest in place of altruism. Truly a poor and sorry substitution, for, as was so well said by Herbert Spencer, none can get golden conduct out of leaden instincts. Yet, when a man thinks only of himself, we must take care that anti-social conduct affects that " self " and recoils upon him. He must be made to feel it does not pay. Laws need not be made vindictive to do this. The calculating criminal is the hardest to catch, but the least difficult to deter. We have but to make the balance of results just unfavourable to the crime's commission, and the contriving criminal will keep away. [2]

---

[1] In a tabular form we may classify thus :

Coercible Crimes are	*Undeterrable Acts* are
Comprehensible	Impulsive
Deliberate	Passionate
Parasitic	Physiological

[2] But the real difficulty is to capture him ; the very genius of competitive " enterprise " is to exploit men in a legal manner.

Although the case which we have been considering was hypothetical, yet a large class of predatory people exist, and differ only in degree. In actual life the devils of the melodrama, the " all blacks " bent on mischief for itself, do not occur ; but there are many selfish folk, who for their own advantage will do anything ; there are plenty of parasites. Of these the worst will most likely escape, but smaller fry who had the will to rob but not the brains to do it cleverly, will fall into the law and be condemned by it.[1]

Men who have forged or coined, stored stolen goods, or spread their nets abroad for the unwary, persons who live by systematic exploitation, professional burglars and habitual thieves, must, one and all, be made to feel and know that these were not the ways to elude work, that these were not the means to live in luxury. The wise old principle of Restitution must guide again.

The old and obvious idea was Like for Like.[2] Then there arose the vague and quasi-metaphysical conception, Pain for Wrong.

Now Like for Like would be the Ideal Justice ; and though it is really unattainable by man, yet it was always aimed at, and to some extent approached, in the immediate and " poetic " punishments of the early days, which gave expression among primitive peoples to the all-life-including instinct of retaliation, which is seen also in the animals. There was some ground for these picturesque punishments, cruel and bloody though they sometimes were. At least they had been short, sharp

---

[1] The degree of responsibility for, or guilt of, an action may be, to some extent, determined by the probability, or otherwise, of its successful accomplishment. I recollect two cases which occurred within a few years' interval at a provincial town. In each of these the criminal made off with funds that totalled into tens of thousands ; neither was ever caught. A better-known offender, one who fleeced in millions, would have got clear, but that the Government itself pursued him with new extradition treaties, and brought him back to suffer a long sentence.

[2] Observe the primitive attempt at this, as shown in the earliest known Code. " 209. If a man strike the daughter of a free man . . . " 210. If that woman die, his daughter shall be slain. " 229. If a builder has built a house for a man . . . and if that house falls and kills the householder, that builder shall be slain. " 230. " If the child of the householder be killed the child of that builder shall be slain." Chilperic Edwards, *The Hammurabi Code.* London, 1904. And see Westermarck, *Origin of Moral Ideas*, i. p. 418, etc. London, 1906.

and conspicuous, and when they were not distorted by taboos or superstitions, they made a rough attempt at paying back in kind, which satisfied the human sense of justice. But Pain for Wrong as a deliberate philosophy is altogether false ; let us examine it.

The common notion in support of punishment is that a crime has to be expiated. Now what is really meant by expiation ? Is it that the deed done should be blotted out ? That is impossible. No act, whether for good or evil, can be recalled ; effects must follow as the night the day, immutably. The past cannot be altered by regret, and punishment brings self-pity, not repentance, remorse perhaps, but never reformation. The hard and clumsy law can reach no heart ; it can give pain of course—that is always easy—but reformation dawns within the soul ; surely no man was ever raised through cowardice and fear ; the wise old East said centuries ago, " By oneself one is purified." [1]

There was much that was fine, and even heroic, in the olden-time vendetta. Ties of kindred, calls of comradeship, courage, devotion, constancy, self-sacrifice, came into action through these sanguinary feuds. But the strong State can claim none of these qualities. That which the individual avenger sought in the smart of injury, and in the vehemence of passion, the Law inflicts with cold-blooded relentlessness : where private revenge would long ago have ceased from shame or pity, the State still torments through the heavy years with unappeased malignity. Punishment implies power, and power should surely be magnanimous. Dickens has well brought out this aspect of the case : " It was a sad sight —all the strength and glitter assembled round one helpless creature." [2] Private revenge might fit a noble cause, and prove a duty though achieved in bloodshed ; but punishment only adds a cold deliberate wrong to the sad sum of all the evil forces that brought the erring individual to the shadow of a cell.

Therefore the future must renounce attempts at expiation. Revenge is indeed sweet, often a balm to bitter

[1] *Dhammapada* xii. 165.
[2] *Barnaby Rudge*, ch. xlvii.

memories ; whenever the injured individual could, he took it to the utmost. Even in modern times the old blood-thirst breaks out against notorious delinquents, and may give rise to worse acts than their crimes. But when the mighty State takes up a case, the hour is passed for outbreaks of ferocity. Hatred and passion-lust, of one or many, have no more place. There shall be order at the seat of Cæsar ; wisdom and method must thenceforth hold sway. The question then to be considered in the future, will not be how to balance the past wrong by a supposed equivalent of inflicted pain, but how to remove the mischief that is working.

Two objects will present themselves in dealing with all criminals in rational times : the compensation and assistance of the victim of aggression ; and the treatment of the particular offender who did the damage, so that he shall not do the like again.[1] The compensation of the despoiled person for loss sustained has been enforced from the earliest times. It was enacted in the Hammurabi Code,[2] and the appeasing of the injured party was the main purpose for which laws were made.[3]

The custom could be traced throughout the world. Like most constructive methods of reform, the task of reparation is neither simple nor always indeed possible. Still nearly all deliberate crime relates to the desire for possession ; ease in luxury is what the criminal has in view at the expense of others. Healthy, hard, wealth-producing work in discipline and abstinence is what the State should carefully contrive for him. He must restore as far as in him lies what he has stolen, he must derive no riches from rapacity.

But with the true, or calculating, criminal, all hangs upon the question of conviction. It is never the severity meted out to the captured, but the certainty of being brought to book, which would deter, could code-makers

[1] See R. Salailles, *L'Individualisation de la Peine*, p. 12. Paris, 1898.
[2] Paragraph 23.
[3] The question of compensation has been referred to by A. R. Whiteway (*Penal Science*, p. 26), and was discussed at the International Prison Congress at Brussels in 1900.
See also Whiteway, *Penal Science*, p. 157. London, 1902.
E. Ferri, *Criminal Sociology*, Morrison's trans., p. 224.
S. E. Baldwin, *Reparation for Crime* (U.S.).
Thomas Holmes, *Known to the Police*. London, 1908

secure it. It is in dealing with the parasite that the deterrent side of treatment cannot be ignored; still, when the social machinery becomes efficient, the temptations to crime will diminish, and the difficulties of committing it without detection will enormously increase.

We must rather look forward to social reforms which have not been tried, than backward after savage penalties which have been worked and wreaked for centuries, to render the exploitation of the people difficult and practically dangerous. But besides the true parasites, whose path the State will try to render fruitless and unprofitable, there yet remain the so-called common criminals.

Truly a mixed and woeful multitude ; in dealing with them we shall get further from the comprehensible, further from rational deliberation, further from (apparent) guilt, and also further than ever from the efficacy of deterrence. At the same time we shall be approaching the second, or impulse, group ; we shall enter the domain of drink and the blight of disease ; we shall reach, and pass, the borderland of reason, and watch the distorted wreckage of humanity through the cells and wards. The mass of the prisoners are not hardened villains—they are indeed only too pliable, and have little strength in them. They are mostly unbalanced, deficient, degenerate. They are weeds which have grown through social neglect. They are the stranded flotsam of society. They are ships without lead in their keels, which blow over at the first squall—and then seldom get right again.

Even the Law looks on them leniently—except that it assumes in them a freedom of choice and action they cannot possess. More than half the people who go to prison are sent there in default of paying fines,[1] while even of those who have to go to gaol,[2] more than 60 per cent. get but two weeks and under, and over 90 per cent. of all the inmates of the prisons are kept there not above three months.[3]

[1] See *Report of the Commissioners of Prisons*, p. 9. London, 1901.
[2] The figures for 1903 were: two weeks or less, 61 per cent. men, 66 per cent. women.
[3] Ninety-four per cent. of the men and 98 per cent. of the women. See *Report of the Commissioners*. London, 1903.
See W. Haldane Porter, " *Civilization and ' Crime,'* " *Pall Mall Gazette*, Oct. 27, 1904.
Evidence of Sir G. Lushington, *D. C. of* 1895, p. 401.

Now it is evident that this shifting crowd, condemned to fines, or mostly, in default, to short terms of imprisonment,[1] will be comparatively little affected by the prevailing system of their cells. The good of the short sentence mainly lies in its deterrent threatening of the disorderly, and in the stern " pull up " it forces on the prisoner.

Unhappily we seldom secure this, without the sacrifice and ruin of the convicted offender, for prison is a desperate expedient. Doubtless it is deterrent to those outside (so far, at least, as regards crimes of Group I), and therefore necessary in competitive communities; but while admitting its negative, or coercive, value, we yet must make it rescue those within. We must continue and develop the work which has been just begun in recent years ; treatment must be constructive, helpful, curative. We want to retain the " pull up " without the fatal subsequent " shove down." All this is easier to talk of than to bring about in practice : social diseases and their remedies lie much deeper than gaols.

" Where are the head springs of Recidivism ? " asks an official report. " Doubtless in a large measure they are to be found in the social conditions of the general population," is its reply. " It is certain," continues the same report, " that the ages when the majority of habitual criminals are made lies between sixteen and twenty-one." [2] The latest Blue Book from the Prison Commissioners, written a decade later, still tells the same story : " 40 per cent. of prisoners convicted of indictable offences are juveniles under twenty-one." [3] Such figures indicate our national neglect.

Conspicuous products of extreme bad training are Hooligans of various degree. These savages are found in all ranks of society—it is the punishments for their

---

[1] The crudity of that thick-headed old theory that there exists equality in punishments, is exposed here. Thus a man earning £50 a year is smitten twenty times as hard as one who has £1,000 per annum, should each of them forfeit a like amount. It has been well suggested that fines should be proportional to the possessions of the offender ; this proposal was carried at an International Congress at Budapest in 1905. See H. Joly, *Problèmes de Science Criminelle*, p. 95. Paris, 1910.

[2] *D. C. of* 1895, *Report*, p. 11.

[3] *P. C. Report*, 1906, p. 17.

excesses that seem reserved unto the poor exclusively. "Young men at Oxford," the Bishop of Stepney is reported to have said, "when they had had a jolly evening, made an infinity of noise and often destroyed a good deal of property that did not belong to them ; only next morning they were brought before a benevolent person like himself and got ' gated,' while young men in another rank of life were hauled up in the police court and were sent to prison." [1]

No doubt the "ragging" tendencies of the rich arise from parents' callousness, from defective education, and from the blending together of animal and ardent spirits in empty heads upon unemployed shoulders. The brutalities which occur from time to time in regiments and the universities could scarcely be outdone in the worst purlieus of the cities, amidst surroundings which give infinitely more excuse for them.

For though there are indeed brawlers and bullies whom the Community must curb and crush into sobriety, yet conduct which may be rough and lawless, or even violently aggressive and mischievous, is often but youth's revolt against those artificial conditions of civilization which render the simple life of the fields and waters the most expensive and most unattainable of all. "The typical hooligan's mode of life is a revolt against the monotony of a city existence. He possesses some imagination. He longs for adventure. His misfortune is that, instead of being born in the backwoods, he was bred in a town." [2]

Yes, and the town has taken little thought for him. It has been stated that of the 1,500,000 young people under twenty-one,[3] belonging to the industrial population in and around London, there are less than 50,000 for whom the means of healthy recreation are provided.[4] It is upon such waste plots that wild oats grow.[5]

---

[1] See *Daily Chronicle*, Nov. 7, 1903.

[2] *The Speaker*, August 1903.

[3] See report of address by W. H. Dickinson, *Daily Chronicle*, Jan. 29, 1903.

[4] At the opening of the York Assizes the Lord Chief Justice declared that he knew of no cause, apart from drink, that led to more crime than young people idling about the streets.—*Pall Mall Gazette*, Dec. 1, 1906.

[5] James Devon, *The Criminal and the Community*, p. 129.

The young are nearer to the savage, and to nature, than elders are ; the blood-trail of the hunter appeals infinitely more to them than Wordsworth's clouds of glory ; we see this in the sort of books turned out for boys. Full of romance, adventure, energy ; these forces, if they find no healthy outlet, will probably make one of their own. " Coltishness," wrote Dr. James Devon, Medical Officer at Glasgow Prison, " is a more common cause of crime than is suspected." [1] " The British public," wrote the Rev. E. Husband of Folkestone, " is to a large extent responsible for the creation of the modern hooligan. I refer to the unkind, unsympathetic way in which the lads of the working class are generally treated in England. Scarcely is there a hand held out to them, although many of us who know these boys not merely by sight in the streets, but in their own private lives at home, know what kind and worthy hearts the majority of them have. The policeman is looked upon as the only suitable being to deal with them. If only our countrymen would turn over a new leaf in this matter, and be kind and friendly and sympathising towards these lads, the hooligan, like the dodo, would soon become extinct." [2]

Mr. Montagu Crackanthorpe, K.C., wrote on the subject: " I believe that the radical cure for it does not lie upon the surface. It lies far deeper, and mainly consists in finding for the turbulent spirits amongst us an active healthy employment either in Great Britain or her colonies." [3] Almost anything would be better than the infliction of unpayable fines, which mostly lead to cellular imprisonment.[4] Official guardians, special schools, colonies,[5] the services,[6] and even imprisonment on the

---

[1] *The Study of the Criminal.* Glasgow, 1902–3.
[2] *Daily Mail*, Aug. 7, 1902.   [3] *Humanitarian*, Feb. 1903.
[4] See the hard, but typical, case under the heading " A Recurrent Problem," *Daily Chronicle*, Jan. 15, 1904.
[5] For an account of what is done and doing with the young in Europe and America, see C. E. B. Russell and L. M. Rigby, *The Making of the Criminal*. London, 1906. W. and V. Carlile, *The Continental Outcast*. London, 1906.
Since this was written the magnificent Boy Scout movement has developed and spread all over the world. I know nothing that has brought out the best in our boy barbarians so well, deflecting energy into healthful channels instead of merely suppressing it to break out in crime.
[6] To make such usage of the army and navy is quite an old and

lines of the Borstal system, must be appealed to for the
rescue of the young.

Drink is the unclean parent of disorder. The bottle is
the wet-nurse of the hooligan in all ranks. But drink-
taking has various degrees; it is present as a habit, a
craving, a disease. The habit we see on all sides, " drink
being the mistaken medium of hospitality, the delusive
sign of personal generosity." [1] The practice set up by
disastrous social customs,[2] and by public-house pressure,[3]
leads to the vice (excesses in normal people) ; thus we
arrive at " Beer Street " and " Gin Lane," and so to
scenes of such intolerable misery and squalor that spirits
were held to be the easiest escape from them.[4]

But as degeneration extends and deepens, whether
produced by drink or other causes, all control passes from
the victim's power, and we perceive the overwhelming
craving ; be it for drink or for some other fatal thing,
which healthy or normal people *do not feel.* Perhaps the
best known of the many pathetic cases of this kind is that
of the notorious Jane Cakebread. " She was not really
a drunkard," says Mr. Thomas Holmes, who has devoted
a chapter to her in his strong and very " human " work.[5]
" But the smallest amount of drink roused the worst ele-

obvious idea. In 1702 the Mutiny Act provided for the impressment
of imprisoned criminals (*vide Law Times,* June 4, 1904) ; and all through
the eighteenth and early nineteenth centuries, convicts, corner-men,
and unemployed of all sorts, were swept away into the services, and
made to fight the battles of their country. Wellington's army was
full of such captures ; how well they fought is testified in history.
The hooligan is the born soldier, the possible empire-builder ; and, far
from shutting him up, we should employ his dangerous energies in the
right way. He would be easy enough to manage under discipline ;
I fancy few will doubt this, who have ever been in uniform. The other
men would in no wise resent his presence ; soldiers and sailors have
their weaknesses, but they are too good-hearted to be pharisaical.
See also Lecky, *History of England in the Eighteenth Century,* vol. vi.
p. 261. London, 1887. For a satirical commentary upon the old-time
methods of recruiting, see R. B. Sheridan, *The Critic,* Act iii. Scene 1.
    [1] John Burns, *Labour and Drink,* p. 5.
    [2] Amongst which " intuitional " cooking may be a cause, in that the
husband or son gets to consider alcohol " as a necessary condiment to
his tasteless and indigestible diet." See Dr. Saleeby, *Daily Chronicle,*
Nov. 15, 1906.
    [3] See Chap. XVII.
    [4] I believe the words employed by one of the Bishops were that
" Drink was the shortest way out of Manchester ! "
    [5] *Pictures and Problems from London Police Courts,* p. 129. London,
1900.

ments within her ; a pennyworth of 'four ale' was quite sufficient, and after the nearest policeman she would go. The police often fled at the sight of her. Many an officer has bribed her to go away when she approached him. I have seen policemen running away and old Jane after them to be taken into custody. . . . During the nine weeks she lay out of doors she touched no drink, and no one could persuade her to take any, but the romantic heart of the old lady had been touched. A gentleman living in the neighbourhood left a shilling a week at a coffee-stall on Stamford Hill that Cakebread might be supplied with two cups of hot coffee daily. That shilling a week loomed large in her eye, and became a pound a day ; that kind act of pity on the gentleman's part she construed into a declaration of love, and she built many hopes upon it. She became a nuisance to the stall-keeper, declaring that she was being robbed and not getting the value for her pound a day. She waited and waited on Stamford Hill for that lover who never came, but fancying every well-dressed man that passed to be her love. Hope deferred made her heart, hopeful as it was, sick at last, so she got her pennyworth of drink and gave herself into custody."

" For over thirty years," continues Mr. Holmes, " this farce had gone on, and all this time a demented woman had been looked upon and treated as a confirmed inebriate." [1] Two hundred and eighty times she had stood in the dock ; at length the prison doctor certified her as insane,[2] and she was sent to an asylum, where she was " sane enough to realize her misery in being surrounded by the insane, too insane to be fit for liberty or to control her actions." [3] She died at the asylum two years later.

Now this Jane Cakebread was but one of many ; she was a type of those " Borderland " victims whom all along the State misunderstood. As I turn over the leaves of my case books, I come upon many other instances.

[1] Holmes, p. 133.

[2] H.M.'s Prison, Holloway, January 27, 1896. Registered No. 17,706. " Jane Cakebread is well known to me. I have always considered her to be of impaired intellect. Her mental condition has however so much deteriorated of late that I am of opinion that she is not now responsible for her actions, and that she should be sent to an asylum."—G. E. W., Medical Officer.

[3] Holmes, p. 141.

Here is Grace Appleyard, 150 convictions; Elizabeth Watts, 223 convictions; [1] Tottie Fay, [2] Margaret Black, and similar men, and who shall tabulate how many more of them ? In the course of years the public, and even the lawyers, began to have doubts. Mr. Stipendiary Lane is stated to have referred to his humiliating, useless piece of duty, on sentencing an old woman to a further seven days.[3] On another occasion Mr. Stipendiary Rose remarked that he must go on applying the clumsy law which so poorly met the prisoner's case.[4]

Of one Kate Henessey, Mr. Holmes wrote : " Two hundred and fifty times she had stood there, two hundred and fifty times she had been sent to the refining influence of prison, to be redeemed and regenerated by the delightful task of oakum picking, sack making and scrubbing floors."[5]

The publicity given to these miserable examples of the entire failure of the old deterrence theory set people thinking,[6] and, what was much more useful, kept them thinking by continually obtruding, in grisly comment on prevailing premises. It was a very slow process (still working and yet far from complete)—as it ever is when the majority enforce what a small minority has to suffer—but it began and grew.

The faith in the power of punishment was assailed and shaken, although the authorities continued to inflict it. The huge machinery of the " clumsy law " was present before them ; there was nothing else—and when it was once set going, it had to grind ; and so it did, and does, uselessly, cruelly. The craving for alcohol, drugs, nauseous substances and strange gratifications,[7] which *do not tempt* the normal man and woman, but are amazing or abhorrent to them, comes from some physical cause.[8]

[1] *Sun*, Dec. 14, 1897. [2] *Evening News*, Nov. 4, 1903.
[3] *Case Book*, i. p. 12. [4] *Ibid.* p. 34.
[5] *Pictures and Problems*, p. 146.
[6] " Nor is this wonderful," say two recent writers ; " for a punishment which only deals with effects and does nothing to get to the root of the matter and remove the causes which have produced and which continue to produce them, can only be expected to prove idle and fruitless."—Russell & Rigby, *The Making of the Criminal*, p. 61. London, 1906.
[7] See Lecture by Dr. Mary Gordon before the Society for the Study of Inebriety, Oct. 9, 1906.
[8] Speaking before the British Association at York in 1906, Mr. W. McAdam Eccles said that he refused to subscribe to the doctrine that a

Till we can touch this *fons et origo*, admonition is futile, and punishment merely cruel ; once really fixed, the craving will prevail. This is a fact, but too painfully proven. If anything on earth has ever been fully tried, it is the world-old and instinctive plan of punishment. If anything has ever been established by the most frightful and persistent vivisection and worse vivisepulture, it is that the all-compelling passions cannot be deterred. The chronic inebriates are one group of those borderland cases which have, so far, been left to the criminal courts. Equally hopeless, and yet even more inhuman, has been the treatment of the sexually abnormal. With these we have the old witch-trial horrors continued in modern times. Largely from the same cause : misapprehension of obscure phenomena. For just as the poor brokendown things, obsessed and overcome by alcohol or by the drug habit—often refined and intellectual people between attacks—have been confounded with the coarsely swinish, so have the inverts and the sexually abnormal been classed among the vicious and the artificially depraved.

The old idea was that sexual inversion was the extreme pitch of abandoned luxury, the last stimulus of exhausted age—at best a substitutional vice, a passing phase of artificial origin.[1]

We now know that, while this may be occasionally the case, the real trouble lies deeper. That the true inverts form a percentage of every population throughout the world. That sexual abnormalities are often manifested before puberty, and in those guarded by the purest surroundings.[2] We know that they may take high forms,

man who took alcohol in excess was a criminal. There was a physical cause for the craving and scientists were engaged in discovering what that cause was.
See also G. V. Poore, **Harveian Oration** for 1899.

[1] " Lorsqu'en 1852 Casper fit cette remarque très judicieuse que la péderastie, considérée jusque-là comme un vice, n'était due en somme qu'à une anomalie congénitale morbide, á une sorte d'hermaphrodisme psychique, personne n'aurait prévu que 40 ans plus tard on trouverait dans les grands ouvrages scientifiques une véritable pathologie psychique de la vie génitale."—Dr. R. von Krafft-Ebing, Preface to Moll's work. Paris, 1893.

[2] Dr. R. von Krafft-Ebing observes, " Tout ami de la vérité et de l'humanité apprendra avec satisfaction que le perverti sexuel est un malheureux et non un criminel."—Preface to Moll's work, p. iv. Paris, 1893.

". . . there is a very clear line of demarcation between the city and low forms—sometimes, as we shall see later, terrible and inconceivable forms, but they are no more amenable to legal control than the tint of the eye or the shade of the hair.

Perhaps upon no other social problem has the law been so futile, inexpedient, and unjust. Futile because framed on false premises, since it ignored human nature in general, and abnormal nature in particular. It took no count either of the origin or the power of the passions it sought to suppress. It drove them in—as they sometimes say of rashes in fevers—with disastrous effect. The wise men of antiquity knew something of the difficulties of the problem—though probably nothing of its physical first-causes. " Who can change the desires of men ? " said Marcus Aurelius. Thucydides declared that it was absurd to think that when human nature was firmly bent upon doing any particular thing, it could be deterred by force or law or any external terror. Gibbon has told us that " it was with the utmost difficulty that ancient Rome could support the institution of six vestals," and not even with these " could the dread of the most horrible death always restrain their incontinence." [1] Lecky expresses his experience in the following paragraph : " No man who knows the world will deny that with the average man the strongest passion or desire will prevail— happy when that desire is not a vice." [2]

In this the criminologists concur. The late Mr. Whiteway pointed out that intimidation was no preventive, because in the face of overwhelming desire people were " more powerfully affected by the certainty of present enjoyment than by the apprehension of possible or probable future pain." [3]

thief and the sexual offender ; many of the latter . . . break the law under the influence of uncontrollable passion and not with the object or purpose of ulterior gain. . . . The sexual offender . . . rarely if ever comes of an habitually criminal stock," etc. *Report of the Commissioners of Prisons*, pp. 17, 18. London, 1897. Thus evidence as to " character " in sexual cases may bear upon the general manner of the accused's life, but not by any means on his sexual nature. We might just as well call evidence to affirm, that Mr. Dot was too honourable to be an albino ; or that Mr. Dash was so highly respected, he could not be colour-blind !

[1] Dr. W. Smith's ed. vol. ii. p. 137. London, 1862.
[2] *Map of Life*, p. 239.
[3] A. R. Whiteway, Pamphlet. London, 1898

" Appellant " says, speaking of the passion-acts : " No system of punishment will have much effect in checking crimes of this kind; " [1] and Letourneau remarks that man obeys with fatal certainty " that which is his strongest impulse." [2]

So much for the views of writers. I would however put in further evidence, from actual facts which all can verify. It is a matter of common knowledge that patients in the latter stages of typhoid grow faint and frantic from the want of food. To take it in this condition means almost certain perforation of the bowels, and that means pain and death in a short time, But eat they will if they can get the chance ; they will beg food from parents, visitors, or nurses, they will steal scraps left anywhere accessible. That gnawing hunger, which, as we saw before, impels men under certain circumstances to devour one another, strives to be stayed though Death attend the meal. Take again prostitution : all men know that a chance meeting and union may result in one of the slowest and most ruinous diseases of the blood—a malady which may break up the constitution, which will defer marriage for two years, and the effects of which may still tell after twenty years. Yet this has never banished illicit intercourse, or frightened men away from risking all things.

But, passing from opinions and general cases, let us now come to the particular and personal. Alas! there are many of these legal tragedies, or else the subject need not have been discussed. As I have said, the grievous results obtained, by punishing the inverts and the other sex offenders, are quite as hopeless and yet even more pathetic than those achieved with the incurable inebriates. We do not find the tens and even hundreds of convictions of the same person for the same kind of offence. But that is because the sentences are so long, and human life is mercifully short, and cannot be drawn out sufficiently for the full demonstration of these hideous experiments. But we still find the long, slow, miserable periods spent in prison, and the same inevitable and unpreventable repetition [3] of what may be called physiological acts.

---

[1] See Romilly Society, Pamphlet No. 7. London.
[2] Preface to French ed. of Lombroso's *L'Homme Criminal*.
[3] Allowing for the much longer sentences inflicted for crimes against

And the same truth is established beyond all doubt : that punishment affords no remedy. The prison directors are being convinced of this. In an official report which had been sent to me from New South Wales I came upon the following significant paragraph : " Another dangerous class is that composed of irresponsible offenders and sexual perverts. They are most difficult persons to deal with, either in or out of gaol. Hovering on the borderland of insanity, they appear to need some special form of treatment, which cannot be applied by prison methods. To turn such people out after completing their sentences is unfair to all concerned. They cannot help their diseased promptings, and it is cruel to expose them to temptation. One such case, who is now serving a long sentence for an indecent assault on a child, has on previous occasions been sentenced to three years, five years, and five years for similar offences. There can be no doubt as to his repentance for the acts he has committed, but when temptation comes to him on his release from prison he simply cannot resist it. Some day there will be special establishments for the treatment of such cases, where surgical and other remedial means will be employed." [1]

Some time ago I received a letter from an eminent criminal lawyer in Melbourne alluding to a prisoner who had five times been flogged for five separate sexual offences (of what kind not stated). But the most terrible case of this sort that ever came to my knowledge took place at home in modern England. Away back in 1877—when the present writer was a child about nine years old— a prosperous and respected bank manager suddenly disappeared. His books and accounts were hurriedly searched, but he was not a common absconder, and they were all correct ; he had been taken for a sexual offence, and he was sent—they passed those shocking sentences lightly then—to penal servitude for life. In 1897 an elderly bald-headed man emerged from that untellable immurement back to the living world. And then immediately succumbed to the old obsession ! He had, I

---

morality, and for the fact that, while those found drunken or demented upon the streets force themselves upon the notice of the police, the sexual secrets are seldom disclosed.

[1] *Report of the Comptroller-General of Prisons*, p. 8. Sydney, 1903.

believe, been free only nine months when he was arrested and stood in the dock again. The judge was indeed amazed, and talked about insanity ; but it was all in his regular work, and the oubliette's door gaped ready and open, so he gave him two years' hard labour—all that the Act allowed for his particular offence. This meant, however, that his licence was cancelled, and he was sent back on the original life sentence—for just as long as the Home Office pleased.[1]

After many more years had passed, the case appears to have attracted the notice of one of the judges and of the Salvation Army, and the poor prisoner was again let out and sent to a settlement in charge of that institution. Would I might end it there, but all was in vain : nature once more prevailed over restraint, over external terrors branded to the bone. He was sent back again, till Death shall intervene. This dreadful history reads like a story of the darkest despotisms. We seem removed into the times of the fourteenth Louis, and gaze out on the Château d'If in the Bay of Marseilles. We think of the Bastille shoemaker by his stone-screened window. We think of the steep trap-door at Nuremberg. We think of the damp-stained dungeons of old Venice, or picture the island citadel of Schlüsselburg as it stands to-day. Yet it has happened where the omnibuses run, within a walking distance of our doors ; only its height of sorrow and distress lifts it above the pavement of commonplace. The *Daily Chronicle* indeed observed,[2] " There is fortunately reason to believe that a case which the Bow Street magistrate was yesterday called upon to deal with, stands alone in the criminal records of our country " ; and so, in a way, it does, but yet withal it represents a class of cases which are survivals of past ignorance and superstition. In the future, such methods as just described with the abnormal or the sexually insane will be considered to have been as amazingly foolish and as cruelly inhuman as we now look upon the witch trials of old. All those who make a study of human habits ; of the real ways and lives of men and women, as distinct from the conventional assumptions made concerning them,

---

[1] Author's **Case Book**, i. 44, ii. 57.
[2] Dec. 20, 1906.

will notice the impotency of the law in matters which, from the very nature of the case, must be so secret and so complex as personal, and, in the widest sense, sexual relationships.[1]

Endeavouring to control the psychic storms and the physiological cravings by external terror, is very much like trying to steer a ship from the outside ; it cannot be done.[2] The mental self-searching restraints of believed religions alone really influence hidden desires ; even then the great passions will mostly break through.[3]

Meanwhile the successive attempts on the part of the State[4] to regulate those matters of private judgment and individual conscience, which were once adjudicated upon purely theological grounds and authority,[5] has resulted in sequelæ widely divergent from, and often directly contrary to, the wishes of empirical law makers.

The first and most obvious was the endowment of blackmail. The blackmailer is a variety of the human parasite, allied to all those others of the tribe of Judas— those traitors, sneaks, and hypocrites who, in some circumstances, may be employed by the State itself at

---

[1] Punishments in these kind of cases bear so small a proportion to the whole number of offences committed, that they are looked upon as being *accidents* occurring to individuals. And the worst accidents, whether at motoring, hunting, or high speeds round railway curves, don't deter any one.

[2] See William Clarke, " The Limits of Collectivism," *Contemp. Review*, Feb. 1893.

[3] Dr. Nordau has observed with regard to possible eugenic marriages : " The religious sanction would be absent from the modern restricted laws, and, in the case of a conflict between passion or desire, and legal prohibition, *this* would weigh as a feather against *that*. In a low state of civilization the masses obey traditional laws without questioning their authority. Highly differentiated cultured persons have a strong critical sense ; they ask of everything the reason why, and they have an irrepressible tendency to be their own law-givers."—*Sociological Papers*, vol. ii. p. 33. London, 1905.

[4] But yet by no means universally : in some parts of the world, not made until the nineteenth century ; in others, again abandoned as impolitic. In England the civil law against homosexual practices, 25 Hen. VIII. c. 6, was repealed 1 Mary, reintroduced 5 Eliz. c. 7, etc. *Vide* C. F. Williams, *American and English Encyclopædia of Law*, vol. xx. p. 828. London, 1893. It should be noted that in later times far less evidence has been required to establish the fact of the commission of an offence. See 9 Geo. IV. c. 31, sec. 18, before which a conviction must have been much more difficult to obtain.

[5] See allusion to instigation by the devil.—J. Bodin, *Demonomanie*, p. 60. Paris, 1580. Also *Statutes at Large*, vol, vi. p. 208. Cambridge, 1763.

a fixed salary, and in others may be found lurking with its most loathed criminals, for speculative and illicit gains. Particularly in an artificial and deliberate offence like blackmailing, Society suffers from the kind of criminals it deserves. Because oppressive puritanical laws serve as the potent instruments of private revenge or selfish extortion,[1] and a scandal-loving, prurient public taste creates the " culture " which the parasite can flourish in. (And, to continue the metaphor, how one bright beam of the sunlight of truth would kill all these unclean things !) The law-makers and politicians, as usual cheaply theorising about things, have assumed the victim of blackmail to be innocent, and have placed frightful penalties in his hands to hurl upon those who shall threaten him.

The blackmailer, being a practical person, knows the accused to be generally guilty, or at any rate compromised, and that, consequently, he will endure almost anything rather than figure in a police-court scandal.[2] The greater his social position, and the higher his general character and reputation—his sexual nature being really a question apart—the more will he dread the odium of publicity ; the safer will the sex blackmailer feel.

And, on the whole it is to be feared with reason, these creatures are extremely hard to catch ;[3] the cases that get into the newspapers represent only *unsuccessful* operations. Effective deals are squared up secretly, and

[1] Though generally impotent and mostly dormant, as Shakespeare, with his immortal insight, showed in *Measure for Measure*.

[2] Perhaps nine times out of ten, but not always. Older people may recollect how a distinguished statesman was once threatened, on which he instantly caused the arrest of his traducer, who was afterwards convicted. Those few who follow and study criminal cases may recall a remarkable incident where a young man, in the open street, was accused of indecency, forthwith seized, and marched towards the nearest police station. On the way, his captor suggested release upon payment, but the " prisoner " calmly elected to stand in the dock. Presently his assailants took fright and bolted, but were afterwards caught and sent to penal servitude, the magistrate warmly commending the prosecutor. Had he, however, been really an invert, the course of events might have been more profitable to the blackmailers and much less satisfactory to the public interest.

[3] Some years ago, in the American Barrister case, an undergraduate, his father, and the tutor of a college were blackmailed for some time before they at last took action. I believe an intrigue with a married woman had been alleged against the student—at any rate the man received ten years.

are never heard of, though many things are pigeonholed at Scotland Yard—In fact a number of most villainous gangs are always badly wanted by the State, whose laws these very criminals get their living by.[1] Certain blackmailers are almost as " known " as politicians or actors, only the witnesses and victims will not come forward, and the police cannot get legal evidence complete enough to put before a jury. But once again I am not theorising from my tranquil study. Let me recall some illustrative cases. D. B., one of the best blackmailers of his day, lives, or did live a very few years ago, in peaceful retirement at a gay town by the sea ; yet men who have committed *one* of his many crimes are toiling through weary years at Portland Prison. R. C., a youth apparently with capabilities worthy of better use, was sent to penal servitude, but was never charged with blackmailing, at which he had been long notorious. Mr. A., a professional man, specialised in obtaining money for compromising letters ; he was ultimately convicted, but never for his blackmailing. Similarly W. H. became an active member of a church, and then proceeded to black-mail his younger acquaintances by writing alarming letters to their parents and employers. Like so many others, this creature escaped the more serious accusations, and was sentenced to only six months' hard labour for false pretences and fraud.[2] The magistrate remarked that he had evidently been living by blackmail.[3]

Sometimes these men are sentenced on other charges, and then we hear something of their previous mode of living, and tales maybe of systematic extortion. Then does the prisoner get all that the judge can give him for the particular offence of which he has been convicted, often accompanied by the grim remark that it was fortu-

---

[1] Mr. Justice Phillimore once remarked, " It is said that England, with all her pretended virtues, is the home of the blackmailer." See *Daily Chronicle*, Dec. 14, *Daily Mail*, Dec. 15, 1905. (Author's Case Book, v. pp. 106, 107).
Curiously enough Balzac said much the same : " Le chantage est une invention de la presse anglaise." See *Monatsbericht des Wissenschaftlich-humanitären Komitees*, p. 156. Charlottenburg-Berlin, July 1906.
[2] *The People*, Jan. 6, 1907.
[3] Some interesting observations on this question were made by the Recorder of London in his charge to the Grand Jury, Feb. 5, 1906. (Author's Case Book, v. pp. 113, 114).

nate for him that he had not been charged with black-mailing. The effrontery of a gang which thinks to have cowed their victim into abject submission was well exemplified some years back at the little town of B. For several years a Mr. M. was somehow in the power of three persons, who got money from him in considerable amounts, and even forced themselves into his country parties. A voyage to far-off lands failed to shake them off ; at last he turned, and the three were arrested. From that moment their case was hopeless ; one fell down in a fit at the magisterial hearing—and afterwards the stern old Hawkins, J., sent two of them to penal servitude for life, and the third, who was very much younger, received fifteen years. I understand they are still in prison.[1]

As an example in sheer audacity, though it belongs to a different variety of blackmailing, and one far less depending on bad laws, I wish to allude to the most remarkable case of the kind present in my collection— the wholesale undertakings of the brothers C.[2] These scoundrels started three small patent medicine companies, and sold, at enormous profit, a fluid purporting to have the same results on pregnant women as are obtained by an illegal operation. As a matter of fact the medicines were quite harmless, but the misguided purchasers did not know it ; and in the winter of 1898, batches of letters totalling some twelve thousand were sent out to the people who had bought drugs, addresses being on the books of the three firms. The recipients were accused, in these letters, of having committed or attempted to perform an act which was punishable with penal servitude —no blackmailing is ever fully effective without the lever of the criminal law—but they were now informed by Mr. " Mitchell, Public Official," that if they would send—I think it was £2—further proceedings might be then averted, if they were truly contrite for their crime. The blackmailer is often a bit of a moralist; one, I remember, quoted from St. Paul.

The panic and terror caused to inexperienced girls can easily be imagined, and the two pounds demanded,

---

[1] Author's Case Book, i. p. 95.
[2] *Ibid.* ii. p. 47.

portions, fractions, shillings, of that sum, were forwarded to " Mitchell " with all haste, accompanied by piteous entreaties to him not to prosecute. More than three thousand letters, containing over fifteen hundred pounds, fell thick into the office of these men, to which an unsuspecting errand boy was sent alone, that he might gather them. But this was too hot to last. Some few out of the numbers had fathers, or maybe husbands, who were not so easily terrified, and who came up on purpose to break Mr. " Mitchell's " head. Some few out of the numbers were desperate and at bay ; these placed the matter in the hands of the police. The end soon came. The messenger was shadowed and followed back, the three brothers were then seized and brought to trial, and sent away to penal servitude. The letters and their remittances were quietly returned.

As might beforehand be anticipated, all the parks, commons, and dark lonely places generally, afford a ready hunting ground for human weasels of various kinds. The usual plan is to pounce upon people in compromising surroundings—genuine or alleged—and to pretend to be one of the plain-clothes constables—who also abound.[1] Such a case, for instance, occurred at Northampton in June 1906, where an admitted blackmailer stalked a soldier and his girl, and in the scuffle which later ensued was killed by the former. The young hussar was afterwards brought to trial, and was acquitted amid cheers in court.[2]

Another example comes to us from Cardiff, where an ex-policeman was sentenced to twelve months' hard labour for attempted blackmail of two lovers who were walking out together.[3] A still more dangerous prowler had somehow obtained possession of an L.C.C. badge,

---

[1] This practice is liable to boundless abuses : see an instance of police collusion and suspicious evidence ; the accused acquitted : *Evening News*, April 21 and 28, 1903, *Case Book*, pp. 97, 101. The purpose of the police should be to prevent offences, not to sneak about and secure cases. The law should be more of a sign-post and less of a man-trap. *Re* Police blackmailing, see W. A. Purrington, "The Police Power and the Police Force," *North American Review*, vol. clxxiv. p. 505. New York, 1897. Also A. Arthur Reade, *The Tragedy of the Streets*, Manchester, 1912.

[2] *Case Book*, vi. p. 23.

[3] *Weekly Dispatch*, Oct. 21, 1906.

with the aid of which he long "worked" Wandsworth Common, till he was captured and got eighteen months' imprisonment.[1] The press furnished these two cases for my collection on the same day. This is exceptional, but these sort of things, in various degrees of meanness and apparent villainy, take place all round us. Doubtless but few of them come under my observation ; what actual proportion of the secret total ever get dragged into publicity at all, is probably quite unknowable.[2]

It will be noticed that everywhere the criminal law is always made the instrument of extortion. The State seems ever to prove itself a clumsy and corrupting influence in regulating personal morality [3]—as it was when it attempted the Contagious Diseases Acts,[4] and as it is on the Continent, where it licenses women. There is no doubt that many of these personal laws become merely lethal weapons left at large, to hand for use by the worst criminals.

Another of the effects by no means intended is the undoubted stimulus of prohibition.[5] Shrewdly wrote Marquis Beccaria in 1764 : " As a general rule, in every crime which by its nature must most frequently go unpunished, the penalty attached to it becomes an incentive."[6] Ages before, Lycurgus had even framed a law upon this principle, " for he ordained that a man should think it shame to be seen going in to his wife or coming out from her. When married people meet in this way, they must feel stronger desire for the company of one another, and whatever offspring is produced must thus be rendered far more robust than if the parents were satiated with each other's society."[7]

Denial always strengthens a desire. We know that

[1] *Reynolds' Newspaper*, Oct. 21, 1906.
[2] **The German** *W. H. K. Monatsbericht* gives lists every month.
[3] See Josephine Butler, *Government by Police*, pp. 7. 15, 17, 33, 63. London, 1879.
[4] Charles Booth, *Life and Labour of the People of London*, final volume, p. 124.
[5] A universal **and** perhaps on the whole a healthy human impulse. Forbid a book, and everyone wants it ; there are advertisements beginning " Don't read this."
[6] *Crimes and Punishments*, p. 229, J. A. Farrer's translation. London, 1880.
[7] Xenophon, *Government of Lacedæmon*, J. S. Watson trans., p. 205. London, 1884.

people perishing with thirst, die thinking, dreaming, raving about rivers of water.[1] So also with hunger: thoughts of the famished always dwell on food—impossible banquets, rare dishes floating in from fairyland; the thoughts are drawn towards the physical craving as the white blood corpuscles are attracted round an injury.[2] Negation and deprivation upset the balance of being. This is no doubt what Blake had in his mind when he once wrote that it was safer for a man to carry a venomous snake with him, than it would be to harbour an unsatisfied desire.[3]

Explosive forces and poisonous gases become most dangerous when they are enclosed. Another result of scandal-making laws has been the influence of advertisement . . . it is notorious that anything which tends to advertise a particular vice or crime invariably tends to produce an epidemic of that particular evil."[4] The imitative impulse has tremendous power, especially on weak and unbalanced natures. Some years ago a young man was found shot under dramatic and suspicious circumstances. A few days later another man killed himself, rehearsing the manner in which it was done. The child repeats her own experiences upon her doll— which fortunately is inanimate—and small boys read of bloody brigands' adventures, and make a police-court copy of the same. Hear of some weird peculiar atrocity; it is quite likely to be done elsewhere. Read of some crime which for the moment fills sensational press columns; the police will shortly be receiving many confessions, from persons who are yet in no way implicated.

---

[1] These facts could be supported by the accounts of adventures innumerable. See for instance R. F. Scott, *Voyage of the " Discovery,"* vol. ii. p. 67. London, 1905.

[2] Savages and children generally gorge themselves from previous scarcity and the anticipation of it. I have seen horses, usually stabled, fly madly round and round a field when first turned out, while those accustomed to wide spaces will graze peacefully. Truly, as Macaulay observed, the cure for excess of liberty is continued liberty.

[3] Victor Hugo has wisely said that we know not " with what fury that sea of the human passion ferments and boils when it is refused all egress —how it gathers strength, swells and overflows—how it wears away the heart—how it breaks forth in inward sobs and stifled convulsions, until it has rent away the dykes, or even burst its bed."—*Notre Dame*, English translation of 1833, vol. ii. p. 210.

[4] *Truth*, Aug. 9, 1894.

And so when some accident or some private feud reveals a case of sexual abnormality, and thus sets the clumsy, indiscriminating law in motion, there can be little doubt but that it prompts and brings about those very practices it is supposed to stay.[1]

We see, then, that the effects resulting from repressive laws, which blindly seek to crush by external terror emotions and feelings implanted from the beginning, fated, and reappearing, thus persisting without end ; have been, the establishment of blackmail, the incentive of prohibition, and the attraction of advertisement.[2]

But the effects of laws which are plainly opposed to personal liberty,[3] and which if we accept as true the saying " Volenti non fit injuria," are even opposed to the first principles of justice, must percolate through the community, spreading the spores of falsehood and mistrust, and leaving deadly toxins in the body politic.[4]

[1] That is, among the neurotic, unbalanced, sexually " neutral " temperaments. The pronounced natures will probably not be influenced one way or the other.

[2] " Societies and private enthusiasts for the suppression of vice should read history." See article by Mr. Justice Gaynor, *North American Review*, vol. clxxvi. p. 19. New York, 1903.

[3] " Pandering to the moral sentiment of the community is one of the daily necessities or pastimes of American political life. The consequence is that the most impossible laws find their way to the statute-book. Nobody seriously believes in them ; nobody intends that they shall ever be really enforced . . . there is a wide gulf between passing a bill and making it operative. To repeal it is hopeless, because no legislator will dare have it said that he favours gambling or Sunday drinking or vice of any kind. Hence follow, especially among the reformers, the most extraordinary devices for getting out of the pit of their own digging."—Sydney Brooks, *Fortnightly Review*, Dec. 1903. On the possibilities of democratic tyranny see also Oliver Goldsmith, *Citizen of the World*.

" It is difficult to observe without some disquiet the manifestly increasing tendency of democracies to consider the regulation of life, character, habits and tastes, within the province of government."— Lecky, *Democracy and Liberty*, p. 462.

" La liberté consiste à pouvoir faire tout ce qui nuit pas à autrui." *Droits de l'Homme*, art. iv.

[4] See *Jahrbuch für sexuelle Zwischenstufen*. Leipzig, Max Spohr. *Elements of Social Science*, p. 249. London, 1886. *Humanité Nouvelle*, March. Brussels, 1900. Havelock-Ellis, *Studies in the Psychology of Sex*, p. 208. Philadelphia, 1901. G. Bernard Shaw, **letter in** *The Adult*, September 1898. John Addington Symonds, *A Problem in Modern Ethics*. The *Vorwärts*. Berlin, Oct and Nov. 1902. **Case Book**, iii. p. 75. *Arbeitzeitung*. Vienna, Oct. and Nov. 1902. *Re* Krupp case. A. R. Whiteway, *Penal Science*, p. 40.

The State of the Future may indeed regulate economics and industry, but it will interfere as little as possible with private life and personal idiosyncrasies.[1] Least of all will it try to intrude itself upon emotional relationships—often so tragic and so irremediable—in which the State, wielding the heavy sword of what is called Justice, seems like a butcher trying to perform an operation. The law, then, will have to be altered and modernised along the lines of Continental Codes (France, Italy, and many other countries).[2]

By these an age of consent is allowed for homosexuality to both sexes, above which the law refrains from interference, except with conduct in a public place. But unfortunately there are other sorts of sexual offences which are against the laws of all civilised countries, as they involve assault against consent, misconduct with children below the age-limit, and irresponsible aberrations which yet involve criminal acts. Of these the crime of rape is governmentally the most important, since it may amount to a true crime—*i.e.* the gratification by a normal person of a selfish desire at the expense of another citizen. The possession of a girl is (like wealth in general) one of those things which most men desire, and would obtain if they were not restrained by conscience or by fear of consequences. It is indeed no part of my purpose to try to estimate moral guilt, or to presume to dogmatise on ultimate responsibility. But cases of rape, especially those involving several persons, present some features of the common possession-struggle ; and just as bigamy[3] is akin to obtaining by false pretences, so certain forms of rape resemble robbery with violence, though rape will always tend to be more of a passion-act, a response to a much more personal and vehement

---

[1] See for instance, Karl Pearson, *Ethic of Free Thought*, p. 440.
H. G. Wells, *Anticipations*, p. 304.
[2] See Havelock-Ellis, *Studies*, Philadelphia, 1901.
F. von Liszt, *Le Droit Criminel des Etats Européens*. Paris, 1884.
Liszt und Crusen, *Aussereuropäische Staaten*. Berlin, 1899. .
C. F. Williams, *American and English Enc. of Law*, vol. xx. London, 1893.
[3] Bigamy is clearly not a *sexual* offence at all, though I have seen it classified as such by a prison official. The sex question, like most other difficulties, is mainly and ultimately an *economic* problem, and is none the less hard and dangerous on that account.

temptation than any form of deliberate robbery. Assaults exhibit various degrees : there may be outrage done by some half-wild beast, taking advantage of a lonely place; or it may be begun by that kind of man, and others, less guilty, but yet perhaps intoxicated and present, may be led on and drawn to the crime. Or again it may assume an altogether different character, and be the outcome of insanity, the irresistible impulse of an abnormal man, which nothing can deter or terrify, and from which he cannot abstain. Many of the offences against children are of this kind, and also some acts of sensuality with animals.[1]

More obviously abnormal and often absolutely maniacal are the sexual aberrations involving algolagny, bloodlust, and sometimes mutilation and murder.[2] There is no doubt that certain people are gratified by witnessing the flagellation of others, and even in receiving pain themselves. Many cases of apparently inexcusable and causeless cruelty, or even of exaggerated " discipline," have had their origin entirely in this.[3]

Other sex maniacs have a craze for wounding people ; of such was the Portsmouth boot-cutter who sliced little girls' shoes, and was never captured so far as I know,[4]

[1] These last-named are not really of public importance, and should not be punished or brought into notice except where cruelty to the animal or open indecency is alleged. Lord Auckland has written shrewdly on this matter : " The unavoidable and general detestation of mankind will always be a strong barrier against so horrid a crime (as bestiality, etc.), but it may be a question whether the public prosecution thereof be founded on wisdom. Some have thought it unsafe and likely rather to solicit the attention than to deter from the crime."— William Eden, Lord Auckland, *Principles of Penal Law*, p. 245. London, 1771.

[2] No doubt in nature, fierce and even fatal ferocity is quite normally associated with the sexual union. For this in animals, see L. Bianchi, *Text-Book of Psychiatry*, J. H. MacDonald's trans. p. 666; and for brutality in marriage by capture see Lord Avebury, *Origin of Civilisation*, etc., etc. Some modern cases of rape and criminal assault may be due to a throw-back to primeval barbarism.

[3] Some might perhaps claim the celebrated Dr. Busby. A terrible example occurred in Germany in the autumn of 1903, when D, a tutor, ill-used one of his pupils till he ultimately died. Author's Case Book, iv. p. 19.

At the last International Congress on Penal Anthropology, the police showed us some frightful whips, etc., which had been used in various disorderly houses to gratify the amazing tastes of a proportion of their frequenters.

[4] Case Book, iii. p. 25.

though the wrong man was very nearly lynched.   Again
there was the stabbing woman—if woman it was—who
but a few years back terrorized Kensington.   She would
accost chance females whom she met, and ask for a
certain street, and as they stopped to direct her she
would stab them in the face and run away.   So great
was the alarm this lunatic occasioned, that women
would shriek and flee on being questioned by a stranger.
Detectives patrolled the region in female dress, and
tried their utmost to secure the offender ; and the crimes
ceased, but the much-wanted woman, or man disguised,
was never secured.   The most notorious instances of
erotic insanity in this country are the extraordinary
Ripper murders, which took place in the East End of
London a good while ago.   That they belonged to this
class of crime was obvious to all criminologists, from the
absolute want of rational motive, the profession of the
victims, and the nature of the mutilations made.   Much
the same thing has occurred in other great cities,[1] and
may happen again whenever there comes a similar combination of luck and lunacy, for no laws can prevent.
Likewise the ghastly wounding of horses and other
creatures, of which we have heard so much in recent years,
must be ascribed to sexual aberration and the power of
the blood-craving.[2]   In these kind of cases, then, the State
will have to interfere—as best it can, and as little as
possible.   But before it moves in the future, there will
have to be allegations involving one or more of the following features : violation of consent ; of the innocence of
childhood ; or of public decency.   One of these being
established, each case will be examined on its merits,
to ascertain its particular nature, and the assumable
responsibility of the offender.   The State must do its
best to determine whether the prisoner is a normal man
who is criminally vicious, or an abnormal person who is
swayed by special and unusual impulses, which may be
quite repellent to the ordinary mind.

[1] See A. Lacassagne, *Vacher et les Crimes sadiques.*
B, Ball, *La Folie Erotique.*
P. Garnier, *Les Fétichistes*, etc.
[2] Always excepting the crimes of this nature which arise from revenge
and the purely imitative outrages which sometimes follow any public
horror which is much advertised and dwelt upon.

The treatment of sexual offences will be of two kinds. (1) Where the offender is assumed to have been normal and responsible. Then he would meet with the deterrent —although always ultimately restorative—penalties incurred by other selfish and unkindly people whom we have spoken of as ranking in Group I. (2) Where there is evidence of abnormality or psychosis ; when he would be placed under special care and supervision and treated for his particular infirmity. Of late years suggestion by hypnotism has been advocated and employed,[1] and this, with a lengthy course of asylum treatment, including what is now known and practised, with perhaps other methods which may be discovered,[2] as we learn more about the functions of the brain, may play a great part in the treatment of disordered impulses.

But while a taste or " twist " artificially acquired or lately developed might readily prove amenable to treatment, or even coercion, an innate instinct accompanied by psychic or somatic abnormalities is held to be altogether irremovable.[3] Moreover hypnotic suggestion and influence, as distinct from any external or physical treatment is somewhat of a dreadful remedy. It is only as a last resource, as an alternative perhaps to prison or annihilation, that we should tamper with the balance of the soul or try to probe the springs of personality.

A word must be said on other crimes of passion which, though not sexual in their origin, are very often physical and pathological. Murder is obviously a grievous, most irrevocable deed, since nothing can bring back a life once taken. Moreover, it need not be an impulse-act at all,

[1] See **Therapeutic Suggestion** in *Psychopathia Sexualis*, by A. von Schrenck-Notzing, C. G. Chaddock's trans. London, 1895.
J. Milne Bramwell, *Hypnotism*, chap. x. London, 1903.
A. Moll, *Pactet et Romme*, trans. p. 271, etc. Paris, 1893.
Hall Caine, *Drink*. London, 1906.
Pall Mall Mag., March, 1903.
C. Lloyd Tuckey, **Paper before Brit. Med. Soc.**, 1891.
T. S. Clouston, *The Hygiene of the Mind*. London, 1907.

[2] It has been found that ascertainable disease may set up sexual aberrations. See D. Ferrier, *The Functions of the Brain*, ch. xii. p. 432. London, 1886 ; and for study of abnormal cerebration, see Morton Prince, *The Dissociation of a Personality*. London, 1906.

[3] L. Bianchi, p. 669. London, 1906.
Otto Weininger, *Sex and Character*, p. 50. London, 1906.
C. G. Chaddock in Peterson & Haines, *Text-Book of Legal Medicine and Toxicology*, p. 683. Philadelphia, 19c3.

but may be planned slowly and carefully, as in revenge, or may arise out of another crime when done by expectant heirs, brigands, or burglars. On the other hand, it does not follow that every murderer is the worst kind of criminal. There are positions in which decent people have found themselves, so maddening and provocative that even the courts of law have held them to have been justified in taking life. And there are people cursed with corrosive or unstable temper, whom drink, or more rarely jealousy, makes mad and frenzied while the fit is on them.[1]

And then how often we read of what seems even more a tragedy than a crime—the sudden act which years will not undo ; the hideous, open, bleeding, accusing, wound, which nothing can close and remorse cannot even heal ! There is small need to punish in such cases ; we want to mend and to restore as far as possible ; the question is, will it occur again ?

Far back in the beginning of this chapter, I said that in the future they will either mend or end a man. All treatment, painful or painless, will have before it a definite object—the reparation of the injury done, and the replacement of the offender back into social fellowship with the community in which he is to live. When the State takes a prisoner in hand, and relegates him to a course of systematic repairing, it will believe that he can be repaired. If he can be reformed, it will entail (1) that he should be taught to lead a useful life, and shall be able in the course of time to regain liberty and character, and (2) it must also mean—for without this all remedies are vain—that he or she is held to be forgivable. The State, by the task it lays upon the prisoner, fixes its own price for the crime committed : not to undo the deed, for that is impossible ; not to punish him for the past, for that would be morbid ; but to prepare him for the future, when he has made amends.

And when once all things possible have been done to right the wronged and to make good the injury, we, the Community, who received our price, must say at length that the debt has been paid, *and not claim it again !*

[1] I was once walking through a Colonial prison with the Governor. "That man," he observed, indicating a prisoner, "I could trust with a bag of gold ; but he has a violent temper, and he struck down another man with his working hammer, and is here for a long term."

In actual practice it is otherwise : Society may cease to imprison, but it seldom ceases to punish, for afterwards it excommunicates. It banishes past prisoners from its sight, and there are now no friendly forests to go to, and foreign lands are too far off to reach ; sometimes disgrace pursues them even there ; " imprisonment is as irrevocable as death."[1] And so they " go under," as people say, and become vaguely of the criminal class, or of the submerged tenth, or are called by any other name that occurs conveniently and means little ; but this is not the end. They are said to go under ; but where ? To the " cave of the depths," or the "grave of the blind,"—what then ? A man is either dead or else he is alive, and if he is alive he is breathing so many times a minute, consuming a certain quantity of food every day, adding wealth to, or taking it away from, the community every year. And, like a fallen pebble in a pond, surely this man upon the sea of souls makes little but yet ever-widening rings of influence around him, if they shall be for good or if they act for evil.

If then a man who has already paid the penalty apportioned, and by law held to have been sufficient for his offence—in the Future this will be expressed in terms of restitution, not of punishment—is still to be treated as an enemy of society, what hope or prospect is there left to him what can he do ? is he not better dead ? I once heard Mr. Stipendiary Chapman say, " Every prisoner has a past, but he has no future."

Yet suppose a man or a woman does something which we refuse to forget and cannot forgive. Here are a few cases which were reported while this part of the present chapter was being written or revised.

There was a man in the Midlands who, while in drink, deliberately set fire to his mother, the unfortunate woman dying from the burns ; he died extremely suddenly. There was a man in India who poisoned his wife, and also the husband of the woman he wanted. There was a man named S, who fired three shots at a passenger in a train through a newspaper, in order to rob him, and then concealed his body under the seat. This most dangerous person had been in prison and in a mad-house.[2] Going

---

[1] Bernard Shaw, *Man and Superman*.
[2] Author's Case Book. vii. p. 95. He received fifteen years.

back a few years, there was a woman in Ireland who was interrupted in a long course of cruelty to her child by its accidental death in a dark cupboard where it had been confined. There was a similar woman in a Western county, who for some reason or other ill-treated *one* of her children in the same savage way ; she escaped with a fine. To my mind these torturers of the weak and helpless are the worst criminals in all the calendar ; at any rate their crimes are the most horrible.[1]

What then is to be done with such as these ? or even, after several convictions, with the baser sort of systematic swindlers, coiners, forgers, and exploiters generally ? For though they do not inspire the same personal hatred, they yet may indirectly cause immeasurable misery, and cannot by any means be tolerated in the commonwealth. The old question recurs : can we forgive them ? Not in words alone, but also in heart and deed. Will we try our best to restore and replace them, and will we ultimately receive them fully and frankly into fellowship again ? This we must mean to do if we intend that they should be kept alive. The tendency of the time is all against capital punishment. I am opposed to every sort of penal retribution, but I think hopeless people should be painlessly removed. The question is not so much what criminals have done, as what we feel compelled to do with them. It is not a matter of blame, but of expediency ; we do not blame a dog for having hydrophobia, but we destroy it as a common danger. It will not be so much what a man (or woman) has done, as his assumed *incurability*, which will convey him to some painless death.

From my point of view a congenital idiot is far more worthy of death than are most murderers, because some of them might yet lead useful lives ; the idiot is beyond remedy.[2]

---

[1] So they are, but as an instance of how bitterness is always found in direct inverse ratio to knowledge (as Nietzsche said), I find in Dr. Devon's admirable work, *The Criminal and the Community* (p. 40), the following sentence, " In fact the proportion of insane among prisoners generally is not greater than among the population outside, but in the case of females admitted for cruelty to children it is enormously in excess." But our old test would always come in : was it a *normal* crime ? Was it done by a stepmother ? Was the child illegitimate ? What the father did ? and so on.

[2] " The small minority, for example, afflicted with . . . hideous incurable habits of mind . . . exists only on sufferance, out of pity and

What, then, has been the practical alternative? In many countries (Belgium, Italy, etc., etc.), lifelong imprisonment under terrible conditions.[1] In England it generally means twenty years.[2]

It is sometimes asserted that the condemned themselves would prefer anything, even lifelong doom, to being hurled at once into the unknown. That might be so; the craven Parolles cried out, "Let me live, sir, in a dungeon, i' the stocks, or anywhere, so I may live."[3] Such people, maddened and stricken by the immediate terror, do not then realize what a life sentence means. Observe that Shelley, in his splendid drama, makes the cold blood-stained villain Cenci say, "I rarely kill the body, which preserves like a strong prison the soul within my power, wherein I feed it with the breath of fear for hourly pain." But even if the criminals preferred prison, others have to be thought of in the commonwealth. "The rulers of the future will grudge making good people into jailors, warders, punishment dealers, nurses and attendants on the bad. People who cannot live happily and freely in the world without spoiling the lives of others are better out of it."[4]

The State which sends forth its sons over the seas—and it is the loss of the *young* which is the deepest tragedy,

patience, and on the understanding that they do not propagate; and I do not suppose that they" (the men of the New Republic) "will hesitate to kill when that sufferance is abused. And I imagine also the plea and proof that a grave criminal is also insane will be regarded by them, not as a reason for mercy, but as an additional reason for death." —H. G. Wells, *Anticipations*, p. 300. London, 1902.

[1] See W. Tallack, *Penological and Preventive Principles*, chap. x. London, 1896).

[2] It has been sometimes contended, and truly enough, that this is a much more dreadful punishment than speedy death. In barbarous times torture preceded execution, and to this day bloodthirsty persons write to the press suggesting flogging before hanging as the only method which will put down this or that.

Early in the last century U.S. Senator Livingston proposed that there should be written over the cell doors of all murderers: "In this cell is confined, to pass his life in solitude and sorrow, A. B., convicted of the murder of C. D.; his food is bread of the coarsest kind, his drink water mingled with his tears; he is dead to the world; this cell is his grave" (F. H. Wines, *Punishment and Reformation*, p. 145). This might be very effective torture, but it were a ghastly mockery to call it humane, and folly indeed to think it reasonable; the inscription is well worthy of "reformers" of those times.

[3] *All's Well that Ends Well*, Act. IV. Sc. iii.

[4] *Anticipations*, p. 302.

because they seem to leave all unfulfilled—to pass on duty through a thousand dangers, or to fill unnamed furrows on the battle-fields, will not spare those it cannot leave at large. The manner of their extinction is a matter of detail ; [1] it will be carried out as painlessly as possible. We shall no more ill-treat the socially incurable than we now blame the physically diseased and loathsome ; they will perish because we can do nothing with them, just as the others die because we can do nothing for them ; and either pass might happen to each one of us.

The body, now buried brutally within prison walls—as though the State could never relax its talons, but vulture-like infixed them in its prey—will ultimately be handed over to the relatives or to such as claim it (but surely there would have been hope for any one who was loved by some one ?) [2]—in any case, to be interred reverently. For he or she that was once convicted will have gone hence : let no one judge ; it is in mightier hands. The more I have tried through these many years to estimate the intrinsic value of acts and motives, the less I have fancied they could be truly weighed. It may be that conduct only balances temptations. At least, when I look on those who were praised or blamed, and who set forth on their lonely way, labelled—by Man—with their assumed journey's end (of which none ever really had the very faintest knowledge), I feel indeed with my whole conviction that fools have rushed, intruding where the angels dare not tread.

[1] See essay on the subject by Dr. J. M. Bleyer, *Scientific Methods of Capital Punishment.* New York, 1887.
I understand that in certain States condemned criminals may to some extent choose how they shall be destroyed, which seems a very wise rule.

[2] " There may be men among us who are so utterly bad that all the State can do with them is to kill them in order to secure the safety of others, but I have not seen them."—Dr. Devon (who was for many years a prison official), *Crim. and Com.*, p. 168.

CHAPTER XX

PRACTICAL PRISONS

On any day, in the streets of London, we might perceive a kind of private cab; it has thick windows of ground glass generally drawn up; within it is a flushed and shivering child being conveyed to one of the great fever hospitals. Or we might meet a special omnibus with long seats and rests, taking cripples to schools. Or we may come upon an ambulance wheeled by policemen. It will have broad strong straps, which can be rapidly buckled, a long leather apron carefully fastened up, and a black hood drawn closely down. And it contains a silent Something, with face concealed; a human form, or all that is left of it; blood-smeared and muddy; maybe mutilated, dead. They pass, and then we realize life's tragedies. Millions have risen up and gone forth at morning, and some of them shall not go home again. For they have been summoned suddenly from the hum of work; watchers shall sit up waiting wearily, counting the tread of feet upon quiet pavements; and desolation shall fill empty rooms, for the lost ones shall lie elsewhere. All this is Life as it has to be; it is the Plan of Creation, it is the Doom of the World, it is man's terrible struggle with nature and circumstances. We are doing the best we can. And as we see these poor things going by, we feel at any rate that they will be well cared for. We know that all will be done for them which kindness can inspire, and which experience has learned. We are assured that they are left in very skilful keeping.

But with the inmates of the prison van it is quite different. Those others whom we just spoke of had come to grief, but they were being taken off for repair and healing. All the appliances which the minds of men

370

have planned and perfected through slow research will be made use of for each special case, and brought to bear that they may be restored. But those whom we dimly see in the passage darkness are merely carted off to be put away. No special remedies are applied to them ; all receive the same, no matter what any did, no matter what *kind* of evil or infirmity has brought each one there. Indeed, apart from the recent and most promising Borstal system, there are no *remedies* of any sort. There is merely a shutting up, as it were, in the sleeping den of a wild beast's cage, and a sullen walking behind the bars by day under keepers' eyes ; for we brutalize well.[1] What shall be aimed at while they brood in cells, what shall have been achieved when they are allowed to leave them, and what they shall find to do when they emerge again outside the wall, has not been thought out or provided for.

In fact, we have found by figures, and by the evidence of years, that probabilities work out against those who have been convicted of dishonesty ; that far from being sent away for cure—although it were through long and painful processes—the greater number of the more serious cases will certainly be dragged down utterly. In practice, we pass upon those who have been condemned, the doom conceived for the ideal hell, of suffering without hope ; for those in the prison van are mostly being driven to absolute destruction. No wonder, then, that " all communities and states are in reality ashamed of jails and penal institutions." [2] No wonder that even those who have worked the punitive machinery officially for years, should perceive no prospect of any real and ultimate regeneration of society by its use.[3] No wonder that every year innumerable cases are never brought to " justice " at all, because more and more thoughtful people are feeling that harm rather than good will probably be done—that the person convicted will be irretrievably ruined, and will never get right again.

Why should he ? What have we done to help, what

---

[1] Many of the modern prisons on the Continent are now very much worse than ours, which have improved in many respects since 1898.
[2] C. S. Darrow, *Resist not Evil*, p. 75. London, 1904.
[3] See Major Arthur Griffiths, *Mysteries of Police and Crime*, ii. p 472. M. Hammard, Chief of the Sûreté, in *The World's Work*, Aug. 1904.

have we done to counteract his defects, to appeal to his better side, to give him a helping hand at the place where he slipped and fell ? [1]

Nothing at all for good in any way; [2] indeed, it is not too much to say, that we have done our worst to demoralize him, to turn him either into a desperado at bay or an abject automaton. [3] And the Community incurs the man it made.

How should he ? Is it likely that a man or woman who went crookedly on the highway of life will be able to keep straight after being, figuratively speaking, hit over the head by the legal truncheon ? [4] Is it likely that a man (or woman) who could not get, or retain, employment under ordinary conditions, should succeed in regaining respect after having been morally tarred and feathered inside prison walls ? Far from having any confidence in the reformative results of the State's penal process, the public will on no account, if they can help it, employ a person who has ever passed its doors. [5]

Then comes the weary fight of the not-wanted, for whom all honest avenues are " up " and no-thoroughfared ; whom the few shun from self-righteousness, and the many avoid from fear of some assumption of complicity, and who are headed off at every turning, and driven to be destitute or desperate. A fight where they mostly fail, and in which you or I, or any one, would probably fail also. [6]

[1] " Whilst we have prisons it matters little which of us occupy the cells."—G. Bernard Shaw, *Man and Superman*, p. 233. London, 1903.

[2] " The professional criminal is in my opinion a prison product."—H. J. B. Montgomery, *National Review*, Aug. 1904, and also in *Humane Review*, April, 1900.

[3] " In fact, our system does not create citizens, but rather habitual criminals."—Edward Carpenter, *Prisons*, p. 15.

[4] " Will a prolonged course of severities and degradations confer the virtues of industrious and orderly citizens on these unhappy men ? On the contrary, the more harshly you punish them the more you reduce the human element which still lies in their hearts. The more you punish them the more certainly you doom them to the awful existence of an habitual criminal."—Rev. W. D. Morrison, LL.D., quoted by E. Carpenter in *Prisons*, p. 16. See also *Daily Mail*, Oct. 28 and 29, 1903 ; Author's Case Book, iv. p. 27. Articles by H. Hamilton Fyfe, *Daily Mirror*, Feb. 27, April 10 Sept. 2, 1907 ; Case Book, vi.

[5] M. B. Booth, quoting from a former Governor of Portland : " I have only known two cases of real reformation in thirty-seven years," and she keenly comments, " What a ghastly confession of unfitness for duty ! " *After Prison What* ? p. 260.

Anxiety of prisoners as to what will become of them on release

As I have indicated all along, the problem of the pariah lies deeper than any prison system. The nuclei of crime are so deep-seated in the origin, and so far-spreading in their ramifications, that they are neither occasioned nor cured by methods of punishment. Thus the absolute ruin which nearly always follows an exposed act of dishonesty is not altogether the fault of the prisons, except in so far that they are not therapeutic, and that they are profoundly hardening to all concerned. For it arises largely from the nature of the case. Amidst the crowds who follow advertisements and seek after places as fish make for breadcrumbs, there is no difficulty in finding plenty of people who are quite poor, though of good character, who will do almost anything for a weekly wage. Moreover, we must admit that any one who has once lost self-respect and reputation from having thieved, and who has been degraded and further stunted and cowed by prison severities, is all too likely to relapse again. We dare not recommend such a man to a decent post without a warning, or at least a reservation, which will most likely deprive him of it. Employers, and societies which now

see *Evidence of Departmental Committee*, 1895, p. 29, etc. " The evidence shows how hard it is for an ex-convict to get on in the world," said Dr. Michael Taylor, holding an inquest on T. C., aged forty-five, of no home and no occupation, who was drowned in the Thames. He had served twenty-seven years' imprisonment. On Easter Monday Detective-Sergeant Allen saw him and gave him a shilling, as he said he had not had a proper meal for some time. " You know how it is, guv'nor : after my career," he said, " nobody will employ me." Detective-Sergeant Allen added that he believed the man made every effort to obtain work (*Daily Chronicle*, April 18, 1904 ; Author's **Case Book**, iv. p. 66). See also remarks of Chief Inspector Watta, of Boston, U.S., in *West. Gaz.* Nov. 1, 1906, **Case Book**, vi. p. 47. " I am sorry to say," observed the magistrate, Sir Joseph Reynals, " that it is quite true that when men who are unfortunately in your position do get honest work, they invariably have to leave it when it is found out that they have been convicts. It is very hard indeed " (*Daily Chronicle*, Sept. 9, 1905 ; **Case Book**, v. p. 86). " Many men on their release carry their prison about with them into the air, and hide it as a secret disgrace in their hearts, and at length, like poor poisoned things, creep into some hole and die. It is wretched that they should have to do so, and it is wrong, terribly wrong of society that it should force them to do so " (Oscar Wilde, *De Profundis*, p. 40. London, 1905).

" There are few persons in the world more to be pitied than the poor fellow who has served his first term of imprisonment or finds himself outside the gaol doors without a character and often without a friend in the world."—General Booth, *In Darkest England.* p. 173. See also J. A. Farrer, *Crimes and Punishments*, p. 57 ; E. DuCane, *Punishment and Prevention of Crime*, p. 171.

insure against loss through dishonesty,[1] will ferret out a person's past from his very boyhood. Whatever such a one may have suffered, hard though he try to get work and atone, the claw-like scar of the State's broad arrow, which brands his name, is always liable to start into sight again, and claim him for its own.

But since we know that difficulties almost insurmountable must needs beset the path of any man who ever stood convicted in the dock, the grim fact must be faced and carefully provided for. It is idle to argue that no one should gain advantage from having been in prison— the hardship is so crushing that we must have a counterpoise to neutralize it. A man *should* be benefited by prison, in the sense that a patient should be benefited by a necessary operation.

Those finally classed as being incurable will be either destroyed swiftly and painlessly, or sent away to wide and open-air settlements, to be treated as patients, semilunatics or children, where they cannot be injured by their own failings, and where the present and also the oncoming generation shall be no longer troubled by their malfeasance. But if men and women are to return again to freedom and citizenship, the aim and purpose of the prison management must be to make them qualified to be at liberty. And this will assuredly not be done through shutting them up in cells, which are too like cellars, or by inflicting periods of " mental cramp ";[2] or by consigning them like wild beasts to the bars, till they have little scope to behave badly and almost none at all to behave well; or by breaking down all personality, for that means likewise losing self-control, the primal need of the majority of prisoners ; or by the unaided ministrations of official clergymen of whatever denomina-

[1] " Am I never to hear the last of that ? " exclaimed a young man who had years before been handed over to the Court Missionary after a week's remand on a charge of theft.

[2] " It is worse than useless to punish them, above all by such an insanitary and vicious method as imprisonment. Full-blooded young men shut up in a cell for six months, nine months, a year! It is a hellish thing to do to any one at any age, but in the heyday of youth, in the prime of manhood ! Here physiology declares the law to be the greater criminal. To kill the murderer has an appearance of equity ; but of what crime is imprisonment the equation ? I know of none." Extract from an article by John Davidson, *Westminster Gazette*, Jan. 21, 1905.

tion : these must become but officers in orders—they have not time to deal with individuals—and sympathy, unlike help, cannot be given out professionally.[1]

The doctor—though as a student he very likely fainted on witnessing the first bad operation—must, and does, grow indifferent to the sight of physical pain. The prison chaplain must, and does, become accustomed [2] to looking upon mental misery ; whatever he may have felt in the beginning he will, in the ordinary course of adaptation, get used to his surroundings and so harden, he will become incapable of responsive pain without which there is no true sympathy ; we see this in the derivation of the word.[3]

The prisoner has not been qualified for anything except prison by the repressive methods practised in the past. The treatment of the Future must be didactic and developmental, looking not so much on what the convict has done before, but rather to what he or she will prove to be when released. The prisoner must be trained, must be taught self-control, must be allowed, within the limits of safety, sufficient liberty to bring that into action, must have innumerable chances of making his, or her, condition rapidly worse or better according to conduct. In the complexity and struggle of life outside, the consequences of actions are mostly too remote, and even uncertain, to be well realized by thoughtless and unbalanced people ; but if they followed swiftly and certainly, as they should in prison, some useful lessons might be inculcated.[4]

[1] " The human will must be left outside prison gates, where it is to be picked up again five, seven or fifteen years afterwards, and refitted to the mental condition which penal servitude has created in the animalized machine which is discharged from custody."—Michael Davitt, quoted by Carpenter, *Prisons*, p. 17.

[2] That fine reformer the Rev. W. D. Morrison observed : " The great difficulty with all of us in prisons is that we are so accustomed to see people under punishment and under suffering that we are apt to get a little hard in the matter, unless we take very great care. We have to bend our minds as much as possible the other way. That is my experience of prisons."—*Departmental Committee*, 1895, Evidence, p. 118.

[3] There may be mute and glorious " Francis Edens," people like Louise Michel, Gordon, or Whitman, who pass the gates ; but they belong to the world's saints and heroes.

[4] This principle is largely in force in many modern reformatories. See for instance V. M. Hamilton, " The World's Model Prison," *Wide World Magazine*, Dec. 1906.
Elmira, *Papers in Penology*, p. 14, etc. 1886.
Borstal, *Reports by Borstal Association*, 2, New Square, W.C. ; also *Westminster Gazette*, Aug. 1, etc. 1907

Clearly for all men, and especially for prisoners, the first necessity will be intelligent employment. In the case of the very short sentences there are great difficulties in the way, and probably to get people clean, tidy, orderly, and disciplined is all that can be attempted with the inmates of this class. There seems, however, to be a tendency to give first offenders further warning,[1] to bind them over, to accept sureties, to suspend sentences, and to release them on parole under special supervision. It is probable that prison will only be resorted to when all else has failed, and that then the initial sentences will be longer and also possibly indeterminate within the limits of the maximum penalty for the particular offence.[2]

For any attempt at mending, or reformation,[3] work is the most important point in prison management. And it must on no account be made intentionally penal—anti-thrift, Charles Reade called the horrible tasks of old— it should be looked on as a blessing and a privilege ; work should be as productive as possible. By all the laws of political economy and well-being we require wealth (1)

---

[1] This principle could be greatly extended ; it might be an excellent thing if certain special officials of the police, or probation officers, were empowered to caution (of course individually and secretly) young persons whom they believed to be drifting into criminal ways. This is already done by the Society for the Prevention of Cruelty to Children ; a letter is written to the man or woman suspected, and with it the intimation that no warning is sent twice. It is obviously better to prevent the commission of an offence, than afterwards to reckon up the wrong-doer and " bring him to a satisfactory criminal total." But we should have to guard carefully against police tyranny, always a very real danger in a democracy which is apt to be tormented by venomous cranks, and through the personal ambitions of unemployed legislators.

[2] See for instance E. P. Hughes, *The Probation System of America.* London: Howard Association.

R. W. McClaughry, *The Parole System as applied to the State Prisons.*

J. L. " The Probation of Offenders Bill," *Glasgow Herald,* Sept. 12, 1907.

S. J. Barrows, *The Indeterminate Sentence.* Washington, 1899.

Thomas Holmes, *Parole Officers and Indeterminate Sentences.*

[3] On the subject of " Which is the most needed Reform ? " Sir Oliver Lodge wrote : " One of the improvements which seems to me the most immediately feasible is prison organization ; whereby prisons could be converted into reforming agencies, with machinery specially adapted to that end, not only in the case of children but in the case of adults also ; age making very little difference to power of self-management in the case of weak characters."—*Evening News,* Feb. 1, 1907. See also *Daily Chronicle,* May 27, 1905, and letter by A. R. Wallace on prison production quoted in *Humane Review,* January 1907, p. 214.

for the community; (2) for the expenses of keeping the prisoner (in the future); (3) for the compensation of his victims; [1] (4) for the convict's family left at home; [2] (5) for small alleviations and luxuries—for we should reward if also we punish—which he may be allowed to earn for himself; (6) for start-money upon his ultimate release. Through the unorganised system, or rather want of system, in Western society, production in prisons has been greatly impeded, especially in democratic countries, by political pressure.[3] The fear of this and the deficiency in land within prison bounds doubtless occasions that look of stagnation so often noticed in prison surroundings.[4]

But all these attempts at restricting production are clearly the worst political economy; they seem to assume that the producer, and not the idler, is the enemy of society; they almost imply that every child who grows to be a citizen appears as a competitor and a rival to be suppressed; they would conflict against the commonwealth, and render prisons worse than plague-houses. The more complex problem of the sale and disposal of gaol-made goods has largely been solved by supplying the State, and this in time may be much more extended. Prison-made goods are better than prison-made *men*![5]

[1] "No method of dealing with first offenders can be satisfactory unless the court can insist on restitution to the person wronged." Thomas Holmes: see "Howard Association," in *Daily Chronicle*, April 16, 1907. To my mind restitution should be the chief aim of the law.
[2] This is apparently being done, under the Swiss Code, art. 31. See E. Jenks.
Law Quarterly Review, vol. xix. p. 21 (Jan. 1903).
See also W. Tallack, *Reparation to the Injured.* London, 1899.
[3] For England, *vide* D. C. of 1895, Evidence, *Re* Resolutions of certain Trades Unions, pp. 375–386. In the State of New York the prisoners passed through a cruel and paralysing period of inaction occasioned by law, made a few years ago. I perceived traces of these restrictions when visiting Melbourne.
[4] See for instance, W. B. N., *Penal Servitude.* London, 1903.
No. 1500, *Life in Sing Sing.* Indianapolis, 1904.
H. J. B. Montgomery, *World's Work*, April, 1905.
The present writer, *Humane Review*, Jan. 1901.
Convict Life, by a Ticket-of-Leave Man, chap. iii. London, 1879.
Report of recent address by Thomas Holmes, *Reynolds'*, Sept. 29, 1907.
[5] It is curious to observe that while the Act prohibiting the importation of prison-made articles from abroad may or may not have been a wise and necessary measure, it yet constituted, for good or for evil, the first step taken in modern times towards establishing protection in England.

It will be those serving the longer terms for whom most can be done; we can afford to take trouble with them, since they are relatively few in number, and they have great and heavy need of help and succour.[1] Among them are good men gone wrong, and stunted, lop-sided, unbalanced creatures, who cannot keep right. The former are made from fine material, which will respond to painstaking treatment, and, in the end, repay a thousandfold. In these we must develop all the great misused faculties of body and brain; we must see that they work hard through the long hours of labour, and then we must yield them rest and give scope to their minds and sympathies when the day is done. I should like to see some of them playing chess—excellent discipline, which teaches patience, combination, consequence—or cultivating some hobby of art or craft, or singing to solemn music at evening.

I should like to see them making beautiful things (I *have* in Greece ; and they do, I am told, in America), engraving, painting, writing, studying ; doing anything and everything that would call forth and kindle their higher nature ; raise them out of the guilt of the past and the doom of the present, and lead them back to fellowship and freedom. It may be said that convicts are not these sort of people. I reply that there are prisoners of all kinds, high and low ; let those then be raised who *can* : hitherto we have levelled, as it were, downwards, making the prisons easiest for the most brutish of their inmates, and ghastly beyond all words for intsllectual prisoners. Let us try if we cannot now at last begin to level up.

The latter, or the degenerates, are far more difficult to reclaim ; apparently less guilty because obviously less responsible than the higher types, some of them may have

---

[1] See Chap. **XIX**.
"Give a man useful work, interesting work, remunerative work: why should he not be paid for his labour ? Don't stunt the moral nature or intellectual being of the convicts. I would make their prison life much more interesting. Why not ? Give them concerts, lectures, interesting employment, light and happy services, a greater selection of ministers to preach to them."—Sir Robert Anderson, late head of the Criminal Investigation Department, Scotland Yard, Interview in *Great Thoughts*.
See also Captain Arthur St. John's very helpful essay on " Prison Régime," *Penal Reform League Series*, No. 11.

fallen through uncontrolled, and, in such simple half-developed cretinous natures, uncontrollable, animalism; many more, however, have probably done nothing very serious taken singly, but a number of things which, from being repeated, have brought on cumulative punishment. With most of these the trouble is not moral or even altogether social, but rather ante-natal and physical. Poor derelicts of life indeed, these chronic prisoners! They are not grotesquely, violently mad enough to be protected in the asylum wards, and they are too unbalanced to go about amidst the snares and passions of the world. What can we do with them? [1] It has been suggested that convicts after a fourth conviction should be painlessly destroyed, and if this had to be the alternative to perpetual, or at any rate constant imprisonment, I should say it was better.

But for the milder, intermediate cases, there might—as has so often been suggested—be asylum-prisons, to which, after a certain number of failures, they could be sent. There, they should all be made as happy as possible, as though still at school; they should be settled in a wide, open country, or upon some island. But they would never be allowed to beget children, and seldom, if ever, would they be let at large to take part in the fierce struggle of life, or move in the great unguarded world again. . . . Still I repeat, that all who cannot ultimately lead useful, human, tolerably happy lives, should be destroyed as soon as ever their condition has been determined.

Now, all along we have been tracing back the causes which bring crime into our midst, and how we should treat the criminals when convicted according to their various distempers. There still remains a hard and grievous problem: what shall become of men and women released, when they emerge again and have to get their livelihood? A patient coming from, say, the small-pox hospital, with his face all red and scarred from the loathsome pits, is received again; we believe that they would not let him out until he was cured; he picks up the thread of his life and labours; he has suffered, and all have helped.

[1] Reported lecture by Mr. Secretary Bonaparte before the National Prison Warders' Association, Chicago. See *Evening Standard*, Sept. 19, 1907.

A person is let out from a lunatic asylum ; he too is received with kindness and compassion, although at first with a certain amount of fear, and even concealed aversion. People are not quite sure that he is safe, they dread that he may relapse, have fits, or perhaps break out in some fresh and appalling way. But in time this will all wear off ; he may pick up the threads again.

But when a man is released from prison, he is tossed back, as it were, on to thorns and briers. Nobody wants him, his place has probably been filled, he is looked upon as having been contaminated rather than cured ; he must hide amongst other outcasts and live as they,[1] for the self-righteous world beyond will have none of him ; the threads of his life and labour are lost and broken, and who shall fix or join them up again ?

" Men with characters branded by their having been convicts,"[2] says the Report of a cruel old Royal Commission, " are exposed to an almost insuperable disadvantage in the strong competition for employment in this country. . . . Even though some masters are willing to employ liberated convicts from motives of charity, it is necessary carefully to conceal their previous condition from their fellow workmen, who would otherwise refuse to work with them." And then it goes on to say, with strange defiance of that Christian rule which these Commissioners followed ostensibly, " This feeling amongst the free working population is one which it is neither possible nor desirable to remove," etc. But this was written in the shallow, selfish, pharisaical nineteenth century, that is dead and damned ; in which they had all the will to ruin and do to death,[3] by slow degrees and

[1] Belonging to a different religion, I know nothing of Salvationist theology, but there is sometimes a splendid human sympathy about them, as in this passage : " A fellow-feeling makes one wondrous kind, and it is an immense advantage to us in dealing with the criminal classes that many of our best officers have themselves been in a prison cell. Our people, thank God, have never learned to regard a prisoner as a mere convict A 234. He is ever a human being to them, who is to be cared for and looked after as a mother looks after her ailing child."— General Booth, *In Darkest England*, p. 174.

[2] *Royal Commission of* 1863 *Report*, pp. 33, 34.

[3] " Nay, take my life and all ; pardon not that:
You take my house when you do take the prop
That doth sustain my house ; you take my life
When you do take the means whereby I live."
Mer. of V. iv. 1.

indirect devices ; though they no longer had the brute courage to hang.

I have tried my best already to drive home the fact that such an attitude on the part of society towards a man or a woman, who has already undergone conviction and punishment, logically involves—and for all parties, far better involve—that the community should *kill* the man or woman in question. A person who is let at large from prison is one whom the State decided not to destroy : then let us act on this and see him through ; so, if he fail again, we can say truthfully that it was his own fault (or his infirmity) and not ours—whereas, at present, we ought to know that most men who have been convicted of dishonesty can only rise up again by quite unusual character or talent.

We set the ex-convict an impossible task ; we make him engage in a kind of conflict with the community, and we tell him to " go in and win " ; and he drifts down and is lost ; and those who should have experience fully expect it, for they keep big books full of thumb-impressions, awaiting him back in prison. This must be altered ; the State must complete its task of restoration. " 'Tis not enough to help the feeble up, but to support him after," [1] and " if these men and women are to live honestly outside prison, work must be found for them somewhere." [2] There is reason to hope that when the young are better looked after, when loafers and idlers are taken in hand, when the accursed public-house is altered in character and is no longer made a training ground for getting drunk, and when all convicted prisoners are scientifically treated and classified, the number of the criminal, or rather the outcast class will diminish enormously.

We must make use of all ancillary aids in the shape of philanthropic societies, work-finding agencies, emigration and colonization. The replacement of any person who has ever been in prison—particularly if the offence has been any form of dishonesty—back into decent work and fellowship with the community, so far presents great practical difficulties arising from the nature of the case. Now that we know more of the origins of crimes, now

[1] *Timon of Athens*, I. i.
[2] Rev. W. Carlile, the head of the Church Army.

that we see more clearly the extent of their excuses and of our own collective guilt and selfishness,[1] we are not likely to come across that spirit of hard, crass cruelty, already alluded to, which yet could be defended by a Royal Commission, in the deep moral darkness of the nineteenth century. But we must always be prepared to meet with the avoidance of ex-prisoners. If they have ever stolen money, we fear that they will do so again, and that we, or worse still, the persons who accepted our recommendation or responded to our appeal will suffer in consequence. Doubtless when they emerge from undergoing new forms of treatment, really directed to apply to each case in hand, the public may acquire confidence in the methods, and may in time become as hopeful of a man's having been reformed, as they are now convinced that he has been incurably degraded in passing through prison. Also, it might not prove impossible to furnish some guarantee to the employers of ex-prisoners against loss through them, up to certain amounts. This is now done on strict business principles by assurance companies for employers of servants possessed of good references; and if the idea were found capable of extension to the more hopeful of the cases discharged from prison, it would give confidence to those who had work to offer. The Government might furnish the guarantee—say up to fifty pounds—and make the prisoner earn his own premium; or the experiment might be thought worth trying by some philanthropic society.

But even if something of this nature were practicable, there is always an instinct to shun the disgraced, especially where they appear to be blameworthy. This is due more to fear than to pharisaism; we see the same avoidance of leaders of unpopular movements, though they may afterwards win and prevail. People will dread association with the ostracised, especially with persons who have

---

[1] There is a great deal to be said for a humane and supervised system of transportation. Our own early experiments gave some great results, though they were marred and disgraced by the ignorance and brutality of the officials and the age. Both France and Russia have done much to develop distant and inhospitable lands by means of their convict labour; and any struggle against nature and disease must be morally healthier and infinitely more hopeful than the slow, passive endurance of artificial penal discipline. See for instance J. S. Balfour, *Weekly Dispatch*, Dec. 9, 1906.

been convicted of acts which they themselves are liable to be suspected of, or towards which they feel themselves drawn secretly. Thus the poor will fear any suspicion of theft, the business man of fraud, the elderly celibate of sexual assault, the young woman of prostitution ; and so on. In fact, it needs much courage and character, in this glass-housed world, to befriend the fallen ; and that is mainly (for conscientious or vindictive impersonal cruelty is now rare) why there are so many castaways.

But we must help them all, for their sake and our own. It *can* be done, if only we should will. Mark how a war, a calamity, even a London fog, draws men together : cannot the spirit of the awakening commonwealth achieve more than these ? But we must teach, and preach, and fight against this deadly, though informal, modern excommunication after prison.[1] I have seen a man, away in North Africa, who looked out on the scene and sunlight, and up at us, with but red sockets where he once had eyes ; he had been blinded by the Government for brigandage, and begged of the passers-by at the wayside. But even such a barbarous mutilation is perhaps not more cruel to the victim than to be set adrift deprived of hope, to roam abroad and find all hearts estranged, all sympathy turned away ; to walk like an earth-bound ghost, unrecognised : alive with all nerves and senses amongst the living, yet treated as one long dead. This is the fate reserved for ex-prisoners ; but it will not be so before the brightness of the Future ; when they will be gathered within the Nation's fold, and comforted.

[1] Since this was written I read an important paper on the reinstatement of persons who have been convicted by F. Reginald Statham, *Fortnightly Review*, Dec. 1907.

INDEX TO AUTHORS

SUBJECT INDEX

A

Abnormal powers possibly existed in certain persons accused of witchcraft, 70

" Accumulation," a word meaning much to prisoners, 225

Acedia, or monastic melancholy, 285

Acton, William, trial of, 20

Africa, West, convicts sent out to, 123

Allen, Dr. C. W., on the need of scientific investigations, 301

Ancyra, Council of, adjudicates upon a case involving a suicide, A.D. 314, 282

Anderson, Major, a Governor at Norfolk Island, 166

Animals acquitted on grounds of character and youth, 259

— considered in all respects amenable to the law, 256

— criminal, kept in the common prisons, 256

— criminous, to be delivered up to the injured party, or damage done to be paid for, 255

— defended by counsel, 256

— domestic, tried by the ordinary criminal courts, 256

— drawn into sexual offences, 258

— duly served with summonses to appear, 260

— guilt fully imputed to, 256

— involved in cases of witchcraft and sorcery, 257

— letters addressed to, 261

— might be called to be witnesses, 256

— occasional imprisonment of, 257

— proclamations issued to, 260

— punishment of, 254

— sometimes put to torture, 257

Animals subjected to ecclesiastical curses, 259, 260

— tried with the reading test, 257

Animals, wild, came within the jurisdiction of the courts Christian, 256

Animism, still shown in the blessing of warships, rivers, houses, etc., 253

Apparitions, suggestion and self-deception in connection with, 62

Aquinas, Thomas, criticism of profit-making, 324

Aristotle on suicide, 271

Arles, Council of, condemns servants who should kill themselves to injure their masters (Fifth Century), 282

Asquith, Mr., committee appointed by, 217

Assignment of convicts to private persons stopped, 142

Assizes, long intervals between, 11

— prisoners linger and die whilst awaiting, 11, 14

Asylum-prisons, need of, for the deficient, 379

Asylums, private, persons imprisoned in, 85

Augustine, St., turns the Christian world against suicide, 281

Auxerre, Council of, refuses to receive oblations for suicides, A.D. 578, 283

B

Baker, Colonel, evidence of, 232

Bambridge, trial of, 20

Bane, anything that occasioned death was called the, 253

Barbadoes, prisoners sent to, 160

Battle, wager of, 23, 24

Baxter, Richard, believes in witchcraft, 67

PATTERSON SMITH REPRINT SERIES IN
CRIMINOLOGY, LAW ENFORCEMENT, AND SOCIAL PROBLEMS

1. Lewis: *The Development of American Prisons and Prison Customs, 1776-1845.*
2. Carpenter: *Reformatory Prison Discipline*
3. Brace: *The Dangerous Classes of New York*
4. Dix: *Remarks on Prisons and Prison Discipline in the United States*
5. Bruce *et al: The Workings of the Indeterminate-Sentence Law and the Parole System in Illinois*
6. Wickersham Commission: *Complete Reports, Including the Mooney-Billings Report.* 14 Vols.
7. Livingston: *Complete Works on Criminal Jurisprudence.* 2 Vols.
8. Cleveland Foundation: *Criminal Justice in Cleveland*
9. Illinois Association for Criminal Justice: *The Illinois Crime Survey*
10. Missouri Association for Criminal Justice: *The Missouri Crime Survey*
11. Aschaffenburg: *Crime and Its Repression*
12. Garofalo: *Criminology*
13. Gross: *Criminal Psychology*
14. Lombroso: *Crime, Its Causes and Remedies*
15. Saleilles: *The Individualization of Punishment*
16. Tarde: *Penal Philosophy*
17. McKelvey: *American Prisons*
18. Sanders: *Negro Child Welfare in North Carolina*
19. Pike: *A History of Crime in England.* 2 Vols.
20. Herring: *Welfare Work in Mill Villages*
21. Barnes: *The Evolution of Penology in Pennsylvania*
22. Puckett: *Folk Beliefs of the Southern Negro*
23. Fernald *et al: A Study of Women Delinquents in New York State*
24. Wines: *The State of the Prisons and of Child-Saving Institutions*
25. Raper: *The Tragedy of Lynching*
26. Thomas: *The Unadjusted Girl*
27. Jorns: *The Quakers as Pioneers in Social Work*
28. Owings: *Women Police*
29. Woolston: *Prostitution in the United States*
30. Flexner: *Prostitution in Europe*
31. Kelso: *The History of Public Poor Relief in Massachusetts: 1820-1920*
32. Spivak: *Georgia Nigger*
33. Earle: *Curious Punishments of Bygone Days*
34. Bonger: *Race and Crime*
35. Fishman: *Crucibles of Crime*
36. Brearley: *Homicide in the United States*
37. Graper: *American Police Administration*
38. Hichborn: *"The System"*
39. Steiner & Brown: *The North Carolina Chain Gang*
40. Cherrington: *The Evolution of Prohibition in the United States of America*
41. Colquhoun: *A Treatise on the Commerce and Police of the River Thames*
42. Colquhoun: *A Treatise on the Police of the Metropolis*
43. Abrahamsen: *Crime and the Human Mind*
44. Schneider: *The History of Public Welfare in New York State: 1609-1866*
45. Schneider & Deutsch: *The History of Public Welfare in New York State: 1867-1940*
46. Crapsey: *The Nether Side of New York*
47. Young: *Social Treatment in Probation and Delinquency*
48. Quinn: *Gambling and Gambling Devices*
49. McCord & McCord: *Origins of Crime*
50. Worthington & Topping: *Specialized Courts Dealing with Sex Delinquency*

TEXAS A&M UNIVERSITY TEXARKANA